"A complex, accomplished life recounted with confidence and candor . . . Every page sparkles with directness and grace."

—Douglas Brinkley, *The Boston Globe*

"More like a novel than a political memoir, the First Lady's book reveals its author as utterly, viscerally human. . . . Beautiful and extraordinary . . . so surprisingly candid, richly emotional, and granularly detailed that it allows readers to feel exactly what Michelle herself felt at various moments in her life."

—Curtis Sittenfeld, *Vanity Fair*

"[*Becoming*] crackles with blunt, often searing observations about politics, race and gender in America."

—Connie Schultz, *The Washington Post*

"A warm, intimate coming-of-age story of a strong-minded girl who grew up to become one of the most powerful and influential women in the country."

—Laurie Hertzel, *Minneapolis Star Tribune*

"A self-aware, vulnerable, and often funny retelling of her life that doubles as a roadmap for women and girls who are similarly navigating unfamiliar territory, even with potentially lower stakes than the White House."

Prachi Gupta, *Jezebel*

"In *Becoming*, Obama doesn't write so much as talks to her readers as she always has to a nation that fell in love with her—in clear, frank and forthcoming terms, as a black woman in America with a bridge called her back and a wisdom to lay bare . . . who Michelle Obama was before she was FLOTUS is a woman you feel glad and grateful to have back in our midst—the striver, an astonishing mix of resilience, joy, pragmatism and grace."

—Rebecca Carroll, *Los Angeles Times*

"An engrossing memoir as well as a lively treatise on what extraordinary grace under extraordinary pressure looks like."

—*Kirkus Reviews*, starred review

A *NEW YORK TIMES* NOTABLE
BOOK OF THE YEAR

NPR, BEST BOOKS OF THE YEAR

PEOPLE, 10 BEST BOOKS
OF THE YEAR

GOODREADS CHOICE
AWARDS, BEST MEMOIR

ESQUIRE,
BEST BOOKS OF THE YEAR

COSMOPOLITAN,
BEST BOOKS OF THE YEAR

PARADE, THE BEST BOOKS
WE READ THIS YEAR.

WINNER OF THE GRAMMY AWARD
FOR BEST SPOKEN WORD ALBUM

Extraordinary praise for
BECOMING

"A serious work of candid reflection by a singular figure of early-21st-century America . . . *Becoming* is refined and forthright, gracefully written and at times laugh-out-loud funny. . . . In finally telling her story, Obama is doing several things with this book. She is taking the country by the hand on an intimate tour of everyday African-American life and ambition, while recounting her rise from modest origins to the closest this country has to nobility. She's meditating on the tensions women face in a world that speaks of gender equality but in which women still bear the greater burdens of balancing career and family, even with a forward-thinking husband like Barack Obama. And she is reminding readers that African-Americans, like any other group, experience the heartbreak of infertility, as she describes the challenges she and her husband confronted in order to become parents. . . . One of the great gifts of Obama's book is her loving and frank bearing-witness to the lived experiences of the black working class, the invisible people who don't make the evening news and whom not enough of us choose to see."

—Isabel Wilkerson, *The New York Times Book Review*

"*Becoming* is inspirational without trying to be. From the first words, the very warmth that permeates its author emanates from the pages. . . . *Becoming* manages to be a coming-of-age tale, a love story and a family saga all in one. More importantly, this book is a reminder that America is still a work-in-progress, and that hope can be an action word if we allow it to be. *Becoming* is a balm that America needs, from a woman America does not yet deserve."

—Angie Thomas, *Time*

"Deeply personal and refreshingly honest . . . She's thoughtful, humorous, bracingly revealing, and when it's time, she does us all the favor of showing us the human side of a man worshipped by so many. . . . It's human and genuine and welcoming to see the layers of humanity she holds open. . . . Michelle Obama's story can maybe inspire you to find a path for your own story."

—Shonda Rhimes, Shondaland

"A sometimes surprisingly intimate look at the life of the former first lady . . . *Becoming* is satisfying for the quiet moments in which Mrs. Obama, the woman who supported a black man named Barack all the way to the presidency, gets to let down her hair and breathe as Michelle LaVaughn Robinson, girl of the South Side."

—Hannah Giorgis, *The Atlantic*

"Every sentence Obama writes makes a statement."

—David Canfield, *Entertainment Weekly*

"Many black women can imagine Michelle Obama as a good girlfriend; her struggles are relatable. It's comforting to read that she, too, battles insecurity, wondering if she's good enough."

—Wendi C. Thomas, *Chicago Tribune*

"An evocative look back . . . and a clear-eyed exposition of what came after."

—Sandra Sobieraj Westfall, *People*

"Candid [and] engaging."

—*The Economist*

"A pioneering and important work . . . Obama has sworn to tell her readers everything, and she delivers on that promise. From the silly to the surreal, from the momentous to the mundane, from the tragic to the transformative, she tells it all. As she shares her story, you are struck that every word is honest, brave and real. . . . As first lady, Obama shattered the mold. . . . *Becoming* shatters the mold, too. . . . The greatest contribution of *Becoming* is the inspiration that Obama gives to press onward."

—Allyson Hobbs, *San Francisco Chronicle*

BECOMING

MICHELLE OBAMA

CROWN
NEW YORK

To all the people who have helped me become:

the folks who raised me—Fraser, Marian, Craig,
and my vast extended family,

my circle of strong women, who always lift me up,

my loyal and dedicated staff, who continue to make me proud.

———————

To the loves of my life:

Malia and Sasha, my two most precious peas,
who are my reasons for being,

and finally, Barack, who always promised me an interesting journey.

Contents

Introduction to the Paperback Edition

I'M PROUD OF THIS BOOK, TRULY, BECAUSE OF WHAT IT means to me. And hopefully, what it will mean to you.

I knew from the outset that if I was going to write a memoir, it had to include more than the shade of blue I chose for a china pattern or who was or wasn't invited to a State Dinner. Those are parts of my story, yes, but to be honest, they aren't very important parts. And I had no interest in using a memoir to settle scores or win a few news cycles, because I don't care about any of that, either.

What I do care about, what I've always cared about, is going deeper to unearth the fullness of our stories, blemishes and all. I know that I am who I am not because of the titles I've held or the celebrities I've met, but because of the snaking paths and winding roads, the frustrations and contradictions, the constant growth that is painful and joyful and full of confusion. So I knew that if this book was going to make any difference at all, it would need to be raw, vulnerable, and unabashedly honest.

And, as a Black woman, all of that was even more important. For the better part of our history, Black women's stories have either gone untold or been told by others—by those who haven't walked in our shoes and sometimes by those who haven't even cared to imagine what it might feel like to do so. That's why it was crucial for me to tell, in my own words and on my own terms, not just the story of the first Black First Lady, but also the story of a little Black girl who studied hard, became a lawyer, and fell in love; the story of a Black woman raising children, building a career, and staying afloat amid a tumultuous world. There is great beauty within every Black woman's story, whether or not we ever become First Lady.

For me, embracing that beauty meant reflecting on my entire history, not just the major events and milestones, but the broader historical and societal context swirling along the way. And I found great joy in redis-covering the tiniest details that I'd long brushed aside: the fresh smell of cleaning products on a spring day, the natural ease with which my grandfather kept the record player humming on a Saturday afternoon, the sound of ice scraped off a windshield on a frozen Chicago morning. While sometimes I think about the stories in this book and wonder if they're too small or trivial, what I've learned and re-learned throughout this process is that these moments may in fact be the most important parts of our stories. These years-old sensory recollections, these dusty emotional bursts can split time in two, overlaying who we are atop who we were. It's that experience—seeing at once the present and the past, the outlines still visible beneath the parchment—that for me was profoundly meaningful, opening up a radiance within my own story I hadn't noticed before.

This isn't to say any of this was easy, particularly the experience of baring this truest version of myself for the entire world to accept or leave behind. In fact, the night before this book first went on sale—after all the chapters had been written, all the copies printed and bound and placed on shelves—I woke up in a panic. The following evening, I was scheduled to discuss my memoir with Oprah Winfrey in front of 14,000 people in a professional basketball arena, an event that would kick off a worldwide tour. I laid awake anxious in my bed, worried that these little stories couldn't bear the enormous load.

What if the book just isn't any good? What if people hate it? Or what if they just don't care at all?

My husband stays up much later than me, and thankfully, he was still awake when my fears came to visit and wouldn't leave. I crawled out of bed, put my slippers on, and went down to talk with him. Maybe the tour wasn't a very smart idea, I told him. Maybe the book will flop. Barack put his arms around me and placed his forehead on mine. "It's good, Miche," he told me. "It really is."

At this point I'd spent eight years as First Lady of the United States. I'd done more interviews than I could count and given more speeches than I can remember. Oprah Winfrey wasn't some high-powered moderator, she was my friend.

But the doubts never leave us for good. We all have our tender spots, and our instinct is to keep them protected.

This book affirmed within me the value in bucking against that instinct, in stepping into our fears. It's where the greatest truths come from—the understanding of what matters and what doesn't, the ability to let go of the things that too often hold us down, the acceptance of ourselves and a belief in our own promise.

I hope that as you read my story, you'll reflect on your own—every one of your bumps and bruises, each of your successes and bursts of laughter. And then I hope you'll share that story, all of it, especially the most tender spots. Because that's how we all can keep becoming.

Michelle Obama
December 2020

Preface

March 2017

WHEN I WAS A KID, MY ASPIRATIONS WERE SIMPLE. I wanted a dog. I wanted a house that had stairs in it—two floors for one family. I wanted, for some reason, a four-door station wagon instead of the two-door Buick that was my father's pride and joy. I used to tell people that when I grew up, I was going to be a pediatrician. Why? Because I loved being around little kids and I quickly learned that it was a pleasing answer for adults to hear. *Oh, a doctor! What a good choice!* In those days, I wore pigtails and bossed my older brother around and managed, always and no matter what, to get As at school. I was ambitious, though I didn't know exactly what I was shooting for. Now I think it's one of the most useless questions an adult can ask a child—*What do you want to be when you grow up?* As if growing up is finite. As if at some point you become something and that's the end.

So far in my life, I've been a lawyer. I've been a vice president at a hospital and the director of a nonprofit that helps young people build meaningful careers. I've been a working-class Black student at a fancy mostly white college. I've been the only woman, the only African American, in all sorts of rooms. I've been a bride, a stressed-out new mother, a daughter torn up by grief. And until recently, I was the First Lady of the United States of America—a job that's not officially a job, but that nonetheless has given me a platform like nothing I could have imagined. It challenged me and humbled me, lifted me up and shrank me down, sometimes all at once. I'm just beginning to process what took place over these last years—from the moment in 2006 when my husband first started talking about running for president to the cold morning this winter when I climbed into a limo with Melania Trump, accompanying her to her husband's inauguration. It's been quite a ride.

When you're First Lady, America shows itself to you in its extremes. I've been to fund-raisers in private homes that look more like art museums, houses where people own bathtubs made from gemstones. I've visited families who lost everything in Hurricane Katrina and were tearful and grateful just to have a working refrigerator and stove. I've encountered people I find to be shallow and hypocritical and others—teachers and military spouses and so many more—whose spirits are so deep and strong it's astonishing. And I've met kids—lots of them, all over the world—who crack me up and fill me with hope and who blessedly manage to forget about my title once we start rooting around in the dirt of a garden.

Since stepping reluctantly into public life, I've been held up as the most powerful woman in the world and taken down as an "angry Black woman." I've wanted to ask my detractors which part of that phrase matters to them the most—is it "angry" or "Black" or "woman"? I've smiled for photos with people who call my husband horrible names on national television, but still want a framed keepsake for their mantel. I've heard about the swampy parts of the internet that question everything about me, right down to whether I'm a woman or a man. A sitting U.S. congressman has made fun of my butt. I've been hurt. I've been furious. But mostly, I've tried to laugh this stuff off.

There's a lot I still don't know about America, about life, about what the future might bring. But I do know myself. My father, Fraser, taught me to work hard, laugh often, and keep my word. My mother, Marian, showed me how to think for myself and to use my voice. Together, in our cramped apartment on the South Side of Chicago, they helped me see the value in our story, in my story, in the larger story of our country. Even when it's not pretty or perfect. Even when it's more real than you want it to be. Your story is what you have, what you will always have. It is something to own.

For eight years, I lived in the White House, a place with more stairs than I can count—plus elevators, a bowling alley, and an in-house florist. I slept in a bed that was made up with Italian linens. Our meals were cooked by a team of world-class chefs and delivered by professionals more highly trained than those at any five-star restaurant or hotel. Secret Service agents, with their earpieces and guns and deliberately flat expressions, stood outside our doors, doing their best to stay out of our family's private life. We got used to it, eventually, sort of—the strange grandeur of our new home and also the constant, quiet presence of others.

The White House is where our two girls played ball in the hallways and climbed trees on the South Lawn. It's where Barack sat up late at night, poring over briefings and drafts of speeches in the Treaty Room, and where Sunny, one of our dogs, sometimes pooped on the rug. I could stand on the Truman Balcony and watch the tourists posing with their selfie sticks and peering through the iron fence, trying to guess at what went on inside. There were days when I felt suffocated by the fact that our windows had to be kept shut for security, that I couldn't get some fresh air without causing a fuss. There were other times when I'd be awestruck by the white magnolias blooming outside, the everyday bustle of government business, the majesty of a military welcome. There were days, weeks, and months when I hated politics. And there were moments when the beauty of this country and its people so overwhelmed me that I couldn't speak.

Then it was over. Even if you see it coming, even as your final weeks are filled with emotional good-byes, the day itself is still a blur. A hand goes on a Bible; an oath gets repeated. One president's furniture gets carried out while another's comes in. Closets are emptied and refilled in the span of a few hours. Just like that, there are new heads on new pillows—new temperaments, new dreams. And when it ends, when you walk out the door that last time from the world's most famous address, you're left in many ways to find yourself again.

So let me start here, with a small thing that happened not long ago. I was at home in the redbrick house that my family recently moved into. Our new house sits about two miles from our old house, on a quiet neighborhood street. We're still settling in. In the family room, our furniture is arranged the same way it was in the White House. We've got mementos around the house that remind us it was all real—photos of our family time at Camp David, handmade pots given to me by Native American students, a book signed by Nelson Mandela. What was strange about this night was that everyone was gone. Barack was traveling. Sasha was out with friends. Malia's been living and working in New York, finishing out her gap year before college. It was just me, our two dogs, and a silent, empty house like I haven't known in eight years.

And I was hungry. I walked down the stairs from our bedroom with the dogs following on my heels. In the kitchen, I opened the fridge. I found a loaf of bread, took out two pieces, and laid them in the toaster oven. I opened a cabinet and got out a plate. I know it's a weird thing to say, but to take a plate from a shelf in the kitchen without anyone first insisting that they get it for me, to stand by myself watching bread turn brown in the toaster, feels as close to a return to my old life as I've come. Or maybe it's my new life just beginning to announce itself.

In the end, I didn't just make toast; I made cheese toast, moving my slices of bread to the microwave and melting a fat mess of gooey cheddar between them. I then carried my plate outside to the backyard. I didn't have to tell anyone I was going. I just went. I was in bare feet, wearing a pair of shorts. The chill of winter had finally lifted. The crocuses were just starting to push up through the beds along our back wall. The air smelled like spring. I sat on the steps of our veranda, feeling the warmth of the day's sun still caught in the slate beneath my feet. A dog started barking somewhere in the distance, and my own dogs paused to listen, seeming momentarily confused. It occurred to me that it was a jarring sound for them, given that we didn't have neighbors, let alone neighbor dogs, at the White House. For them, all this was new. As the dogs loped off to explore the perimeter of the yard, I ate my toast in the dark, feeling alone in the best possible way. My mind wasn't on the group of guards with guns sitting less than a hundred yards away at the custom-built command post inside our garage, or the fact that I still can't walk down a street without a security detail. I wasn't thinking about the new president or for that matter the old president, either.

I was thinking instead about how in a few minutes I would go back inside my house, wash my plate in the sink, and head up to bed, maybe opening a window so I could feel the spring air—how glorious that would be. I was thinking, too, that the stillness was affording me a first real opportunity to reflect. As First Lady, I'd get to the end of a busy week and need to be reminded how it had started. But time is beginning to feel different. My girls, who arrived at the White House with their Polly Pockets, a blanket named Blankie, and a stuffed tiger named Tiger, are now teenagers, young women with plans and voices of their own. My husband is making his own adjustments to life after the White House, catching his own breath. And here I am, in this new place, with a lot I want to say.

BECOMING

Becoming Me

1

I SPENT MUCH OF MY CHILDHOOD LISTENING TO THE sound of striving. It came in the form of bad music, or at least amateur music, coming up through the floorboards of my bedroom—the *plink plink plink* of students sitting downstairs at my great-aunt Robbie's piano, slowly and imperfectly learning their scales. My family lived in the South Shore neighborhood of Chicago, in a tidy brick bungalow that belonged to Robbie and her husband, Terry. My parents rented an apartment on the second floor, while Robbie and Terry lived on the first. Robbie was my mother's aunt and had been generous to her over many years, but to me she was kind of a terror. Prim and serious, she directed the choir at a local church and was also our community's resident piano teacher. She wore sensible heels and kept a pair of reading glasses on a chain around her neck. She had a sly smile but didn't appreciate sarcasm the way my mother did. I'd sometimes hear her chewing out her students for not having practiced enough or chewing out their parents for delivering them late to lessons.

"Good night!" she'd exclaim in the middle of the day, with the same blast of exasperation someone else might say, "Oh, for God's sake!" Few, it seemed, could live up to Robbie's standards.

The sound of people trying, however, became the soundtrack to our life. There was plinking in the afternoons, plinking in the evenings. Ladies from church sometimes came over to practice hymns, belting their piety through our walls. Under Robbie's rules, kids who took piano lessons were allowed to work on only one song at a time. From my room, I'd listen to them attempting, note by uncertain note, to win her approval, graduating from "Hot Cross Buns" to "Brahms's Lullaby," but only after many tries. The music was never annoying; it was just persistent. It crept up the stairwell that separated our space from Robbie's. It drifted through open windows in summertime, accompanying my thoughts as I played with my Barbies or built little kingdoms made out of blocks. The only respite came when my father got home from an early shift at the city's water treatment plant and put the Cubs game on TV, boosting the volume just enough to blot it all out.

This was the tail end of the 1960s on the South Side of Chicago. The Cubs weren't bad, but they weren't great, either. I'd sit on my dad's lap in his recliner and listen to him narrate how the Cubs were in the middle of a late-season swoon or why Billy Williams, who lived just around the corner from us on Constance Avenue, had such a sweet swing from the left side of the plate. Outside the ballparks, America was in the midst of a massive and uncertain shift. The Kennedys were dead. Martin Luther King Jr. had been killed standing on a balcony in Memphis, setting off riots across the country, including in Chicago. The 1968 Democratic National Convention turned bloody as police went after Vietnam War protesters with batons and tear gas in Grant Park, about nine miles north of where we lived. White families, meanwhile, were moving out of the city in droves, lured by the suburbs—the promise of better schools, more space, and probably more whiteness, too.

None of this really registered with me. I was just a kid, a girl with Barbies and blocks, with two parents and an older brother who slept each night with his head about three feet from mine. My family was my world, the center of everything. My mother taught me how to read early, walking me to the public library, sitting with me as I sounded out words on a page. My father went to work every day dressed in the blue uniform of a city laborer, but at night he showed us what it meant to love jazz and art.

As a boy, he'd taken classes at the Art Institute of Chicago, and in high school he'd painted and sculpted. He'd been a competitive swimmer and boxer in school, too, and as an adult was a fan of every televised sport, from professional golf to the NHL. He appreciated seeing strong people excel. When my brother, Craig, got interested in basketball, my father propped coins above the doorframe in our kitchen, encouraging him to leap for them.

Everything that mattered was within a five-block radius—my grand-parents and cousins, the church on the corner where we were not quite regulars at Sunday school, the gas station where my mother sometimes sent me to pick up a pack of Newports, and the liquor store, which also sold Wonder bread, penny candy, and gallons of milk. On hot summer nights, Craig and I dozed off to the sound of cheers from the adult-league softball games going on at the nearby public park, where by day we climbed on the playground jungle gym and played tag with other kids.

Craig and I are not quite two years apart in age. He's got my father's soft eyes and optimistic spirit, my mother's implacability. The two of us have always been tight, in part thanks to an unwavering and somewhat inexplicable allegiance he seemed to feel for his baby sister right from the start. There's an early family photograph, a black and white of the four of us sitting on a couch, my mother smiling as she holds me on her lap, my father appearing serious and proud with Craig perched on his. We're dressed for church or maybe a wedding. I'm about eight months old, a pudge-faced, no-nonsense bruiser in diapers and an ironed white dress, looking ready to slide out of my mother's clutches, staring down the camera as if I might eat it. Next to me is Craig, gentlemanly in a little bow tie and suit jacket, bearing an earnest expression. He's two years old and already the portrait of brotherly vigilance and responsibility—his arm extended toward mine, his fingers wrapped protectively around my fat wrist.

At the time the photo was taken, we were living across the hall from my father's parents in Parkway Gardens, an affordable housing project on the South Side made up of modernist apartment buildings. It had been built in the 1950s and was designed as a co-op, meant to ease a post–World War II housing shortage for Black working-class families. Later, it would deteriorate under the grind of poverty and gang violence, becoming one of the city's more dangerous places to live. Long before this, though, when I was still a toddler, my parents—who had met as teenagers and married in their mid-twenties—accepted an offer to move a few miles south to Robbie and Terry's place in a nicer neighborhood.

On Euclid Avenue, we were two households living under one not very big roof. Judging from the layout, the second-floor space had probably been designed as an in-law apartment meant for one or two people, but four of us found a way to fit inside. My parents slept in the lone bedroom, while Craig and I shared a bigger area that I assume was intended to be the living room. Later, as we grew, my grandfather—Purnell Shields, my mother's father, who was an enthusiastic if not deeply skilled carpenter—brought over some cheap wooden paneling and built a makeshift partition to divide the room into two semiprivate spaces. He added a plastic accordion door to each space and created a little common play area in front where we could keep our toys and books.

I loved my room. It was just big enough for a twin bed and a narrow desk. I kept all my stuffed animals on the bed, painstakingly tucking them around my head each night as a form of ritual comfort. On his side of the wall, Craig lived a sort of mirror existence with his own bed pushed up against the paneling, parallel to mine. The partition between us was so flimsy that we could talk as we lay in bed at night, often tossing a balled sock back and forth through the ten-inch gap between the partition and the ceiling as we did.

Aunt Robbie, meanwhile, kept her part of the house like a mausoleum, the furniture swathed in protective plastic that felt cold and sticky on my bare legs when I dared sit on it. Her shelves were loaded with porcelain figurines we weren't allowed to touch. I'd let my hand hover over a set of sweet-faced glass poodles—a delicate-looking mother and three tiny puppies—and then pull it back, fearing Robbie's wrath. When lessons weren't happening, the first floor was deadly silent. The television was never on, the radio never played. I'm not even sure the two of them talked much down there. Robbie's husband's full name was William Victor Terry, but for some reason we called him only by his last name. Terry was like a shadow, a distinguished-looking man who wore three-piece suits every day of the week and pretty much never said a word.

I came to think of upstairs and downstairs as two different universes, ruled over by competing sensibilities. Upstairs, we were noisy and unapologetically so. Craig and I threw balls and chased each other around the apartment. We sprayed Pledge furniture polish on the wood floor of the hallway so we could slide farther and faster in our socks, often crashing into the walls. We held brother-sister boxing matches in the kitchen, using the two sets of gloves my dad had given us for Christmas, along with personalized instructions on how to land a proper jab. At night, as a family, we played board games, told stories and jokes, and cranked Jackson 5 records on the stereo. When it got to be too much for Robbie down below, she'd emphatically flick the light switch in our shared stairwell, which also controlled the lightbulb in our upstairs hallway, off and on, again and again—her polite-ish way of telling us to pipe down.

Robbie and Terry were older. They grew up in a different era, with different concerns. They'd seen things our parents hadn't—things that Craig and I, in our raucous childishness, couldn't begin to guess. This was some version of what my mother would say if we got too wound up about the grouchiness downstairs. Even if we didn't know the context, we were instructed to remember that context existed. Everyone on earth, they'd tell us, was carrying around an unseen history, and that alone deserved some tolerance. Robbie, I'd learn many years later, had sued Northwestern University for discrimination, having registered for a choral music workshop there in 1943 and been denied a room in the women's dorm. She was instructed to stay instead in a rooming house in town—a place "for coloreds," she was told. Terry, meanwhile, had once been a Pullman porter on one of the overnight passenger rail lines running in and out of Chicago. It was a respectable if not well-paying profession, made up entirely of Black men who kept their uniforms immaculate while also hauling luggage, serving meals, and generally tending to the needs of train passengers, including shining their shoes.

Years after his retirement, Terry still lived in a state of numbed formality—impeccably dressed, remotely servile, never asserting himself in any way, at least that I would see. It was as if he'd surrendered a part of himself as a way of coping. I'd watch him mow our lawn in the high heat of summer in a pair of wing tips, suspenders, and a thin-brimmed fedora, the sleeves of his dress shirt carefully rolled up. He'd indulge himself by having exactly one cigarette a day and exactly one cocktail a month, and even then he wouldn't loosen up the way my father and mother would after having a highball or a Schlitz, which they did a few times a month. Some part of me wanted Terry to talk, to spill whatever secrets he carried. I imagined that he had all sorts of interesting stories about cities he'd visited and how rich people on trains behaved or maybe didn't. But we wouldn't hear any of it. For some reason, he'd never tell.

I WAS ABOUT FOUR when I decided I wanted to learn piano. Craig, who was in the first grade, was already making trips downstairs for weekly lessons on Robbie's upright and returning relatively unscathed. I figured I was ready. I was pretty convinced I already *had* learned piano, in fact, through straight-up osmosis—all those hours spent listening to other kids fumbling through their songs. The music was already in my head. I just wanted to go downstairs and demonstrate to my exacting great-aunt what a gifted girl I was, how it would take no effort at all for me to become her star student.

Robbie's piano sat in a small square room at the rear of the house, close to a window that overlooked the backyard. She kept a potted plant in one corner and a folding table where students could fill out music work sheets in the other. During lessons, she sat straight spined in an uphol-stered high-back armchair, tapping out the beat with one finger, her head cocked as she listened keenly for each mistake. Was I afraid of Robbie? Not exactly, but there was a scariness to her; she represented a rigid kind of authority I hadn't yet encountered elsewhere. She demanded excel-lence from every kid who sat on her piano bench. I saw her as someone to win over, or maybe to somehow conquer. With her, it always felt like there was something to prove.

At my first lesson, my legs dangled from the piano bench, too short to reach the floor. Robbie gave me my own elementary music workbook, which I was thrilled about, and showed me how to position my hands properly over the keys.

"All right, pay attention," she said, scolding me before we'd even begun. "Find middle C."

When you're little, a piano can look like it has a thousand keys. You're staring at an expanse of black and white that stretches farther than two small arms can reach. Middle C, I soon learned, was the anchoring point. It was the territorial line between where the right hand and the left hand traveled, between the treble and the bass clefs. If you could lay your thumb on middle C, everything else automatically fell into place. The keys on Robbie's piano had a subtle unevenness of color and shape, places where bits of the ivory had broken off over time, leaving them looking like a set of bad teeth. Helpfully, the middle C key had a full corner missing, a wedge about the size of my fingernail, which got me centered every time.

It turned out I liked the piano. Sitting at it felt natural, like something I was meant to do. My family was loaded with musicians and music lovers, especially on my mother's side. I had an uncle who played in a professional band. Several of my aunts sang in church choirs. I had Robbie, who in addition to her choir and lessons directed something called the Operetta Workshop, a shoestring musical theater program for kids, which Craig and I attended every Saturday morning in the basement of her church. The musical center of my family, though, was my grandfather Shields, the carpenter, who was also Robbie's younger brother. He was a carefree, round-bellied man with an infectious laugh and a scraggly salt-and-pepper beard. When I was younger, he'd lived on the West Side of the city and Craig and I had referred to him as Westside. But he moved into our neighborhood the same year I started taking piano lessons, and we'd duly rechristened him Southside.

Southside had separated from my grandmother decades earlier, when my mother was in her teens. He lived with my aunt Carolyn, my mom's oldest sister, and my uncle Steve, her youngest brother, just two blocks from us in a cozy one-story house that he'd wired top to bottom for music, putting speakers in every room, including the bathroom. In the dining room, he built an elaborate cabinet system to hold his stereo equipment, much of it scavenged at yard sales. He had two mismatched turntables plus a rickety old reel-to-reel tape player and shelves packed with records he'd collected over many years.

There was a lot about the world that Southside didn't trust. He was kind of a classic old-guy conspiracy theorist. He didn't trust dentists, which led to his having virtually no teeth. He didn't trust the police, and he didn't always trust white people, either, being the grandson of a Georgia slave and having spent his early childhood in Alabama during the time of Jim Crow before coming north to Chicago in the 1920s. When he had kids of his own, Southside had taken pains to keep them safe— scaring them with real and imagined stories about what might happen to Black kids who crossed into the wrong neighborhood, lecturing them about avoiding the police.

Music seemed to be an antidote to his worries, a way to relax and crowd them out. When Southside had a payday for his carpentry work, he'd sometimes splurge and buy himself a new album. He threw regular parties for the family, forcing everyone to talk loudly over whatever he put on the stereo, because the music always dominated. We celebrated most major life events at Southside's house, which meant that over the years we unwrapped Christmas presents to Ella Fitzgerald and blew out birthday candles to Coltrane. According to my mother, as a younger man Southside had made a point of pumping jazz into his seven children, often waking everyone at sunrise by playing one of his records at full blast.

His love for music was infectious. Once Southside moved to our neighborhood, I'd pass whole afternoons at his house, pulling albums from the shelf at random and putting them on his stereo, each one its own immersing adventure. Even though I was small, he put no restrictions on what I could touch. He'd later buy me my first album, Stevie Wonder's *Talking Book,* which I'd keep at his house on a special shelf he designated for my favorite records. If I was hungry, he'd make me a milk shake or fry us a whole chicken while we listened to Aretha or Miles or Billie. To me, Southside was as big as heaven. And heaven, as I envisioned it, had to be a place full of jazz.

. . .

A T HOME, I continued to work on my own progress as a musician. Sitting at Robbie's upright piano, I was quick to pick up the scales— that osmosis thing was real—and I threw myself into filling out the sight-reading work sheets she gave me. Because we didn't have a piano of our own, I had to do my practicing downstairs on hers, waiting until nobody else was having a lesson, often dragging my mom with me to sit in the upholstered chair and listen to me play. I learned one song in the piano book and then another. I was probably no better than her other students, no less fumbling, but I was driven. To me, there was magic in the learning. I got a buzzy sort of satisfaction from it. For one thing, I'd picked up on the simple, encouraging correlation between how long I practiced and how much I achieved. And I sensed something in Robbie as well— too deeply buried to be outright pleasure, but still, a pulse of something lighter and happier coming from her when I made it through a song without messing up, when my right hand picked out a melody while my left touched down on a chord. I'd notice it out of the corner of my eye: Robbie's lips would unpurse themselves just slightly; her tapping finger would pick up a little bounce.

This, it turns out, was our honeymoon phase. It's possible that we might have continued this way, Robbie and I, had I been less curious and more reverent when it came to her piano method. But the lesson book was thick enough and my progress on the opening few songs slow enough that I got impatient and started pecking ahead—and not just a few pages ahead but deep into the book, checking out the titles of the more advanced songs and beginning, during my practice sessions, to fiddle around with playing them. When I proudly debuted one of my late-in-the-book songs for Robbie, she exploded, slapping down my achievement with a vicious "Good *night!*" I got chewed out the way I'd heard her chewing out plenty of students before me. All I'd done was try to learn more and faster, but Robbie viewed it as a crime approaching treason. She wasn't impressed, not even a little bit.

Nor was I chastened. I was the kind of kid who liked concrete answers to my questions, who liked to reason things out to some logical if exhausting end. I was lawyerly and also veered toward dictatorial, as my brother, who often got ordered out of our shared play area, would attest. When I thought I had a good idea about something, I didn't like being told no. Which is how my great-aunt and I ended up in each other's faces, both of us hot and unyielding.

"How could you be mad at me for wanting to learn a new song?"

"You're not ready for it. That's not how you learn piano."

"But I *am* ready. I just played it."

"That's not how it's done."

"But *why*?"

Piano lessons became epic and trying, largely due to my refusal to follow the prescribed method and Robbie's refusal to see anything good in my freewheeling approach to her songbook. We went back and forth, week after week, as I remember it. I was stubborn and so was she. I had a point of view and she did, too. In between disputes, I continued to play the piano and she continued to listen, offering a stream of corrections. I gave her little credit for my improvement as a player. She gave me little credit for improving. But still, the lessons went on.

Upstairs, my parents and Craig found it all so very funny. They cracked up at the dinner table as I recounted my battles with Robbie, still seething as I ate my spaghetti and meatballs. Craig, for his part, had no issues with Robbie, being a cheerful kid and a by-the-book, marginally invested piano student. My parents expressed no sympathy for my woes and none for Robbie's, either. In general, they weren't ones to intervene in matters outside schooling, expecting early on that my brother and I should handle our own business. They seemed to view their job as mostly to listen and bolster us as needed inside the four walls of our home. And where another parent might have scolded a kid for being sassy with an elder as I had been, they also let that be. My mother had lived with Robbie on and off since she was about sixteen, following every arcane rule the woman laid down, and it's possible she was secretly happy to see Robbie's authority challenged. Looking back on it now, I think my parents appreciated my feistiness and I'm glad for it. It was a flame inside me they wanted to keep lit.

. . .

ONCE A YEAR, Robbie held a fancy recital so that her students could perform for a live audience. To this day, I'm not sure how she managed it, but she somehow got access to a practice hall at Roosevelt University in downtown Chicago, holding her recitals in a grand stone building on Michigan Avenue, right near where the Chicago Symphony Orchestra played. Just thinking about going there made me nervous. Our apartment on Euclid Avenue was about nine miles south of the Chicago Loop, which with its glittering skyscrapers and crowded sidewalks felt otherworldly to me. My family made trips into the heart of the city only a handful of times a year, to visit the Art Institute or see a play, the four of us traveling like astronauts in the capsule of my dad's Buick.

My father loved any excuse to drive. He was devoted to his car, a bronze-colored two-door Buick Electra 225, which he referred to with pride as "the Deuce and a Quarter." He kept it buffed and waxed and was religious about the maintenance schedule, taking it to Sears for tire rotations and oil changes the same way my mom carted us kids to the pediatrician for checkups. We loved the Deuce and a Quarter, too. It had smooth lines and narrow taillights that made it look cool and futuristic. It was roomy enough to feel like a house. I could practically stand up inside it, running my hands over the cloth-covered ceiling. This was back when wearing a seat belt was optional, so most of the time Craig and I just flopped around in the rear, draping our bodies over the front seat when we wanted to talk to our parents. Half the time I'd pull myself up on the headrest and jut my chin forward so that my face could be next to my dad's and we'd have the exact same view.

The car provided another form of closeness for my family, a chance to talk and travel at once. In the evenings after dinner, Craig and I would sometimes beg my dad to take us out for an aimless drive. As a treat on summer nights, we'd head to a drive-in theater southwest of our neighborhood to watch Planet of the Apes movies, parking the Buick at dusk and settling in for the show, my mother handing out a dinner of fried chicken and potato chips she'd brought from home, Craig and I eating it on our laps in the backseat, careful to wipe our hands on our napkins and not the seat.

It would be years before I fully understood what driving the car meant to my father. As a kid, I could only sense it—the liberation he felt behind the wheel, the pleasure he took in having a smooth-running engine and perfectly balanced tires humming beneath him. He'd been in his thirties when a doctor informed him that the odd weakness he'd started to feel in one leg was just the beginning of a long and probably painful slide toward immobility, that odds were that someday, due to a mysterious unsheathing of neurons in his brain and spinal cord, he'd find himself unable to walk at all. I don't have the precise dates, but it seems that the Buick came into my father's life at roughly the same time that multiple sclerosis did. And though he never said it, the car had to provide some sort of sideways relief.

The diagnosis was not something he or my mother dwelled upon. We were decades, still, from a time when a simple Google search would bring up a head-spinning array of charts, statistics, and medical explainers that either gave or took away hope. I doubt he would have wanted to see them anyway. Although my father was raised in the church, he wouldn't have prayed for God to spare him. He wouldn't have looked for alternative treatments or a guru or some faulty gene to blame. In my family, we have a long-standing habit of blocking out bad news, of trying to forget about it almost the moment it arrives. Nobody knew how long my father had been feeling poorly before he first took himself to the doctor, but my guess is it had already been months if not years. He didn't like medical appointments. He wasn't interested in complaining. He was the sort of person who accepted what came and just kept moving forward.

I do know that on the day of my big piano recital, he was already walking with a slight limp, his left foot unable to catch up to his right. All my memories of my father include some manifestation of his disability, even if none of us were quite willing to call it that yet. What I knew at the time was that my dad moved a bit more slowly than other dads. I sometimes saw him pausing before walking up a flight of stairs, as if needing to think through the maneuver before actually attempting it. When we went shopping at the mall, he'd park himself on a bench, content to watch the bags or sneak in a nap while the rest of the family roamed freely.

Riding downtown for the piano recital, I sat in the backseat of the Buick wearing a nice dress and patent leather shoes, my hair in pigtails, experiencing the first cold sweat of my life. I was anxious about performing, even though back at home in Robbie's apartment I'd practiced my song practically to death. Craig, too, was in a suit and prepared to play his own song. But the prospect of it wasn't bothering him. He was sound asleep, in fact, knocked out cold in the backseat, his mouth agape, his expression blissful and unworried. This was Craig. I'd spend a lifetime admiring him for his ease. He was playing by then in a Biddy Basketball league that had games every weekend and apparently had already tamed his nerves around performing.

My father would often pick a lot as close to our destination as possible, shelling out more money for parking to minimize how far he'd have to walk on his unsteady legs. That day, we found Roosevelt University with no trouble and made our way up to what seemed like an enormous, echoing hall where the recital would take place. I felt tiny inside it. The room had elegant floor-to-ceiling windows through which you could see the wide lawns of Grant Park and, beyond that, the white-capped swells of Lake Michigan. There were steel-gray chairs arranged in orderly rows, slowly filling with nervous kids and expectant parents. And at the front, on a raised stage, were the first two baby grand pianos I'd ever laid eyes on, their giant hardwood tops propped open like black bird wings. Robbie was there, too, bustling about in a floral-print dress like the belle of the ball—albeit a matronly belle—making sure all her students had arrived with sheet music in hand. She shushed the room to silence when it was time for the show to begin.

I don't recall who played in what order that day. I only know that when it was my turn, I got up from my seat and walked with my very best posture to the front of the room, mounting the stairs and finding my seat at one of the gleaming baby grands. The truth is I was ready. As much as I found Robbie to be snippy and inflexible, I'd also internalized her devotion to rigor. I knew my song so well I hardly had to think about it. I just had to start moving my hands.

And yet there was a problem, one I discovered in the split second it took to lift my little fingers to the keys. I was sitting at a perfect piano, it turned out, with its surfaces carefully dusted, its internal wires precisely tuned, its eighty-eight keys laid out in a flawless ribbon of black and white. The issue was that I wasn't used to flawless. In fact, I'd never once in my life encountered it. My experience of the piano came entirely from Robbie's squat little music room with its scraggly potted plant and view of our modest backyard. The only instrument I'd ever played was her less-than-perfect upright, with its honky-tonk patchwork of yellowed keys and its conveniently chipped middle C. To me, that's what a piano was—the same way my neighborhood was my neighborhood, my dad was my dad, my life was my life. It was all I knew.

Now, suddenly, I was aware of people watching me from their chairs as I stared hard at the high gloss of the piano keys, finding nothing there but sameness. I had no clue where to place my hands. With a tight throat and chugging heart, I looked out to the audience, trying not to telegraph my panic, searching for the safe harbor of my mother's face. Instead, I spotted a figure rising from the front row and slowly levitating in my direction. It was Robbie. We had brawled plenty by then, to the point where I viewed her a little bit like an enemy. But here in my moment of comeuppance, she arrived at my shoulder almost like an angel. Maybe she understood my shock. Maybe she knew that the disparities of the world had just quietly shown themselves to me for the first time. It's possible she needed simply to hurry things up. Either way, without a word, Robbie gently laid one finger on middle C so that I would know where to start. Then, turning back with the smallest smile of encouragement, she left me to play my song.

2

I STARTED KINDERGARTEN AT BRYN MAWR ELEMEN-
tary School in the fall of 1969, showing up with the twin advantages
of knowing in advance how to read basic words and having a well-liked
second-grade brother ahead of me. The school, a four-story brick building with a yard in front, sat just a couple of blocks from our house on
Euclid. Getting there involved a two-minute walk or, if you did it like
Craig, a one-minute run.

I liked school right away. I liked my teacher, a diminutive white lady
named Mrs. Burroughs, who seemed ancient to me but was probably in
her fifties. Her classroom had big sunny windows, a collection of baby
dolls to play with, and a giant cardboard playhouse in the back. I made
friends in my class, drawn to the kids who, like me, seemed eager to be
there. I was confident in my ability to read. At home, I'd plowed through
the Dick and Jane books, courtesy of my mom's library card, and thus
was thrilled to hear that our first job as kindergartners would be learning to read new sets of words by sight. We were assigned a list of colors
to study, not the hues, but the words themselves—"red," "blue," "green,"
"black," "orange," "purple," "white." In class, Mrs. Burroughs quizzed
us one student at a time, holding up a series of large manila cards and

asking us to read whatever word was printed in black letters on the front. I watched one day as the girls and boys I was just getting to know stood up and worked through the color cards, succeeding and failing in varying degrees, and were told to sit back down at whatever point they got stumped. It was meant to be something of a game, I think, the way a spelling bee is a game, but you could see a subtle sorting going on and a knowing slump of humiliation in the kids who didn't make it past "red." This, of course, was 1969, in a public school on the South Side of Chicago. Nobody was talking about self-esteem or growth mind-sets. If you'd had a head start at home, you were rewarded for it at school, deemed "bright" or "gifted," which in turn only compounded your confidence. The advantages aggregated quickly. The two smartest kids in my kindergarten class were Teddy, a Korean American boy, and Chiaka, an African American girl, who both would remain at the top of the class for years to come.

I was driven to keep up with them. When it came my turn to read the words off the teacher's manila cards, I stood up and gave it everything I had, rattling off "red," "green," and "blue" without effort. "Purple" took a second, though, and "orange" was hard. But it wasn't until the letters W-H-I-T-E came up that I froze altogether, my throat instantly dry, my mouth awkward and unable to shape the sound as my brain glitched madly, trying to dig up a color that resembled "wuh-haaa." It was a straight-up choke. I felt a weird airiness in my knees, as if they might buckle. But before they did, Mrs. Burroughs instructed me to sit back down. And that's exactly when the word hit me in its full and easy perfection. *White. Whiiiite.* The word was "white."

Lying in bed that night with my stuffed animals packed around my head, I thought only of "white." I spelled it in my head, forward and backward, chastising myself for my own stupidity. The embarrassment felt like a weight, like something I'd never shake off, even though I knew my parents wouldn't care whether I'd read every card correctly. I just wanted to achieve. Or maybe I didn't want to be dismissed as incapable of achieving. I was sure my teacher had now pegged me as someone who couldn't read or, worse, didn't try. I obsessed over the dime-sized gold-foil stars that Mrs. Burroughs had given to Teddy and Chiaka that day to wear on their chests as an emblem of their accomplishment, or maybe a sign that they were marked for greatness when the rest of us weren't. The two of them, after all, had read every last color card without a hitch.

The next morning in class, I asked for a do-over.

When Mrs. Burroughs said no, cheerily adding that we kindergartners had other things to get to, I demanded it.

Pity the kids who then had to watch me face the color cards a second time, going slower now, pausing deliberately to breathe after I'd pronounced each word, refusing to let my nerves short-circuit my brain. And it worked, through "black," "orange," "purple," and especially "white." I was practically shouting the word "white" before I'd even seen the letters on the card. I like to imagine now that Mrs. Burroughs was impressed with this little Black girl who'd found the courage to advocate for herself. I didn't know whether Teddy and Chiaka had even noticed. I was quick to claim my trophy, though, heading home that afternoon with my head up and one of those gold-foil stars stuck on my shirt.

A T HOME, I lived in a world of high drama and intrigue, immersing myself in an ever-evolving soap opera of dolls. There were births, feuds, and betrayals. There was hope, hatred, and sometimes sex. My preferred way to pass the time between school and dinner was to park myself in the common area outside my room and Craig's and spread my Barbies across the floor, spinning out scenarios that felt as real to me as life itself, sometimes inserting Craig's G.I. Joe action figures into the plotlines. I kept my dolls' outfits in a child-sized vinyl suitcase covered in a floral print. I assigned every Barbie and every G.I. Joe a personality. I also recruited into service the worn-out alphabet blocks my mother had used years earlier to teach us our letters. They, too, were given names and inner lives.

I rarely chose to join the neighborhood kids who played outside after school, nor did I invite school friends home with me, in part because I was a fastidious kid and didn't want anyone meddling with my dolls. I'd been to other girls' houses and seen the horror-show scenarios—Barbies whose hair had been hacked off or whose faces had been crosshatched with Magic Marker. And one thing I was learning at school was that kid dynamics could be messy. Whatever sweet scenes you might witness on a playground, beneath them lay a tyranny of shifting hierarchies and alliances. There were queen bees, bullies, and followers. I wasn't shy, but I also wasn't sure I needed any of that messiness in my life outside school. Instead, I sank my energy into being the sole animating force in my little common-area universe. If Craig showed up and had the audacity to move a single block, I'd start shrieking. I was also not above hitting him when necessary—usually a direct fist blow to the middle of his back. The point was that the dolls and blocks needed me to give them life, and I dutifully gave it to them, imposing one personal crisis after another. Like any good deity, I was there to see them suffer and grow.

Meanwhile, from my bedroom window, I could observe most of the real-world happenings on our block of Euclid Avenue. In the late afternoons, I'd see Mr. Thompson, the tall African American man who owned the three-unit building across the street, loading his big bass guitar into the back of his Cadillac, setting off for a gig in one jazz club or another. I'd watch the Mendozas, the Mexican family next door, arriving home in their pickup loaded with ladders after a long day of painting houses, greeted at the fence by their yapping dogs.

Our neighborhood was middle-class and racially mixed. Kids found one another based not on the color of their skin but on who was outside and ready to play. My friends included a girl named Rachel, whose mother was white and had a British accent; Susie, a curly-haired redhead; and the Mendozas' granddaughter whenever she was visiting. We were a motley mix of last names—Kansopant, Abuasef, Yacker, Robinson—and were too young to register that things around us were changing fast. In 1950, fifteen years before my parents moved to South Shore, the neighborhood had been 96 percent white. By the time I'd leave for college in 1981, it would be about 96 percent Black.

Craig and I were raised squarely in the crosscurrents of that flux. The blocks surrounding us were home to Jewish families, immigrant families, white and Black families, folks who were thriving and some who were not. In general, people tended to their lawns and kept track of their children. They wrote checks to Robbie so their kids could learn piano. My family, in fact, was probably on the poor side of the neighborhood spectrum. We were among the few people we knew who didn't own their own home, stuffed as we were into Robbie and Terry's second floor. South Shore hadn't yet tilted the way other neighborhoods had—with the better-off people long departed for the suburbs, the neighborhood businesses closing one by one, the blight setting in—but the tilt was clearly beginning.

We were starting to feel the effects of this transition, especially at school. My second-grade classroom turned out to be a mayhem of unruly kids and flying erasers, which had not been the norm in either my experience or Craig's. All this seemed due to a teacher who couldn't figure out how to assert control—who didn't seem to like children, even. Beyond that, it wasn't clear that anyone was particularly bothered by the fact that the teacher was incompetent. The students used it as an excuse to act out, and she seemed to think only the worst of us. In her eyes, we were a class of "bad kids," though we had no guidance and no structure and had been sentenced to a grim, underlit room in the basement of the school. Every hour there felt hellish and long. I sat miserably at my desk, in my puke-green chair—puke green being the official color of the 1970s—learning nothing and waiting for the midday lunch break, when I could go home and have a sandwich and complain to my mom.

When I got angry as a kid, I almost always funneled it through my mother. As I fumed about my new teacher, she listened placidly, saying things like "Oh, dear" and "Oh, really?" She never indulged my outrage, but she took my frustration seriously. If my mother were somebody different, she might have done the polite thing and said, "Just go and do your best." But she knew the difference. She knew the difference between whining and actual distress. Without telling me, she went over to the school and began a weeks-long process of behind-the-scenes lobbying, which led to me and a couple of other high-performing kids getting quietly pulled out of class, given a battery of tests, and about a week later reinstalled permanently into a bright and orderly third-grade class upstairs, governed by a smiling, no-nonsense teacher who knew her stuff.

It was a small but life-changing move. I didn't stop to ask myself then what would happen to all the kids who'd been left in the basement with the teacher who couldn't teach. Now that I'm an adult, I realize that kids know at a very young age when they're being devalued, when adults aren't invested enough to help them learn. Their anger over it can manifest itself as unruliness. It's hardly their fault. They aren't "bad kids." They're just trying to survive bad circumstances. At the time, though, I was just happy to have escaped. But I'd learn many years later that my mother, who is by nature wry and quiet but generally also the most forthright person in any room, made a point of seeking out the second-grade teacher and telling her, as kindly as possible, that she had no business teaching and should be working as a drugstore cashier instead.

A S TIME WENT BY, my mother started nudging me to go outside and engage with kids in the neighborhood. She was hoping that I'd learn to glide socially the way my brother had. Craig, as I've mentioned, had a way of making hard things look easy. He was by then a growing sensation on the basketball court, high-spirited and agile and quickly growing tall. My father pushed him to seek out the toughest competition he could find, which meant that he would later send Craig across town on his own to play with the best kids in the city. But for now, he left him to wrangle the neighborhood talent. Craig would take his ball and carry it across the street to Rosenblum Park, passing the monkey bars and swing set where I liked to play, and then cross an invisible line, disappearing through a veil of trees to the far side of the park, where the basketball courts were. I thought of it as an abyss over there, a mythic dark forest of drunks and thugs and criminal goings-on, but Craig, once he started visiting that side of the park, would set me straight, saying that really nobody over there was all that bad.

Basketball, for my brother, seemed to unlock every frontier. It taught him how to approach strangers when he wanted to snag a spot in a pickup game. He learned how to talk a friendly form of smack, trash-talking his bigger, faster opponents on the court. It helped, too, to debunk various myths about who was who and what was what around the neighborhood, reinforcing the possibility—something that had long been a credo of my dad's—that most people were good people if you just treated them well. Even the sketchy guys who hung out in front of the corner liquor store lit up when they spotted Craig, calling his name and high-fiving him as we passed by.

"How do you even know them?" I'd ask, incredulous.

"I don't know. They just know me," he'd say with a shrug.

I was ten when I finally mellowed enough to start venturing out myself, a decision driven in large part by boredom. It was summer and school was out. Craig and I rode a bus to Lake Michigan every day to go to a rec camp run by the city at a beachfront park, but we'd be back home by four, with many daylight hours still to fill. My dolls were becoming less interesting, and without air-conditioning our apartment got unbearably hot in the late afternoons. And so I started tailing Craig around the neighborhood, meeting the kids I didn't already know from school. Across the alley behind our house, there was a mini housing community called Euclid Parkway, where about fifteen homes had been built around a common green space. It was a kind of paradise, free from cars and full of kids playing softball and jumping double Dutch or sitting on stoops, just hanging out. But before I could find my way into the fold of girls my age who hung out at the Parkway, I faced a test. It came in the form of DeeDee, a girl who went to a nearby Catholic school. DeeDee was athletic and pretty, but she wore her face in a pout and was always ready with an eye roll. She often sat on her family's stoop next to another, more popular girl named Deneen.

Deneen was always friendly, but DeeDee didn't seem to like me. I don't know why. Every time I went over to Euclid Parkway, she'd make quiet, cutting remarks, as if just by showing up I'd managed to ruin everyone's day. As the summer went on, DeeDee's comments only grew louder. My morale began to sink. I understood that I had choices. I could continue on as the picked-on new girl, I could give up on the Parkway and just go back to my toys at home, or I could attempt to earn DeeDee's respect. And inside that last choice lay another one: I could try to reason with DeeDee, to win her over with words or some other form of kid diplomacy, or I could just shut her up.

The next time DeeDee made one of her remarks, I lunged for her, summoning everything my dad had taught me about how to throw a punch. The two of us fell to the ground, fists flailing and legs thrashing, every kid in Euclid Parkway instantly clustered in a tight knot around us, their hollers fueled by excitement and grade school bloodlust. I can't remember who finally pulled us apart, whether it was Deneen or my brother or maybe a parent who'd been called to the scene, but when it was done, some sort of silent baptism had taken place. I was officially an accepted member of the neighborhood tribe. DeeDee and I were unharmed, dirt stained and panting and destined never to be close friends, but at least I'd earned her respect.

M Y DAD'S BUICK continued to be our shelter, our window to the world. We took it out on Sundays and summer evenings, cruising for no reason but the fact that we could. Sometimes we'd end up in a neighborhood to the south, an area known as Pill Hill due to an apparently large number of African American doctors living there. It was one of the prettier, more affluent parts of the South Side, where people kept two cars in the driveway and had abundant beds of flowers blooming along their walkways.

My father viewed rich people with a shade of suspicion. He didn't like people who were uppity and had mixed feelings about home ownership in general. There was a short period when he and my mom considered buying a home for sale not far from Robbie's house, driving over one day to inspect the place with a real estate agent, but ultimately deciding against it. At the time, I'd been all for it. In my mind, I thought it would mean something if my family could live in a place with more than one floor. But my father was innately cautious, aware of the trade-offs, understanding the need to maintain some savings for a rainy day. "You never want to end up house poor," he'd tell us, explaining how some people handed over their savings and borrowed too much, ending up with a nice home but no freedom at all.

My parents talked to us like we were adults. They didn't lecture, but rather indulged every question we asked, no matter how juvenile. They never hurried a discussion for the sake of convenience. Our talks could go on for hours, often because Craig and I took every opportunity to grill my parents about things we didn't understand. When we were little, we'd ask, "Why do people go to the bathroom?" or "Why do you need a job?" and then blitz them with follow-ups. One of my early Socratic victories came from a question driven by self-interest: "Why do we have to eat eggs for breakfast?" Which led to a discussion about the necessity of protein, which led me to ask why peanut butter couldn't count as protein, which eventually, after more debate, led to my mother revising her stance on eggs, which I had never liked to eat in the first place. For the next nine years, knowing that I'd earned it, I made myself a fat peanut butter and jelly sandwich for breakfast each morning and consumed not a single egg.

As we grew, we spoke more about drugs and sex and life choices, about race and inequality and politics. My parents didn't expect us to be saints. My father, I remember, made a point of saying that sex was and should be fun. They also never sugarcoated what they took to be the harder truths about life. Craig, for example, got a new bike one summer and rode it east to Lake Michigan, to the paved pathway along Rainbow Beach, where you could feel the breeze off the water. He'd been promptly picked up by a police officer who accused him of stealing it, unwilling to accept that a young Black boy would have come across a new bike in an honest way. (The officer, an African American man himself, ultimately got a brutal tongue-lashing from my mother, who made him apologize to Craig.) What had happened, my parents told us, was unjust but also unfortunately common. The color of our skin made us vulnerable. It was a thing we'd always have to navigate.

My father's habit of driving us through Pill Hill was a bit of an aspirational exercise, I would guess, a chance to show us what a good education could yield. My parents had spent almost their entire lives living within a couple of square miles in Chicago, but they had no illusions that

Craig and I would do the same. Before they were married, both of them had briefly attended community colleges, but each had abandoned the exercise long before getting a degree. My mother had been studying to become a teacher but realized she'd rather work as a secretary. My father had simply run out of money to pay tuition, joining the Army instead. He'd had no one in his family to talk him into returning to school, no model of what that sort of life looked like. Instead, he served two years moving between different military bases. If finishing college and becoming an artist had been a dream for my father, he quickly redirected his hopes, using his wages to help pay for his younger brother's degree in architecture instead.

Now in his late thirties, my dad was focused on saving for us kids. Our family was never going to be house poor, because we weren't going to own a house. My father operated from a practical place, sensing that resources were limited and maybe so, too, was time. When he wasn't driving, he now used a cane to get around. Before I finished elementary school, that cane would become a crutch and soon after that two crutches. Whatever was eroding inside my father, withering his muscles and stripping his nerves, he viewed it as his own private challenge, as something to silently withstand.

As a family, we sustained ourselves with humble luxuries. When Craig and I got our report cards at school, our parents celebrated by ordering in a pizza from Italian Fiesta, our favorite place. During hot weather, we'd buy hand-packed ice cream—a pint each of chocolate, butter pecan, and black cherry—and make it last for days. Every year for the Air and Water Show, we packed a picnic and drove north along Lake Michigan to the fenced-off peninsula where my father's water filtration plant was located. It was one of the few times a year when employee families were allowed through the gates and onto a grassy lawn overlooking the lake, where the view of fighter jets swooping in formation over the water rivaled that of any penthouse on Lake Shore Drive.

Each July, my dad would take a week off from his job tending boilers at the plant, and we'd pile into the Buick with an aunt and a couple of cousins, seven of us in that two-door for hours, taking the Skyway out of Chicago, skirting the south end of Lake Michigan, and driving until we landed in White Cloud, Michigan, at a place called Dukes Happy Holiday Resort. It had a game room, a vending machine that sold glass bottles of pop, and most important to us, a big outdoor swimming pool. We rented a cabin with a kitchenette and passed our days jumping in and out of the water.

My parents barbecued, smoked cigarettes, and played cards with my aunt, but my father also took long breaks to join us kids in the pool. He was handsome, my dad, with a mustache that tipped down the sides of his lips like a scythe. His chest and arms were thick and roped with muscle, testament to the athlete he'd once been. During those long afternoons in the pool, he paddled and laughed and tossed our small bodies into the air, his diminished legs suddenly less of a liability.

DECLINE CAN BE a hard thing to measure, especially when you're in the midst of it. Every September, when Craig and I showed up back at Bryn Mawr Elementary, we'd find fewer white kids on the playground. Some had transferred to a nearby Catholic school, but many had left the neighborhood altogether. At first it felt as if just the white families were leaving, but then that changed, too. It soon seemed that anyone who had the means to go was now going. Much of the time, the departures went unannounced and unexplained. We'd see a "For Sale" sign in front of the Yacker family's house or a moving van in front of Teddy's and know what was coming.

Perhaps the biggest blow to my mother came when her friend Velma Stewart announced that she and her husband had put a down payment on a house in a suburb called Park Forest. The Stewarts had two kids and lived down the block on Euclid. Like us, they were apartment dwellers. Mrs. Stewart had a wicked sense of humor and a big infectious laugh, which drew my mother to her. The two of them swapped recipes and kept up with each other, but never fell into the neighborhood's gossip cycle the way other mothers did. Mrs. Stewart's son, Donny, was Craig's age and just as athletic, giving the two of them an instant bond. Her daughter, Pamela, was a teenager already and not so interested in me, though I found all teenagers intriguing. I don't remember much about Mr. Stewart, except that he drove a delivery truck for one of the big bakery companies in the city and that he and his wife and their kids were the lightest-skinned Black people I'd ever met.

How they afforded a place in the suburbs, I couldn't guess. Park Forest, it turns out, was one of America's first fully planned communities—not just a housing subdivision, but a full village designed for about thirty thousand people, with shopping malls, churches, schools, and parks. Founded in 1948, it was, in many ways, meant to be the paragon of suburban life, with mass-produced houses and cookie-cutter yards. There were also quotas for how many Black families could live on a given block, though by the time the Stewarts got there, the quotas had apparently been abolished.

Not long after they moved, the Stewarts invited us to come visit them on one of my dad's days off. We were excited. For us, it would be a new kind of outing, a chance to glimpse the fabled suburbs. The four of us took the Buick south on the expressway, following the road out of Chicago, exiting about forty minutes later near a sterile-looking shopping plaza. We were soon winding through a network of quiet streets, following Mrs. Stewart's directions, turning from one nearly identical block to the next. Park Forest was like a miniature city of tract homes—modest ranch-style places with soft gray shingles and newly planted saplings and bushes out front.

"Now why would anyone want to live all the way out here?" my father asked, staring over the dashboard. I agreed that it made no sense. As far as I could see, there were no big trees like the giant oak that sat outside my bedroom window at home. Everything in Park Forest was new and wide and uncrowded. There was no corner liquor store with ratty guys hanging out in front of it. There were no cars honking or sirens. There was no music floating from anybody's kitchen. The windows in the houses all looked to be shut.

Craig would remember our visit there as heavenly, namely because he played ball all day long in the wide-open lots under a blue sky with Donny Stewart and his new pack of suburban brethren. My parents had a pleasant enough catch-up with Mr. and Mrs. Stewart, and I followed Pamela around, gaping at her hair, her fair skin and teenager jewelry. At some point, we all had lunch.

It was evening when we finally said good-bye. Leaving the Stewarts, we walked in the dusk to the curb where my dad had parked the car. Craig was sweaty, dead on his feet after all the running he'd done. I, too, was fatigued and ready to go home. Something about the place had put me on edge. I wasn't a fan of the suburbs, though I couldn't articulate exactly why.

My mother would later make an observation about the Stewarts and their new community, based on the fact that almost all of their neighbors on the street seemed to be white.

"I wonder," she said, "if nobody knew that they're a Black family until we came to visit."

She thought that maybe we'd unwittingly outed them, arriving from the South Side with a housewarming gift and our conspicuous dark skin. Even if the Stewarts weren't deliberately trying to hide their race, they probably didn't speak of it one way or another with their new neighbors. Whatever vibe existed on their block, they hadn't overtly disrupted it. At least not until we came to visit.

Was somebody watching through a window as my father approached our car that night? Was there a shadow behind some curtain, waiting to see how things would go? I'll never know. I just remember the way my dad's body stiffened slightly when he reached the driver's side door and saw what was there. Someone had scratched a line across the side of his beloved Buick, a thin ugly gulch that ran across the door and toward the tail of the car. It had been done with a key or a rock and was in no way accidental.

I've said before that my father was a withstander, a man who never complained about small things or big, who cheerily ate liver when it was served to him, who had a doctor give him what amounted to a death sentence and then just carried on. This thing with the car was no different. If there was some way to fight it, if there was some door to pound in response, my dad wouldn't have done it anyway.

"Well, I'll be damned," he said, before unlocking the car.

We rode back to the city that night without much discussion about what had happened. It was too exhausting, maybe, to parse. In any event, we were done with the suburbs. My father must have had to drive the car to work the next day looking the way it did, and I'm sure that didn't sit well with him. But the gash in his chrome didn't stay for long. As soon as there was time, he took the car over to the body shop at Sears and had it erased.

3

SOMEWHERE ALONG THE WAY, MY NORMALLY LAID-back brother started to sprout worries. I can't say exactly when or why this began, but Craig—the boy who could high-five and what-up his way around the neighborhood, who blithely catnapped anytime he had ten free minutes, regardless of his surroundings—grew more fretful and vigilant at home, convinced that catastrophe was creeping our way. In the evenings at our apartment, he rehearsed for every outcome, immersing himself in hypotheticals the rest of us found bizarre. Worried he'd lose his sight, he took to wearing a blindfold around the house, learning to navigate our living room and kitchen by feel. Worried he might go deaf, he began teaching himself sign language. There was also apparently the threat of amputation, prompting Craig to fumble his way through various meals and homework sessions with his right arm tied behind his back. Because you never did know.

Craig's biggest fear, however, was also probably the most realistic, and that was fire. House fires were a regular occurrence in Chicago, in part due to slumlords who let their buildings slide into disrepair and were all too happy to reap the insurance benefits when a fire tore through, and in part because home smoke detectors were a relatively new development and still expensive for working-class people to afford. Either way, inside our tight city grid, fire was almost a fact of life, a random but persistent snatcher of homes and hearts. My grandfather Southside had moved to our neighborhood after a fire destroyed his old house on the West Side, though luckily nobody'd been hurt. (According to my mother, Southside stood on the curb outside the burning house, shouting for the firefighters to direct their hoses away from his precious jazz albums.) More recently, in a tragedy almost too giant for my young mind to take in, one of my fifth-grade classmates—a boy with a sweet face and a tall Afro named Lester McCullom, who lived around the corner from us in a town house on Seventy-Fourth Street—had died in a fire that also killed his brother and sister, the three of them trapped by flames in bedrooms upstairs.

Theirs was the first wake I ever attended: every kid in the neighborhood sobbing at the funeral parlor as a Jackson 5 album played softly in the background; the adults stunned into silence, no prayer or platitude capable of filling the void. There were three closed caskets at the front of the room, each one with a framed photograph of a smiling child on its lid. Mrs. McCullom, who with her husband had managed to survive the fire by jumping out a window, sat before them, so slumped and broken that it hurt to look in her direction.

For days afterward, the skeleton of the McCulloms' burned-out town house continued to hiss and cave in on itself, dying far more slowly than its young occupants had. The smell of smoke lingered heavily in the neighborhood.

As time passed, Craig's anxieties only grew. At school, we'd been put through the paces of teacher-led evacuation drills, dutifully enduring lectures on how to stop, drop, and roll. And as a result, Craig decided that we needed to step it up on safety at home, electing himself the family fire marshal, with me as his lieutenant, ready to clear exit pathways during drills or boss around our parents as needed. We weren't so much convinced we'd have a fire as we were fixated on being ready for one. Preparation mattered. Our family was not just punctual; we arrived early to everything, knowing that it made my dad less vulnerable, sparing him from having to worry about finding a parking spot that didn't require him to walk a long way or an accessible seat in the bleachers at one of

Craig's basketball games. The lesson being that in life you control what you can.

To this end, as kids, we ran through our escape-route possibilities, trying to guess whether we could jump from a window to the oak tree in front of the house or to a neighbor's rooftop in the event of a fire. We imagined what would happen if a grease fire broke out in the kitchen, or if an electrical fire started in the basement, or if lightning struck from above. Craig and I had little concern about our mom in an emergency. She was small and agile and one of those people who, if her adrenaline got going, could probably bench-press a car off a baby. What was harder to talk about was Dad's disability—the obvious but unstated truth that he couldn't readily leap from a window like the rest of us, and it had been years since we'd seen him run.

Should things get scary, we realized, our rescue wouldn't unfold the way rescues did in the tidy after-school movies we watched on TV. It would not be our dad who'd throw us over his shoulder with Herculean grace and carry us to safety. If anyone, it would have to be Craig, who would eventually tower over my father but was then still a narrow-shouldered, spindle-legged boy who seemed to understand that any heroics on his part would require practice. Which is why during our family fire drills, he started conjuring the worst-case scenarios, ordering my dad to the floor, instructing him to lie there limp and heavy as a sack, as if he'd passed out from smoke inhalation.

"Oh, good Lord," Dad would say, shaking his head. "You're really going to do this?"

My father was not accustomed to being helpless. He lived his life in defiance of that very prospect, assiduously looking after our car, paying the bills on time, never discussing his advancing multiple sclerosis nor missing a day of work. To the contrary, my father loved to be the rock for others. What he couldn't do physically, he substituted with emotional and intellectual guidance and support, which is why he enjoyed his work as a precinct captain for the city's Democratic Party. He'd held the post for years, in part because loyal service to the party machine was more or less expected of city employees. Even if he'd been half forced into it, though, my dad loved the job, which baffled my mother given the amount of time it demanded. He paid weekend visits to a nearby neighborhood to check in on his constituents, often with me reluctantly in tow. We'd park the car and walk along streets of modest bungalows, landing on a doorstep to find a hunched-over widow or a big-bellied factory worker with a can of Michelob peering through the screen door. Often, these people were delighted by the sight of my father smiling broadly on their porch, propped up by his cane.

"Well, *Fraser*!" they'd say. "What a surprise. Get on in here."

For me, this was never good news. It meant we were going inside. It meant that my whole Saturday afternoon would now get sucked up as I got parked on a musty sofa or with a 7UP at a kitchen table while my dad fielded feedback—complaints, really—that he'd then pass on to the elected alderman who controlled the ward. When somebody had problems with garbage pickup or snow plowing or was irritated by a pothole, my dad was there to listen. His purpose was to help people feel cared for by the Democrats—and to vote accordingly when elections rolled around. To my dismay, he never rushed anyone along. Time, as far as my father was concerned, was a gift you gave to other people. He clucked approvingly at pictures of cute grandkids, patiently endured gossip and long litanies of health woes, and nodded knowingly at stories about how money was tight. He hugged the old ladies as we finally left their houses, assuring them he'd do his best to be useful—to get the fixable issues fixed.

My dad had faith in his own utility. It was a point of pride. Which is why at home during our fire drills he had little interest in being a passive prop, even in a pretend crisis. He had no intention, under any circumstance, of being a liability—of winding up the unconscious guy on the floor. But still, some part of him seemed to understand that this mattered to us—to Craig in particular. When we asked him to lie down, he'd humor us, dropping first to his knees, then to his butt, then spreading himself out obligingly, faceup on the living room carpet. He'd exchange glances with my mother, who found it all a little funny, as if to say, *These damn kids*.

With a sigh, he'd close his eyes, waiting to feel Craig's hands hook themselves solidly beneath his shoulders to start the rescue operation. My mother and I would then watch as, with no small amount of effort and a good deal of awkwardness, my brother managed to drag 170 or so pounds of paternal deadweight backward through the imaginary inferno that raged in his preadolescent mind, hauling my father across the floor, rounding the couch, and finally making it to the stairwell.

From here, Craig figured he could probably slide my dad's body down the stairs and out the side door to safety. My father always refused to let him practice this part, saying gently, "That's enough now," and insisting on getting back to his feet before Craig could try to lug him down the stairs. But between the small man and the grown man, the point had been made. None of this would be easy or comfortable if it came to it, and there were, of course, no guarantees that any of us would survive. But if the very worst happened, we at least had a plan.

S LOWLY, I WAS becoming more outward and social, more willing to open myself up to the messes of the wider world. My natural resistance to chaos and spontaneity had been worn down somewhat through all the hours I'd spent trailing my father through his precinct visits, plus all the other weekend outings we made, dropping in on our dozens of aunts, uncles, and cousins, sitting in thick clouds of barbecue smoke in someone's backyard or running around with neighborhood kids in a neighborhood that wasn't ours.

My mother was one of seven children in her family. My father was the oldest of five. My mom's relatives tended to gather at Southside's house around the corner—drawn by my grandfather's cooking, the ongoing games of bid whist, and the exuberant blasting of jazz. Southside acted as a magnet for all of us. He was forever mistrustful of the world beyond his own yard—worried primarily about everyone's safety and well-being—and as a result poured his energy into creating an environment where we were always well fed and entertained, likely with the hope we'd never want to move away from it. He even got me a dog, an affable, cinnamon-colored shepherd mutt we called Rex. Per my mother's orders, Rex wasn't allowed to live at our house, but I'd visit him all the time at Southside's, lying on the floor with my face buried in his soft fur, listening to his tail *thwap* appreciatively anytime Southside walked past. Southside spoiled the dog the same way he spoiled me, with food and love and tolerance, all of it a silent, earnest plea never to leave him.

My father's family, meanwhile, sprawled across Chicago's broader South Side and included an array of great-aunts and third cousins, plus a few stray outliers whose blood connection remained cloudy. We orbited between all of them. I quietly assessed where we were going by the number of trees I'd see on the street outside. The poorer neighborhoods often had no trees at all. But to my dad, everyone was kin. He lit up when he saw his uncle Calio, a skinny, wavy-haired little man who looked like Sammy Davis Jr. and was almost always drunk. He adored his aunt Verdelle, who lived with her eight children in a neglected apartment building next to the Dan Ryan Expressway, in a neighborhood where Craig and I understood that the rules of survival were very different.

On Sunday afternoons, all four of us normally took the ten-minute drive north to Parkway Gardens to eat dinner with my dad's parents, whom we called Dandy and Grandma, and his three youngest siblings, Andrew, Carleton, and Francesca, who'd been born more than a decade after my father and thus seemed more like sister and brothers to us than aunt and uncles. My father, I thought, seemed more like a father and less like a brother with the three of them, offering them advice and slipping them cash when they needed it. Francesca was smart and beautiful and sometimes let me brush her long hair. Andrew and Carleton were in their early twenties and dazzlingly hip. They wore bell-bottoms and turtlenecks. They owned leather jackets, had girlfriends, and talked about things like Malcolm X and "soul power." Craig and I passed hours in their bedroom at the back of the apartment, just trying to sponge up their cool.

My grandfather, also named Fraser Robinson, was decidedly less fun to be around, a cigar-puffing patriarch who'd sit in his recliner with a newspaper open on his lap and the evening news blaring on the television nearby. His demeanor was nothing like my father's. For Dandy, everything was an irritant. He was galled by the day's headlines, by the state of the world as shown on TV, by the young Black men—"boo-boos," he called them—whom he perceived to be hanging uselessly around the neighborhood, giving Black people everywhere a bad name. He shouted at the television. He shouted at my grandmother, a sweet, soft-spoken woman and devout Christian named LaVaughn. (My parents had named me Michelle LaVaughn Robinson, in honor of her.) By day, my grandmother expertly managed a thriving Bible bookstore on the Far South Side, but in her off-hours with Dandy she was reduced to a meekness I found perplexing, even as a young girl. She cooked his meals and absorbed his barrage of complaints and said nothing in her own defense. Even at a young age, there was something about my grandmother's silence and passivity in her relationship with Dandy that got under my skin.

According to my mother, I was the only person in the family to talk back to Dandy when he yelled. I did it regularly, from the time I was very young and over many years, in part because it drove me crazy that my grandmother wouldn't speak up for herself, in part because everyone else fell silent around him, and lastly because I loved Dandy as much as he confounded me. His stubbornness was something I recognized, something I'd inherited myself, though I hoped in a less abrasive form. There was also a softness in Dandy, which I caught only in glimmers. He tenderly rubbed my neck sometimes when I sat at the foot of his reclining chair. He smiled when my dad said something funny or one of us kids managed to slip a sophisticated word into a conversation. But then something would set him off and he'd start snarling again.

"Quit shouting at everyone, Dandy," I'd say. Or, "Don't be mean to Grandma." Often, I'd add, "What's got you so mad anyway?"

The answer to that question was both complicated and simple. Dandy himself would leave it unanswered, shrugging crankily in response to my interference and returning to his newspaper. Back at home, though, my parents would try to explain.

Dandy was from the South Carolina Low Country, having grown up in the humid seaport of Georgetown, where thousands of slaves once labored on vast plantations, harvesting crops of rice and indigo and making their owners rich. My grandfather, born in 1912, was the grandson of slaves, the son of a millworker, and the oldest of what would be ten children in his family. A quick-witted and intelligent kid, he'd been nicknamed "the Professor" and set his sights early on the idea of someday going to college. But not only was he Black and from a poor family, he also came of age during the Great Depression. After finishing high school, Dandy went to work at a lumber mill, knowing that if he stayed in Georgetown, his options would never widen. When the mill eventually closed, like many African Americans of his generation he took a chance and moved north to Chicago, joining what became known as the Great Migration, in which six million southern Blacks relocated to big northern cities over the course of five decades, fleeing racial oppression and chasing industrial jobs.

If this were an American Dream story, Dandy, who arrived in Chicago in the early 1930s, would have found a good job and a pathway to college. But the reality was far different. Jobs were hard to come by, limited at least somewhat by the fact that managers at some of the big factories in Chicago regularly hired European immigrants over African American workers. Dandy took what work he could find, setting pins in a bowling alley and freelancing as a handyman. Gradually, he downgraded his hopes, letting go of the idea of college, thinking he'd train to become an electrician instead. But this, too, was quickly thwarted. If you wanted to work as an electrician (or as a steelworker, carpenter, or plumber, for that matter) on any of the big job sites in Chicago, you needed a union card. And if you were Black, the overwhelming odds were that you weren't going to get one.

This particular form of discrimination altered the destinies of generations of African Americans, including many of the men in my family, limiting their income, their opportunity, and, eventually, their aspirations. As a carpenter, Southside wasn't allowed to work for the larger construction firms that offered steady pay on long-term projects, given that he couldn't join a labor union. My great-uncle Terry, Robbie's husband, had abandoned a career as a plumber for the same reason, instead becoming a Pullman porter. There was also Uncle Pete, on my mother's side, who'd been unable to join the taxi drivers' union and instead turned to driving an unlicensed jitney, picking up customers who lived in the less safe parts of the West Side, where normal cabs didn't like to go. These were highly intelligent, able-bodied men who were denied access to stable high-paying jobs, which in turn kept them from being able to buy homes, send their kids to college, or save for retirement. It pained them, I know, to be cast aside, to be stuck in jobs that they were overqualified for, to watch white people leapfrog past them at work, sometimes training new employees they knew might one day become their bosses. And it bred within each of them at least a basic level of resentment and mistrust: You never quite knew what other folks saw you to be.

As for Dandy, life wasn't all bad. He met my grandmother while attending church on the South Side and ultimately found work through the federal government's Works Progress Administration, the relief program that hired unskilled laborers for public construction projects during the Depression. He then went on to log thirty years as a postal worker before retiring with a pension that helped allow him all that time to yell at the boo-boos on TV from the comfort of his recliner.

In the end, he had five kids who were as smart and disciplined as he was. Nomenee, his second child, would end up with a degree from Harvard Business School. Andrew and Carleton would go on to become a train conductor and an engineer, respectively. Francesca worked as a creative director in advertising for a time and eventually became a grade school teacher. But still, Dandy would remain unable to see his children's accomplishments as any sort of extension of his. As we saw every Sunday arriving at Parkway Gardens for dinner, my grandfather lived with the bitter residue of his own dashed dreams.

I F MY QUESTIONS for Dandy were hard and unanswerable, I soon learned that many questions are just that way. In my own life, I was starting to encounter questions I couldn't readily answer. One came from a girl whose name I can't remember—one of the distant cousins who played with us in the backyard of one of my great-aunts' bungalows farther west of us, part of the loosely related crowd that often turned up when my parents drove over for a visit. As the adults drank coffee and laughed in the kitchen, a parallel scene would unfold outside as Craig and I joined whatever pack of kids came with those adults. Sometimes it was awkward, all of us managing a forced camaraderie, but generally it worked out. Craig almost always disappeared into a basketball game. I'd jump double Dutch or try to fall into whatever banter was going on.

One summer day when I was about ten, I sat on a stoop, chatting with a group of girls my age. We were all in pigtails and shorts and basically just killing time. What were we discussing? It could have been anything—school, our older brothers, an anthill on the ground.

At one point, one of the girls, a second, third, or fourth cousin of mine, gave me a sideways look and said, just a touch hotly, "How come you talk like a white girl?"

The question was pointed, meant as an insult or at least a challenge, but it also came from an earnest place. It held a kernel of something that was confusing for both of us. We seemed to be related but of two different worlds.

"I don't," I said, looking scandalized that she'd even suggest it and mortified by the way the other girls were now staring at me.

But I knew what she was getting at. There was no denying it, even if I just had. I *did* speak differently than some of my relatives, and so did Craig. Our parents had drilled into us the importance of using proper diction, of saying "going" instead of "goin'" and "isn't" instead of "ain't." We were taught to finish off our words. They bought us a dictionary and a full *Encyclopaedia Britannica* set, which lived on a shelf in the stairwell to our apartment, its titles etched in gold. Any time we had a question about a word, or a concept, or some piece of history, they directed us toward those books. Dandy, too, was an influence, meticulously correcting our grammar or admonishing us to enunciate our words when we went over for dinner. The idea was we were to transcend, to get ourselves further. They'd planned for it. They encouraged it. We were expected not just to be smart but to own our smartness—to inhabit it with pride—and this filtered down to how we spoke.

Yet it also could be problematic. Speaking a certain way—the "white" way, as some would have it—was perceived as a betrayal, as being uppity, as somehow denying our culture. Years later, after I'd met and married my husband—a man who is light-skinned to some and dark-skinned to others, who speaks like an Ivy League–educated Black Hawaiian raised by white middle-class Kansans—I'd see this confusion play out on the national stage among whites and Blacks alike, the need to situate someone inside his or her ethnicity and the frustration that comes when it can't easily be done. America would bring to Barack Obama the same questions my cousin was unconsciously putting to me that day on the stoop: Are you what you appear to be? Do I trust you or not?

I passed the rest of that day trying to say less to my cousin, feeling put off by her hostility, but also wanting her to see me as genuine—not trying to flaunt some advantage. It was hard to know what to do. All the while, I could hear the trickle of conversation going on between the adults in the kitchen nearby, my parents' laughter ringing easy and loud over the yard. I watched my brother in the flow of a sweaty game with a group of boys on the adjacent street corner. Everyone seemed to fit in, except for me. I look back on the discomfort of that moment now and recognize the more universal challenge of squaring who you are with where you come from and where you want to go. I also realize that I was a long way, still, from finding my voice.

4

A T SCHOOL, WE WERE GIVEN AN HOUR-LONG BREAK for lunch each day. Because my mother didn't work and our apartment was so close by, I usually marched home with four or five other girls in tow, all of us talking nonstop, ready to sprawl on the kitchen floor to play jacks and watch *All My Children* while my mom handed out sandwiches. This, for me, began a habit that has sustained me for life, keeping a close and high-spirited council of girlfriends—a safe harbor of female wisdom. In my lunch group, we dissected whatever had gone on that morning at school, any beefs we had with teachers, any assignments that struck us as useless. Our opinions were largely formed by committee. We idolized the Jackson 5 and weren't sure how we felt about the Osmonds. Watergate had happened, but none of us understood it. It seemed like a lot of old guys talking into microphones in Washington, D.C., which to us was just a faraway city filled with a lot of white buildings and white men.

My mom, meanwhile, was plenty happy to serve us. It gave her an easy window into our world. As my friends and I ate and gossiped, she often stood by quietly, engaged in some household chore, not hiding the fact that she was taking in every word. In my family, with four of us packed into less than nine hundred square feet of living space, we'd never had any privacy anyway. It mattered only sometimes. Craig, who was suddenly interested in girls, had started taking his phone calls behind closed doors in the bathroom, the phone's curlicue cord stretched taut across the hallway from its wall-mounted base in the kitchen.

As Chicago schools went, Bryn Mawr fell somewhere between a bad school and a good school. Racial and economic sorting in the South Shore neighborhood continued through the 1970s, meaning that the student population only grew Blacker and poorer with each year. There was, for a time, a citywide integration movement to bus kids to new schools, but Bryn Mawr parents had successfully fought it off, arguing that the money was better spent improving the school itself. As a kid, I had no perspective on whether the facilities were run-down or whether it mattered that there were hardly any white kids left. The school ran from kindergarten all the way through eighth grade, which meant that by the time I'd reached the upper grades, I knew every light switch, every chalkboard and cracked patch of hallway. I knew nearly every teacher and most of the kids. For me, Bryn Mawr was practically an extension of home.

As I was entering seventh grade, the *Chicago Defender,* a weekly newspaper that was popular with African American readers, ran a vitriolic opinion piece that claimed Bryn Mawr had gone, in the span of a few years, from being one of the city's best public schools to a "run-down slum" governed by a "ghetto mentality." Our school principal, Dr. Lavizzo, immediately hit back with a letter to the editor, defending his community of parents and students and deeming the newspaper piece "an outrageous lie, which seems designed to incite only feelings of failure and flight."

Dr. Lavizzo was a round, cheery man who had an Afro that puffed out on either side of his bald spot and who spent most of his time in an office near the building's front door. It's clear from his letter that he understood precisely what he was up against. Failure is a feeling long before it becomes an actual result. It's vulnerability that breeds with self-doubt and then is escalated, often deliberately, by fear. Those "feelings of failure" he mentioned were everywhere already in my neighborhood, in the form of parents who couldn't get ahead financially, of kids who were starting to suspect that their lives would be no different, of families who watched their better-off neighbors leave for the suburbs or transfer their children to Catholic schools. There were predatory real estate agents roaming South Shore all the while, whispering to home owners that they should sell before it was too late, that they'd help them *get out while you still can*. The inference being that failure was coming, that it was inevitable, that it had already half arrived. You could get caught up in the ruin or you could escape it. They used the word everyone was most afraid of— "ghetto"—dropping it like a lit match.

My mother bought into none of this. She'd lived in South Shore for ten years already and would end up staying another forty. She didn't buy into fearmongering and at the same time seemed equally inoculated against any sort of pie-in-the-sky idealism. She was a straight-down-the-line realist, controlling what she could.

At Bryn Mawr, she became one of the most active members of the PTA, helping raise funds for new classroom equipment, throwing appreciation dinners for the teachers, and lobbying for the creation of a special multigrade classroom that catered to higher-performing students. This last effort was the brainchild of Dr. Lavizzo, who'd gone to night school to get his PhD in education and had studied a new trend in grouping students by ability rather than by age—in essence, putting the brighter kids together so they could learn at a faster pace.

The idea was controversial, criticized as being undemocratic, as all "gifted and talented" programs inherently are. But it was also gaining steam as a movement around the country, and for my last three years at Bryn Mawr I was a beneficiary. I joined a group of about twenty students from different grades, set off in a self-contained classroom apart from the rest of the school with our own recess, lunch, music, and gym schedules. We were given special opportunities, including weekly trips to a community college to attend an advanced writing workshop or dissect a rat in the biology lab. Back in the classroom, we did a lot of independent work, setting our own goals and moving at whatever speed best suited us.

We were given dedicated teachers, first Mr. Martinez and then Mr. Bennett, both gentle and good-humored African American men, both keenly focused on what their students had to say. There was a clear sense that the school had invested in us, which I think made us all try harder and feel better about ourselves. The independent learning setup only served to fuel my competitive streak. I tore through the lessons, quietly keeping tabs on where I stood among my peers as we charted our progress from long division to pre-algebra, from writing single paragraphs to turning in full research papers. For me, it was like a game. And as with any game, like most any kid, I was happiest when I was ahead.

I TOLD MY MOTHER everything that happened at school. Her lunchtime update was followed by a second update, which I'd deliver in a rush as I walked through the door in the afternoon, slinging my book bag on the floor and hunting for a snack. I realize I don't know exactly what my mom did during the hours we were at school, mainly because in the self-centered manner of any child I never asked. I don't know what she thought about, how she felt about being a traditional homemaker as opposed to working a different job. I only knew that when I showed up at home, there'd be food in the fridge, not just for me, but for my friends. I knew that when my class was going on an excursion, my mother would almost always volunteer to chaperone, arriving in a nice dress and dark lipstick to ride the bus with us to the community college or the zoo.

In our house, we lived on a budget but didn't often discuss its limits. My mom found ways to compensate. She did her own nails, dyed her own hair (one time accidentally turning it green), and got new clothes only when my dad bought them for her as a birthday gift. She'd never be rich, but she was always crafty. When we were young, she magically turned old socks into puppets that looked exactly like the Muppets. She crocheted doilies to cover our tabletops. She sewed a lot of my clothes, at least until middle school, when suddenly it meant everything to have a Gloria Vanderbilt swan label on the front pocket of your jeans, and I insisted she stop.

Every so often, she'd change the layout of our living room, putting a new slipcover on the sofa, swapping out the photos and framed prints that hung on our walls. When the weather turned warm, she did a ritualistic spring cleaning, attacking on all fronts—vacuuming furniture, laundering curtains, and removing every storm window so she could Windex the glass and wipe down the sills before replacing them with screens to allow the spring air into our tiny, stuffy apartment. She'd then often go downstairs to Robbie and Terry's, particularly as they got older and less able, to scour that as well. It's because of my mother that still to this day I catch the scent of Pine-Sol and automatically feel better about life.

At Christmastime, she got especially creative. One year, she figured out how to cover our boxy metal radiator with corrugated cardboard printed to look like red bricks, stapling everything together so that we'd have a faux chimney that ran all the way to the ceiling and a faux fireplace, complete with a mantel and hearth. She then enlisted my father— the family's resident artist—to paint a series of orange flames on pieces of very thin rice paper, which, when backlit with a lightbulb, made for a half-convincing fire. On New Year's Eve, as a matter of tradition, she'd buy a special hors d'oeuvre basket, the kind that came filled with blocks of cheese, smoked oysters in a tin, and different kinds of salami. She'd invite my dad's sister Francesca over to play board games. We'd order a pizza for dinner and then snack our way elegantly through the rest of the evening, my mom passing around trays of pigs in a blanket, fried shrimp, and a special cheese spread baked on Ritz crackers. As midnight drew close, we'd each have a tiny glass of champagne.

My mother maintained the sort of parental mind-set that I now recognize as brilliant and nearly impossible to emulate—a kind of unflappable Zen neutrality. I had friends whose mothers rode their highs and lows as if they were their own, and I knew plenty of other kids whose parents were too overwhelmed by their own challenges to be much of a presence at all. My mom was simply even-keeled. She wasn't quick to judge and she wasn't quick to meddle. Instead, she monitored our moods and bore benevolent witness to whatever travails or triumphs a day might bring. When things were bad, she gave us only a small amount of pity. When we'd done something great, we received just enough praise to know she was happy with us, but never so much that it became the reason we did what we did.

Advice, when she offered it, tended to be of the hard-boiled and pragmatic variety. "You don't have to *like* your teacher," she told me one day after I came home spewing complaints. "But that woman's got the kind of math in her head that you need in yours. Focus on that and ignore the rest."

She loved us consistently, Craig and me, but we were not overmanaged. Her goal was to push us out into the world. "I'm not raising babies," she'd tell us. "I'm raising adults." She and my dad offered guidelines rather than rules. It meant that as teenagers we'd never have a curfew. Instead, they'd ask, "What's a reasonable time for you to be home?" and then trust us to stick to our word.

Craig tells a story about a girl he liked in eighth grade and how one day she issued a kind of loaded invitation, asking him to come by her house, pointedly letting him know that her parents wouldn't be home and they'd be left alone.

My brother had privately agonized over whether to go or not— titillated by the opportunity but knowing it was sneaky and dishonorable, the sort of behavior my parents would never condone. This didn't, however, stop him from telling my mother a preliminary half-truth, letting her know about the girl but saying they were going to meet in the public park.

Guilt-ridden before he'd even done it, guilt-ridden for even thinking about it, Craig finally confessed the whole home-alone scheme, expecting or maybe just hoping that my mom would blow a gasket and forbid him to go.

But she didn't. She wouldn't. It wasn't how she operated.

She listened, but she didn't absolve him from the choice at hand. Instead, she returned him to his agony with a blithe shrug of her shoulders. "Handle it how you think best," she said, before turning back to the dishes in the sink or the pile of laundry she had to fold.

It was another small push out into the world. I'm sure that in her heart my mother knew already that he'd make the right choice. Every move she made, I realize now, was buttressed by the quiet confidence that she'd raised us to be adults. Our decisions were on us. It was our life, not hers, and always would be.

. . .

B Y THE TIME I was fourteen, I basically thought of myself as half
a grown-up anyway—maybe even as two-thirds of a grown-up.
I'd gotten my period, which I announced immediately and with huge
excitement to everyone in the house, because that was just the kind
of household we had. I'd graduated from a training bra to one that
looked vaguely more womanly, which also thrilled me. Instead of coming home for lunch, I now ate with my classmates in Mr. Bennett's room
at school. Instead of dropping in at Southside's house on Saturdays to
listen to his jazz records and play with Rex, I rode my bike right past,
headed east to the bungalow on Oglesby Avenue where the Gore sisters
lived.

The Gore sisters were my best friends and also a little bit my idols.
Diane was in my grade, and Pam a grade behind. Both were beautiful
girls—Diane was fair-skinned, and Pam was darker—each with a kind
of self-possessed grace that seemed to come naturally. Even their little
sister, Gina, who was a few years younger, emanated a robust femininity
that I came to think of simply as Gore-like. Theirs was a home with few
men. Their father didn't live there and was rarely discussed. There was
one much older brother who was a peripheral presence. Mrs. Gore was
an upbeat, attractive woman who worked full-time. She had a makeup
table laden with perfume bottles and face powder compacts and various ointments in tiny pots, which given my mother's modest practicality
seemed as exotic as jewels to me. I loved spending time at their house.
Pam, Diane, and I talked endlessly about which boys we liked. We put on
lip gloss and took turns trying on one another's clothes, suddenly aware
that certain pairs of pants made our hips look curvier. Much of my energy in those days was spent inside my own head, sitting alone in my
room listening to music, daydreaming about a slow dance with a cute
boy, or glancing out the window, hoping for a crush to ride his bike down
the block. So it was a blessing to have found some sisters to ride through
these years with together.

Boys weren't allowed inside the Gore house, but they buzzed around it like flies. They rode their bikes back and forth on the sidewalk. They sat on the front stoop, hoping Diane or Pam might come out to flirt. It was fun to be around all this expectancy, even as I was unsure of what it all meant. Everywhere I looked, bodies were changing. Boys from school were suddenly man-sized and awkward, their energy twitchy and their voices deep. Some of my girlfriends, meanwhile, looked like they were eighteen, walking around in short-shorts and halter tops, their expressions cool and confident as if they knew some secret, as if they now existed on a different plane, while the rest of us remained uncertain and slightly dumbfounded, waiting for our call-up to the adult world, foal-like on our growing legs and young in a way that no amount of lip gloss could yet fix.

Like a lot of girls, I became aware of the liabilities of my body early, long before I began to even look like a woman. I moved around the neighborhood now with more independence, less tied to my parents. I'd catch a city bus to go to late-afternoon dance classes at Mayfair Academy on Seventy-Ninth Street, where I was taking jazz and acrobatics. I ran errands for my mom sometimes. With the new freedoms came new vulnerabilities. I learned to keep my gaze fixed firmly ahead anytime I passed a group of men clustered on a street corner, careful not to register their eyes roving over my chest and legs. I knew to ignore the catcalls when they came. I learned which blocks in our neighborhood were thought to be more dangerous than others. I knew never to walk alone at night.

At home, my parents made one major concession to the fact they were housing two growing teenagers, renovating the back porch off our kitchen and converting it into a bedroom for Craig, who was now a sophomore in high school. The flimsy partition that Southside had built for us years earlier came down. I moved into what had been my parents' room, they rotated into what had been the kids' room, and for the first time my brother and I had actual space for ourselves. My new bedroom was dreamy, complete with a blue-and-white floral bed skirt and pillow shams, a crisp navy-blue rug, and a white princess-style bed with a matching dresser and lamp—a near-exact replica of a full-page bedroom layout I'd liked in the Sears catalog and been allowed to get. Each of us was given our own phone extension, too—my phone was a light blue to match my new decor, while Craig's was a manly black—which meant we could conduct our personal business semi-privately.

I arranged my first real kiss, in fact, over the phone. It was with a boy named Ronnell. Ronnell didn't go to my school or live in my immediate neighborhood, but he sang in the Chicago Children's Choir with my classmate Chiaka, and with Chiaka acting as intermediary, we somehow had decided we liked each other. Our phone calls were a little awkward, but I didn't care. I liked the feeling of being liked. I felt a zing of anticipation every time the phone rang. *Could it be Ronnell?* I don't remember which one of us proposed that we meet outside my house one afternoon to give kissing a try, but there was no nuance to it; no shy euphemisms needed to be applied. We weren't going to "hang out" or "take a walk." We were going to make out. And we were both all for it.

Which is how I landed on the stone bench that sat near the side door of my family's house, in full view of the south-facing windows and surrounded by my great-aunt's flower beds, lost in a warm splishy kiss with Ronnell. There was nothing earth-shattering or especially inspiring about it, but it was fun. Being around boys, I was slowly coming to realize, was fun. The hours I passed watching Craig's games from the bleachers of one gym or another began to feel less like a sisterly obligation. Because what was a basketball game if not a showcase of boys? I'd wear my snuggest jeans and lay on some extra bracelets and sometimes bring one of the Gore sisters along to boost my visibility in the stands. And then I'd enjoy every minute of the sweaty spectacle before me—the leaping and charging, the rippling and roaring, the pulse of maleness and all its mysteries on full display. When a boy on the JV team smiled at me as he left the court one evening, I smiled right back. It felt like my future was just beginning to arrive.

I was slowly separating from my parents, gradually less inclined to blurt every last thought in my head. I rode in silence behind them in the backseat of the Buick as we drove home from those basketball games, my feelings too deep or too jumbled to share. I was caught up in the lonely thrill of being a teenager now, convinced that the adults around me had never been there themselves.

Sometimes in the evenings I'd emerge from brushing my teeth in the bathroom and find the apartment dark, the lights in the living room and kitchen turned off for the night, everyone settled into their own sphere. I'd see a glow beneath the door to Craig's room and know he was doing homework. I'd catch the flicker of television light coming from my parents' room and hear them murmuring quietly, laughing to themselves. Just as I never wondered what it was like for my mother to be a full-time, at-home mother, I never wondered then what it meant to be married. I took my parents' union for granted. It was the simple solid fact upon which all four of our lives were built.

Much later, my mother would tell me that every year when spring came and the air warmed up in Chicago, she entertained thoughts about leaving my father. I don't know if these thoughts were actually serious or not. I don't know if she considered the idea for an hour, or for a day, or for most of the season, but for her it was an active fantasy, something that felt healthy and maybe even energizing to ponder, almost as ritual.

I understand now that even a happy marriage can be a vexation, that it's a contract best renewed and renewed again, even quietly and privately—even alone. I don't think my mother announced whatever her doubts and discontents were to my father directly, and I don't think she let him in on whatever alternative life she might have been dreaming about during those times. Was she picturing herself on a tropical island somewhere? With a different kind of man, or in a different kind of house, or with a corner office instead of kids? I don't know, and I suppose I could ask my mother, who is now in her eighties, but I don't think it matters.

If you've never passed a winter in Chicago, let me describe it: You can live for a hundred straight days beneath an iron-gray sky that claps itself like a lid over the city. Frigid, biting winds blow in off the lake. Snow falls in dozens of ways, in heavy overnight dumps and daytime, sideways squalls, in demoralizing sloppy sleet and fairy-tale billows of fluff. There's ice, usually, lots of it, that shellacs the sidewalks and windshields that then need to be scraped. There's the sound of that scraping in the early mornings—the *hack hack hack* of it—as people clear their cars to go to work. Your neighbors, unrecognizable in the thick layers they wear against the cold, keep their faces down to avoid the wind. City snowplows thunder through the streets as the white snow gets piled up and sooty, until nothing is pristine.

Eventually, however, something happens. A slow reversal begins. It can be subtle, a whiff of humidity in the air, a slight lifting of the sky. You feel it first in your heart, the possibility that winter might have passed. You may not trust it at the beginning, but then you do. Because now the sun is out and there are little nubby buds on the trees and your neighbors have taken off their heavy coats. And maybe there's a new airiness to your thoughts on the morning you decide to pull out every window in your apartment so you can spray the glass and wipe down the sills. It allows you to think, to wonder if you've missed out on other possibilities by becoming a wife to this man in this house with these children.

Maybe you spend the whole day considering new ways to live before finally you fit every window back into its frame and empty your bucket of Pine-Sol into the sink. And maybe now all your certainty returns, because yes, truly, it's spring and once again you've made the choice to stay.

5

M Y MOTHER ULTIMATELY DID GO BACK TO WORK, right about the time I began high school, catapulting herself out of the house and the neighborhood and into the dense, skyscrapered heart of Chicago, where she found a job as an executive assistant at a bank. She bought a work wardrobe and began commuting each morning, catching the bus north on Jeffery Boulevard or riding along with my dad in the Buick, if their start times happened to line up. The job, for her, was a welcome shift in routine, and for our family it was also more or less a financial necessity. My parents had been paying tuition for Craig to go to Catholic school. He was starting to think about college, with me coming up right behind him.

My brother was now full grown, a graceful giant with uncanny spring in his legs, and considered one of the best basketball players in the city. At home, he ate a lot. He drained gallons of milk, devoured entire large pizzas in one sitting, and often snacked from dinner to bedtime. He managed, as he'd always done, to be both easygoing and deeply focused, maintaining scads of friends and good grades while also turning heads as an athlete. He'd traveled around the Midwest on a summer rec-league team that featured an incubating superstar named Isiah Thomas, who would later go on to a Hall of Fame career in the NBA. As he approached high school, Craig had been sought after by some of Chicago's top public school coaches looking to fill gaps in their rosters. These teams pulled in big rowdy crowds as well as college scouts, but my parents were adamant that Craig not sacrifice his intellectual development for the short-lived glory of being a high school phenom.

Mount Carmel, with its strong Catholic-league basketball team and rigorous curriculum, had seemed the best solution—worth the thousands of dollars it was costing my parents. Craig's teachers were brown-robed priests who went by "Father." About 80 percent of his classmates were white, many of them Irish Catholic kids who came from outlying working-class white neighborhoods. By the end of his junior year, he was already being courted by Division I college teams, a couple of which would probably offer him a free ride. Still, my parents held fast to the idea that he should keep all options open, aiming to get himself into the best college possible. They alone would worry about the cost.

My high school experience blessedly cost us nothing except for bus fare. I was lucky enough to test into Chicago's first magnet high school, Whitney M. Young High School, which sat in what was then a run-down area just west of the Loop and was, after a few short years in existence, on its way to becoming a top public school in the city. Whitney Young was named for a civil rights activist and had been opened in 1975 as a positive-minded alternative to busing. Located squarely on the dividing line between the North and the South Sides of the city and featuring forward-thinking teachers and brand-new facilities, the school was designed as a kind of equal-opportunity nirvana, meant to draw high-performing students of all colors. Admissions quotas set by the Chicago school board called for a student body that would be 40 percent Black, 40 percent white, and 20 percent Hispanic or other. But the reality of who enrolled looked slightly different. When I attended, about 80 percent of the students were nonwhite.

Just getting to school for my first day of ninth grade was a whole new odyssey, involving ninety minutes of nerve-pummeling travel on two different city bus routes as well as a transfer downtown. Hauling myself out of bed at five o'clock that morning, I'd put on all new clothes and a pair of nice earrings, unsure of how any of it would be received on the other end of my bus trek. I'd eaten breakfast, having no idea where lunch would be. I said good-bye to my parents, unclear on whether I'd even still be myself at the end of the day. High school was meant to be transformative. And Whitney Young, for me, was pure frontier.

The school itself was striking and modern, like no school I'd ever seen—made up of three large, cube-shaped buildings, two of them connected by a fancy-looking glass skyway that crossed over the Jackson Boulevard thoroughfare. The classrooms were open concept and thoughtfully designed. There was a whole building dedicated to the arts, with special rooms for the choir to sing and bands to play, and other rooms that had been outfitted for photography and pottery. The whole place was built like a temple for learning. Students streamed through the main entryway, purposeful already on day one.

There were about nineteen hundred kids at Whitney Young, and from my point of view they appeared universally older and more confident than I'd ever be, in full command of every brain cell, powered by every multiple-choice question they'd nailed on the citywide standardized test. Looking around, I felt small. I'd been one of the older kids at Bryn Mawr and was now among the youngest of the high schoolers. Getting off the bus, I'd noticed that along with their book bags a lot of the girls carried actual purses.

My worries about high school, if they were to be cataloged, could mostly be filed under one general heading: *Am I good enough?* It was a question that dogged me through my first month, even as I began to settle in, even as I got used to the predawn wake-ups and navigating between buildings for class. Whitney Young was subdivided into five "houses," each one serving as a home base for its members and meant to add intimacy to the big-school experience. I was in the Gold House, led by an assistant principal named Mr. Smith, who happened to live a few doors down from my family on Euclid Avenue. I'd been doing odd jobs for Mr. Smith and his family for years, having been hired to do everything from babysitting his kids and giving them piano lessons to attempting to train their untrainable puppy. Seeing Mr. Smith at school was a mild comfort, a bridge between Whitney Young and my neighborhood, but it did little to offset my anxiety.

Just a few kids from my neighborhood had come to Whitney Young. My neighbor and friend Terri Johnson had gotten in, and so had my classmate Chiaka, whom I'd known and been in friendly competition with since kindergarten, as well as one or two boys. Some of us rode the bus together in the mornings and back home at the end of the day, but at school we were scattered between houses, mostly on our own. I was also operating, for the first time ever, without the tacit protection of my older brother. Craig, in his ambling and smiley way, had conveniently broken every trail for me. At Bryn Mawr, he'd softened up the teachers with his sweetness and earned a certain cool-kid respect on the playground. He'd created sunshine that I could then just step into. I had always, pretty much everywhere I'd gone, been known as Craig Robinson's little sister.

Now, though, I was just Michelle Robinson, with no Craig attached. At Whitney Young, I had to work to ground myself. My initial strategy involved keeping quiet and trying to observe my new classmates. Who were these kids anyway? All I knew was that they were smart. Demonstrably smart. Selectively smart. The smartest kids in the city, apparently. But wasn't I as well? Hadn't all of us—me and Terri and Chiaka—landed here because we were smart like them?

The truth is I didn't know. I had no idea whether we were smart like them.

I knew only that we were the best students coming out of what was thought to be a middling, mostly Black school in a middling, mostly Black neighborhood. But what if that wasn't enough? What if, after all this fuss, we were just the best of the worst?

This was the doubt that sat in my mind through student orientation, through my first sessions of high school biology and English, through my somewhat fumbling get-to-know-you conversations in the cafeteria with new friends. *Not enough. Not enough.* It was doubt about where I came from and what I'd believed about myself until now. It was like a malignant cell that threatened to divide and divide again, unless I could find some way to stop it.

· · ·

CHICAGO, I WAS LEARNING, was a much bigger city than I'd ever imagined it to be. This was a revelation formed in part over the three hours I now logged daily on the bus, boarding at Seventy-Fifth Street and chuffing through a maze of local stops, often forced to stand because it was too crowded to find a seat.

Through the window, I got a long slow view of the South Side in what felt like its entirety, its corner stores and barbecue joints still shuttered in the gray light of early morning, its basketball courts and paved playgrounds lying empty. We'd go north on Jeffery and then west on Sixty-Seventh Street, then north again, zagging and stopping every two blocks to collect more people. We crossed Jackson Park Highlands and Hyde Park, where the University of Chicago campus sat hidden behind a massive wrought-iron gate. After what felt like an eternity, we'd finally accelerate onto Lake Shore Drive, following the curve of Lake Michigan north toward downtown.

There's no hurrying a bus ride, I can tell you. You get on and you endure. Every morning, I'd switch buses downtown at Michigan Avenue at the height of rush hour, catching a westbound ride along Van Buren Street, where the view at least got more interesting as we passed bank buildings with big gold doors and bellhops standing outside the fancy hotels. Through the window, I watched men and women in smart outfits—in suits and skirts and clicking heels—carrying their coffee to work with a bustle of self-importance. I didn't yet know that people like this were called professionals. I hadn't yet tracked the degrees they must have earned to gain access to the tall corporate castles lining Van Buren. But I did like how determined they looked.

Meanwhile, at school I was quietly collecting bits of data, trying to sort out my place inside the teenage intelligentsia. Until now, my experiences with kids from other neighborhoods had been limited to visits with various cousins and a few summers of city-run day camp at Rainbow Beach, where every camper still came from some part of the South Side and nobody was well-off. At Whitney Young, I met white kids who lived on the North Side—a part of Chicago that felt like the dark side of the moon, a place I'd never thought about nor had reason to go to. More intriguing was my early discovery that there was such a thing as an African American elite. Most of my new high school friends were Black, but that didn't necessarily translate, it turned out, to any sort of uniformity in our experience. A number of them had parents who were lawyers or doctors and seemed to know one another through an African American social club called Jack and Jill. They'd been on ski vacations and trips that required passports. They talked about things that were foreign to me, like summer internships and historically Black colleges. One of my Black classmates, a nerdy boy who was always kind to everyone, had parents who'd founded a big beauty-supply company and lived in one of the ritziest high-rises downtown.

This was my new world. It's not to say that everyone at the school was rich or overly sophisticated, because that wasn't the case. There were plenty of kids who came from neighborhoods just like mine, who struggled with far more than I ever would. But my first months at Whitney Young gave me a glimpse of something that had previously been invisible—the apparatus of privilege and connection, what seemed like a network of half-hidden ladders and guide ropes that lay suspended overhead, ready to connect some but not all of us to the sky.

M Y FIRST ROUND of grades at school turned out to be pretty good, and so did my second. Over the course of my freshman and sophomore years, I began to build the same kind of confidence I'd had at Bryn Mawr. With each little accomplishment, with every high school screwup I managed to avoid, my doubts slowly took leave. I liked most of my teachers. I wasn't afraid to raise my hand in class. At Whitney Young, it was safe to be smart. The assumption was that everyone was working toward college, which meant that you never hid your intelligence for fear of someone saying you talked like a white girl.

I loved any subject that involved writing and labored through precalc. I was a half-decent French student. I had peers who were always a step or two ahead of me, whose achievements seemed effortless, but I tried not to let that get to me. I was beginning to understand that if I put in extra hours of studying, I could often close the gap. I wasn't a straight-A student, but I was always trying, and there were semesters when I got close.

Craig, meanwhile, had enrolled at Princeton University, vacating his back-porch room on Euclid Avenue, leaving a six-foot-six, two-hundred-pound gap in our daily lives. Our fridge was considerably less loaded with meat and milk, the phone line no longer tied up by girls calling to chat him up. He'd been recruited by big universities offering scholarships and what amounted to a celebrity existence playing basketball, but with my parents' encouragement he'd chosen Princeton, which cost more but, as they saw it, promised more as well. My father burst with pride when Craig became a starter as a sophomore on Princeton's basketball team. Wobbly on his feet and using two canes to walk, he still relished a long drive. He'd traded in his old Buick for a new Buick, another 225, this one a shimmering deep maroon. When he could get the time off from his job at the filtration plant, he'd drive twelve hours across Indiana, Ohio, Pennsylvania, and New Jersey to catch one of Craig's games.

By nature of my long commute to Whitney Young, I saw less of my parents, and looking back at it, I'd guess that it was a lonely time for them, or at least required some adjustment. I was now gone more than I was home. Tired of standing through the ninety-minute bus ride to school, Terri Johnson and I had figured out a kind of trick, which involved leaving our houses fifteen minutes earlier in the morning and catching a bus that was headed in the opposite direction from school. We rode a few stops south to a less busy neighborhood, then jumped out, crossed the street, and hailed our regular northbound bus, which was reliably emptier than it would be at Seventy-Fifth, where we normally boarded. Pleased by our own cleverness, we'd smugly claim a seat and then talk or study the whole way to school.

In the evenings, I dragged myself back through the door around six or seven o'clock, in time for a quick dinner and a chance to talk to my parents about whatever had gone on that day. But once the dishes had been washed, I disappeared into homework, often taking my books downstairs to the encyclopedia nook off the stairwell next to Robbie and Terry's apartment for privacy and quiet.

My parents never once spoke of the stress of having to pay for college, but I knew enough to appreciate that it was there. When my French teacher announced that she'd be leading an optional class trip to Paris over one of our breaks for those who could come up with the money to do it, I didn't even bother to raise the issue at home. This was the difference between me and the Jack and Jill kids, many of whom were now my close friends. I had a loving and orderly home, bus fare to get me across town to school, and a hot meal to come home to at night. Beyond that, I wasn't going to ask my parents for a thing.

Yet one evening my parents sat me down, looking puzzled. My mom had learned about the France trip through Terri Johnson's mom.

"Why didn't you tell us?" she said.

"Because it's too much money."

"That's actually not for you to decide, Miche," my dad said gently, almost offended. "And how are we supposed to decide, if we don't even know about it?"

I looked at them both, unsure of what to say. My mother glanced at me, her eyes soft. My father had changed out of his work uniform and into a clean white shirt. They were in their early forties then, married nearly twenty years. Neither one of them had ever vacationed in Europe. They never took beach trips or went out to dinner. They didn't own a house. We were their investment, me and Craig. Everything went into us.

A few months later, I boarded a flight to Paris with my teacher and a dozen or so of my classmates from Whitney Young. We would stay in a hostel, tour the Louvre and the Eiffel Tower. We'd buy *crêpes au fromage* from stands on the street and walk along the banks of the Seine. We'd speak French like a bunch of high school kids from Chicago, but we'd at least speak French. As the plane pulled away from its gate that day, I looked out my window and back at the airport, knowing that my mother stood somewhere behind its black-glass windows, dressed in her winter coat and waving me on. I remember the jet engines firing, shockingly loud. And then we were rattling down the runway and beginning to tilt upward as the acceleration seized my chest and pressed me backward into my seat for that strange, in-between half moment that comes before finally you feel lifted.

. . . .

I N THE MANNER of all high schoolers everywhere, my friends and I liked to loiter. We loitered boisterously and we loitered in public. On days when school got out early or when homework was light, we flocked from Whitney Young to downtown Chicago, landing in the eight-story mall at Water Tower Place. Once there, we rode the escalators up and down, spent our money on gourmet popcorn from Garrett's, and commandeered tables at McDonald's for more hours than was reasonable, given how little food we ordered. We browsed the designer jeans and the purses at Marshall Field's, often surreptitiously tailed by security guards who didn't like the look of us. Sometimes we went to a movie.

We were happy—happy with our freedom, happy with one another, happy with the way the city seemed to glitter more on days when we weren't thinking about school. We were city kids learning how to range.

I spent a lot of my time with a classmate named Santita Jackson, who in the mornings boarded the Jeffery bus a few stops after I did and who became one of my best friends in high school. Santita had beautiful dark eyes, full cheeks, and the bearing of a wise woman, even at sixteen. At school, she was one of those kids who signed up for every AP class available and seemed to ace them all. She wore skirts when everyone else wore jeans and had a singing voice so clear and powerful that she'd end up touring years later as a backup singer for Roberta Flack. She was also deep. It's what I loved most about Santita. Like me, she could be frivolous and goofy when we were with a larger group, but on our own we'd get ponderous and intense, two girl-philosophers together trying to sort out life's issues, big and small. We passed hours sprawled on the floor of Santita's room on the second floor of her family's white Tudor house in Jackson Park Highlands, a more affluent section of South Shore, talking about things that irked us and where our lives were headed and what we did and didn't understand about the world. As a friend, she was a good listener and insightful, and I tried to be the same.

Santita's father was famous. This was the primary, impossible-to-get-around fact of her life. She was the eldest child of the Reverend Jesse

Jackson, the firebrand Baptist preacher and increasingly powerful political leader. Jackson had worked closely with Martin Luther King Jr. and risen to national prominence himself in the early 1970s as the founder of a political organization called Operation PUSH, which advocated for the rights of underserved African Americans. By the time we were in high school, he'd become an outright celebrity—charismatic, well connected, and constantly on the move. He toured the country, mesmerizing crowds with thundering calls for Black people to shake off the undermining ghetto stereotypes and claim their long-denied political power. He preached a message of relentless, let's-do-this self-empowerment. "Down with dope! Up with hope!" he'd call to his audiences. He had schoolkids sign pledges to turn off the TV and devote two hours to their homework each night. He made parents promise to stay involved. He pushed back against the feelings of failure that permeated so many African American communities, urging people to quit with the self-pity and take charge of their own destiny. "Nobody, but nobody," he'd yell, "is too poor to turn off the TV two hours a night!"

Hanging around Santita's house could be exciting. The place was roomy and a little chaotic, home to the family's five children and stuffed with heavy Victorian furniture and antique glassware that Santita's mom, Jacqueline, liked to collect. Mrs. Jackson, as I called her, had an expansive spirit and a big laugh. She wore colorful, billowy clothes and served meals at a massive table in the dining room, hosting anyone who turned up, mostly people who belonged to what she called "the movement." This included business leaders, politicians, and poets, plus a coterie of famous people, from singers to athletes.

When Reverend Jackson was at home, a different energy pulsed through the house. Routines were cast aside; dinner conversations lasted late into the night. Advisers came and went. Plans were always being made. Unlike at my apartment on Euclid, where life ran at an orderly and predictable pace, where my parents' concerns rarely extended beyond keeping our family happy and on track for success, the Jacksons seemed caught up in something larger, messier, and seemingly more impactful. Their engagement was outward; their community was big, their mission important. Santita and her siblings were being raised to be politically active. They knew how and what to boycott. They marched for their father's causes. They went on his work trips, visiting places like Israel and Cuba, New York and Atlanta. They'd stood on stages in front of big crowds and were learning to absorb the anxiety and controversy that came with having a father, maybe especially a Black father, in public life. Reverend Jackson had bodyguards—large, silent men who traveled with him. At the time, it only half registered with me that there had been threats against his life.

Santita adored her father and was proud of his work, but she was also trying to live her own life. She and I were all for strengthening the character of Black youth across America, but we also needed rather desperately to get to Water Tower Place before the K-Swiss sneaker sale ended. We often found ourselves looking for rides or to borrow a car. Because I lived in a one-car family with two working parents, the odds were usually better at the Jacksons' house, where Mrs. Jackson had both a wood-paneled station wagon and a little sports car. Sometimes we'd hitch rides with the various staff members or visitors who buzzed in and out. What we sacrificed was control. This would become one of my early, unwitting lessons about life in politics: Schedules and plans never seemed to stick. Even standing on the far edge of the vortex, you still felt its spin. Santita and I were often stuck waiting out some delay that related to her father—a meeting that was running long or a plane that was still circling the airport—or detouring through a series of last-minute stops. We'd think we were getting a ride home from school or going to the mall, but instead we'd end up at a political rally on the West Side or stranded for hours at the Operation PUSH headquarters in Hyde Park.

One day we found ourselves marching with a crowd of Jesse Jackson supporters in the Bud Billiken Day Parade. The parade, named for a fictional character from a long-ago newspaper column, is one of the South Side's grandest traditions, held every August—an extravaganza of marching bands and floats that runs for almost two miles along Martin Luther King Jr. Drive, through the heart of the African American neighborhood that was once referred to as the Black Belt but was later rechristened Bronzeville. The Bud Billiken Day Parade had been going on since 1929, and it was all about African American pride. If you were any sort of community leader or politician, it was—and still is, to this day—more or less mandatory that you show up and walk the route.

I didn't know it at the time, but the vortex around Santita's father was starting to spin faster. Jesse Jackson was a few years from formally launching a run to be president of the United States, which means he was likely beginning to actively consider the idea during the time we were in high school. Money had to be raised. Connections needed to be made. Running for president, I understand now, is an all-consuming, full-body effort for every person involved, and good campaigns tend to involve a stage-setting, groundwork-laying preamble, which can add whole years to the effort. Setting his sights on the 1984 election, Jesse Jackson would become the second African American ever to run a serious national campaign for the presidency, after Congresswoman Shirley Chisholm's unsuccessful run in 1972. My guess is that at least some of this was on his mind at the time of the parade.

What I knew was that I personally didn't love the feeling of being out there, thrust under a baking sun amid balloons and bullhorns, amid trombones and throngs of cheering people. The fanfare was fun and even intoxicating, but there was something about it, and about politics in general, that made me queasy. For one thing, I was someone who liked things to be neat and planned in advance, and from what I could tell, there seemed to be nothing especially neat about a life in politics. The parade had not been part of my plan. As I remember it, Santita and I hadn't intended on joining at all. We'd been conscripted at the last minute, maybe by her mother or father, or by someone else in the movement who'd caught us before we could follow through on whatever ideas we'd had for ourselves that day. But I loved Santita dearly, and I was also a polite kid who for the most part went along with what adults told me to do, and so I'd done it. I'd plunged myself deep into the hot, spinning noisiness of the Bud Billiken Day Parade.

I arrived home at Euclid Avenue that evening to find my mother laughing.

"I just saw you on TV," she said.

She'd been watching the news and spotted me marching alongside Santita, waving and smiling and going along. What made her laugh, I'd guess, is that she also picked up on the queasiness—the fact that maybe I'd been caught up in something I'd rather not do.

W HEN IT CAME time to look at colleges, Santita and I both were interested in schools on the East Coast. She went to check out Harvard but was disheartened when an admissions officer pointedly harassed her about her father's politics, when all she wanted was to be taken on her own terms. I spent a weekend visiting Craig at Princeton, where he seemed to have slipped into a productive rhythm of playing basketball, taking classes, and hanging out at a campus center designed for minority students. The campus was large and pretty—an Ivy League school covered with ivy—and Craig's friends seemed nice enough. I didn't overthink it from there. No one in my immediate family had much in the way of direct experience with college, so there was little, anyway, to debate or explore. As had always been the case, I figured that whatever Craig liked, I would like, too, and that whatever he could accomplish, I could as well. And with that, Princeton became my top choice for school.

Early in my senior year at Whitney Young, I went for an obligatory first appointment with the school college counselor to whom I'd been assigned.

I can't tell you much about the counselor, because I deliberately and almost instantly blotted this experience out. I don't remember her age or race or how she happened to look at me that day when I turned up in her office doorway, full of pride at the fact that I was on track to graduate in the top 10 percent of my class at Whitney Young, that I'd been elected treasurer of the senior class, made the National Honor Society, and managed to vanquish pretty much every doubt I'd arrived with as a nervous ninth grader. I don't remember whether she inspected my transcript before or after I announced my interest in joining my brother at Princeton the following fall.

It's possible, in fact, that during our short meeting the college counselor said things to me that might have been positive and helpful, but I recall none of it. Because rightly or wrongly, I got stuck on one single sentence the woman uttered.

"I'm not sure," she said, giving me a perfunctory, patronizing smile, "that you're Princeton material."

Her judgment was as swift as it was dismissive, probably based on a quick-glance calculus involving my grades and test scores. It was some version, I imagine, of what this woman did all day long and with practiced efficiency, telling seniors where they did and didn't belong. I'm sure she figured she was only being realistic. I doubt that she gave our conversation another thought.

But as I've said, failure is a feeling long before it's an actual result. And for me, it felt like that's exactly what she was planting—a suggestion of failure long before I'd even tried to succeed. She was telling me to lower my sights, which was the absolute reverse of every last thing my parents had ever told me.

Had I decided to believe her, her pronouncement would have toppled my confidence all over again, reviving the old thrum of *not enough, not enough.*

But three years of keeping up with the ambitious kids at Whitney Young had taught me that I was something more. I wasn't going to let one person's opinion dislodge everything I thought I knew about myself. Instead, I switched my method without changing my goal. I would apply to Princeton and a scattershot selection of other schools, but without any more input from the college counselor. Instead, I sought help from someone who actually knew me. Mr. Smith, my assistant principal and neighbor, had seen my strengths as a student and furthermore trusted me with his own kids. He agreed to write me a recommendation letter.

I've been lucky enough now in my life to meet all sorts of extraordinary and accomplished people—world leaders, inventors, musicians, astronauts, athletes, professors, entrepreneurs, artists and writers, pioneering doctors and researchers. Some (though not enough) of them are women. Some (though not enough) are Black or of color. Some were born poor or have lived lives that to many of us would appear to have been unfairly heaped with adversity, and yet still they seem to operate as if they've had every advantage in the world. What I've learned is this: All of them have had doubters. Some continue to have roaring, stadium-sized collections of critics and naysayers who will shout *I told you so* at every little misstep or mistake. The noise doesn't go away, but the most successful people I know have figured out how to live with it, to lean on the people who believe in them, and to push onward with their goals.

That day I left the college counselor's office at Whitney Young, I was fuming, my ego bruised more than anything. My only thought, in the moment, was *I'll show you.*

But then I settled down and got back to work. I never thought getting into college would be easy, but I was learning to focus and have faith in my own story. I tried to tell the whole thing in my college essay. Rather than pretending that I was madly intellectual and thought I'd fit right in inside the ivy-strewn walls of Princeton, I wrote about my father's MS and my family's lack of experience with higher education. I owned the fact that I was reaching. Given my background, reaching was really all I could do.

And ultimately, I suppose that I did show that college counselor, because six or seven months later, a letter arrived in our mailbox on Euclid Avenue, offering me admission to Princeton. My parents and I celebrated that night by having pizza delivered from Italian Fiesta. I called Craig and shouted the good news. The next day I knocked on Mr. Smith's door to tell him about my acceptance, thanking him for his help. I never did stop in on the college counselor to tell her she'd been wrong—that I was Princeton material after all. It would have done nothing for either of us. And in the end, I hadn't needed to show her anything. I was only showing myself.

6

M Y DAD DROVE ME TO PRINCETON IN THE SUMMER of 1981, across the flat highways connecting Illinois to New Jersey. But it was more than a simple father-daughter road trip. My boyfriend, David, came along for the ride. I'd been invited to attend a special three-week summer orientation program, meant to close a "preparation gap," giving certain incoming freshmen extra time and help settling into college. It was unclear exactly how we were identified—what part of our admissions applications had tipped the university off to the idea that we might benefit from lessons on how to read a syllabus or advance practice navigating the pathways between campus buildings—but Craig had done it two years earlier, and it seemed like an opportunity. So I packed up my stuff, said good-bye to my mom—neither of us teary or sentimental—and climbed into the car.

My eagerness to leave town was fueled in part by the fact I'd spent the last couple of months working an assembly-line job, operating what was basically an industrial-sized glue gun at a small bookbinding factory in downtown Chicago—a soul-killing routine that went on for eight hours a day, five days a week, and served as possibly the single most reinforcing reminder that going to college was a good idea. David's mom worked at the bookbindery and had helped get the two of us jobs there. We'd worked shoulder to shoulder all summer, which made the whole endeavor more palatable. David was smart and gentle, a tall, good-looking guy who was two years older than I was. He'd first befriended Craig on the neighborhood basketball court in Rosenblum Park a few years earlier, joining pickup games when he came to visit relatives who lived on Euclid Parkway. Eventually, he started hanging around with me. During the school year, David went away to college out of state, which conveniently kept him from being any sort of distraction from my studies. During holiday breaks and over the summer, though, he came home to stay with his mom on the far southwest side of the city and drove over almost every day to pick me up in his car.

David was easygoing and also more of an adult than any boyfriend I'd had. He sat on the couch and watched ball games with my father. He joked around with Craig and made polite conversation with my mom. We went on real dates, going for what we considered upscale dinners at Red Lobster and to the movies. We fooled around and smoked pot in his car. By day at the bookbindery, we glue gunned our way into a companionable oblivion, wisecracking until there was nothing left to say. Neither of us was particularly invested in the job, beyond trying to save up money for school. I'd be leaving town soon anyway, and had little intention of ever coming back to the bookbinding plant. In a sense, I was already half departed—my mind flown off in the direction of Princeton.

Which is to say that on the early August evening when our father-daughter-boyfriend trio finally pulled off Route 1 and turned onto the wide leafy avenue leading to campus, I was fully ready to get on with things. I was ready to cart my two suitcases into the summer-session dorm, ready to pump the hands of the other kids who'd come (minority and low-income students primarily, with a few athletes mixed in). I was ready to taste the dining-hall food, memorize the campus map, and conquer whatever syllabi they wanted to throw my way. I was there. I had landed. I was seventeen years old, and my life was under way.

There was only one problem, and that was David, who as soon as we crossed the state line from Pennsylvania had begun to look a little doleful. As we wrestled my luggage out of the back of my dad's car, I could tell he was feeling lonely already. We'd been dating for over a year. We'd professed love, but it was love in the context of Euclid Avenue and Red Lobster and the basketball courts at Rosenblum Park. It was love in the context of the place I'd just left. While my father took his customary extra minute to get out of the driver's seat and steady himself on his canes, David and I stood wordlessly in the dusk, surveying the immaculate diamond of green lawn outside my stone fortress of a dorm. It was hitting us both, I assumed, that there were perhaps important things we hadn't discussed, that we had perhaps divergent views on whether this was a temporary farewell or an outright, geographically induced breakup. Were we going to visit? Write love letters? How hard were we going to work at this?

David held my hand in an earnest way. It was confusing. I knew what I wanted but couldn't find the words. I hoped that someday my feelings for a man would knock me sideways, that I'd get swept into the upending, tsunami-like rush that seemed to power all the best love stories. My parents had fallen in love as teenagers. My dad took my mother to her high school prom, even. I knew that teenage affairs were sometimes real and lasting. I wanted to believe that there was a guy who'd materialize and become everything to me, who'd be sexy and solid and whose effect would be so immediate and deep that I'd be willing to rearrange my priorities.

It just wasn't the guy standing in front of me right now.

My father finally broke the silence between me and David, saying that it was time for us to get my stuff up to the dorm. He'd booked a motel room in town for the two of them. They planned to take off the next day, headed back to Chicago.

In the parking lot, I hugged my father tight. His arms had always been strong from his youthful devotion to boxing and swimming and were now further maintained by the effort required to move around by cane.

"Be good, Miche," he said, releasing me, his face betraying no emotion other than pride.

He then got into the car, kindly giving me and David some privacy.

We stood together on the pavement, both of us sheepish and stalling. My heart lurched with affection as he leaned in to kiss me. This part always felt good.

And yet I knew. I knew that while I had my arms around a good-hearted Chicago guy who genuinely cared about me, there was also, just beyond us, a lit path leading out of the parking lot and up a slight hill toward the quad, which would in a matter of minutes become my new context, my new world. I was nervous about living away from home for the first time, about leaving the only life I'd ever known. But some part of me understood it was better to make a clean, quick break and not hold on to anything. The next day David would call me at my dorm, asking if we could meet up for a quick meal or a final walk around town before he left, and I would mumble something about how busy I was already at school, how I didn't think it would work. Our good-bye that night was for real and forever. I probably should have said it directly in the moment, but I chickened out, knowing it would hurt, both to say and to hear. Instead, I just let him go.

IT TURNED OUT there were a lot of things I had yet to learn about life, or at least life on the Princeton campus in the early 1980s. After I spent several energizing weeks as a summer student, surrounded by a few dozen other kids who seemed both accessible and familiar to me, the fall semester officially began, opening the floodgates to the student population at large. I moved my belongings into a new dorm room, a one-room triple in Pyne Hall, and then watched through my third-floor window as several thousand mostly white students poured onto campus, carting stereos and duvet sets and racks of clothes. Some kids arrived in limos. One girl brought two limos—stretch limos—to accommodate all her stuff.

Princeton was extremely white and very male. There was no avoiding the facts. Men on campus outnumbered women almost two to one. Black students made up less than 9 percent of my freshman class. If during the orientation program we'd begun to feel some ownership of the space, we were now a glaring anomaly—poppy seeds in a bowl of rice. While Whitney Young had been somewhat diverse, I'd never been part of a predominantly white community before. I'd never stood out in a crowd or a classroom because of the color of my skin. It was jarring and uncomfortable, at least at first, like being dropped into a strange new terrarium, a habitat that hadn't been built for me.

As with anything, though, you learn to adapt. Some of the adjustment was easy—a relief almost. For one thing, nobody seemed much concerned about crime. Students left their rooms unlocked, their bikes casually kickstanded outside buildings, their gold earrings unattended on the sink in the dorm bathrooms. Their trust in the world seemed infinite, their forward progress in it entirely assured. For me, it was something to get used to. I'd spent years quietly guarding my possessions on the bus ride to and from Whitney Young. Walking home to Euclid Avenue in the evenings, I carried my house key wedged between two knuckles and pointed outward, in case I needed it to defend myself.

At Princeton, it seemed the only thing I needed to be vigilant about was my studies. Everything otherwise was designed to accommodate our well-being as students. The dining halls served five different kinds of breakfast. There were enormous spreading oak trees to sit under and open lawns where we could throw Frisbees to relieve our stress. The main library was like an old-world cathedral, with high ceilings and glossy hardwood tables where we could lay out our textbooks and study in silence. We were protected, cocooned, catered to. A lot of kids, I was coming to realize, had never in their lifetimes known anything different.

Attached to all of this was a new vocabulary, one I needed to master. What was a precept? What was a reading period? Nobody had explained to me the meaning of "extra-long" bedsheets on the school packing list, which meant that I bought myself too-short bedsheets and would thus spend my freshman year sleeping with my feet resting on the exposed plastic of the dorm mattress. There was an especially distinct learning curve when it came to understanding sports. I'd been raised on the bedrock of football, basketball, and baseball, but it turned out that East Coast prep schoolers did more. Lacrosse was a thing. Field hockey was a thing. Squash, even, was a thing. For a kid from the South Side, it could be a little dizzying. "You row crew?" What does that even mean?

I had only one advantage, the same one I'd had when starting kindergarten: I was still Craig Robinson's little sister. Craig was now a junior and a top player on the varsity basketball team. He was, as he'd always been, a man with fans. Even the campus security guards greeted him by name. Craig had a life, and I managed at least partially to slip into it. I got to know his teammates and their friends. One night I went to a dinner with him off campus, at the well-appointed home of one of the basketball team's boosters, where sitting at the dining room table I was met by a confounding sight, a food item that like so many other things at Princeton required a lesson in gentility—a spiny green artichoke laid out on a white china plate.

Craig had found himself a plum housing arrangement for the year, living rent-free as a caretaker in an upstairs bedroom at the Third World Center, a poorly named but well-intentioned offshoot of the university with a mission to support students of color. (It would be a full twenty years before the Third World Center was rechristened the Carl A. Fields Center for Equality and Cultural Understanding—named for Princeton's first African American dean.) The center was housed in a brick building on a corner lot on Prospect Avenue, whose prime blocks were dominated by the grand, mansion-like stone and Tudor-style eating clubs that substituted for fraternities.

The Third World Center—or TWC, as most of us called it—quickly became a kind of home base for me. It hosted parties and co-op meals. There were volunteer tutors to help with homework and spaces just to hang out. I'd made a handful of instant friends during the summer program, and many of us gravitated toward the center during our free time. Among them was Suzanne Alele. Suzanne was tall and thin with thick eyebrows and luxurious dark hair that fell in a shiny wave down her back.

She had been born in Nigeria and raised in Kingston, Jamaica, though her family had moved to Maryland when she was a teenager. Perhaps as a result, she seemed unhooked from any single cultural identity. People were drawn to Suzanne. It was hard not to be. She had a wide-open smile and a slight island lilt in her voice that became more pronounced anytime she was tired or a little drunk. She carried herself with what I think of as a Caribbean breeziness, a lightness of spirit that caused her to stand out among Princeton's studious masses. She was unafraid to plunge into parties where she didn't know a soul. Even though she was premed, she made a point of taking pottery and dance classes for the simple reason that they made her happy.

Later, during our sophomore year, Suzanne would take another plunge, deciding to bicker at an eating club called Cap and Gown— "bicker" being a verb with a meaning particular to Princeton, signifying the social vetting that goes on when clubs choose new members. I loved the stories Suzanne brought back from the eating-club banquets and parties she went to, but I had no interest in bickering myself. I was happy with the community of Black and Latino students I'd found through the TWC, content to remain at the margins of Princeton's larger social scene. Our group was small but tight. We threw parties and danced half the night. At meals, we often packed ten or more around a table, laid-back and laughing. Our dinners could stretch into hours, not unlike the long communal meals my family used to have around the table at Southside's house.

I imagine that the administrators at Princeton didn't love the fact that students of color largely stuck together. The hope was that all of us would mingle in heterogeneous harmony, deepening the quality of student life across the board. It's a worthy goal. I understand that when it comes to campus diversity, the ideal would be to achieve something resembling what's often shown on college brochures—smiling students working and socializing in neat, ethnically blended groups. But even today, with white students continuing to outnumber students of color on college campuses, the burden of assimilation is put largely on the shoulders of minority students. In my experience, it's a lot to ask.

At Princeton, I needed my Black friends. We provided one another relief and support. So many of us arrived at college not even aware of what our disadvantages were. You learn only slowly that your new peers had been given SAT tutoring or college-caliber teaching in high school or had gone to boarding school and thus weren't grappling with the difficulties of being away from home for the first time. It was like stepping onstage at your first piano recital and realizing that you'd never played anything but an instrument with broken keys. Your world shifts, but you're asked to adjust and overcome, to play your music the same as everyone else.

This is doable, of course—minority and underprivileged students rise to the challenge all the time—but it takes energy. It takes energy to be the only Black person in a lecture hall or one of a few nonwhite people trying out for a play or joining an intramural team. It requires effort, an extra level of confidence, to speak in those settings and own your presence in the room. Which is why when my friends and I found one another at dinner each night, it was with some degree of relief. It's why we stayed a long time and laughed as much as we could.

My two white roommates in Pyne Hall were both perfectly nice, but I wasn't around the dorm enough to strike up any sort of deep friendship. I didn't, in fact, have many white friends at all. In retrospect, I realize it was my fault as much as anyone's. I was cautious. I stuck to what I knew. It's hard to put into words what sometimes you pick up in the ether, the quiet, cruel nuances of not belonging—the subtle cues that tell you to not risk anything, to find your people and just stay put.

Cathy, one of my roommates, would surface in the news many years later, describing with embarrassment something I hadn't known when we lived together: Her mother, a schoolteacher from New Orleans, had been so appalled that her daughter had been assigned a Black roommate that she'd badgered the university to separate us. Her mother also gave an interview, confirming the story and providing more context. Having been raised in a home where the *n*-word was a part of the family lexicon, having had a grandfather who'd been a sheriff and used to brag about chasing Black people out of his town, she'd been "horrified," as she put it, by my proximity to her daughter.

All I knew at the time is that midway through our freshman year,

Cathy moved out of our triple and into a single room. I'm happy to say that I had no idea why.

M Y FINANCIAL AID package at Princeton required me to get a work-study job, and I ended up with a good one, getting hired as an assistant to the director of the TWC. I helped out about ten hours a week when I wasn't in class, sitting at a desk alongside Loretta, the full-time secretary, typing memos, answering the phone, and directing students who came in with questions about dropping a class or signing up for the food co-op. The office sat in the front corner of the building, with sun-flooded windows and mismatched furniture that made it more homey than institutional. I loved the feeling of being there, of having office work to do. I loved the little jolt of satisfaction I got anytime I finished off some small organizational task. But more than anything, I loved my boss, Czerny Brasuell.

Czerny was a smart and beautiful Black woman, barely thirty years old, a swift-moving and lively New Yorker who wore flared jeans and wedge sandals and seemed always to be having four or five ideas at once. For students of color at Princeton, she was like an über-mentor, our ultra-hip and always outspoken defender in chief, and for this she was universally appreciated. In the office, she juggled multiple projects—lobbying the university administration to enact more inclusive policies for minorities, advocating for individual students and their needs, and spinning out new ideas for how all of us could improve our lot. She was often running late, blasting out the center's front door at a full sprint, clutching a sheaf of loose papers with a lit cigarette in her mouth and a purse draped over her shoulder, shouting directives to me and Loretta as she went. It was a heady experience, being around her—as close-up as I'd ever been to an independent woman with a job that thrilled her. She was also, not incidentally, a single mother raising a dear, precocious boy named Jonathan, whom I often babysat.

Czerny saw some sort of potential in me, though I was also clearly short on life experience. She treated me like an adult, asking for my thoughts, listening keenly as I described the various worries and administrative tangles students had brought in. She seemed determined to awaken more boldness in me. A good number of her questions began with "Have you ever. . . .?" Had I ever, for example, read the work of James Cone? Had I ever questioned Princeton's investments in South Africa or whether more could be done to recruit minority students? Most of the time the answer was no, but once she mentioned it, I became immediately interested.

"Have you ever been to New York?" she asked at one point.

The answer was again no, but Czerny soon rectified that. One Saturday morning, we piled into her car—me and young Jonathan and another friend who also worked at the TWC—and rode along as Czerny drove full speed toward Manhattan, talking and smoking all the way. You could almost feel something lifting off her as we drove, an unspooling of tension as the white-fenced horse farms surrounding Princeton gave way to choked highways and finally the spires of the city rising in front of us. New York was home for Czerny, the same way Chicago was home for me. You don't really know how attached you are until you move away, until you've experienced what it means to be dislodged, a cork floating on the ocean of another place.

Before I knew it, we were in the teeming heart of New York, locked into a flow of yellow taxis and blaring car horns as Czerny floored it between stoplights, hitting her brakes at the absolute last second before a red light caught her short. I don't remember exactly what we did that day: I know we had pizza. We saw Rockefeller Center, drove through Central Park, and caught sight of the Statue of Liberty with her hopeful hoisted torch. But we were mainly there for practical reasons. Czerny seemed to be recharging her soul by running through a list of mundane errands. She had things to pick up, things to drop off. She double-parked on busy cross streets as she dashed in and out of buildings, provoking an avalanche of honking ire from other drivers, while the rest of us sat helplessly in the car. New York overwhelmed me. It was fast and noisy, a less patient place than Chicago. But Czerny was full of life there, unfazed by jaywalking pedestrians and the smell of urine and stacked garbage wafting from the curb.

She was about to double-park again when she sized up the traffic in her rearview and suddenly seemed to think better of it. Instead, she gestured to me in the passenger seat, indicating I should slide over and take her place behind the steering wheel.

"You have a license, right?" she asked. When I answered with an affirmative nod, she said, "Great. Take the wheel. Just do a slow loop around the block. Or maybe two. Then come back around. I'll be five minutes or less, I promise."

I looked at her like she was nuts. She *was* nuts, in my opinion, for thinking I could drive in Manhattan—me being just a teenager, a foreigner in this unruly city, inexperienced and fully incapable, as I saw it, of taking not just her car but her young son for an uncertain, time-killing spin in the late-afternoon traffic. But my hesitancy only triggered something in Czerny that I will forever associate with New Yorkers—an instinctive and immediate push back against thinking small. She climbed out of the car, giving me no choice but to drive. *Get over it and just live a little* was her message.

I WAS LEARNING ALL the time now. I was learning in the obvious academic ways, holding my own in classes, doing most of my studying in a quiet room at the Third World Center or in a carrel at the library. I was learning how to write efficiently, how to think critically. I'd inadvertently signed up for a 300-level theology class as a freshman and floundered my way through, ultimately salvaging my grade with an eleventh-hour, leave-it-all-on-the-field effort on the final paper. It wasn't pretty, but I found it encouraging in the end, proof that I could work my way out of just about any hole. Whatever deficits I might have arrived with, coming from an inner-city high school, it seemed that I could make up for them by putting in extra time, asking for help when I needed it, and learning to pace myself and not procrastinate.

Still, it was impossible to be a Black kid at a mostly white school and not feel the shadow of affirmative action. You could almost read the scrutiny in the gaze of certain students and even some professors, as if they wanted to say, "I know why *you're* here." These moments could be demoralizing, even if I'm sure I was just imagining some of it. It planted a seed of doubt. Was I here merely as part of a social experiment?

Slowly, though, I began to understand that there were many versions of quotas being filled at the school. As minorities, we were the most visible, but it became clear that special dispensations were made to admit all kinds of students whose grades or accomplishments might not measure up to the acknowledged standard. It was hardly a straight meritocracy. There were the athletes, for example. There were the legacy kids, whose fathers and grandfathers had been Tigers or whose families had funded the building of a dorm or a library. I also learned that being rich didn't protect you from failure. Around me, I saw students flaming out—white, Black, privileged or not. Some were seduced by weeknight keg parties, some were crushed by the stress of trying to live up to some scholarly ideal, and others were just plain lazy or so out of their element they needed to flee. My job, as I saw it, was to hold steady, earn the best grades I could, and get myself through.

By sophomore year, when Suzanne and I moved into a double room together, I'd figured out how to better manage. I was more accustomed now to being one of a few students of color in a packed lecture hall. I tried not to feel intimidated when classroom conversation was dominated by male students, which it often was. Hearing them, I realized that they weren't at all smarter than the rest of us. They were simply emboldened, floating on an ancient tide of superiority, buoyed by the fact that history had never told them anything different.

Some of my peers felt their otherness more acutely than I did. My friend Derrick remembers white students refusing to yield the sidewalk when he walked in their path. Another girl we knew had six friends over to her dorm room one night to celebrate her birthday and promptly got hauled into the dean's office, informed that her white roommate evidently hadn't felt comfortable with having "big Black guys" in the room. There were so few of us minority kids at Princeton, I suppose, that our presence was always conspicuous. I mainly took this as a mandate to overperform, to do everything I possibly could to keep up with or even plow past the more privileged people around me. Just as it had been at Whitney Young, my intensity was spawned at least in part by a feeling of *I'll show you.* If in high school I'd felt as if I were representing my neighborhood, now at Princeton I was representing my race. Anytime I found my voice in class or nailed an exam, I quietly hoped it helped make a larger point.

Suzanne, I was learning, was not an overthinker. I nicknamed her Screwzy, for the impractical, sidewinding course of her days. She based most of her decisions—who she'd date, what classes she took—primarily on how fun it was likely to be. And when things weren't fun, she quickly changed direction. While I joined the Organization for Black Unity and generally stuck close to the Third World Center, Suzanne ran track and managed the lightweight football team, enjoying the fact that it kept her close to cute, athletic men. Through the eating club, she had friends who were white and wealthy, including a bona fide teenage movie star and a European student rumored to be a princess. Suzanne had felt some pressure from her parents to pursue medicine though eventually gave up on it, finding that it messed with her joy. At some point, she was put on academic probation, but even that didn't seem to bother her much. She was the Laverne to my Shirley, the Ernie to my Bert. Our shared room resembled an ideological battlefield, with Suzanne presiding over a wrecked landscape of tossed clothing and strewn papers on her side and me perched on my bed, surrounded by fastidious order.

"You really gotta do that?" I'd say, watching Suzanne arrive back from track practice and head to the shower, stripping off her sweaty workout outfit and dropping it on the floor where it would live, intermingled with clean clothes and unfinished school assignments, for the next week.

"Do what?" she'd say back, flashing her wholesome smile.

I sometimes had to block out Suzanne's chaos so I could think straight. I sometimes wanted to yell at her, but I never did. Suzanne was who she was. She wasn't going to change. When it got to be too much, I'd scoop up her junk and pile it on her bed without comment.

I see now that she provoked me in a good way, introducing me to the idea that not everyone needs to have their file folders labeled and alphabetized, or even to have files at all. Years later, I'd fall in love with a guy who, like Suzanne, stored his belongings in heaps and felt no compunction, really ever, to fold his clothes. But I was able to coexist with it, thanks to Suzanne. I am still coexisting with that guy to this day. This is what a control freak learns inside the compressed otherworld of college, maybe above all else: There are simply other ways of being.

H AVE YOU EVER," Czerny said to me one day, "thought about starting a little after-school program for kids?"

She was asking out of compassion, I would guess. Over time, I'd grown so dedicated to Jonathan, who was now in elementary school, that a good number of my afternoons were spent wandering around Princeton with him as my sidekick, or at the Third World Center, the two of us playing duets on its poorly tuned piano or reading on a saggy couch. Czerny paid me for my time but seemed to think it wasn't enough.

"I'm serious," she said. "I know plenty of faculty members who're always looking for after-school care. You could run it out of the center. Just try it and see how it goes."

With Czerny's word-of-mouth advertising, it wasn't long before I had a gaggle of three or four children to look after. These were the kids of Black administrators and professors at Princeton, who themselves were a profound minority and like the rest of us tended to gravitate toward the TWC. Several afternoons a week, after public elementary school let out, I fed them healthy snacks and ran around with them on the lawn. If they had homework, we worked on it together.

For me, the hours flew. Being around children had a wonderful obliterative effect, wiping out school stress, forcing me out of my head and into the moment. As a girl, I'd passed whole days playing "mommy" to my dolls, pretending that I knew how to dress and feed them, brushing their hair, and tenderly putting Band-Aids on their plastic knees. Now I was doing it for real, finding the whole undertaking a lot messier but no less gratifying than what I'd imagined. I'd go back to my dorm after a few hours with the kids, drained but happy.

Once a week or so, if I found a quiet moment, I'd pick up the phone and dial the number for our apartment on Euclid. If my father was working early shifts, I could catch him in the late afternoon, sitting—or so I imagined—with his legs up in his reclining chair in our living room, watching TV, and waiting for my mom to get home from work. In the evenings, it was usually my mother who picked up the phone. I narrated my college life in exacting detail to both my parents like a homesteader dutifully providing dispatches from the frontier. I spilled every observation I had—from how I didn't like my French professor to the antics of the little kids in my after-school program to the fact that Suzanne and I had a dedicated, mutual crush on an African American engineering student with transfixing green eyes who, even though we doggedly shadowed his every move, seemed to barely know we were alive.

My dad chuckled at my stories. "Is that right?" he'd say. And, "How about that?" And, "Maybe that engineer-boy doesn't deserve either one of you girls."

When I was done talking, he ran through the news from home. Dandy and Grandma had moved back to Dandy's hometown of Georgetown, South Carolina, and Grandma, he reported, was finding herself a bit lonely. He described how my mother was working overtime trying to care for Robbie, who was now in her seventies, widowed, and struggling with an array of health issues. He never mentioned his own struggles, but I knew they were there. At one point when Craig had a home basketball game on a Saturday, my parents drove all the way to Princeton to see it, and I got my first look at their shifting reality—at what never got said on the phone. After pulling into the vast parking lot outside Jadwin Gym, my father reluctantly slid into a wheelchair and allowed my mother to push him inside.

I almost didn't want to see what was happening to my father. I couldn't bear it. I'd done some research on multiple sclerosis in the Princeton library, photocopying medical journal articles to send to my parents. I'd tried to insist that they call a specialist or sign Dad up for some physical therapy, but they—my dad, primarily—didn't want to hear any of it. For all the hours we spent talking on the phone while I was at college, his health was the one topic he wouldn't touch.

If I asked how he was feeling, the answer was always "I feel good." And that would be that.

I let his voice be my comfort. It bore no trace of pain or self-pity, carrying only good humor and softness and just the tiniest hint of jazz. I lived on it as if it were oxygen. It was sustaining, and it was always enough. Before hanging up, he always asked if I needed anything—money, for instance—but I never said yes.

7

HOME GRADUALLY BEGAN TO FEEL MORE DISTANT, almost like a place in my imagination. While I was in college, I kept up with a few of my high school friends, most especially Santita, who'd landed at Howard University in Washington, D.C. I went to visit her there over a long weekend and we laughed and had deep conversations, same as we always had. Howard's campus was urban—"Girl, you're still in the *hood*!" I teased, after a giant rat charged past us outside her dorm—and its student population, twice the size of Princeton's, was almost entirely Black. I envied Santita for the fact she was not isolated by her race—she didn't have to feel that everyday drain of being in a deep minority—but still, I was content returning to the emerald lawns and vaulted stone archways of Princeton, even if few people there could relate to my background.

I was majoring in sociology, pulling good grades. I started dating a football player who was smart and spontaneous, who liked to have fun. Suzanne and I were now rooming with another friend, Angela Kennedy, a wiry, fast-talking kid from Washington, D.C. Angela had a quick, wacky wit and made a game of making us laugh. Despite being an urban Black girl, she dressed like a preppy out of central casting, wearing saddle shoes and pink sweaters and somehow managing to pull off the look.

I was from one world but now lived fully in another, one in which people fretted about their LSAT scores and their squash games. It was a tension that never quite went away. At school, when anyone asked where I was from, I answered, "Chicago." And to make clear that I wasn't one of the kids who came from well-heeled northern suburbs like Evanston or Winnetka and staked some false claim on Chicago, I would add, with a touch of pride or maybe defiance, "the South Side." I knew that if those words conjured anything at all, it was probably stereotyped images of a Black ghetto, given that gang battles and violence in housing projects were what most often showed up in the news. But again, I was trying, if only half consciously, to represent the alternative. I belonged at Princeton, as much as anybody. And I came from the South Side of Chicago. It felt important to say out loud.

For me, the South Side was something entirely different from what got shown on TV. It was home. And home was our apartment on Euclid Avenue, with its fading carpet and low ceilings, my dad kicked back in the bucket of his easy chair. It was our tiny yard with Robbie's blooming flowers and the stone bench where, what seemed like eons ago, I'd kissed that boy Ronnell. Home was my past, connected by gossamer threads to where I was now.

We did have one blood relative in Princeton, Dandy's younger sister, whom we knew as Aunt Sis. She was a simple, bright woman who lived in a simple, bright house on the edge of town. I don't know what brought Aunt Sis to Princeton originally, but she'd been there for a long time, doing domestic work for local families and never losing her Georgetown accent, which sits between a Low Country drawl and a Gullah lilt. Like Dandy, Aunt Sis had been raised in Georgetown, which I remembered from a couple of summer visits we'd made with my parents when I was a kid. I remembered the thick heat of the place and the heavy green drape of Spanish moss on the live oaks, the cypress trees rising from the swamps and the old men fishing on the muddy creeks. There were insects in Georgetown, alarming numbers of them, buzzing and whirring in the evening air like little helicopters.

We stayed with my great-uncle Thomas during our visits, another sibling of Dandy's. He was a genial high school principal who'd take me over to his school and let me sit at his desk, who graciously bought me a tub of peanut butter when I turned my nose up at the enormous breakfasts of bacon, biscuits, and yellow grits that Aunt Dot, his wife, served every morning. I both loved and hated being in the South, for the simple reason that it was so different from what I knew. On the roads outside town, we'd drive past the gateways to what were once slave plantations, though they were enough of a fact of life that nobody ever bothered to remark on them. Down a lonely dirt road deep in the woods, we ate venison in a falling-down country shack belonging to some more distant cousins. One of them took Craig out back and showed him how to shoot a gun. Late at night, back at Uncle Thomas's house, both of us had a hard time sleeping, given the deep silence, which was punctuated only by cicadas throbbing in the trees.

The hum of those insects and the twisting limbs of the live oaks stayed with us long after we'd gone north again, beating in us almost like a second heart. Even as a kid, I understood innately that the South was knit into me, part of my heritage that was meaningful enough for my father to make return visits to see his people there. It was powerful enough that Dandy wanted to move back to Georgetown, even though as a young man he'd needed to escape it. When he did return, it wasn't to some idyllic little river cottage with a white fence and tidy backyard but rather (as I saw when Craig and I made a trip to visit) a bland, cookie-cutter home near a teeming strip mall.

The South wasn't paradise, but it meant something to us. There was a push and pull to our history, a deep familiarity that sat atop a deeper and uglier legacy. Many of the people I knew in Chicago—the kids I'd gone to Bryn Mawr with, many of my friends at Whitney Young—knew something similar, though it was not explicitly discussed. Kids simply went "down south" every summer—shipped out sometimes for the whole season to run around with their second cousins back in Georgia, or Louisiana, or Mississippi. It seems likely that they'd had grandparents or other relatives who'd joined the Great Migration north, just as Dandy had from South Carolina, and Southside's mother had from Alabama. Somewhere in the background was another more-than-decent likelihood—that they, like me, were descended from slaves.

The same was true for many of my friends at Princeton, but I was also coming to understand that there were other versions of being Black in America. I was meeting kids from East Coast cities whose roots were Puerto Rican, Cuban, and Dominican. One of my good friends, David Maynard, had been born into a wealthy Bahamian family. And there was Suzanne, with her Nigerian birth certificate and her collection of beloved aunties in Jamaica. We were all different, our lineages half buried or maybe just half forgotten. We didn't talk about our ancestry. Why would we? We were young, focused only on the future—though of course we knew nothing of what lay ahead.

Once or twice a year, Aunt Sis invited me and Craig to dinner at her house on the other side of Princeton. She piled our plates with succulent fatty ribs and steaming collard greens and passed around a basket with neatly cut squares of corn bread, which we slathered with butter. She refilled our glasses with impossibly sweet tea and urged us to go for seconds and then thirds. As I remember it, we never discussed anything of significance with Aunt Sis. It was an hour or so of polite, go-nowhere small talk, accompanied by a hot, hearty South Carolina meal, which we shoveled in appreciatively, tired as we were of dining-hall food. I saw Aunt Sis simply as a mild-mannered, accommodating older lady, but she was giving us a gift we were still too young to recognize, filling us up with the past—ours, hers, our father's and grandfather's—without once needing to comment on it. We just ate, helped clean the dishes, and then walked our full bellies back to campus, thankful for the exercise.

HERE'S A MEMORY, which like most memories is imperfect and subjective—collected long ago like a beach pebble and slipped into the pocket of my mind. It's from sophomore year of college and involves Kevin, my football-player boyfriend.

Kevin is from Ohio and a near-impossible combination of tall, sweet, and rugged. He's a safety for the Tigers, fast on his feet and fearless with his tackles, and at the same time pursuing premed studies. He's two years ahead of me at school, in the same class as my brother, and soon to graduate. He's got a cute, slight gap in his smile and makes me feel special. We're both busy and have different sets of friends, but we like being together. We get pizza and go out for brunch on weekends. Kevin enjoys every meal, in part because of the need to maintain his weight for football and because, beyond that, he has a hard time sitting still. He's restless, always restless, and impulsive in ways I find charming.

"Let's go driving," Kevin says one day. Maybe he says it over the phone or it's possible we're already together when he gets the idea. Either way, we're soon in his car—a little red compact—driving across campus toward a remote, undeveloped corner of Princeton's property, turning down an almost-hidden dirt road. It's spring in New Jersey, a warm clear day with open sky all around us.

Are we talking? Holding hands? I don't recall, but the feeling is easy and light, and after a minute Kevin hits the brakes, rolling us to a stop. He's halted alongside a wide field, its high grass stunted and straw-like after the winter but shot through with tiny early-blooming wildflowers. He's getting out of the car.

"Come on," he says, motioning for me to follow.

"What are we doing?"

He looks at me as if it should be obvious. "We're going to run through this field."

And we do. We run through that field. We dash from one end to the other, waving our arms like little kids, puncturing the silence with cheerful shouts. We plow through the dry grass and leap over the flowers. Maybe it wasn't obvious to me initially, but now it is. *We're supposed to run through this field! Of course we are!*

Plopping ourselves back in the car, Kevin and I are panting and giddy, loaded up on the silliness of what we've just done.

And that's it. It's a small moment, insignificant in the end. It's still with me for no reason but the silliness, for how it unpinned me just briefly from the more serious agenda that guided my every day. Because while I was a social student who continued to lounge through communal mealtimes and had no problem trying to own the dance floor at Third

World Center parties, I was still privately and at all times focused on the agenda. Beneath my laid-back college-kid demeanor, I lived like a half-closeted CEO, quietly but unswervingly focused on achievement, bent on checking every box. My to-do list lived in my head and went with me everywhere. I assessed my goals, analyzed my outcomes, counted my wins. If there was a challenge to vault, I'd vault it. One proving ground only opened onto the next. Such is the life of a girl who can't stop wondering, *Am I good enough?* and is still trying to show herself the answer.

Kevin, meanwhile, was someone who swerved—who even relished the swerve. He and Craig graduated from Princeton at the end of my sophomore year. Craig would end up moving to Manchester, England, to play basketball professionally. Kevin, I'd thought, was headed to medical school, but then he swerved, deciding to put off schooling and instead pursue a sideline interest in becoming a sports mascot.

Yes, that's right. He'd set his sights on trying out for the Cleveland Browns—not as a player, but rather as a contender for the role of a wide-eyed, gape-mouthed faux animal named Chomps. It was what he wanted. It was a dream—another field to run through, because why the heck not? That summer, Kevin even came up to Chicago from his family's home outside Cleveland, purportedly to visit me but also, as he announced shortly after arriving, because Chicago was the kind of city where an aspiring mascot could find the right kind of furry-animal suit for his upcoming audition. We spent a whole afternoon driving around to shops and looking at costumes together, evaluating whether they were roomy enough to do handsprings in. I don't remember whether Kevin actually found the perfect animal suit that day. I'm not sure whether he landed the mascot job in the end, though he did ultimately become a doctor, evidently a very good one, and married another Princeton classmate of ours.

At the time—and unfairly, I think now—I judged him for the swerve. I had no capacity to understand why someone would take an expensive Princeton education and not immediately convert it into the kind of leg up in the world that such a degree was meant to yield. Why, when you could be in medical school, would you be a dog who does handsprings?

But that was me. And as I've said, I was a box checker—marching to the resolute beat of effort/result, effort/result—a devoted follower of the established path, if only because nobody in my family (aside from Craig) had ever set foot on the path before. I wasn't particularly imaginative in how I thought about the future, which is another way of saying I was already thinking about law school.

Life on Euclid Avenue had taught me—maybe forced me—to be hard-edged and practical about both time and money. The biggest swerve I'd ever made was a decision to spend the first part of the summer after sophomore year working for basically nothing as a camp counselor in New York's Hudson Valley, looking after urban kids who were having their first experiences in the woods. I'd loved the job but came out of it more or less broke, more dependent on my parents financially than I wanted to be. Though they never once complained, I'd feel guilty about it for years to come.

This was the same summer, too, when people I loved started to die. Robbie, my great-aunt, my rigid taskmaster of a piano teacher, passed away in June, bequeathing her house on Euclid to my parents, allowing them to become home owners for the first time. Southside died a month later after having suffered with advanced lung cancer, his long-held view that doctors were untrustworthy having kept him from any sort of timely intervention. After Southside's funeral, my mother's enormous family piled into his snug little home, along with a smattering of friends and neighbors. I felt the warm tug of the past and the melancholy of absence—all of it a little jarring, accustomed as I was to the hermetic and youthful world of college. It was something deeper than what I normally felt at school, the slow shift of generational gears. My kid cousins were full grown; my aunts had grown old. There were new babies and new spouses. A jazz album roared from the home-built stereo shelves in the dining room, and we dined on a potluck brought by loved ones—baked ham, Jell-O molds, and casseroles. But Southside himself was gone. It was painful, but time pushed us all forward.

EACH SPRING, CORPORATE recruiters descended on the Princeton campus, aiming themselves at the graduating seniors. You'd see a classmate who normally dressed in ratty jeans and an untucked shirt crossing campus in a pin-striped suit and understand that he or she was destined for a Manhattan skyscraper. It happened quickly, this vocational sorting—the bankers, lawyers, doctors, and executives of tomorrow hastily migrating toward their next launchpad, whether it was graduate school or a cushy Fortune 500 training-program job. I'm certain there were others among us who followed their hearts into education, the arts, and nonprofit work or who went off on Peace Corps missions or to serve in the military, but I knew very few of them. I was busy climbing my ladder, which was sturdy and practical and aimed straight up.

If I'd stopped to think about it, I might have realized that I was burned-out by school—by the grind of lectures, papers, and exams—and probably would have benefited from doing something different. Instead I took the LSAT, wrote my senior thesis, and dutifully reached for the next rung, applying to the best law schools in the country. I saw myself as smart, analytical, and ambitious. I'd been raised on feisty dinner table debates with my parents. I could argue a point down to its theoretical essence and prided myself on never rolling over in a conflict. Was this not the stuff lawyers were made of? I figured it was.

I can admit now that I was driven not just by logic but by some reflexive wish for other people's approval, too. When I was a kid, I quietly basked in the warmth that floated my way anytime I announced to a teacher, a neighbor, or one of Robbie's church-choir friends that I wanted to be a pediatrician. *My, isn't that impressive?* their expressions would say, and I reveled in it. Years later, it was really no different. Professors, relatives, random people I met, asked what was next for me, and when I mentioned I was bound for law school—Harvard Law School, as it turned out—the affirmation was overwhelming. I was applauded just for getting in, even if the truth was I'd somehow squeaked in off the wait list. But I was in. People looked at me as if already I'd made my mark on the world.

This may be the fundamental problem with caring a lot about what others think: It can put you on the established path—the *my-isn't-that-impressive* path—and keep you there for a long time. Maybe it stops you from swerving, from ever even considering a swerve, because what you risk losing in terms of other people's high regard can feel too costly. Maybe you spend three years in Massachusetts, studying constitutional law and discussing the relative merits of exclusionary vertical agreements in antitrust cases. For some, this might be truly interesting, but for you it is not. Maybe during those three years you make friends you'll love and respect forever, people who seem genuinely called to the bloodless intricacies of the law, but you yourself are not called. Your passion stays low, yet under no circumstance will you underperform. You live, as you always have, by the code of effort/result, and with it you keep achieving until you think you know the answers to all the questions—including the most important one. *Am I good enough? Yes, in fact I am.*

What happens next is that the rewards get real. You reach for the next rung of the ladder, and this time it's a job with a salary in the Chicago offices of a high-end law firm called Sidley & Austin. You're back where you started, in the city where you were born, only now you go to work on the forty-seventh floor in a downtown building with a wide plaza and a sculpture out front. You used to pass by it as a South Side kid riding the bus to high school, peering mutely out the window at the people who strode like titans to their jobs. Now you're one of them. You've worked yourself out of that bus and across the plaza and onto an upward-moving elevator so silent it seems to glide. You've joined the tribe. At the age of twenty-five, you have an assistant. You make more money than your parents ever have. Your co-workers are polite, educated, and mostly white. You wear an Armani suit and sign up for a subscription wine service. You make monthly payments on your law school loans and go to step aerobics after work. Because you can, you buy yourself a Saab.

Is there anything to question? It doesn't seem that way. You're a lawyer now. You've taken everything ever given to you—the love of your parents, the faith of your teachers, the music from Southside and Robbie, the meals from Aunt Sis, the vocabulary words drilled into you by Dandy—and converted it to this. You've climbed the mountain. And part of your job, aside from parsing abstract intellectual property issues for big corporations, is to help cultivate the next set of young lawyers being courted by the firm. A senior partner asks if you'll mentor an incoming summer associate, and the answer is easy: Of course you will. You have yet to understand the altering force of a simple yes. You don't know that when a memo arrives to confirm the assignment, some deep and unseen fault line in your life has begun to tremble, that some hold is already starting to slip. Next to your name is another name, that of some hotshot law student who's busy climbing his own ladder. Like you, he's Black and from Harvard. Other than that, you know nothing—just the name, and it's an odd one.

8

BARACK OBAMA WAS LATE ON DAY ONE. I SAT IN MY office on the forty-seventh floor, waiting and not waiting for him to arrive. Like most first-year lawyers, I was busy. I put in long hours at Sidley & Austin, often eating both lunch and dinner at my desk while combating a continuous flow of documents, all of them written in precise and decorous lawyer-language. I read memos, I wrote memos, I edited other people's memos. At this point, I thought of myself basically as trilingual. I knew the relaxed patois of the South Side and the high-minded diction of the Ivy League, and now on top of that I spoke Lawyer, too. I'd been hired into the firm's marketing and intellectual property practice group, which was considered internally more freewheeling and creative than other groups, I suppose because we dealt at least some of the time with advertising. Part of my job involved poring over scripts for our clients' TV and radio ads, making sure they didn't violate Federal Communications Commission standards. I would later be awarded the honor of looking after the legal concerns of Barney the Dinosaur. (Yes, this is what passes for freewheeling in a law firm.)

The problem for me was that as a junior associate my work didn't involve much actual interaction with clients and I was a Robinson, raised in the boisterous scrum of my extended family, molded by my father's instinctive love of a crowd. I craved interaction of any sort. To offset the solitude, I joked around with Lorraine, my assistant, a hyperorganized, good-humored African American woman several years my senior who sat just outside my office and answered my phone. I had friendly professional relationships with some of the senior partners and perked up at any chance I had to chitchat with my fellow associates, but in general everyone was overloaded with work and careful not to waste one billable minute of the day. Which put me back at my desk, alone with my documents.

If I had to spend seventy hours a week somewhere, my office was a pleasant enough place. I had a leather chair, a buffed walnut desk, and wide windows with a southeastern view. I could look out over the hodgepodge of the business district and see the white-capped waves of Lake Michigan, which in summertime were dotted with bright sailboats. If I angled myself a certain way, I could trace the coastline and glimpse a narrow seam of the South Side with its low-rise rooftops and intermittent stands of trees. From where I sat, the neighborhoods appeared placid and almost toylike, but the reality was in many cases far different. Parts of the South Side had become desolate as businesses shut down and families continued to move out. The steel mills that had once provided stability were cutting thousands of jobs. The crack epidemic, which had ravaged African American communities in places like Detroit and New York, was only just reaching Chicago, but its course was no less destructive. Gangs battled for market share, recruiting young boys to run their street-corner operations, which, while dangerous, was far more lucrative than going to school. The city's murder rate was starting to tick upward—a sign of even more trouble to come.

I made good money at Sidley but was pragmatic enough to take a bird in the hand when it came to housing. Since finishing law school, I'd been living back in my old South Shore neighborhood, which was still relatively untouched by gangs and drugs. My parents had moved downstairs into Robbie and Terry's old space, and at their invitation I'd taken over the upstairs apartment, where we'd lived when I was a kid, sprucing it up with a crisp white couch and framed batik prints on the walls. I wrote my parents an occasional check that loosely covered my share of the utilities. It hardly counted as paying rent, but they insisted it was plenty. Though my apartment had a private entrance, I most often tromped through the downstairs kitchen as I came and went from work—in part because my parents' back door opened directly to the garage and in part because I was still and always would be a Robinson. Even if I now fancied myself the sort of suit-wearing, Saab-driving independent young professional I'd always dreamed of being, I didn't much like being alone. I fortified myself with daily check-ins with my mom and dad. I'd hugged them that very morning, in fact, before dashing out the door and driving through a heavy rainstorm to get to work. To get to work, I might add, *on time*.

I looked at my watch.

"Any sign of this guy?" I called to Lorraine.

Her sigh was audible. "Girl, no," she called back. She was amused, I could tell. She knew how tardiness drove me nuts—how I saw it as nothing but hubris.

Barack Obama had already created a stir at the firm. For one thing, he'd just finished his first year of law school, and normally we only hired second-year students for summer positions. But rumor had it he was exceptional. Word had spread that one of his professors at Harvard—the daughter of a managing partner—claimed he was the most gifted law student she'd ever encountered. Some of the secretaries who'd seen the guy come in for his interview were saying that on top of this apparent brilliance he was also cute.

I was skeptical of all of it. In my experience, you put a suit on any half-intelligent Black man and white people tended to go bonkers. I was doubtful he'd earned the hype. I'd checked out his photo in the summer edition of our staff directory—a less-than-flattering, poorly lit head shot of a guy with a big smile and a whiff of geekiness—and remained unmoved. His bio said he was originally from Hawaii, which at least made him a comparatively exotic geek. Otherwise, nothing stood out. The only surprise had come weeks earlier when I made a quick obligatory phone call to introduce myself. I'd been pleasantly startled by the voice on the other end of the line—a rich, even sexy, baritone that didn't seem to match his photo one bit.

It was another ten minutes before he checked in at the reception area on our floor and I walked out to meet him, finding him seated on a couch—one Barack Obama, dressed in a dark suit and still a little damp from the rain. He grinned sheepishly and apologized for his lateness as he shook my hand. He had a wide smile and was taller and thinner than I'd imagined he'd be—a man who was clearly not much of an eater, who also looked fully unaccustomed to wearing business clothes. If he knew he was arriving with a whiz-kid reputation, it didn't show. As I walked him through the corridors to my office, introducing him to the cushy mundanities of corporate law—showing him the word-processing center and the coffee machine, explaining our system for tracking billable hours—he was quiet and deferential, listening attentively. After about twenty minutes, I delivered him to the senior partner who'd be his actual supervisor for the summer and went back to my desk.

Later that day, I took Barack to lunch at the fancy restaurant on the first floor of our office building, a place packed with well-groomed bankers and lawyers power lunching over meals priced like dinners. This was the boon of having a summer associate to advise: It was an excuse to eat out and eat well, and to do it on the firm's expense account. As Barack's adviser, I was meant to act as a social conduit more than anything. My assignment was to make sure he was happy in the job, that he had someone to come to if he needed advice, and that he felt connected to the larger team. It was the start of a larger wooing process—the idea being, as it was with all summer associates, that the firm might want to recruit him for a full-time job once he had his law degree.

Very quickly, I realized that Barack would need little in the way of advice. He was three years older than I was—about to turn twenty-eight. Unlike me, he'd worked for several years after finishing his undergrad degree at Columbia before moving on to law school. What struck me was how assured he seemed of his own direction in life. He was oddly free from doubt, though at first glance it was hard to understand why. Compared with my own lockstep march toward success, the direct arrow shot of my trajectory from Princeton to Harvard to my desk on the forty-seventh floor, Barack's path was an improvisational zigzag through disparate worlds. I learned over lunch that he was in every sense a hybrid—the son of a Black Kenyan father and a white mother from Kansas whose marriage had been both youthful and short-lived. He'd been born and raised in Honolulu but had spent four years of his childhood flying kites and catching crickets in Indonesia. After high school, he'd passed two relatively laid-back years as a student at Occidental College in Los Angeles before transferring to Columbia, where by his own account he'd behaved nothing like a college boy set loose in 1980s Manhattan and instead lived like a sixteenth-century mountain hermit, reading lofty works of literature and philosophy in a grimy apartment on 109th Street, writing bad poetry, and fasting on Sundays.

We laughed about all of it, swapping stories about our backgrounds and what led us to the law. Barack was serious without being self-serious. He was breezy in his manner but powerful in his mind. It was a strange, stirring combination. Surprising to me, too, was how well he knew Chicago.

Barack was the first person I'd met at Sidley who had spent time in the barbershops, barbecue joints, and Bible-thumping Black parishes of the Far South Side. Before going to law school, he'd worked in Chicago for three years as a community organizer, earning $12,000 a year from a nonprofit that bound together a coalition of churches. His task was to help rebuild neighborhoods and bring back jobs. As he described it, it had been two parts frustration to one part reward: He'd spend weeks planning a community meeting, only to have a dozen people show up. His efforts were scoffed at by union leaders and picked apart by Black folks and white folks alike. Yet over time, he'd won a few incremental victories, and this seemed to encourage him. He was in law school, he explained, because grassroots organizing had shown him that meaningful societal change required not just the work of the people on the ground but stronger policies and governmental action as well.

Despite my resistance to the hype that had preceded him, I found myself admiring Barack for both his self-assuredness and his earnest demeanor. He was refreshing, unconventional, and weirdly elegant. Not once, though, did I think about him as someone I'd want to date. For one thing, I was his mentor at the firm. I'd also recently sworn off dating altogether, too consumed with work to put any effort into it. And finally, appallingly, at the end of lunch Barack lit a cigarette, which would have been enough to snuff any interest, if I'd had any to begin with.

He would be, I thought to myself, a good summer mentee.

O VER THE NEXT couple of weeks, we fell into a kind of routine. In the late afternoon, Barack would wander down the hall and flop onto one of the chairs in my office, as if he'd known me for years. Sometimes it felt as if he had. Our banter was easy, our mind-sets alike. We gave each other sideways glances when people around us got stressed to the point of mania, when partners made comments that seemed condescending or out of touch. What was unspoken but obvious was that he was a brother, and in our office, which employed more than four hundred lawyers, only about five full-time attorneys were African American. Our pull toward each other was evident and easy to understand.

Barack bore no resemblance to the typical eager-beaver summer associate (as I myself had been two years earlier at Sidley), networking furiously and anxiously wondering whether a golden-ticket job offer was coming. He sauntered around with calm detachment, which seemed only to increase his appeal. Inside the firm, his reputation was continuing to grow. Already, he was being asked to sit in on high-level partner meetings. Already, he was being pressed to give input on whatever issues were under discussion. At some point early in the summer, he pumped out a thirty-page memo about corporate governance that was evidently so thorough and cogent it became instantly legendary. Who was this guy? Everyone seemed intrigued.

"I brought you a copy," Barack said one day, sliding his memo across my desk with a smile.

"Thanks," I said, taking the file. "Looking forward to it."

After he left, I tucked it into a drawer.

Did he know I'd never read it? I think he probably did. He'd given it to me half as a joke. We were in different specialty groups, so there was no material overlap in our work anyway. I had plenty of my own documents to contend with. And I didn't need to be wowed. We were friends now, Barack and I, comrades in arms. We ate lunch out at least once a week and sometimes more often than that, always, of course, billing Sidley & Austin for the pleasure. Gradually, we learned more about each other. He knew that I lived in the same house as my parents, that my happiest memories of Harvard Law School stemmed from the work I'd done in the Legal Aid Bureau. I knew that he consumed volumes of political philosophy as if it were beach reading, that he spent all his spare change on books. I knew that his father had died in a car crash in Kenya and that he'd made a trip there to try to understand more about the man. I knew he loved basketball, went for long runs on the weekends, and spoke wistfully of his friends and family on Oahu. I knew he'd had plenty of girlfriends in the past, but didn't have one now.

This last bit was something I thought I could rectify. My life in Chicago was nothing if not crowded with accomplished and eligible Black women. My marathon work hours notwithstanding, I liked to socialize. I had friends from Sidley, friends from high school, friends developed through professional networking, and friends I'd met through Craig, who was newly married and making his living as an investment banker in town. We were a merry co-ed crew, congregating when we could in one downtown bar or another and catching up over long, lavish meals on weekends. I'd gone out with a couple of guys in law school but hadn't met anyone special upon returning to Chicago and had little interest anyway. I'd announced to everyone, including potential suitors, that my career was my priority. I did, though, have plenty of girlfriends who were looking for someone to date.

One evening early in the summer, I brought Barack along with me to a happy hour at a downtown bar, which served as an unofficial monthly mixer for Black professionals and was where I often met up with friends. He'd changed out of his work clothes, I noticed, and was wearing a white linen blazer that looked as if it'd come straight out of the *Miami Vice* costume closet. Ah well.

There was no arguing with the fact that even with his challenged sense of style, Barack was a catch. He was good-looking, poised, and successful. He was athletic, interesting, and kind. What more could anyone want? I sailed into the bar, certain I was doing everyone a favor—him and all the ladies. Almost immediately, he was corralled by an acquaintance of mine, a beautiful and high-powered woman who worked in finance. She perked up instantly, I could see, talking to Barack. Pleased with this development, I got myself a drink and moved on toward others I knew in the crowd.

Twenty minutes later, I caught sight of Barack across the room, in the grips of what looked to be an endless conversation with the woman, who was doing a large portion of the talking. He shot me a look, implying that he'd like to be rescued. But he was a grown man. I let him rescue himself.

"Do you know what she asked me?" he said the next day, turning up in my office, still slightly incredulous. "She asked if I liked to go *riding*. She meant on horseback." He said they'd discussed their favorite movies, which also hadn't gone well.

Barack was cerebral, probably too cerebral for most people to put up with. (This, in fact, would be my friend's assessment of him when we next spoke.) He wasn't a happy-hour guy, and maybe I should have realized that earlier. My world was filled with hopeful, hardworking people who were obsessed with their own upward mobility. They had new cars and were buying their first condos and liked to talk about it all over martinis after work. Barack was more content to spend an evening alone, reading up on urban housing policy. As an organizer, he'd spent weeks and months listening to poor people describe their challenges. His insistence on hope and the potential for mobility, I was coming to see, came from an entirely different and not easily accessible place.

There was a time, he told me, when he'd been looser, more wild. He'd spent the first twenty years of his life going by the nickname Barry. As a teen, he smoked pot in the lush volcanic foothills of Oahu. At Occidental, he rode the waning energy of the 1970s, embracing Hendrix and the Stones. Somewhere along the way, though, he'd stepped into the fullness of his birth name—Barack Hussein Obama—and the complicated rubric of his identity. He was white and Black, African and American. He was modest and lived modestly, yet knew the richness of his own mind and the world of privilege that would open up to him as a result. He took it all seriously, I could tell. He could be lighthearted and jokey, but he never strayed far from a larger sense of obligation. He was on some sort of quest, though he didn't yet know where it would lead. All I knew was that it didn't translate over drinks. Next time happy hour rolled around, I left him at the office.

W HEN I WAS A KID, my parents smoked. They lit cigarettes in the evenings as they sat in the kitchen, talking through their workdays. They smoked while they cleaned the dinner dishes later at night, sometimes opening a window to let in some fresh air. They weren't heavy smokers, but they were habitual smokers, and defiant ones, too. They smoked long after the research made clear that it was bad for you.

The whole thing drove me crazy, and Craig as well. We made an elaborate show of coughing when they lit up. We ran sabotage missions on their supplies. When Craig and I were very young, we pulled a brand-new carton of Newports from a shelf and set about destroying them, snapping them like beans over the kitchen sink. Another time, we dipped the ends of their cigarettes in hot sauce and returned them to the pack. We lectured our parents about lung cancer, explaining the horrors that had been shown to us on filmstrips during health class at school—images of smokers' lungs, desiccated and black as charcoal, death in the making, death right inside your chest. For contrast, we'd been shown pictures of florid pink lungs that were healthy, uncontaminated by smoke. The paradigm was simple enough to make their behavior confounding: Good/Bad. Healthy/Sick. You choose your own future. It was everything our parents had ever taught us. And yet it would be years before they finally quit.

Barack smoked the way my parents did—after meals, walking down a city block, or when he was feeling anxious and needed to do something with his hands. In 1989, smoking was more prevalent than it is now, more embedded in everyday life. Research on the effects of secondhand smoke was relatively new. People smoked in restaurants, offices, and airports. But still, I'd seen the filmstrips. To me, and to every sensible person I knew, smoking was pure self-destruction.

Barack knew exactly how I felt about it. Our friendship was built on a plainspoken candor that I think we both enjoyed.

"Why would someone as smart as you do something as dumb as

that?" I'd blurted on the very first day we met, watching him cap off our lunch with a smoke. It was an honest question.

As I recall, he just shrugged, acknowledging that I was right. There was no fight to be put up, no finer point to be argued. Smoking was the one topic where Barack's logic seemed to leave him altogether.

Whether I was going to admit it or not, though, something between us had started to change. On days when we were too busy to check in face-to-face, I found myself wondering what he'd been up to. I talked myself out of being disappointed when he didn't surface in my office doorway. I talked myself out of being too excited when he did. I had feelings for the guy, but they were latent, buried deep beneath my resolve to keep my life and career tidy and forward focused—free from any drama. My annual reviews at work were solid. I was on track to become an equity partner at Sidley & Austin, probably before I hit thirty-two. It was everything I wanted—or so I was trying to convince myself.

I might have been ignoring whatever was growing between us, but he wasn't.

"I think we should go out," Barack announced one afternoon as we sat finishing a meal.

"What, you and me?" I feigned shock that he even considered it a possibility. "I told you, I don't date. And I'm your adviser."

He gave a wry laugh. "Like that counts for anything. You're not my boss," he said. "And you're pretty cute."

Barack had a smile that seemed to stretch the whole width of his face. He was a deadly combination of smooth and reasonable. More than once in the coming days, he laid out the evidence for why we should be going out. We were compatible. We made each other laugh. We were both available, and furthermore we confessed to being almost immediately uninterested in anyone else we met. Nobody at the firm, he argued, would care if we dated. In fact, maybe it would be seen as a positive. He presumed that the partners wanted him to come work for them, eventually. If he and I were an item, it would improve the odds of his committing.

"You mean I'm like some sort of bait?" I said, laughing. "You flatter yourself."

Over the course of the summer, the firm organized a series of events and outings for its associates, sending around sign-up sheets for anyone who wanted to go. One was a weeknight performance of *Les Misérables* at a theater not far from the office. I put us on the list for two tickets, which was standard behavior for a junior-associate adviser and her summer-associate charge. We were supposed to be attending firm functions together. I was supposed to be ensuring that his experience with Sidley & Austin was bright and positive. That was the whole point.

We sat side by side in the theater, both of us worn out after a long day of work. The curtain went up and the singing began, giving us a gray, gloomy version of Paris. I don't know if it was my mood or whether it was just *Les Misérables* itself, but I spent the next hour feeling helplessly pounded by French misery. Grunts and chains. Poverty and rape. Injustice and oppression. Millions of people around the world had fallen in love with this musical, but I squirmed in my seat, trying to rise above the inexplicable torment I felt every time the melody repeated.

When the lights went up for intermission, I stole a glance at Barack. He was slumped down, with his right elbow on the armrest and index finger resting on his forehead, his expression unreadable.

"What'd you think?" I said.

He gave me a sideways look. "Horrible, right?"

I laughed, relieved that he felt the same way.

Barack sat up in his seat. "What if we got out of here?" he said. "We could just leave."

Under normal circumstances, I wouldn't bolt. I wasn't that sort of person. I cared too much what the other lawyers thought of me—what they'd think if they spotted our empty seats. I cared too much, in general, about finishing what I'd started, about seeing every last little thing through to the absolute heart-stopping end, even if it was an overwrought Broadway musical on an otherwise beautiful Wednesday night. This, unfortunately, was the box checker in me. I endured misery for the sake of appearances. But now, it seemed, I'd joined up with someone who did not.

Avoiding everyone we knew from work—the other advisers and their summer associates bubbling effusively in the lobby—we slipped out of the theater and into a balmy evening. The last light was draining from a purple sky. I exhaled, my relief so palpable that it caused Barack to laugh.

"Where are we going now?" I asked.

"How 'bout we grab a drink?"

We walked to a nearby bar in the same manner we always seemed to walk, with me a step forward and him a step back. Barack was an ambler. He moved with a loose-jointed Hawaiian casualness, never given to hurry, even and especially when instructed to hurry. I, on the other hand, power walked even during my leisure hours and had a hard time decelerating. But I remember how that night I counseled myself to slow down, just a little—just enough so that I could hear what he was saying, because it was beginning to dawn on me that I cared about hearing everything he said.

Until now, I'd constructed my existence carefully, tucking and folding every loose and disorderly bit of it, as if building some tight and airless piece of origami. I had labored over its creation. I was proud of how it looked. But it was delicate. If one corner came untucked, I might discover that I was restless. If another popped loose, it might reveal I was uncertain about the professional path I'd so deliberately put myself on, about all the things I told myself I wanted. I think now it's why I guarded myself so carefully, why I still wasn't ready to let him in. He was like a wind that threatened to unsettle everything.

A day or two later, Barack asked if I could give him a ride to a barbecue for summer associates, which was happening that weekend at a senior partner's home in one of the wealthy lakefront suburbs north of the city. The weather, as I remember it, was clear that day, the lake sparkling at the edge of a well-tended lawn. A caterer served food as music blared over stereo speakers and people remarked on the tasteful grandeur of the house. The whole milieu was a portrait of affluence and ease, a less-than-subtle reminder of the payoff that came when you committed yourself wholeheartedly to the grind. Barack, I knew, wrestled with what he wanted to do with his life, which direction his career would take. He had an uneasy relationship with wealth. Like me, he'd never had it, and he didn't aspire to it, either. He wanted to be effective far more than he wanted to be rich but was still trying to figure out how.

We walked through the party not quite like a couple but still mostly together, drifting between clusters of colleagues, drinking beer and lemonade, eating hamburgers and potato salad from plastic plates. We'd get separated and then find each other again. It all felt natural. He was quietly flirty with me and I was flirty back. Some of the men started playing pickup basketball, and I watched as Barack moseyed on over to the court in his flip-flops to join. He had an easy rapport with everyone at the firm. He addressed all the secretaries by name and got along with everyone—from the older, stuffier lawyers to the ambitious young bucks who were now playing basketball. *He's a good person,* I thought to myself, watching him pass the ball to another lawyer.

Having sat through scores of high school and college games, I recognized a good player when I saw one, and Barack quickly passed the test. He played an athletic, artful form of basketball, his lanky body moving quickly, showing power I hadn't before noticed. He was swift and graceful, even in his Hawaiian footwear. I stood there pretending to listen to what somebody's perfectly nice wife was saying to me, but my eyes stayed fixed on Barack. I was struck for the first time by the spectacle of him—this strange mix-of-everything man.

As we drove back to the city in the early evening, I felt a new ache, some freshly planted seed of longing. It was July. Barack would be leaving sometime in August, disappearing into law school and whatever else life held for him there. Nothing had changed outwardly—we were kidding around, as we always did, gossiping about who'd said what at the barbecue—but there was a certain kind of heat climbing my spine. I was acutely aware of his body in the small space of my car—his elbow resting on the console, his knee within reach of my hand. As we followed the southward curve of Lake Shore Drive, passing bicyclists and runners on the pedestrian pathways, I was arguing silently with myself. Was there a way to do this unseriously? How badly could it hurt my job? I had no clarity about anything—about what was proper, about who would find out and whether that mattered—but it hit me that I was done waiting for clarity.

He was living in Hyde Park, subletting an apartment from a friend. By the time we pulled into the neighborhood, the tension lay thick in the air between us, like something inevitable or predestined was finally about to happen. Or was I imagining it? Maybe I'd shut him down too many times. Maybe he'd given up and now just saw me as a good, stalwart friend—a girl with an air-conditioned Saab who'd drive him around when he needed it.

I halted the car in front of his building, my mind still in blurry overdrive. We let an awkward beat pass, each waiting for the other to initiate a good-bye. Barack cocked his head at me.

"Should we get some ice cream?" he said.

This is when I knew the game was on, one of the few times I decided to stop thinking and just live. It was a warm summer evening in the city that I loved. The air felt soft on my skin. There was a Baskin-Robbins on the block near Barack's apartment, and we got ourselves two cones, taking them outside to eat, finding ourselves a spot on the curb. We sat close together with our knees pulled up, pleasantly tired after a day spent outdoors, eating our ice cream quickly and wordlessly, trying to stay ahead of the melt. Maybe Barack read it on my face or sensed it in my posture—the fact that everything for me had now begun to loosen and unfold.

He was looking at me curiously, with the trace of a smile.

"Can I kiss you?" he asked.

And with that, I leaned in and everything felt clear.

Becoming Us

9

———

A S SOON AS I ALLOWED MYSELF TO FEEL ANYTHING for Barack, the feelings came rushing—a toppling blast of lust, gratitude, fulfillment, wonder. Any worries I'd been harboring about my life and career and even about Barack himself seemed to fall away with that first kiss, replaced by a driving need to know him better, to explore and experience everything about him as fast as I could.

Maybe because he was due back at Harvard in a month, we wasted no time being casual. Not quite ready to have a boyfriend sleeping under the same roof as my parents, I began spending nights at Barack's apartment, a cramped, second-floor walk-up above a storefront on a noisy section of Fifty-Third Street. The guy who normally lived there was a University of Chicago law student and he'd furnished it like any good student would, with mismatched garage-sale finds. There was a small table, a couple of rickety chairs, and a queen-sized mattress on the floor. Piles of Barack's books and newspapers covered the open surfaces and a good deal of the floor. He hung his suit jackets on the backs of the kitchen chairs and kept very little in the fridge. It wasn't homey, but now that I viewed everything through the lens of our fast-moving romance, it felt like home.

Barack intrigued me. He was not like anyone I'd dated before, mainly because he seemed so secure. He was openly affectionate. He told me I was beautiful. He made me feel good. To me, he was sort of like a unicorn—unusual to the point of seeming almost unreal. He never talked about material things, like buying a house or a car or even new shoes. His money went largely toward books, which to him were like sacred objects, providing ballast for his mind. He read late into the night, often long after I'd fallen asleep, plowing through history and biographies and Toni Morrison, too. He read several newspapers daily, cover to cover. He kept tabs on the latest book reviews, the American League standings, and what the South Side aldermen were up to. He could speak with equal passion about the Polish elections and which movies Roger Ebert had panned and why.

With no air-conditioning, we had little choice but to sleep with the windows open at night, trying to cool the sweltering apartment. What we gained in comfort, we sacrificed in quiet. In those days, Fifty-Third Street was a hub of late-night activity, a thoroughfare for cruising lowriders with unmuffled tailpipes. Almost hourly, it seemed, a police siren would blare outside the window or someone would start shouting, unloading a stream of outrage and profanity that would startle me awake on the mattress. If I found it unsettling, Barack did not. I sensed already that he was more at home with the unruliness of the world than I was, more willing to let it all in without distress. I woke one night to find him staring at the ceiling, his profile lit by the glow of streetlights outside. He looked vaguely troubled, as if he were pondering something deeply personal. Was it our relationship? The loss of his father?

"Hey, what're you thinking about over there?" I whispered.

He turned to look at me, his smile a little sheepish. "Oh," he said. "I was just thinking about income inequality."

This, I was learning, was how Barack's mind worked. He got himself fixated on big and abstract issues, fueled by some crazy sense that he might be able to do something about them. It was new to me, I have to say. Until now, I'd hung around with good people who cared about important enough things but who were focused primarily on building their careers and providing for their families. Barack was just different. He was dialed into the day-to-day demands of his life, but at the same time, especially at night, his thoughts seemed to roam a much wider plane.

The bulk of our time, of course, was still spent at work, in the plush stillness of the Sidley & Austin offices, where every morning I shook off any dreaminess and zipped myself back into my junior-associate existence, returning dutifully to my stack of documents and the demands of corporate clients I'd never once meet. Barack, meanwhile, worked on his own documents in a shared office down the hall, increasingly fawned over by partners who found him impressive.

Still concerned about propriety, I insisted we keep our blooming relationship out of sight of our colleagues, though it hardly worked. Lorraine, my assistant, gave Barack a knowing smile each time he surfaced in my office. We'd even been busted the very first night we'd been out in public as a couple, shortly after our first kiss, having gone to the Art Institute and then to see Spike Lee's movie *Do the Right Thing* at Water Tower Place, where we bumped into one of the firm's most high-ranking partners, Newt Minow, and his wife, Josephine, in the popcorn line. They'd greeted us warmly, even approvingly, and made no comment on the fact we were together. But still, there we were.

Work, during this time, felt like a distraction—the thing we had to do before we were allowed to charge back toward each other again. Away from the office, Barack and I talked endlessly, over leisurely walks around Hyde Park dressed in shorts and T-shirts and meals that seemed short to us but in reality went on for hours. We debated the merits of every single Stevie Wonder album before doing the same thing with Marvin Gaye. I was smitten. I loved the slow roll of his voice and the way his eyes softened when I told a funny story. I was coming to appreciate how he ambled from one place to the next, never worried about time.

Each day brought small discoveries: I was a Cubs fan, while he liked the White Sox. I loved mac and cheese, and he couldn't stand it. He liked dark, dramatic movies, while I went all-in for rom-coms. He was a lefty with immaculate handwriting; I had a heavy right-hand scrawl. In the month before he went back to Cambridge, we shared what felt like every memory and stray thought, running through our childhood follies, teenage blunders, and the thwarted starter romances that had gotten us to each other. Barack was especially intrigued by my upbringing—the year-to-year, decade-to-decade sameness of life on Euclid Avenue, with me and Craig and Mom and Dad making up four corners of a sturdy square. Barack had spent a lot of time in churches during his time as a community organizer, which had left him with an appreciation for organized religion, but at the same time he remained less traditional. Marriage, he told me early on, struck him as an unnecessary and overhyped convention.

I don't remember introducing Barack to my family that summer, though Craig tells me I did. He says that the two of us walked up to the house on Euclid Avenue one evening. Craig was over for a visit, sitting on the front porch with my parents. Barack, he recalls, was friendly and confident and made a couple of minutes of easy small talk before we ran up to my apartment to pick something up.

My father appreciated Barack instantly, but still didn't like his odds. After all, he'd seen me jettison my high school boyfriend David at the gates of Princeton. He'd watched me dismiss Kevin the college football player as soon as I'd seen him in a furry mascot outfit. My parents knew better than to get too attached. They'd raised me to run my own life, and that's basically what I did. I was too focused and too busy, I'd told my parents plenty of times, to make room for any man.

According to Craig, my father shook his head and laughed as he watched me and Barack walk away.

"Nice guy," he said. "Too bad he won't last."

I F MY FAMILY was a square, then Barack's was a more elaborate piece of geometry, one that reached across oceans. He'd spent years trying to make sense of its lines. His mother, Ann Dunham, had been a seventeen-year-old college student in Hawaii in 1960, when she fell for a Kenyan student named Barack Obama. Their marriage was brief and confusing—especially given that her new husband, it turned out, already had a wife in Nairobi. After their divorce, Ann went on to marry a Javanese geologist named Lolo Soetoro and moved to Jakarta, bringing along the junior Barack Obama—*my* Barack Obama—who was then six years old.

As Barack described it to me, he'd been happy in Indonesia and got along well with his new stepfather, but his mother had concerns about the quality of his schooling. In 1971, Ann Dunham sent her son back to Oahu to attend private school and live with her parents. She was a free spirit who would go on to spend years moving between Hawaii and Indonesia. Aside from making one extended trip back to Hawaii when Barack was ten, his father—a man who by all accounts had both a powerful mind and a powerful drinking problem—remained absent and unengaged.

And yet Barack was loved deeply. His grandparents on Oahu doted on both him and his younger half sister Maya. His mother, though still living in Jakarta, was warm and supportive from afar. Barack also spoke affectionately of another half sister in Nairobi, named Auma. He'd grown up with far less stability than I had, but he didn't lament it. His story was his story. His family life had left him self-reliant and curiously hard-wired for optimism. The fact he'd navigated his unusual upbringing so successfully seemed only to reinforce the idea that he was ready to take on more.

On a humid evening, I went with him as he did a favor for an old friend. One of his former community-organizer co-workers had asked if he could lead a training at a Black parish in Roseland, on the Far South Side, an area that had been crippled by the steel mill closings of the mid-1980s. For Barack, it was a welcome one-night return to his old job and the part of Chicago where he'd once worked. It occurred to me as we walked into the church, both of us still dressed in our office clothes, that I'd never thought much about what a community organizer actually did. We followed a stairwell down to a low-ceilinged, fluorescent-lit basement area, where fifteen or so parishioners—mostly women, as I remember—were sitting in folding chairs in what looked to be a room that doubled as a day-care center, fanning themselves in the heat. I took a seat in the back as Barack walked to the front of the room and said hello.

To them, he must have seemed young and lawyerly. I could see that they were sizing him up, trying to figure out whether he was some sort of opinionated outsider or in fact had something of value to offer. The atmosphere was plenty familiar to me. I'd grown up attending my great-aunt Robbie's weekly Operetta Workshop in an African Methodist Episcopal church not unlike this one. The women in the room were no different from the ladies who sang in Robbie's choir or who'd turned up with casseroles after Southside died. They were well-intentioned, community-minded women, often single mothers or grandmothers, the type who inevitably stepped in to help when no one else would volunteer.

Barack hung his suit jacket on the back of his chair and took off his wristwatch, laying it on the table in front of him to keep an eye on the time. After introducing himself, he facilitated a conversation that would last about an hour, asking people to share their stories and describe their concerns about life in the neighborhood. Barack, in turn, shared his own story, tying it to the principles of community organizing. He was there to convince them that our stories connected us to one another, and through those connections, it was possible to harness discontent and convert it to something useful. Even they, he said—a tiny group inside a small church, in what felt like a forgotten neighborhood—could build real political power. It took effort, he cautioned. It required mapping strategy and listening to your neighbors and building trust in communities where trust was often lacking. It meant asking people you'd never met to give you a bit of their time or a tiny piece of their paycheck. It involved being told no in a dozen or a hundred different ways before hearing the "yes" that would make all the difference. (This, it seemed, was a large part of what an organizer did.) But he assured them they could have influence. They could make change. He'd seen the process work, if not always smoothly, in the Altgeld Gardens public-housing project, where a group just like this one had managed to register new voters, rally residents to meet with city officials about asbestos contamination, and persuade the mayor's office to fund a neighborhood job-training center.

The heavyset woman sitting next to me bounced a toddler on her knee and did nothing to hide her skepticism. She inspected Barack with her chin lifted and her bottom lip stuck out, as if to say, *Who are you to be telling us what to do?*

But skepticism didn't bother him, the same way long odds didn't seem to bother him. Barack was a unicorn, after all—shaped by his unusual name, his odd heritage, his hard-to-pin-down ethnicity, his missing dad, his unique mind. He was used to having to prove himself, pretty much anywhere he went.

The idea he was presenting wasn't an easy sell, nor should it have been. Roseland had taken one hit after another, from the exodus of white families and the bottoming out of the steel industry to the deterioration of its schools and the flourishing of the drug trade. As an organizer working in urban communities, Barack had told me, he'd contended most often with a deep weariness in people—especially Black people—a cynicism bred from a thousand small disappointments over time. I understood it. I'd seen it in my own neighborhood, in my own family. A bitterness, a lapse in faith. It lived in both of my grandfathers, spawned by every goal they'd abandoned and every compromise they'd had to make. It was inside the harried second-grade teacher who'd basically given up trying to teach us at Bryn Mawr. It was inside the neighbor who'd stopped mowing her lawn or keeping track of where her kids went after school. It lived in every piece of trash tossed carelessly in the grass at our local park and every ounce of malt liquor drained before dark. It lived in every last thing we deemed unfixable, including ourselves.

Barack didn't talk down to the people of Roseland, and he wasn't trying to win them over, either, by hiding his privilege and acting more "Black." Amid the parishioners' fears and frustrations, their disenfranchisement and sinking helplessness, he was somewhat brashly pointing an arrow in the opposite direction.

I'd never been someone who dwelled on the more demoralizing parts of being African American. I'd been raised to think positively. I'd absorbed my family's love and my parents' commitment to seeing us succeed. I'd stood with Santita Jackson at Operation PUSH rallies, listening to her father call for Black people to remember their pride. My purpose had always been to see past my neighborhood—to look ahead and overcome. And I had. I'd scored myself two Ivy League degrees. I had a seat at the table at Sidley & Austin. I'd made my parents and grandparents proud. But listening to Barack, I began to understand that his version of hope reached far beyond mine: It was one thing to get yourself out of a stuck place, I realized. It was another thing entirely to try and get the place itself unstuck.

I was gripped all over again by a sense of how special he was. Slowly, all around me, too, the church ladies began nodding their approval, punctuating his sentences with calls of "Mmmm-hmm" and "That's right!"

His voice climbed in intensity as he got to the end of his pitch. He wasn't a preacher, but he was definitely preaching something—a vision. He was making a bid for our investment. The choice, as he saw it, was this: You give up or you work for change. "What's better for us?" Barack called to the people gathered in the room. "Do we settle for the world as it is, or do we work for the world as it should be?"

It was a phrase borrowed from a book he'd read when he first started out as an organizer, and it would stay with me for years. It was as close as I'd come to understanding what motivated Barack. *The world as it should be.*

Next to me, the woman with the toddler on her lap all but exploded. "That's right!" she bellowed, finally convinced. "Amen!"

Amen, I thought to myself. Because I was convinced, too.

B EFORE HE RETURNED to law school, sometime in the middle of August, Barack told me he loved me. The feeling had flowered between us so quickly and naturally that there was nothing especially memorable about the moment itself. I don't recall when or how exactly it happened. It was just an articulation, tender and meaningful, of the thing that had caught us both by surprise. Even though we'd known each other only a couple of months, even though it was kind of impractical, we were in love.

But now we had to navigate the more than nine hundred miles that would separate us. Barack had two years of school left and said he hoped to settle in Chicago when he was done. There was no expectation that I would leave my life there in the interim. As a still-newish associate at Sidley, I understood that the next phase of my career was critical—that my accomplishments would determine whether I made partner or not. Having been through law school myself, I also knew how busy Barack would be. He'd been chosen as an editor on the *Harvard Law Review,* a monthly student-run journal that was considered one of the top legal publications in the country. It was an honor to be picked for the editorial team, but it was also like tacking a full-time job onto the already-heavy load of being a law student.

What did this leave us with? It left us with the phone. Keep in mind that this was 1989, when phones didn't live in our pockets. Texting wasn't a thing; no emoji could sub for a kiss. The phone required both time and mutual availability. Personal calls happened usually at home, at night, when you were dog tired and in need of sleep.

Barack told me, ahead of leaving, that he preferred letter writing.

"I'm not much of a phone guy" was how he put it. As if that settled it.

But it settled nothing. We'd just spent the whole summer talking. I wasn't going to relegate our love to the creeping pace of the postal service. This was another small difference between us: Barack could pour his heart out through a pen. He'd been raised on letters, sustenance arriving in the form of wispy airmail envelopes from his mom in Indonesia. I, meanwhile, was an in-your-face sort of person—brought up on Sunday dinners at Southside's, where you sometimes had to shout to be heard.

In my family, we gabbed. My dad, who'd recently traded in his car for a specialized van to accommodate his disability, still made a point of showing up in his cousins' doorways as often as possible for in-person visits. Friends, neighbors, and cousins of cousins also regularly turned up on Euclid Avenue and planted themselves in the living room next to my father in his recliner to tell stories and ask for advice. Even David, my old high school boyfriend, sometimes dropped in to seek his counsel. My dad had no problem with the phone, either. For years, I'd seen him call my grandmother in South Carolina almost daily, asking for her news.

I informed Barack that if our relationship was going to work, he'd better get comfortable with the phone. "If I'm not talking to you," I announced, "I might have to find another guy who'll listen." I was joking, but only a little.

And so it was that Barack became a phone guy. Over the course of that fall, we spoke as often as we could manage, both of us locked into our respective worlds and schedules but still sharing the little details of our days, commiserating over the heap of corporate tax cases he had to read, or laughing about how I'd taken to sweating out my office frustrations at after-work aerobics. As months passed, our feelings stayed steady and reliable. For me, it became one less thing in life to question.

At Sidley & Austin, I was part of the Chicago office's recruiting team, tasked with interviewing Harvard Law School students for summer-associate jobs. It was essentially a wooing process. As a student, I'd experienced for myself the power and temptation of the corporate-law industrial complex, having been given a binder as thick as a dictionary that listed law firms across the country and told that every one of them was interested in landing Harvard-educated lawyers. It would seem that with the imprimatur of a Harvard JD, you had a shot at working in any city, in any field of law, whether it be at a mammoth litigation firm in Dallas or a boutique real-estate firm in New York. If you were curious about any of them, you requested an on-campus interview. If that went well, you were then treated to a "fly-out," which amounted to a plane ticket, a five-star hotel room, and another round of interviews at the firm's office, followed by some extravagant wine-and-dine experience with recruiters like me. While at Harvard, I'd availed myself of fly-outs to San Francisco and Los Angeles, in part to check out entertainment-law practices there but also, if I was honest, because I'd never been to California.

Now that I was at Sidley and on the other side of the recruiting experience, my goal was to bring in law students who were not just smart and hard-driving but also something other than male and white. There was exactly one other African American woman on the recruiting team, a senior associate named Mercedes Laing. Mercedes was about ten years older than I was and became a dear friend and mentor. Like me, she had two Ivy League degrees and routinely sat at tables where nobody looked like her. The struggle, we agreed, was not to get used to it or accept it. In meetings on recruitment, I argued insistently—and I'm sure brazenly, in some people's opinion—that the firm cast a wider net when it came to finding young talent. The long-held practice was to engage students from a select group of law schools—Harvard, Stanford, Yale, Northwestern, the University of Chicago, and the University of Illinois, primarily—the places where most of the firm's lawyers had earned their degrees. It was a circular process: one generation of lawyers hiring new lawyers whose life experience mirrored their own, leaving little room for diversity of any sort. In fairness to Sidley, this was a problem (whether recognized or not) at virtually every big firm in the country. A *National Law Journal* survey from the time found that in large firms African Americans made up not quite 3 percent of all associates and less than 1 percent of all partners.

Trying to help remedy the imbalance, I pushed for us to consider law students coming from other state schools and from historically Black colleges like Howard University. When the recruiting team gathered in a conference room in Chicago with a pile of student résumés to review, I objected anytime a student was automatically dismissed for having a B on a transcript or for having gone to a less prestigious undergraduate program. If we were serious about bringing in minority lawyers, I asserted, we'd have to look more holistically at candidates. We'd need to think about how they'd used whatever opportunities life had afforded them rather than measuring them simply by how far they'd made it up an elitist academic ladder. The point wasn't to lower the firm's high standards: It was to realize that by sticking with the most rigid and old-school way of evaluating a new lawyer's potential, we were overlooking all sorts of people who could contribute to the firm's success. We needed to interview more students, in other words, before writing them off.

For this reason, I loved making recruiting trips to Cambridge, because it gave me some influence in which Harvard students got chosen for an interview. It also, of course, gave me an excuse to see Barack. The first time I visited, he picked me up in his car, a snub-nosed, banana-yellow Datsun he'd bought used on his loan-strapped student budget. When he turned the key, the engine revved and the car spasmed violently before settling into a loud, sustained juddering that shook us in our seats. I looked at Barack in disbelief.

"You drive this thing?" I said, raising my voice over the noise.

He flashed me the impish, *I-got-this-covered* grin that melted me every time. "Just give it a minute or two," he said, shifting the car into gear. "It goes away." After another few minutes, having steered us onto a busy road, he added, "Also, maybe don't look down."

I'd already spotted what he wanted me to avoid—a rusted-out, four-inch hole in the floor of his car, through which I could see the pavement rushing beneath us.

Life with Barack would never be dull. I knew it even then. It would be some version of banana yellow and slightly hair-raising. It occurred to me, too, that quite possibly the man would never make any money.

He was living in a spartan one-bedroom apartment in Somerville, but during my recruiting trips Sidley put me up at the luxe Charles Hotel adjacent to campus, where we slept on smooth high-quality sheets and Barack, rarely one to cook for himself, could load up on a hot breakfast before his morning classes. In the evenings, he parked himself in my room and did his schoolwork, giddily dressed in one of the hotel's thick terry-cloth robes.

At Christmastime that year, we flew to Honolulu. I'd never been to Hawaii before but was pretty certain I'd like it. I was coming from Chicago, after all, where winter stretched through April, where it was normal to keep a snow shovel stashed in the trunk of your car. I owned an unsettling amount of wool. For me, getting away from winter had always felt like a joyride. During college, I'd made a trip to the Bahamas with my Bahamian classmate David, and another to Jamaica with Suzanne. In both instances, I'd reveled in the soft air on my skin and the simple buoyancy I felt anytime I got close to the ocean. Maybe it was no accident that I was drawn to people who'd been raised on islands.

In Kingston, Suzanne had taken me to powdery white beaches where we dodged waves in water that looked like jade. She'd piloted us expertly through a chaotic market, jabbering with street vendors.

"Try dis!" she'd shouted at me, going full throttle with the accent, exuberantly handing me pieces of grilled fish to taste, handing me fried yams, stalks of sugarcane, and cut-up pieces of mango. She demanded I try everything, intent on getting me to see how much there was to love.

It was no different with Barack. By now he'd spent more than a decade on the mainland, but Hawaii still mattered to him deeply. He wanted me to take it all in, from the splaying palm trees that lined the streets of Honolulu and the crescent arc of Waikiki Beach to the green drape of hills surrounding the city. For about a week, we stayed in a borrowed apartment belonging to family friends and made trips every day to the ocean, to swim and laze about in the sun. I met Barack's half sister Maya, who at nineteen was kind and smart and getting a degree at Barnard. She had round cheeks and wide brown eyes and dark hair that curled in a rich tangle around her shoulders. I met his grandparents Madelyn and Stanley Dunham, or "Toot and Gramps," as he called them. They lived in the same high-rise where they'd raised Barack, in a small apartment decorated with Indonesian textiles that Ann had sent home over the years.

And I met Ann herself, a plump, lively woman with dark frizzy hair and the same angular chin as Barack. She wore chunky silver jewelry, a bright batik dress, and the kind of sturdy sandals I would guess an anthropologist might wear. She was friendly toward me and curious about my background and my career. It was clear she adored her son—almost revered him—and she seemed most eager to sit down and talk with him, describing her dissertation work and swapping book recommendations as if catching up with an old friend.

Everyone in the family still called him Barry, which I found endearing. Though they'd left their home state of Kansas back in the 1940s, his grandparents seemed to me like the misplaced midwesterners Barack had always described them as. Gramps was big and bearlike and told silly jokes. Toot, a stout, gray-haired woman who'd worked her way up to becoming the vice president of a local bank, made us tuna salad sandwiches for lunch. In the evenings, she served Ritz crackers piled with sardines for appetizers and put dinner on TV trays so that everyone could watch the news or play a heated game of Scrabble. They were a modest, middle-class family, in many ways not at all unlike my own.

There was something comforting in this, for both me and Barack. As different as we were, we fit together in an interesting way. It was as if the reason for the ease and attraction between us was now being explained.

In Hawaii, Barack's intense and brainy side receded somewhat, while the laid-back part of him flourished. He was at home. And home was where he didn't feel the need to prove anything to anyone. We were late for everything we did, but it didn't matter—not even to me. Barack's high school buddy Bobby, who was a commercial fisherman, took us out on his boat one day for some snorkeling and an aimless cruise. It was then that I saw Barack as relaxed as I'd ever seen him, lounging under a blue sky with a cold beer and an old friend, no longer fixated on the day's news or law school reading, or what should be done about income inequality. The sun-bleached mellowness of the island opened up space for the two of us, in part by giving us time we'd never before had.

So many of my friends judged potential mates from the outside in, focusing first on their looks and financial prospects. If it turned out the person they'd chosen wasn't a good communicator or was uncomfortable with being vulnerable, they seemed to think time or marriage vows would fix the problem. But Barack had arrived in my life a wholly formed person. From our very first conversation, he'd shown me that he wasn't self-conscious about expressing fear or weakness and that he valued being truthful. At work, I'd witnessed his humility and willingness to sacrifice his own needs and wants for a bigger purpose.

And now in Hawaii, I could see his character reflected in other small ways. His long-lasting friendships with his high school buddies showed his consistency in relationships. In his devotion to his strong-willed mother, I saw a deep respect for women and their independence. Without needing to discuss it outright, I knew he could handle a partner who had her own passions and voice. These were things you couldn't teach in a relationship, things that not even love could really build or change. In opening up his world to me, Barack was showing me everything I'd ever need to know about the kind of life partner he'd be.

One afternoon, we borrowed a car and drove to the North Shore of Oahu, where we sat on a ribbon of soft beach and watched surfers rip across enormous waves. We stayed for hours, just talking, as one wave tipped into the next, as the sun dropped toward the horizon and the other beachgoers packed up to go home. We talked as the sky turned pink and then purple and finally went dark, as the bugs started to bite, as we began to get hungry. If I'd come to Hawaii to sample something of Barack's past, we were now sitting at the edge of a giant ocean, trying on a version of the future, discussing what kind of house we'd want to live in someday, what kind of parents we wanted to be. It felt speculative and a little daring to talk like this, but it was also reassuring, because it seemed as if maybe we'd never stop, that maybe this conversation between us could go on for life.

B ACK IN CHICAGO, separated again from Barack, I still sometimes went to my old happy-hour gatherings, though I rarely stayed out late. Barack's dedication to reading had brought out a new bookishness in me. I was now content to spend a Saturday night reading a good novel on the couch.

When I got bored, I called up old friends. Even now that I had a serious boyfriend, my girlfriends were the ones who held me steady. Santita Jackson was now traveling the country as a backup singer for Roberta Flack, but we spoke when we could. A year or so earlier, I'd sat with my parents in their living room, bursting with pride as we watched Santita and her siblings introduce their father at the 1988 Democratic National Convention. Reverend Jackson had made a respectable run for the presidency, winning about a dozen primaries before ceding the nomination to Michael Dukakis. Along the way, he'd filled households like ours with a new and profound level of hope and excitement, even if in our hearts we understood that he was a long shot's long shot.

I spoke regularly with Verna Williams, a close friend from law school, who until recently had been living in Cambridge. She'd met Barack a couple of times and liked him a lot but teased me that I'd let my insanely high standards slip, having allowed a smoker into my life. Angela Kennedy and I still laughed hard together, even though she was working as a teacher in New Jersey while also parenting a young son and trying to hold herself steady as her marriage slowly imploded. We'd known each other as goofy, half-mature college girls, and now we were adults, with adult lives and adult concerns. That idea alone sometimes struck us as hilarious.

Suzanne, meanwhile, was the same free spirit she'd been when we roomed together at Princeton—flitting in and out of my life with varying predictability, continuing to measure the value of her days purely by whether they were pleasurable or not. We'd go long stretches without talking but then pick up the thread of our friendship with ease. As always, I called her Screwzy and she called me Miche. Our worlds continued to be as different as they'd been at school, when she was trekking off to eating-club parties and kicking her dirty laundry beneath the bed and I was color coding my Sociology 201 notes. Even then, Suzanne was like a sister whose life I could only track from afar, across the gulf of our inherent differences. She was maddening, charming, and always important to me. She'd ask my advice and then willfully ignore it. Would it be bad to date a philandering semi-famous pop star? Why, yes it would, but she'd do it anyway, because *why not?* Most galling to me was when she turned down an opportunity to go to an Ivy League business school after college, deciding that it would be too much work and therefore no fun. Instead, she got her MBA from a not-so-stressful program at a state school, which I viewed as kind of a lazy move.

Suzanne's choices sometimes seemed like an affront to my way of doing things, a vote in favor of easing up and striving less. I can say now that I judged her unfairly for them. At the time, though, I just thought I was right.

Not long after I'd started dating Barack, I called Suzanne to gush about my feelings for him. She'd been thrilled to hear me so happy—happiness being her currency. She also had news of her own: She was ditching her job as a computer specialist at the Federal Reserve and going traveling—not for weeks, but for months. Suzanne and her mom were soon to head off on some round-the-world-style adventure. Because *why not?*

I could never guess whether Suzanne knew unconsciously that something strange was happening in the cells of her body, that a silent hijacking was already under way. What I did know was that during the fall of 1989, while I wore patent leather pumps and sat through long, dull conference-room meetings at Sidley, Suzanne and her mother were trying not to spill curry on their sundresses in Cambodia and dancing at dawn on the grand walkways of the Taj Mahal. As I balanced my checkbook, picked up my dry cleaning, and watched the leaves wither and drop from the trees along Euclid Avenue, Suzanne was careening through hot, humid Bangkok in a *tuk-tuk,* hooting—as I imagined it—with joy. I don't, in fact, know what any of her travels looked like or where she actually went, because she wasn't one to send postcards or keep in touch. She was too busy living, stuffing herself full of what the world had to give.

By the time she got home to Maryland and found a moment to reach out to me, the news was different—so clanging and dissonant from my image of her that I could hardly take it in.

"I have cancer," Suzanne told me, her voice husky with emotion. "A lot of it."

Her doctors had just diagnosed it, an aggressive form of lymphoma, already ravaging her organs. She described a plan for treatment, pegging some hope to what the results could be, but I was too overwhelmed to note the details. Before hanging up, she told me that in a cruel twist of fate her mother had fallen gravely ill as well.

I'm not sure that I ever believed that life was fair, but I had always thought that you could work your way out of just about any problem. Suzanne's cancer was the first real challenge to that notion, a sabotage of my ideals. Because even if I didn't have the specifics nailed down yet, I did have ideas about the future. I had that agenda I'd been assiduously maintaining since freshman year of college, stemming from the neat line of boxes I was meant to check.

For me and Suzanne, it was supposed to go like this: We'd be the maids of honor at each other's weddings. Our husbands would be really different, of course, but they'd like each other a lot anyway. We'd have babies at the same time, take family beach trips to Jamaica, remain mildly critical of each other's parenting techniques, and be favorite fun aunties to each other's kids as they grew. I'd get her kids books for their birthdays; she'd get mine pogo sticks. We'd laugh and share secrets and roll our eyes at what we perceived as the other person's ridiculous idio-syncrasies, until one day we'd realize we were two old ladies who'd been best friends forever, flummoxed suddenly by where the time had gone.

That, for me, was the world as it should be.

WHAT I FIND remarkable in hindsight is how, over the course of that winter and spring, I just did my job. I was a lawyer, and lawyers worked. We worked all the time. We were only as good as the hours we billed. There was no choice, I told myself. The work was important, I told myself. And so I kept showing up every morning in downtown Chicago, at the corporate ant mound known as One First National Plaza. I put my head down and billed my hours.

Back in Maryland, Suzanne was living with her disease. She was coping with medical appointments and surgeries and at the same time trying to care for her mother, who was also fighting an aggressive cancer that was, the doctors insisted, completely unrelated to Suzanne's. It was bad luck, bad fortune, freakish to the point of being too scary to contemplate. The rest of Suzanne's family was not particularly close-knit, except for two of her favorite female cousins who helped her out as much as they could. Angela drove down from New Jersey to visit sometimes, but she was juggling both a toddler and a job. I enlisted Verna, my law school friend, to go by when she could, as a sort of proxy for me. Verna had met Suzanne a couple of times while we were at Harvard and by sheer coincidence was now living in Silver Spring, in a building just across the parking lot from Suzanne's.

It was a lot to ask of Verna, who'd recently lost her father and was wrestling with her own grief. But she was a true friend, a compassionate person. She phoned my office one day in May to relay the details of a visit.

"I combed her hair," she said.

That Suzanne needed to have her hair combed should have told me everything, but I'd walled myself off from the truth. Some part of me still insisted this wasn't happening. I held on to the idea that Suzanne's health would turn around, even as the evidence against it stacked up.

It was Angela, finally, who called me in June and got right to the point. "If you're going to come, Miche," she said, "you'd better get to it."

By then, Suzanne had been moved to a hospital. She was too weak to talk, slipping in and out of consciousness. There was nothing left to feed my denial. I hung up the phone and bought a plane ticket. I flew east, caught a taxi to the hospital, took the elevator to the right floor, walked the hallway to her room, and found her there, lying in bed as Angela and her cousin watched over her, everyone silent. Suzanne's mother, it turned out, had died just a few days earlier, and now Suzanne was in a coma. Angela made room for me to perch on the side of her bed.

I stared hard at Suzanne, at her perfect heart-shaped face and reddish-brown skin, feeling comforted somehow by the youthful smoothness of her cheeks and the girlish curve in her lips. She seemed oddly undiminished by the illness. Her dark hair was still lustrous and long; someone had put it in two ropy braids that reached almost to her waist. Her track runner's legs lay hidden beneath the blankets. She looked young, like a sweet, beautiful twenty-six-year-old who was maybe in the middle of a nap.

I regretted not coming earlier. I regretted the many times, over the course of our seesawing friendship, that I'd insisted she was making a wrong move, when possibly she'd been doing it right. I was suddenly glad for all the times she'd ignored my advice. I was glad that she hadn't over-worked herself to get some fancy business school degree. That she'd gone off for a lost weekend with a semi-famous pop star, just for fun. I was happy that she'd made it to the Taj Mahal to watch the sunrise with her mom. Suzanne had lived in ways that I had not.

That day, I held her limp hand and watched as her breathing grew ragged, as eventually there were long pauses between her inhales. At some point, the nurse gave us a knowing nod. It was happening. Suzanne was leaving. My mind went dark. I had no deep thoughts. I had no revelations about life or loss. If anything, I was mad.

To say that it was unfair that Suzanne got sick and died at twenty-six seems too simple a thing. But it was a fact, as cold and ugly as they come. What I was thinking as I finally left her body in that hospital room was this: *She's gone and I'm still here.* Outside in the hallway, there were people wandering in hospital gowns who were far older and sicker looking than Suzanne, and they were still here. I would take a packed flight back to Chicago, drive along a busy highway, ride an elevator up to my office. I'd see all these people looking happy in their cars, walking the sidewalk in their summer clothes, sitting idly in cafés, and working at their desks, all of them oblivious to what happened to Suzanne—apparently unaware that they, too, could die at any moment. It felt perverse, how the world just carried on. How everyone was still here, except for my Suzanne.

10

———

THAT SUMMER, I STARTED KEEPING A JOURNAL. I bought myself a clothbound black book with purple flowers on the cover and kept it next to my bed. I took it with me when I went on business trips for Sidley & Austin. I was not a daily writer, or even a weekly writer: I picked up a pen only when I had the time and energy to sort through my jumbled feelings. I'd write a few entries in a single week and then lay the journal down for a month or sometimes more. I was not, by nature, especially introspective. The whole exercise of recording one's thoughts was new to me—a habit I'd picked up in part, I suppose, from Barack, who viewed writing as therapeutic and clarifying and had kept journals on and off over the years.

He'd come back to Chicago over his summer break from Harvard, this time skipping the sublet and moving directly into my apartment on Euclid Avenue. This meant not only that we were learning, in a real way, how to cohabit as a couple but also that Barack got to know my family in a more intimate way. He'd talk sports with my dad as he headed out for a shift at the water plant. He sometimes helped my mother carry her groceries in from the garage. It was a good feeling. Craig had already assessed Barack's character in the most thorough and revealing way he could—by including him in a high-octane weekend basketball game with a bunch of his buddies, most of them former college players. He'd done this, actually, at my request. Craig's opinion of Barack mattered to me, and my brother knew how to read people, especially in the context of a game. Barack had passed the test. He was smooth on the floor, my brother said, and knew when to make the right pass, but he also wasn't afraid to shoot when he was open. "He's no ball hog," Craig said. "But he's got guts."

Barack had accepted a summer-associate job with a downtown firm whose offices were close to Sidley's, but his time in Chicago was short. He'd been elected president of the *Harvard Law Review* for the coming academic year, which meant he'd be responsible for turning out eight issues of about three hundred pages each and would need to get back to Cambridge early in order to get started. The competition to lead the *Review* was ferocious every year, involving rigorous vetting and a vote by eighty student editors. Being picked for the position was an enormous achievement for anyone. It turned out that Barack was also the first African American in the publication's 103-year history to be selected— a milestone so huge that it had been written up in the *New York Times*, accompanied by a photo of Barack, smiling in a scarf and winter coat.

My boyfriend, in other words, was a big deal. He could have landed any number of fat-salaried law firm jobs at that point, but instead he was thinking about practicing civil rights law once he got his degree, even if it would then take twice as long to pay off his student loans. Practically everyone he knew was urging him to follow the lead of many previous *Review* editors and apply for what would be a shoo-in clerkship with the Supreme Court. But Barack wasn't interested. He wanted to live in Chicago. He had ideas for writing a book about race in America and planned, he said, to find work that aligned with his values, which most likely meant he wouldn't end up in corporate law. He steered himself with a certainty I found astounding.

All this inborn confidence was admirable, of course, but honestly, try living with it. For me, coexisting with Barack's strong sense of purpose— sleeping in the same bed with it, sitting at the breakfast table with it—was something to which I had to adjust, not because he flaunted it, exactly,

but because it was so alive. In the presence of his certainty, his notion that
he could make some sort of difference in the world, I couldn't help but
feel a little bit lost by comparison. His sense of purpose seemed like an
unwitting challenge to my own.

Hence the journal. On the very first page, in careful handwriting, I
spelled out my reasons for starting it:

> One, I feel very confused about where I want my life to go. What kind of
> person do I want to be? How do I want to contribute to the world?
> Two, I am getting very serious in my relationship with Barack and I
> feel that I need to get a better handle on myself.

This little flowered book has now survived a couple of decades and
multiple moves. It sat on a shelf in my dressing room at the White House
for eight years, until very recently, when I pulled it out from a box in
my new home to try to reacquaint myself with who I'd been as a young
lawyer. I read those lines today and see exactly what I was trying to
tell myself—what a no-nonsense female mentor might have said to me
directly. Really, it was simple: The first thing was that I hated being a
lawyer. I wasn't suited to the work. I felt empty doing it, even if I was
plenty good at it. This was a distressing thing to admit, given how hard
I'd worked and how in debt I was. In my blinding drive to excel, in my
need to do things perfectly, I'd missed the signs and taken the wrong
road.

The second was that I was deeply, delightfully in love with a guy
whose forceful intellect and ambition could possibly end up swallowing
mine. I saw it coming already, like a barreling wave with a mighty under-
tow. I wasn't going to get out of its path—I was too committed to Barack
by then, too in love—but I did need to quickly anchor myself on two feet.

This meant finding a new profession, and what shook me most was
that I had no concrete ideas about what I wanted to do. Somehow, in all
my years of schooling, I hadn't managed to think through my own passions and how they might match up with work I found meaningful. As a
young person, I'd explored exactly nothing. Barack's maturity, I realized,
came in part from the years he'd logged as a community organizer and

even, prior to that, a decidedly unfulfilling year he'd spent as a researcher at a Manhattan business consulting firm immediately after college. He'd tried out some things, gotten to know all sorts of people, and learned his own priorities along the way. I, meanwhile, had been so afraid of floundering, so eager for respectability and a way to pay the bills, that I'd marched myself unthinkingly into the law.

In the span of a year, I'd gained Barack and lost Suzanne, and the power of those two things together had left me spinning. Suzanne's sudden death had awakened me to the idea that I wanted more joy and meaning in my life. I couldn't continue to live with my own complacency. I both credited and blamed Barack for the confusion. "If there were not a man in my life constantly questioning me about what drives me and what pains me," I wrote in my journal, "would I be doing it on my own?"

I mused about what I might do, what skills I might possibly have. Could I be a teacher? A college administrator? Could I run some sort of after-school program, a professionalized version of what I'd done for Czerny at Princeton? I was interested in possibly working for a foundation or a nonprofit. I was interested in helping underprivileged kids. I wondered if I could find a job that engaged my mind and still left me enough time to do volunteer work, or appreciate art, or have children. I wanted a life, basically. I wanted to feel whole. I made a list of issues that interested me: education, teen pregnancy, Black self-esteem. A more virtuous job, I knew, would inevitably involve a pay cut. More sobering was my next list, this one of my essential expenses—what was left after I let go of the luxuries I'd allowed myself on a Sidley salary, things like my subscription wine service and health-club membership. I had a $600 monthly payment on my student loans, a $407 car payment, money spent on food, gas, and insurance, plus the roughly $500 a month I'd need for rent if I ever moved out of my parents' house.

Nothing was impossible, but nothing looked simple, either. I started asking around about opportunities in entertainment law, thinking perhaps that it might be interesting and would also spare me the sting of a lower salary. But in my heart, I felt a slow-growing certainty of my own: I wasn't built to practice law. One day I made note of a *New York Times* article I'd read that reported widespread fatigue, stress, and unhappiness among American lawyers—most especially female ones. "How depressing," I wrote in my journal.

I SPENT A GOOD chunk of that August toiling in a rented conference room at a hotel in Washington, D.C., having been dispatched to help prepare a case. Sidley & Austin was representing the chemical conglomerate Union Carbide in an antitrust trial involving the sale of one of its business holdings. I stayed in Washington for about three weeks but managed to see very little of the city, because my life was wholly dedicated to sitting in that room with several Sidley peers, opening file boxes that had been shipped from the company headquarters, and reviewing the thousands of pages of documents inside.

You wouldn't think I'd be the type of person to find psychic relief in the intricacies of the urethane polyether polyol trade, but I did. I was still practicing law, but the specificity of the work and the change of scenery distracted me just enough from the bigger questions beginning to bubble up in my mind.

Ultimately, the chemical case was settled out of court, which meant that much of my document reviewing had been for nothing. This was an irksome but expected trade-off in the legal field, where it was not uncommon to prepare for a trial that never came to pass. On the evening I flew home to Chicago, I felt a heavy dread settling over me, knowing that I was about to step back into my everyday routine and the fog of my confusion.

My mother was kind enough to meet my flight at O'Hare. Just seeing her gave me comfort. She was in her early fifties now, working full-time as an executive assistant at a downtown bank, which as she described it was basically a bunch of men sitting at desks, having gone into the business because their fathers had been bankers before them. My mother was a force. She had little tolerance for fools. She kept her hair short and wore practical, unfussy clothes. Everything about her radiated competence and calm. As it had been when Craig and I were kids, she didn't get involved with our private lives. Her love came in the form of reliability. She showed up when your flight came in. She drove you home and offered food if you were hungry. Her even temper was like shelter to me, a place to seek refuge.

As we drove downtown toward the city, I heaved a big sigh.

"You okay?" my mom asked.

I looked at her in the half-light of the freeway. "I don't know," I began. "It's just . . ."

And with that, I unloaded my feelings. I told her that I wasn't happy with my job, or even with my chosen profession—that I was seriously *unhappy*, in fact. I told her about my restlessness, how I was desperate to make a major change but worried about not making enough money if I did. My emotions were raw. I let out another sigh. "I'm just not fulfilled," I said.

I see now how this must have come across to my mother, who was then in the ninth year of a job she'd taken primarily so she could help finance my college education, after years of *not* having a job so that she'd be free to sew my school clothes, cook my meals, and do laundry for my dad, who for the sake of our family spent eight hours a day watching gauges on a boiler at the filtration plant. My mom, who'd just driven an hour to fetch me from the airport, who was letting me live rent-free in the upstairs of her house, and who would have to get herself up at dawn the next morning in order to help my disabled dad get ready for work, was hardly ready to indulge my angst about fulfillment.

Fulfillment, I'm sure, struck her as a rich person's conceit. I doubt that my parents, in their thirty years together, had even once discussed it.

My mother didn't judge me for being ponderous. She wasn't one to give lectures or draw attention to her own sacrifices. She'd quietly supported every choice I'd ever made. This time, though, she gave me a wry, sideways look, hit her turn signal to get us off the highway and back to our neighborhood, and chuckled just a little. "If you're asking me," she said, "I say make the money first and worry about your happiness later."

THERE ARE TRUTHS we face and truths we ignore. I spent the next six months quietly trying to empower myself without making any sort of abrupt change. At work, I met with the partner in charge of my division, asking to be given more challenging assignments. I tried to focus on the projects I found most meaningful, including my efforts to recruit a new and more diverse crop of summer associates. All the while, I kept an eye on job listings in the newspaper and did my best to network with more people who weren't lawyers. One way or another, I figured I'd work myself toward some version of feeling whole.

At home on Euclid Avenue, I felt powerless in the face of a new reality. My father's feet had started to swell for no obvious reason. His skin looked strangely mottled and dark. Anytime I asked how he was feeling, though, he gave me the same answer, with the same degree of insistence that he'd given me for years.

"I'm fine," he'd say, as if the question were never worth asking. He'd then change the subject.

It was winter again in Chicago. I woke in the mornings to the sound of the neighbors chipping ice from their windshields on the street. The wind blew and the snow piled up. The sun stayed wan and weak. Through my office window on the forty-seventh floor at Sidley, I looked out at a tundra of gray ice on Lake Michigan and a gunmetal sky above. I wore my wool and hoped for a thaw. In the Midwest, as I've mentioned, winter is an exercise in waiting—for relief, for a bird to sing, for the first purple crocus to push up through the snow. You have no choice in the meantime but to pep-talk yourself through.

My dad hadn't lost his jovial good humor. Craig came by for family dinners once in a while, and we sat around the table and laughed the same as always, though we were now joined by Janis, Craig's wife. Janis was happy and hard-driving, a telecommunications analyst who worked downtown and was, like everyone else, completely smitten with my dad. Craig, meanwhile, was a poster child for the post-Princeton urban-professional dream. He was getting an MBA and had a job as a vice president at Continental Bank, and he and Janis had bought a nice condo in Hyde Park. He wore tailored suits and had driven over for dinner in his red Porsche 944 Turbo. I didn't know it then, but none of this made him happy. Like me, he had his own crisis brewing and in coming years would wrestle with questions about whether his work was meaningful, whether the rewards he'd felt compelled to seek were the rewards he actually wanted. Knowing, though, how thrilled our father was by what his kids had managed to accomplish, neither of us ever brought up our discontent over dinner.

Saying good-bye at the end of a visit, Craig would give my dad a final, concerned look and pose the usual question about his health, only to be given the merry brush-off of "I'm fine."

We accepted this, I believe, because it was steadying, and steady was how we liked to be. Dad had lived with MS for years and had managed always to be fine. We were happy to extend the rationalization, even as he was visibly declining. He was fine, we told each other, because he still got up and went to work every day. He was fine because we'd watched him have a second helping of meat loaf that night. He was fine, especially if you didn't look too hard at his feet.

I had several tense conversations with my mom, asking why it was that Dad wouldn't go to the doctor. But like me, she'd all but given up, having prodded him and been shut down enough times already. For my father, doctors had never brought good news and therefore were to be avoided. As much as he loved to talk, he didn't want to talk about his problems. He viewed it as self-indulgent. He wanted to get by in his own way. To accommodate his bulging feet, he'd simply asked my mother to buy him a bigger pair of work boots.

The stalemate over a doctor's visit continued through January and into February that year. My dad moved with a pained slowness, using an aluminum walker to get himself around the house, pausing often to catch his breath. It took longer in the mornings now for him to maneuver from bed to bathroom, bathroom to kitchen, and finally to the back door and down the three stairs to the garage so that he could drive himself to work. Despite what was happening at home, he insisted that all was well at the filtration plant. He used a motorized scooter to pilot himself from boiler to boiler and took pride in his own indispensability. In twenty-six years, he hadn't missed a single shift. If a boiler happened to overheat, my dad claimed to be one of only a few workers with enough experience to swiftly and ably contain a disaster. In a true reflection of his optimism, he'd recently put his name in for a promotion.

My mom and I tried to reconcile what he told us with what we saw with our own eyes. It grew increasingly hard to do. At home in the evenings, my father spent much of his time watching basketball and hockey games on TV, appearing weak and exhausted in his chair. In addition to his feet, there seemed to be something swelling in his neck now, we'd noticed. It put an odd rattle in his voice.

We finally staged a sort of intervention one night. Craig was never one to be the bad cop, and my mother stuck to her self-imposed ceasefire on matters of my father's health. In a conversation like this, the role of tough talker almost always fell to me. I told my dad that he owed it to us to get some help and that I planned to call his doctor in the morning. Grudgingly, my dad agreed, promising that if I made the appointment, he would go. I urged him to let himself sleep late the next morning, to give his body a rest.

We went to bed that night, my mother and I, feeling relieved that we'd finally gained some control.

M Y FATHER, HOWEVER, had divided loyalties. Rest, for him, was a form of giving in. I came downstairs in the morning to find my mother already departed for work and my dad sitting at the kitchen table with his walker parked next to him. He was dressed in his navy-blue city uniform and struggling to put on his shoes. He was going to work.

"Dad," I said, "I thought you were going to rest. We're getting you that doctor's appointment . . ."

He shrugged. "I know, sweetie," he said, his voice gravelly from whatever new thing was wrong in his neck. "But right now, I'm fine."

His stubbornness was packed beneath so many layers of pride that it was impossible for me to be angry. There was no dissuading him. My parents had raised us to handle our own business, which meant that I had to trust him to handle his, even if he could, at that point, barely put on his shoes. So I let him handle it. I stuffed down my worries, gave my dad a kiss, and took myself back upstairs to get ready for my own workday. I figured I'd call my mother later at her office, telling her we'd need to strategize about how to force the man to take some time off.

I heard the back door click shut. A few minutes later, I returned to the kitchen to find it empty. My father's walker sat by the back door. On an impulse, I went over and looked through the little glass peephole in the door, which gave a wide-angle view of the back stoop and pathway to the garage, just to confirm that his van was gone.

But the van was there, and so, too, was my dad. He was dressed in a cap and his winter jacket and had his back to me. He'd made it only partway down the stairs before needing to sit down. I could see the exhaustion in the angle of his body, in the sideways droop of his head and the half-collapsed heaviness with which he was resting against the wooden railing. He wasn't in a crisis so much as he looked just too weary to carry on. It seemed clear he was trying to summon enough strength to turn around and come back inside.

I was seeing him, I realized, in a moment of pure defeat.

How lonely it must have been to live twenty-some years with such a disease, to persist without complaint as your body is slowly and inexorably consumed. Seeing my dad on the stoop, I ached in a way I never had. My instinct was to rush outside and help him back into the warm house, but I fought it, knowing it would be just another blow to his dignity. I took a breath and turned away from the door.

I'd see him when he came back in, I thought. I'd help take off his work boots, get him some water, and usher him to his chair, with the silent acknowledgment between us that now without question he would need to accept some help.

Upstairs in my apartment again, I sat listening for the sound of the back door. I waited for five minutes and then five minutes more, before finally I went downstairs and back to the peephole to make sure he'd made it to his feet. But the stoop was empty now. Somehow my father, in defiance of everything that was swollen and off-kilter in his body, had willed himself down those stairs and across the icy walkway and into his van, which was now probably almost halfway to the filtration plant. He was not giving in.

FOR MONTHS NOW, Barack and I had danced around the idea of marriage. We'd been together a year and a half and remained, it seemed, unshakably in love. He was in his final semester at Harvard and caught up in his *Law Review* work but would soon head back my way to take the Illinois bar and look for a job. The plan was that he'd move back to Euclid Avenue, this time in a way that felt more permanent. For me, it was another reason why winter couldn't end soon enough.

We'd talked in abstract ways about how each of us viewed marriage, and it worried me sometimes how different those views seemed to be. For me, getting married had been a given, something I'd grown up expecting to do someday—the same way having children had always been a given, dating back to the attention I'd heaped on my baby dolls as a girl. Barack wasn't opposed to getting married, but he was in no particular rush. For him, our love meant everything already. It was foundation enough for a full and happy life together—with or without rings.

We were both, of course, products of how we'd been raised. Barack had experienced marriage as ephemeral: His mother had married twice, divorced twice, and in each instance managed to move on with her life, career, and young children intact. My parents, meanwhile, had locked in early and for life. For them, every decision was a joint decision, every endeavor a joint endeavor. In thirty years, they'd hardly spent a night apart.

What did Barack and I want? We wanted a modern partnership that suited us both. He saw marriage as the loving alignment of two people who could lead parallel lives but without forgoing any independent dreams or ambitions. For me, marriage was more like a full-on merger, a reconfiguring of two lives into one, with the well-being of a family taking precedence over any one agenda or goal. I didn't exactly want a life like my parents had. I didn't want to live in the same house forever, work the same job, and never claim any space for myself, but I did want the year-to-year, decade-to-decade steadiness they had. "I do recognize the value of individuals having their own interests, ambitions, and dreams," I wrote in my journal. "But I don't believe that the pursuit of one person's dreams should come at the expense of the couple."

We'd work out our feelings, I figured, when Barack came back to Chicago, when the weather warmed up, when we had the luxury of spending weekends together again. I just had to wait, though waiting was hard. I craved permanence. From the living room of my apartment, I could sometimes hear the murmur of my parents talking on the floor below. I heard my mother laughing as my father told some sort of story. I heard them shutting off the TV to get ready for bed. I was twenty-seven years old now, and there were days when all I wanted was to feel complete. I wanted to grab every last thing I loved and stake it ruthlessly to the ground. I'd known just enough loss by then to know that there was more coming.

I T WAS I who made the appointment for my father to see a doctor, but it was my mother who ultimately got him there—by ambulance, as it turned out. His feet had ballooned and grown tender to the point that he finally admitted that walking on them felt like walking on needles. When it was time to go, he couldn't stand on them at all. I was at work that day, but my mother described it to me later—Dad being carried out of the house by burly paramedics, trying to joke with them as they went.

He was taken directly to the hospital at the University of Chicago. What followed was a string of lost days spent in the purgatory of blood draws, pulse checks, untouched meal trays, and squads of doctors making rounds. All the while, my father continued to swell. His face puffed up, his neck got thicker, his voice grew weak. Cushing's syndrome was the official diagnosis, possibly related to his MS and possibly not. Either way, we were well past the point of any sort of stopgap treatment. His endocrine system was now going fully haywire. A scan showed that he had a growth in his throat that had become so enlarged he was practically choking on it.

"I don't know how I missed that," my father said to the doctor, sounding genuinely perplexed, as if he hadn't felt a single symptom leading up to this point, as if he hadn't spent weeks and months, if not years, ignoring his pain.

We cycled through hospital visits to be with him—my mom, Craig, Janis, and me. We came and went over days as the doctors blasted him with medicine, as tubes were added and machines were hooked up. We tried to grasp what the specialists were telling us but could make little sense of it. We rearranged my dad's pillows and talked uselessly about college basketball and the weather outside, knowing that he was listening, though it exhausted him now to speak. We were a family of planners, but now everything seemed unplanned. Slowly, my father was sinking away from us, enveloped by some invisible sea. We called him back with old memories, seeing how they put a little brightness in his eyes. Remember the Deuce and a Quarter and how we used to roll around in that giant backseat on our summer outings to the drive-in? Remember the boxing gloves you gave us, and the swimming pool at Dukes Happy Holiday Resort? What about how you used to build the props for Robbie's Operetta Workshop? What about dinners at Dandy's house? Remember when Mom made us fried shrimp on New Year's Eve?

One evening I stopped by and found my father alone, my mother having gone home for the night, the nurses clustered outside at their hallway station. The room was quiet. The whole floor of the hospital was quiet. It was the first week of March, the winter snow having just melted, leaving the city in what felt like a perpetual state of dampness. My dad had been in the hospital about ten days then. He was fifty-five years old, but he looked like an old man, with yellowed eyes and arms too heavy to move. He was awake but unable to speak, whether due to the swelling or due to emotion, I'll never know.

I sat in a chair next to his bed and watched him laboring to breathe. When I put my hand in his, he gave it a comforting squeeze. We looked at each other silently. There was too much to say, and at the same time it felt as if we'd said everything. What was left was only one truth. We were reaching the end. He would not recover. He was going to miss the whole rest of my life. I was losing his steadiness, his comfort, his everyday joy. I felt tears spilling down my cheeks.

Keeping his gaze on me, my father lifted the back of my hand to his lips and kissed it again and again and again. It was his way of saying, *Hush now, don't cry.* He was expressing sorrow and urgency, but also something calmer and deeper, a message he wanted to make clear. With those kisses, he was saying that he loved me with his whole heart, that he was proud of the woman I'd become. He was saying that he knew he should have gone to the doctor a lot sooner. He was asking for forgiveness. He was saying good-bye.

I stayed with him until he fell asleep that night, leaving the hospital in icy darkness and driving back home to Euclid Avenue, where my mother had already turned off the lights. We were alone in the house now, just me and my mom and whatever future we were now meant to have. Because by the time the sun came up, he'd be gone. My father— Fraser Robinson III—had a heart attack and passed away that night, having given us absolutely everything.

11

I T HURTS TO LIVE AFTER SOMEONE HAS DIED. IT JUST does. It can hurt to walk down a hallway or open the fridge. It hurts to put on a pair of socks, to brush your teeth. Food tastes like nothing. Colors go flat. Music hurts, and so do memories. You look at something you'd otherwise find beautiful—a purple sky at sunset or a playground full of kids—and it only somehow deepens the loss. Grief is so lonely this way.

The day after my father died, we drove to a South Side funeral parlor—me, my mother, and Craig—to pick out a casket and plan a service. *To make arrangements,* as they say in funeral parlors. I don't remember much about our visit there, except for how stunned we were, each of us bricked inside our private grief. Still, as we went through the obscene ritual of shopping for the right box in which to bury our dad, Craig and I managed to have our first and only fight as adult siblings.

It boiled down to this: I wanted to buy the fanciest, most expensive casket in the place, complete with every extra handle and cushion a casket could possibly have. I had no particular rationale for wanting this. It was something to do when there was nothing else to do. The practical, pragmatic part of our upbringing wouldn't allow me to put much stock in the gentle, well-intentioned platitudes people would heap on us a few days later at the funeral. I couldn't be easily comforted by the suggestion that my dad had gone to a better place or was sitting with angels. As I saw it, he just deserved a nice casket.

Craig, meanwhile, insisted that Dad would want something basic—modest and practical and nothing more. It suited our father's personality, he said. Anything else would be too showy.

We started quiet, but soon exploded, as the kindly funeral director pretended not to listen and our mother just stared at us implacably, through the fog of her own pain.

We were yelling for reasons that had nothing to do with the actual argument. Neither of us was invested in the outcome. In the end, we'd bury our dad in a compromise casket—nothing too fancy, nothing too plain—and never once discuss it again. We were having an absurd and inappropriate argument because in the wake of death every single thing on earth feels absurd and inappropriate.

Later, we drove Mom back to Euclid Avenue. The three of us sat downstairs at the kitchen table, spent and sullen now, our misery provoked all over again by the sight of the fourth empty chair. Soon, we were weeping. We sat for what felt like a long time, blubbering until we were exhausted and out of tears. My mother, who hadn't said much all day, finally offered a comment.

"Look at us," she said, a little ruefully.

And yet there was a touch of lightness in how she said it. She was pointing out that we Robinsons had been reduced to a true and ridiculous mess—unrecognizable with our swollen eyelids and dripping noses, our hurt and strange helplessness here in our own kitchen. Who were we? Didn't we know? Hadn't he shown us? She was calling us back from our loneliness with three blunt words, as only our mom could do.

Mom looked at me and I looked at Craig, and suddenly the moment seemed a little funny. The first chuckle, we knew, would normally have come from that empty chair. Slowly, we started to titter and crack up, collapsing finally into full-blown fits of laughter. I realize that might seem strange, but we were so much better at this than we were at crying. The point was he would have liked it, and so we let ourselves laugh.

. . .

L OSING MY DAD exacerbated my sense that there was no time to
sit around and ponder how my life should go. My father was just
fifty-five when he died. Suzanne had been twenty-six. The lesson there
was simple: Life is short and not to be wasted. If I died, I didn't want
people remembering me for the stacks of legal briefs I'd written or the
corporate trademarks I'd helped defend. I felt certain that I had something more to offer the world. It was time to make a move.

Still unsure of where I hoped to land, I typed up letters of introduction and sent them to people all over the city of Chicago. I wrote to the
heads of foundations, community-oriented nonprofits, and big universities in town, reaching out specifically to their legal departments—not
because I wanted to do legal work, but because I figured they were more
likely to respond to my résumé. Thankfully, a number of people did respond, inviting me to have lunch or come in for a meeting, even if they
had no job to offer. Over the course of the spring and summer of 1991, I
put myself in front of anyone I thought might be able to give me advice.
The point was less to find a new job than to widen my understanding of
what was possible and how others had gone about it. I was realizing that
the next phase of my journey would not simply unfold on its own, that
my fancy academic degrees weren't going to automatically lead me to fulfilling work. Finding a career as opposed to a job wouldn't just come from
perusing the contact pages of an alumni directory; it required deeper
thought and effort. I would need to hustle and learn. And so, again and
again, I laid out my professional dilemma for the people I met, quizzing
them on what they did and whom they knew. I asked earnest questions
about what kind of work might be available to a lawyer who didn't, in
fact, want to practice law.

One afternoon, I visited the office of a friendly, thoughtful man
named Art Sussman, who was the in-house legal counsel for the University of Chicago. It turned out that my mother had once spent about
a year working for him as a secretary, taking dictation and maintaining
the legal department's files. This was back when I was a sophomore in
high school, before she'd taken her job at the bank. Art was surprised

to learn that I hadn't ever visited her at work—that I'd never actually set foot on the university's pristine Gothic campus before now, despite having grown up just a few miles away.

If I was honest, there'd been no reason for me to visit the campus. My neighborhood school didn't run field trips there. If there were cultural events open to the community when I was a kid, my family hadn't known about them. We had no friends—no acquaintances, even—who were students or alumni. The University of Chicago was an elite school, and to most everyone I knew growing up, elite meant *not for us*. Its gray stone buildings almost literally had their backs turned to the streets surrounding campus. Driving past, my dad used to roll his eyes at the flocks of students haplessly jaywalking across Ellis Avenue, wondering how it was that such smart people had never learned to properly cross a street.

Like many South Siders, my family maintained what was an admittedly dim and limited view of the university, even if my mom had passed a year happily working there. When it came time for me and Craig to think about college, we didn't even consider applying to the University of Chicago. Princeton, for some strange reason, had struck us as more accessible.

Hearing all this, Art was incredulous. "You've really never been here?" he said. "Never?"

"Nope, not once."

There was an odd power in saying it out loud. I hadn't given the idea much thought before now, but it occurred to me that I'd have made a perfectly fine University of Chicago student, if only the town-gown divide hadn't been so vast—if I'd known about the school and the school had known about me. Thinking about this, I felt an internal prick, a small subterranean twinge of purpose. The combination of where I came from and what I'd made of myself gave me a certain, possibly meaningful perspective. Being Black and from the South Side, I suddenly saw, helped me recognize problems that a man like Art Sussman didn't even realize existed.

In several years, I'd get my chance to work for the university and reckon with some of these community-relations problems directly, but right now Art was just kindly offering to pass around my résumé.

"I think you should talk to Susan Sher," he told me then, unwittingly setting off what to this day feels like an inspired chain reaction. Susan was about fifteen years older than I was. She'd been a partner at a big law firm but had ultimately bailed out of the corporate world, just as I was hoping to do, though she was still practicing law with the Chicago city government. Susan had slate-gray eyes, the kind of fair skin that belongs on a Victorian queen, and a laugh that often ended with a mischievous snort. She was gently confident and highly accomplished and would become a lifelong friend. "I'd hire you right now," she told me when we finally met. "But you just finished telling me how you don't want to be a lawyer."

Instead, Susan proposed what now seems like another fated introduction, steering me and my résumé toward a new colleague of hers at city hall—another ship-jumping corporate lawyer with a yen for public service, this one a fellow daughter of the South Side and someone who would end up altering my course in life, not once, but repeatedly. "The person you really need to meet," Susan said, "is Valerie Jarrett."

Valerie Jarrett was the newly appointed deputy chief of staff to the mayor of Chicago and had deep connections across the city's African American community. Like Susan, she'd been smart enough to land herself a job in a blue-chip firm after law school and had then been self-aware enough to realize that she wanted out. She'd moved to city hall largely because she was inspired by Harold Washington, who'd been elected mayor in 1983 when I was away at college and was the first African American to hold the office. Washington was a voluble politician with an exuberant spirit. My parents loved him for how he could pepper an otherwise folksy speech with Shakespeare quotes and for the famous, mouth-stuffing vigor with which he ate fried chicken at community events on the South Side. Most important, he had a distaste for the entrenched Democratic machinery that had long governed Chicago, awarding lucrative city contracts to political donors and generally keeping Blacks in service to the party but rarely allowing them to advance into official elected roles.

Building his campaign around reforming the city's political system and better tending to its neglected neighborhoods, Washington won the election by a hair. His style was brassy and his temperament was bold. He was able to eviscerate opponents with his eloquence and intellect. He was a Black, brainy superhero. He clashed regularly and fearlessly with the mostly white old-guard members of the city council and was viewed as something of a walking legend, especially among the city's Black citizens, who saw his leadership as kindling a larger spirit of progressivism. His vision had been an early inspiration for Barack, who arrived in Chicago to work as an organizer in 1985.

Valerie, too, was drawn by Washington. She was thirty years old when she joined Washington's staff in 1987, at the start of his second term. She was also the mother of a young daughter and soon to be divorced, which made it a deeply inconvenient time to take the sort of pay cut one does when leaving a swishy law firm and landing in city government. And within months of her starting the job, tragedy struck: Harold Washington abruptly had a heart attack and died at his desk, thirty minutes after holding a press conference about low-income housing. In the aftermath, a Black alderman was appointed by the city council to take Washington's place, but his tenure was relatively short. In a move many African Americans saw as a swift and demoralizing return to the old white ways of Chicago politics, voters went on to elect Richard M. Daley, the son of a previous mayor, Richard J. Daley, who was broadly considered the godfather of Chicago's famous cronyism.

Though she had reservations about the new administration, Valerie had decided to stay on at city hall, moving out of the legal department and directly into Mayor Daley's office. She was glad to be there, as much for the contrast as anything. She described to me how her transition from corporate law into government felt like a relief, an energizing leap out of the super-groomed unreality of high-class law being practiced on the top floors of skyscrapers and into the real world—the very real world.

Chicago's City Hall and County Building is a flat-roofed, eleven-story, gray-granite monolith that occupies an entire block between Clark and LaSalle north of the Loop. Compared with the soaring office towers surrounding it, it's squatty but not without grandeur, featuring tall Corinthian columns out front and giant, echoing lobbies made primarily of marble. The county runs its business out of the east-facing half of the building; the city uses the western half, which houses the mayor and city council members as well as the city clerk. City hall, as I learned on the sweltering summer day I showed up to meet Valerie for a job interview, was both alarmingly and upliftingly packed with people.

There were couples getting married and people registering cars. There were people lodging complaints about potholes, their landlords, their sewer lines, and everything else they felt the city could improve. There were babies in strollers and old ladies in wheelchairs. There were journalists and lobbyists, and also homeless people just looking to get out of the heat. Out on the sidewalk in front of the building, a knot of activists waved signs and shouted chants, though I can't remember what it was they were angry about. What I do know is that I was simultaneously taken aback and completely enthralled by the clunky, controlled chaos of the place. City hall belonged to the people. It had a noisy, gritty immediacy that I never felt at Sidley.

Valerie had reserved twenty minutes on her schedule to talk to me that day, but our conversation ended up stretching for an hour and a half. A thin, light-skinned African American woman dressed in a beautifully tailored suit, she was soft-spoken and strikingly serene, with a steady brown-eyed gaze and an impressive grasp of how the city functioned. She enjoyed her job but didn't try to gloss over the bureaucratic headaches of government work. Something about her caused me instantly to relax. Years later, Valerie would tell me that to her surprise I'd managed to reverse the standard interview process on her that day—that I'd given her some basic, helpful information about myself, but otherwise I'd grilled her, wanting to understand every last feeling she had about the work she did and how responsive the mayor was to his employees. I was testing the suitability of the work for me as much as she was testing the suitability of me for the work.

Looking back on it, I'm sure I was only capitalizing on what felt like a rare opportunity to speak with a woman whose background mirrored mine but who was a few years ahead of me in her career trajectory. Valerie was calm, bold, and wise in ways that few people I'd met before were. She was someone to learn from, to stick close to. I saw this right away.

Before I left, she offered me a job, inviting me to join her staff as an assistant to Mayor Daley, beginning as soon as I was ready. I would no longer be practicing law. My salary would be $60,000, about half of what I was currently making at Sidley & Austin. She told me I should take some time and think about whether I was truly prepared to make this sort of change. It was my leap to consider, my leap to make.

I had never been one to hold city hall in high regard. Having grown up Black and on the South Side, I had little faith in politics. Politics had traditionally been used against Black folks, as a means to keep us isolated and excluded, leaving us undereducated, unemployed, and underpaid. I had grandparents who'd lived through the horror of Jim Crow laws and the humiliation of housing discrimination and basically mistrusted authority of any sort. (Southside, as you may recall, thought that even the dentist was out to get him.) My father, who was a city employee most of his life, had essentially been conscripted into service as a Democratic precinct captain in order to even be considered for promotions at his job. He relished the social aspect of his precinct duties but had always been put off by city hall cronyism.

And yet I was suddenly considering a city hall job. I'd winced at the pay cut, but on some visceral level I was just intrigued. I was feeling another twinge, a quiet nudge toward what might be a whole different future from the one I'd planned for. I was almost ready to leap, but for one thing. It wasn't just about me anymore. When Valerie called me a few days later to follow up, I told her I was still thinking the offer over. I then asked a final and probably strange question. "Could I please," I said, "also introduce you to my fiancé?"

I SUPPOSE I SHOULD back up here, rewinding us through the heavy heat of that summer, through the disorienting haze of those long months after my father died. Barack had flown back to Chicago to be with me for as long as he could around my dad's funeral before returning to finish at Harvard. After graduation in late May, he packed up his things, sold his banana-yellow Datsun, and flew back to Chicago, delivering himself to 7436 South Euclid Avenue and into my arms. I loved him. I felt loved by him. We'd made it almost two years as a long-distance couple, and now, finally, we could be a short-distance couple. It meant that we once again had weekend hours to linger in bed, to read the newspaper and go out for brunch and share every thought we had. We could have Monday night dinners and Tuesday, Wednesday, and Thursday night dinners, too. We could shop for groceries and fold laundry in front of the TV. On the many evenings when I still got weepy over the loss of my dad, Barack was now there to curl himself around me and kiss the top of my head.

Barack was relieved to be done with law school, eager to get out of the abstract realm of academia and into work that felt more engaging and real. He'd also sold his idea for a nonfiction book about race and identity to a New York publisher, which for someone who worshipped books as he did felt like an enormous and humbling boon. He'd been given an advance and had about a year to complete the manuscript.

Barack had, as he always seemed to, plenty of options. His reputation—the gushing reports by his law school professors, the *New York Times* story about his selection as president of the *Law Review*—seemed to bring a flood of opportunity. The University of Chicago offered him an unpaid fellowship that came with a small office for the year, the idea being that he'd write his book there and maybe eventually sign on to teach as an adjunct professor at the law school. My colleagues at Sidley & Austin, still hoping Barack would come work full-time at the firm, provided him with a desk to use during the eight or so weeks leading up to his bar exam in July. He was now also considering taking a job at Davis, Miner, Barnhill & Galland, a small public interest firm that did civil rights and fair housing work and whose attorneys had been aligned closely with Harold Washington, which was a huge draw for Barack.

There's something innately bolstering about a person who sees his opportunities as endless, who doesn't waste time or energy questioning whether they will ever dry up. Barack had worked hard and dutifully for everything he was now being given, but he wasn't notching achievements or measuring his progress against that of others, as so many people I knew did—as I sometimes did myself. He seemed, at times, beautifully oblivious to the giant rat race of life and all the material things a thirty-something lawyer was supposed to be going after, from a car that wasn't embarrassing to a house with a yard in the suburbs or a swank condo in the Loop. I'd observed this quality in him before, but now that we were living together and I was considering making the first real swerve of my life, I came to value it even more.

In a nutshell, Barack believed and trusted when others did not. He had a simple, buoying faith that if you stuck to your principles, things would work out. I'd had so many careful, sensible conversations at this point, with so many people, about how to extract myself from a career in which, by all outward measures, I was flourishing. Again and again, I'd read the caution and concern on so many faces when I spoke of having loans to pay off, of not yet having managed to buy a house. I couldn't help but think about how my father had kept his aims deliberately modest, avoiding every risk in order to give us constancy at home. I still walked around with my mother's advice ringing in my ear: *Make the money first and worry about your happiness later.* Compounding my anxiety was the one deep longing that far outmatched any material wish: I knew I wanted to have children, sooner rather than later. And how would that work if I abruptly started over in a brand-new field?

Barack, when he showed up back in Chicago, became a kind of soothing antidote. He absorbed my worries, listened as I ticked off every financial obligation I had, and affirmed that he, too, was excited to have children. He acknowledged that there was no way we could predict how exactly we'd manage things, given that neither of us wanted to be locked into the comfortable predictability of a lawyer's life. But the bottom line was that we were far from poor and our future was promising, maybe even more promising for the fact that it couldn't easily be planned.

His was the lone voice telling me to just go for it, to erase the worries and go toward whatever I thought would make me happy. It was okay to make my leap into the unknown, because—and this would count as startling news to most every member of the Shields/Robinson family, going back all the way to Dandy and Southside—the unknown wasn't going to kill me.

Don't worry, Barack was saying. *You can do this. We'll figure it out.*

. . .

A WORD NOW ABOUT the bar exam: It's a necessary chore, a rite of passage for any just-hatched lawyer wishing to practice, and though the content and structure of the test itself vary somewhat from state to state, the experience of taking it—a two-day, twelve-hour exam meant to prove your knowledge of everything from contract law to arcane rules about secured transactions—is pretty much universally recognized as hellish. Just as Barack was intending to, I had sat for the Illinois bar exam three years earlier, the summer after finishing up at Harvard, submitting myself beforehand to what was supposed to be a self-disciplined two months of logging hours as a first-year associate at Sidley while also taking a bar review class and pushing myself through a dauntingly fat book of practice tests.

This was the same summer that Craig was getting married to Janis in her hometown of Denver. Janis had asked me to be a bridesmaid, and for a whole set of reasons—not the least of which being that I'd just spent seven years grinding nonstop at Princeton and Harvard—I hurled myself, early and eagerly, into the role. I oohed and aahed at wedding dresses and helped plan the bachelorette activities. There was nothing I wouldn't do to help make the anointed day merrier. I was far more excited about the prospect of my brother taking his wedding vows, in other words, than I was about reviewing what constituted a tort.

This was in the old days, back when test results arrived via the post office. That fall, with both the bar exam and the wedding behind me, I called my father from work one day and asked if he'd check to see if the mail had come in. It had. I asked if there was an envelope in there for me. There was. Was it a letter from the Illinois State Bar Association? Why, yes, that's what it said on the envelope. I next asked if he'd open it for me, which is when I heard some rustling and then a long, damning pause on the other end of the line.

I had failed.

I had never in my entire life failed a test, unless you want to count the moment in kindergarten when I stood up in class and couldn't read the word "white" off the manila card held by my teacher. But I'd blown it with the bar. I was ashamed, sure that I'd let down every person who'd ever taught, encouraged, or employed me. I wasn't used to blundering. If anything, I generally overdid things, especially when it came to preparing for a big moment or test, but this one I'd let slip by. I think now that it was a by-product of the disinterest I'd felt all through law school, burned out as I was on being a student and bored by subjects that struck me as esoteric and far removed from real life. I wanted to be around people and not books, which is why the best part of law school for me had been volunteering at the school's Legal Aid Bureau, where I could help someone get a Social Security check or stand up to an out-of-line landlord.

But still, I didn't like to fail. The sting of it would stay with me for months, even as plenty of my colleagues at Sidley confessed that they, too, hadn't passed the bar exam the first time. Later that fall, I buckled down and studied for a do-over test, going on to pass it handily. In the end, aside from issues of pride, my screwup would make no difference at all.

Several years later, though, the memory was causing me to regard Barack with extra curiosity. He was attending bar review classes and carrying around his own bar review books, and yet didn't seem to be cracking them as often as I thought maybe he should—as I would, anyway, knowing what I knew now. But I wasn't going to nag him or even offer myself as an example of what could go wrong. We were built so differently, he and I. For one thing, Barack's head was an overpacked suitcase of information, a mainframe from which he could seemingly pull disparate bits of data at will. I called him "the fact guy," for how he seemed to have a statistic to match every little twist in a conversation. His memory seemed not-quite-but-almost photographic. The truth was, I wasn't worried about whether he'd pass the bar and, somewhat annoyingly, neither was he.

So we celebrated early, on the very same day he finished the exam— July 31, 1991—booking ourselves a table at a downtown restaurant called Gordon. It was one of our favorite places, a special-occasion kind of joint, with soft Art Deco lighting and crisp white tablecloths and things like caviar and artichoke fritters on the menu. It was the height of summer and we were happy.

At Gordon, Barack and I always ordered every course. We had martinis and appetizers. We picked a nice wine to go with our entrées. We talked idly, contentedly, maybe a little sappily. As we were reaching the end of the meal, Barack smiled at me and raised the subject of marriage. He reached for my hand and said that as much as he loved me with his whole being, he still didn't really see the point. Instantly, I felt the blood rise in my cheeks. It was like pushing a button in me—the kind of big blinking red button you might find in some sort of nuclear facility surrounded by warning signs and evacuation maps. Really? We were going to do this now?

In fact, we were. We'd had the hypothetical marriage discussion plenty of times already, and nothing much ever changed. I was a traditionalist and Barack was not. It seemed clear that neither one of us could be swayed. But still, this didn't stop us—two lawyers, after all—from taking up the topic with hot gusto. Surrounded by men in sport coats and women in nice dresses enjoying their fancy meals, I did what I could to keep my voice calm.

"If we're committed," I said, as evenly as I could muster, "why wouldn't we formalize that commitment? What part of your dignity would be sacrificed by that?"

From here, we traversed all the familiar loops of the old argument. Did marriage matter? Why did it matter? What was wrong with him? What was wrong with me? What kind of future did we have if we couldn't sort this out? We weren't fighting, but we were quarreling, and doing it attorney-style. We punched and counterpunched, dissected and cross-examined, though it was clearly I who was more inflamed. It was I who was doing most of the talking.

Eventually, our waiter came around holding a dessert plate, covered by a silver lid. He slid it in front of me and lifted the cover. I was almost too miffed to even look down, but when I did, I saw a dark velvet box where the chocolate cake was supposed to be. Inside it was a diamond ring.

Barack looked at me playfully. He'd baited me. It had all been a ruse. It took me a second to dismantle my anger and slide into joyful shock. He'd riled me up because this was the very last time he would invoke his inane marriage argument, ever again, as long as we both should live. The case was closed. He dropped to one knee then and with an emotional hitch in his voice asked sincerely if I'd please do him the honor of marrying him. Later, I'd learn that he'd already gone to both my mother and my brother to ask for their approval ahead of time. When I said yes, it seemed that every person in the whole restaurant started to clap.

For a full minute or two, I stared dumbfounded at the ring on my finger. I looked at Barack to confirm that this was all real. He was smiling. He'd completely surprised me. In a way, we'd both won. "Well," he said lightly, "that should shut you up."

I SAID YES TO BARACK, and shortly after that I said yes to Valerie Jarrett, accepting her offer to come work at city hall. Before committing, I made a point of following through on my request to introduce Barack and Valerie, scheduling a dinner during which the three of us could talk.

I did this for a couple of reasons. For one, I liked Valerie. I was impressed by her, and whether or not I ended up taking the job, I was excited to get to know her better. I knew that Barack would be impressed, too. More important, though, I wanted him to hear Valerie's story. Like Barack, she'd spent part of her childhood in a different country—in her case, Iran, where her father had been a doctor at a hospital—and returned to the United States for her schooling, giving her the same kind of clear-eyed perspective I saw in Barack. Barack had concerns about my working at city hall. Like Valerie, he'd been inspired by the leadership of Harold Washington when he was mayor, but felt decidedly less affinity for the old-school establishment represented by Richard M. Daley. It was the community organizer in him: Even while Washington was in office, he'd had to battle relentlessly and sometimes fruitlessly with the city in order to get even the smallest bit of support for grassroots projects. Though he'd been nothing but encouraging about my job prospects, I think he was quietly worried I might end up disillusioned or disempowered working under Daley.

Valerie was the right person to address any concerns. She'd rearranged her entire life in order to work for Washington and then lost him almost immediately. The void that followed Washington's death offered a kind of cautionary tale for the future, one I'd eventually find myself trying to explain to people across America: In Chicago, we'd made the mistake of putting all our hopes for reform on the shoulders of one person without building the political apparatus to support his vision. Voters, especially liberal and Black voters, viewed Washington as a kind of golden savior, a symbol, the man who could change everything. He'd carried the load admirably, inspiring people like Barack and Valerie to move out of the private sector and into community work and public service. But when Harold Washington died, most of the energy he'd generated did, too.

Valerie's decision to stay on with the mayor's office had required some thought, but she explained to us why she felt it was the right choice. She described feeling supported by Daley and knowing that she was being useful to the city. Her loyalty, she said, had been to Harold Washington's principles more than to the man himself. Inspiration on its own was shallow; you had to back it up with hard work. This idea resonated with both me and Barack, and inside that one dinner I felt as if something had been cemented: Valerie Jarrett was now a part of our lives. Without our ever discussing it, it seemed almost as if the three of us had somehow agreed to carry one another a good long way.

THERE WAS ONE last thing to do, now that we were engaged, now that I'd taken a new job and Barack had made a commitment to Davis, Miner, Barnhill & Galland, the public interest law firm that had been courting him: We took a vacation, or maybe more accurately we went on a sort of pilgrimage. We flew out of Chicago on a Wednesday in late August, had a long wait in the airport in Frankfurt, Germany, and then flew another eight hours to arrive in Nairobi just before dawn, stepping outside in the Kenyan moonlight and into what felt like a different world altogether.

I had been to Jamaica and the Bahamas, and to Europe a few times, but this was my first time being this far from home. I felt Nairobi's foreignness—or really, my own foreignness in relation to it—immediately, even in the first strains of morning. It's a sensation I've come to love as I've traveled more, the way a new place signals itself instantly and without pretense. The air has a different weight from what you're used to; it carries smells you can't quite identify, a faint whiff of wood smoke or diesel fuel, maybe, or the sweetness of something blooming in the trees. The same sun comes up, but looking slightly different from what you know.

Barack's half sister Auma met us at the airport, greeting us both warmly. The two of them had met only a handful of times, beginning six years earlier when Auma had visited Chicago, but they had a close bond. Auma is a year older than Barack. Her mother, Grace Kezia, had been pregnant with Auma when Barack Obama Sr. left Nairobi to study in Hawaii in 1959. (They also had a son, Abongo, who was a toddler at the time.) After he returned to Kenya in the mid-1960s, Barack senior and Kezia went on to have two more children together.

Auma had ebony skin and brilliant white teeth and spoke with a strong British accent. Her smile was enormous and comforting. Arriving in Kenya, I was so tired from the travel I could barely make conversation, but riding into the city in the backseat of Auma's rattletrap Volkswagen Bug, I took note of how the quickness of her smile was just like Barack's, how the curve of her head also resembled his. Auma also clearly had inherited the family brains: She'd been raised in Kenya and returned there often, but she'd gone to college in Germany and was still living there, studying for a PhD. She was fluent in English, German, Swahili, and her family's local language, called Luo. Like us, she was just here for a visit.

Auma had arranged for me and Barack to stay in a friend's empty apartment, a spartan one-bedroom in a nondescript cinder-block building that had been painted bright pink. For the first couple of days, we were so zonked by jet lag it felt as if we were moving at half speed. Or maybe it was just the pace of Nairobi, which ran on an entirely different logic than Chicago did, its roads and British-style roundabouts clogged by a mix of pedestrians, bikers, cars, and *matatus*—the tottering, informal jitney-like buses that could be seen everywhere, painted brightly with murals and tributes to God, their roofs piled high with strapped-on luggage, so crowded that passengers sometimes just rode along, clinging precariously to the exterior.

I was in Africa now. It was heady, draining, and wholly new to me.

Auma's sky-blue VW was so old that it often needed to be pushed in order to get the engine into gear. I'd ill-advisedly bought new white sneakers to wear on the trip, and within a day, after all the pushing we did, they'd turned reddish brown, stained with the cinnamon-hued dust of Nairobi.

Barack was more at home in Nairobi than I was, having been there once before. I moved with the awkwardness of a tourist, aware that we were outsiders, even with our Black skin. People sometimes stared at us on the street. I hadn't been expecting to fit right in, obviously, but I think I arrived there naively believing I'd feel some visceral connection to the continent I'd grown up thinking of as a sort of mythic motherland, as if going there would bestow on me some feeling of completeness. But Africa, of course, owed us nothing. It's a curious thing to realize, the in-betweenness one feels being African American in Africa. It gave me a hard-to-explain feeling of sadness, a sense of being unrooted in both lands.

Days later, I was still feeling dislocated, and we were both nursing sore throats. Barack and I got into a fight—about what exactly, I can't remember. For every bit of awe we felt in Kenya, we were also tired, which led to quibbling, which led finally, for whatever reason, to rage. "I'm so angry at Barack," I wrote in my journal. "I don't think we have anything in common." My thoughts trailed off there. As a measure of my frustration, I drew a long emphatic gash across the rest of the page.

Like any newish couple, we were learning how to fight. We didn't fight often, and when we did, it was typically over petty things, a string of pent-up aggravations that surfaced usually when one or both of us got overly fatigued or stressed. But we did fight. And for better or worse, I tend to yell when I'm angry. When something sets me off, the feeling can be intensely physical, a kind of fireball running up my spine and exploding with such force that I sometimes later don't remember what I said in the moment. Barack, meanwhile, tends to remain cool and rational, his words coming in an eloquent (and therefore irritating) cascade. It's taken us time—years—to understand that this is just how each of us is built, that we are each the sum total of our respective genetic codes as well as everything instilled in us by our parents and their parents before them. Over time, we have figured out how to express and overcome our irritations and occasional rage. When we fight now, it's far less dramatic, often more efficient, and always with our love for each other, no matter how strained, still in sight.

We woke the next morning in Nairobi to blue skies and fresh energy, less zonked by the jet lag and feeling like our happy, regular selves. We met Auma at a downtown train station, and the three of us boarded a passenger train with slatted windows to head west out of the city and toward the Obama family's ancestral home. Sitting by a window in a cabin packed with Kenyans, some of whom were traveling with live chickens in baskets, others with hefty pieces of furniture they'd bought in the city, I was again struck by how strange my girl-from-Chicago, lawyer-at-a-desk life had suddenly become—how this man sitting next to me had shown up at my office one day with his weird name and quixotic smile and brilliantly upended everything. I sat glued to the window as the sprawling community of Kibera, the largest urban slum in Africa, streamed past, showing us its low-slung shanties with corrugated-tin roofs, its muddy roads and open sewers, and a kind of poverty I'd never seen before nor could hardly have imagined.

We were on the train for several hours. Barack finally opened a book, but I continued to stare transfixed out the window as the Nairobi slums gave way to jewel-green countryside and the train rattled north to the town of Kisumu, where Auma, Barack, and I disembarked into the broiling equatorial heat and took a last, jackhammering ride on a *matatu* through the maize fields to their grandmother's village of Kogelo.

I will always remember the deep red clay of the earth in that part of Kenya, so rich it looked almost primordial, how its dust caked the dark skin and hair of the children who shouted greetings to us from the side of the road. I remember being sweaty and thirsty as we walked the last bit of the way to Barack's grandmother's compound, to the well-kept concrete home where she'd lived for years, farming an adjacent vegetable patch and tending several cows. Granny Sarah, they called her. She was a short, wide-built lady with wise eyes and a crinkling smile. She spoke no English, only Luo, and expressed delight that we'd come all this way to see her. Next to her, I felt very tall. She studied me with an extra, bemused curiosity, as if trying to place where I came from and how precisely I'd landed on her doorstep. One of her first questions for me was, "Which one of your parents is white?"

I laughed and explained, with Auma's help, that I was Black through and through, basically as Black as we come in America.

Granny Sarah found this funny. She seemed to find everything funny, teasing Barack for not being able to speak her language. I was bowled over by her easy joy. As evening fell, she butchered us a chicken and made us a stew, which she served with a cornmeal mush called *ugali*. All the while, neighbors and relatives popped in to say hello to the younger Obamas and to congratulate us on our engagement. I gobbled the food gratefully as the sun dropped and night settled over the village, which had no electricity, leaving a bright spray of stars overhead. That I was in this place seemed like a little miracle. I was sharing a rudimentary bedroom with Barack, listening to the stereo sound of crickets in the cornfields all around us, the rustle of animals we couldn't see. I remember feeling awed by the scope of land and sky around me and at the same time snug and protected inside that tiny home. I had a new job, a fiancé, and an expanded family—an approving Kenyan granny, even. It was true: I'd been flung out of my world, and for the moment it was all good.

———

12

B ARACK AND I GOT MARRIED ON A SUNNY OCTOBER Saturday in 1992, the two of us standing before more than three hundred of our friends and family at Trinity United Church of Christ on the South Side. It was a big wedding, and big was how it needed to be. If we were having the wedding in Chicago, there was no trimming the guest list. My roots went too deep. I had not just cousins but also cousins of cousins, and those cousins of cousins had kids, none of whom I'd ever leave out and all of whom made the day more meaningful and merry.

My father's younger siblings were there. My mother's family turned out in its entirety. I had old school friends and neighbors who came, people from Princeton, people from Whitney Young. Mrs. Smith, the wife of my high school assistant principal who still lived down the street from us on Euclid Avenue, helped organize the wedding, while our across-the-street neighbors Mr. and Mrs. Thompson and their jazz band played later that day at our reception. Santita Jackson, ebullient in a black dress with a plunging neckline, was my maid of honor. I'd invited old colleagues from Sidley and new colleagues from city hall. The law partners from Barack's firm were there, as were his old organizer friends.

Barack's rowdy Hawaiian high school guy posse mingled happily with a handful of his Kenyan relatives, who wore brightly colored East African hats. Sadly, we'd lost Gramps—Barack's grandfather—the previous winter to cancer, but his mother and grandmother had made the trip to Chicago, as had Auma and Maya, half sisters from different continents, united in their affection for Barack. It was the first time our two families had met, and the feeling was joyful.

We were surrounded by love—the eclectic, multicultural Obama kind and the anchoring Robinsons-from-the-South-Side kind, all of it now interwoven visibly, pew to pew, inside the church. I held tightly to Craig's elbow as he walked me down the aisle. As we reached the front, I caught my mother's gaze. She was sitting in the first row, looking regal in a floor-length black-and-white sequined dress we'd picked out together, her chin lifted and her eyes proud. We still ached for my father every day, though as he would've wanted, we were also continuing on.

Barack had woken up that morning with a nasty head cold, but it had miraculously cleared as soon as he arrived at the church. He was now smiling at me, bright-eyed, from his place at the altar, dressed in a rented tux and a buffed pair of new shoes. Marriage was still more mysterious to him than it was to me, but in the fourteen months we'd been engaged, he'd been nothing but all in. We'd chosen everything about this day carefully. Barack, having initially declared he was not interested in wedding minutiae, had ended up lovingly, assertively—and predictably—inserting his opinion into everything from the flower arrangements to the canapés that would get served at the South Shore Cultural Center in another hour or so. We'd picked our wedding song, which Santita would sing with her stunning voice, accompanied by a pianist.

It was a Stevie Wonder tune called "You and I (We Can Conquer the World)." I'd first heard it as a kid, in third or fourth grade, when South-side gave me the *Talking Book* album as a gift—my first record album, utterly precious to me. I kept it at his house and was allowed to play it anytime I came to visit. He'd taught me how to care for the vinyl, how to wipe the record's grooves clean of dust, how to lift the needle from the turntable and set it down delicately in the right spot. Usually he'd left me alone with the music, making himself scarce so that I could learn, in privacy, everything that album had to teach, mostly by belting out the lyrics again and again with my little-girl lungs. *Well, in my mind, we can conquer the world / In love you and I, you and I, you and I . . .*

I was nine years old at the time. I knew nothing about love and commitment or conquering the world. All I could do was conjure for myself shimmery ideas about what love might be like and who might come along someday to make me feel that strong. Would it be Michael Jackson? José Cardenal from the Cubs? Someone like my dad? I couldn't even begin to imagine him, really, the person who would become the "you" to my "I."

But now here we were.

Trinity Church had a dynamic and soulful reputation. Barack had first started going there during his days as an organizer, and more recently the two of us had formally become members, following the lead of many of our young, professional African American friends in town. The church's pastor, the Reverend Jeremiah Wright, was known as a sensational preacher with a passion for social justice and was now officiating at our wedding. He welcomed our friends and family and then held up our wedding bands for all to see. He spoke eloquently of what it meant to form a union and have it witnessed by a caring community, these people who collectively knew every dimension of Barack and every dimension of me.

I felt it then—the power of what we were doing, the significance of the ritual—as we stood there with our future still unwritten, with every unknown still utterly unknown, just gripping each other's hands as we said our vows.

Whatever was out there, we'd step into it together. I'd poured myself into planning this day, the elegance of the entire affair had somehow mattered to me, but I understood now that what really mattered, what I'd remember forever, was the grip. It settled me like nothing else ever had. I had faith in this union, faith in this man. To declare it was the easiest thing in the world. Looking at Barack's face, I knew for sure that he felt the same. Neither one of us cried that day. Nobody's voice quavered. If anything, we were a little giddy. From here, we'd gather up all several hundred of our witnesses and roll on over to the reception. We'd eat and drink and dance until we'd exhausted ourselves with our joy.

. . .

OUR HONEYMOON was meant to be restful, a low-key road trip in Northern California, involving wine, sleep, mud baths, and good food. The day after the wedding, we flew to San Francisco, spent several days in Napa, and then drove down Highway 1 to Big Sur to read books, stare at the blue bowl of ocean, and clear our minds. It was glorious, despite the fact that Barack's head cold managed to return in full force, and also despite the mud baths, which we deemed to be unsoothing and kind of icky.

After a busy year, we were more than ready to kick back. Barack had originally planned to spend the months leading up to our wedding finishing his book and working at his new law firm, but he'd ended up putting most of it on an abrupt hold. Sometime early in 1992, he'd been approached by the leaders of a national nonpartisan organization called Project VOTE!, which spearheaded efforts to register new voters in states where minority turnout was traditionally low. They asked if Barack would run the process in Illinois, opening a field office in Chicago to enroll Black voters ahead of the November elections. It was estimated that about 400,000 African Americans in the state were eligible to vote but still unregistered, the majority in and around Chicago.

The pay was abysmal, but the job appealed to Barack's core beliefs. In 1983, a similar voter-registration drive in Chicago had helped propel Harold Washington into office. In 1992, the stakes again felt high: Another African American candidate, Carol Moseley Braun, had surprised everyone by narrowly winning the Democratic nomination for the U.S. Senate race and was locked in what would become a tight race in the general election. Bill Clinton, meanwhile, would be running against George H. W. Bush for president. It was no time for minority voters to be sitting out.

To say that Barack threw himself into the job would be an understatement. The goal of Project VOTE! was to sign up new Illinois voters at a staggering pace of ten thousand per week. The work was similar to what he'd done as a grassroots organizer: Over the course of the spring and summer, he and his staff had tromped through plenty of church basements, gone house to house to talk with unregistered voters. He net-worked regularly with community leaders and made his pitch countless times to wealthy donors, helping to fund the production of radio ads and informational brochures that could be handed out in Black neighbor-hoods and public-housing projects. The organization's message was un-wavering and clear, and a straight reflection of what I knew Barack felt in his heart: There was power in voting. If you wanted change, you couldn't stay home on Election Day.

In the evenings, Barack came home to our place on Euclid Avenue and often flopped on the couch, reeking of the cigarettes he still smoked when he was out of my sight. He appeared tired but never depleted. He kept careful track of the registration tallies: They were averaging an im-pressive seven thousand a week in midsummer but were still falling short of the goal. He strategized about how to get the message across, how to wrangle more volunteers and find pockets of people who remained un-found. He seemed to view the challenges as a Rubik's Cube–like puzzle that could be solved if only he could swivel the right blocks in the right order. The hardest people to reach, he told me, were the younger folks, the eighteen- to thirty-year-olds who seemed to have no faith in govern-ment at all.

I, meanwhile, was fully steeped in government. I'd spent a year now working with Valerie in the mayor's office, acting as a liaison to several of the city's departments, including Health and Human Services. The job was broad and people oriented enough to be energizing and almost always interesting. Whereas I'd once spent my days writing briefs in a quiet, plush-carpeted office with a view of the lake, I now worked in a windowless room on one of the top floors of city hall, with citizens streaming noisily through the building every hour of the day.

Government issues, I was learning, were elaborate and unending. I shuttled between meetings with various department heads, worked with the staffs of city commissioners, and was dispatched sometimes to differ-ent neighborhoods around Chicago to follow up on personal complaints received by the mayor. I went on missions to inspect fallen trees that needed removing, talked to neighborhood pastors who were upset about traffic or garbage collection, and often represented the mayor's office at community functions. I once had to break up a shoving match at a senior citizens' picnic on the North Side. None of this was what a corporate lawyer did, and for this reason I found it compelling. I was experiencing Chicago in a way I never had before.

I was learning something else of value, too, spending much of my time in the presence of Susan Sher and Valerie Jarrett, two women who— I was seeing—managed to be both tremendously confident and tremendously human at the same time. Susan ran meetings with a steely and unflappable grace. Valerie thought nothing of speaking her mind in a roomful of opinionated men, often managing to deftly bring people around to whatever side she was arguing. She was like a fast-moving comet, someone who was clearly going places. Not long before my wedding, she'd been promoted to the role of commissioner in charge of planning and economic development for the city and had offered me a job as an assistant commissioner. I was going to begin work as soon as we got back from our honeymoon.

I saw more of Valerie than I did of Susan, but I took careful note of everything each of them did, similarly to how I'd observed Czerny, my college mentor. These were women who knew their own voices and were unafraid to use them. They could be humorous and humble when the moment called for it, but they were unfazed by blowhards and didn't second-guess the power in their own points of view. Also, importantly, they were working moms. I watched them closely in this regard as well, knowing that I wanted someday to be one myself. Valerie never hesitated to step out of a big meeting when a call came in from her daughter's school. Susan, likewise, dashed out in the middle of the day if one of her sons spiked a fever or was performing in a preschool music show. They were unapologetic about prioritizing the needs of their children, even if it meant occasionally disrupting the flow at work, and didn't try to compartmentalize work and home the way I'd noticed male partners at Sidley seemed to do. I'm not sure compartmentalization was even a choice for Valerie and Susan, given that they were juggling the expectations unique to mothers and were also both divorced, which came with its own emotional and financial challenges. They weren't striving for perfect, but managed somehow to be always excellent, the two of them bound in a deep and mutually helpful friendship, which also made a real impression on me. They'd dropped any masquerade and were just wonderfully, powerfully, and instructively themselves.

B ARACK AND I came back from our honeymoon in Northern California to both good and bad news. The good news came in the form of the November election, which brought what felt like a tide of encouraging change. Bill Clinton won overwhelmingly in Illinois and across the country, moving President Bush out of office after only one term. Carol Moseley Braun also won decisively, becoming the first African American woman ever to hold a Senate seat. What was even more exciting to Barack was that the Election Day turnout had been nothing short of epic: Project VOTE! had directly registered 110,000 new voters, and its broader get-out-the-vote campaign had likely boosted overall turnout as well.

For the first time in a decade, over half a million Black voters in Chicago went to the polls, proving that they had the collective power to shape political outcomes. This sent a clear message to lawmakers and future politicians and reestablished a feeling that seemed to have been lost when Harold Washington died: The African American vote mattered. It would be costly politically for anyone to ignore or discount Black people's needs and concerns. Inside of this, too, was a secondary message to the Black community itself, a reminder that progress was possible, that our worth was measurable. All this was heartening for Barack. As tiring as it was, he'd loved his job for what it taught him about Chicago's complex political system and for proving that his organizing instincts could work on a larger scale. He'd collaborated with grassroots leaders, everyday citizens, and elected officials, and almost miraculously it had yielded results. Several media outlets noted the impressive impact of Project VOTE! A writer for *Chicago* magazine described Barack as "a tall, affable workaholic," suggesting that he should someday run for office, an idea that he simply shrugged off.

And here was the bad news: That tall, affable workaholic I'd just married had also blown his book deadline, having been so caught up in registering voters that he'd managed to turn in only a partial manuscript.

We got home from California to learn that the publisher had canceled his contract, sending word through his literary agent that Barack was now on the hook to pay back his $40,000 advance.

If he panicked, he didn't do it in front of me. I was busy enough shifting into my new role at city hall, which entailed going to more zoning board meetings and fewer senior citizen picnics than my previous job had. Though I was no longer working corporate-lawyer hours, the city's everyday fracas left me spent in the evenings, less interested in processing any stresses at home and more ready to pour a glass of wine, switch my brain off, and watch TV on the couch. If I'd learned anything from Barack's obsessive involvement with Project VOTE!, anyway, it was that it wasn't helpful for me to worry about his worries—in part because I seemed to find them more overwhelming than he ever did. Chaos agitated me, but it seemed to invigorate Barack. He was like a circus performer who liked to set plates spinning: If things got too calm, he took it as a sign that there was more to do. He was a serial over-committer, I was coming to understand, taking on new projects without much regard for limits of time and energy. He'd said yes, for example, to serving on the boards of a couple of nonprofits while also saying yes to a part-time teaching job at the University of Chicago for the coming spring semester while also planning to work full-time at the law firm.

And then there was the book. Barack's agent felt sure she could resell the idea to a different publisher, though he'd have to get a draft finished soon. With his teaching gig yet to begin and having obtained the blessing of the law firm that had waited a year already for him to start full-time, he came up with a solution that seemed to suit him perfectly: He'd write the book in isolation, removing his everyday distractions by renting a little cabin somewhere and drilling down hard on the work. It was the equivalent of pulling a frantic all-nighter to get a paper done in college, only Barack was estimating it would take him roughly a couple of months to get the book finished. He relayed all of this to me one night at home about six weeks after our wedding, before delicately dropping a final bit of information: His mother had found him the perfect cabin. In fact, she'd already rented it for him. It was cheap, quiet, and on the beach. In Sanur. Which was on the Indonesian island of Bali, some nine thousand miles away from me.

I T SOUNDS A little like a bad joke, doesn't it? What happens when a solitude-loving individualist marries an outgoing family woman who does not love solitude one bit?

The answer, I'm guessing, is probably the best and most sustaining answer to nearly every question arising inside a marriage, no matter who you are or what the issue is: You find ways to adapt. If you're in it forever, there's really no choice.

Which is to say that at the start of 1993, Barack flew to Bali and spent about five weeks living alone with his thoughts while working on a draft of his book *Dreams from My Father*, filling yellow legal pads with his fastidious handwriting, distilling his ideas during languid daily walks amid the coconut palms and lapping tide. I, meanwhile, stayed home on Euclid Avenue, living upstairs from my mother as another leaden Chicago winter descended, shellacking the trees and sidewalks with ice. I kept myself busy, seeing friends and hitting workout classes in the evenings. In my regular interactions at work or around town, I'd find myself casually uttering this strange new term—"my husband." *My husband and I are hoping to buy a home. My husband is a writer finishing a book.* It was foreign and delightful and conjured memories of a man who simply wasn't there. I missed Barack terribly, but I rationalized our situation as I could, understanding that even if we were newlyweds, this interlude was probably for the best.

He had taken the chaos of his unfinished book and shipped himself out to do battle with it. Possibly this was out of kindness to me, a bid to keep the chaos out of my view. I'd married an outside-the-box thinker, I had to remind myself. He was handling his business in what struck him as the most sensible and efficient manner, even if outwardly it appeared to be a beach vacation—a honeymoon with himself (I couldn't help but think in my lonelier moments) to follow his honeymoon with me.

You and I, you and I, you and I. We were learning to adapt, to knit ourselves into a solid and forever form of *us*. Even if we were the same two people we'd always been, the same couple we'd been for years, we now had new labels, a second set of identities to wrangle. He was my husband. I was his wife. We'd stood up at church and said it out loud, to each other and to the world. It did feel as if we owed each other new things.

For many women, including myself, "wife" can feel like a loaded word. It carries a history. If you grew up in the 1960s and 1970s as I did, wives seemed to be a genus of white women who lived inside television sitcoms—cheery, coiffed, corseted. They stayed at home, fussed over the children, and had dinner ready on the stove. They sometimes got into the sherry or flirted with the vacuum-cleaner salesman, but the excitement seemed to end there. The irony, of course, was that I used to watch those shows in our living room on Euclid Avenue while my own stay-at-home mom fixed dinner without complaint and my own clean-cut dad recovered from a day at work. My parents' arrangement was as traditional as anything we saw on TV. Barack sometimes jokes, in fact, that my upbringing was like a Black version of *Leave It to Beaver,* with the South Shore Robinsons as steady and fresh-faced as the Cleaver family of Mayfield, U.S.A., though of course we were a poorer version of the Cleavers, with my dad's blue city worker's uniform subbing for Mr. Cleaver's suit. Barack makes this comparison with a touch of envy, because his own childhood was so different, but also as a way to push back on the entrenched stereotype that African Americans primarily live in broken homes, that our families are somehow incapable of living out the same stable, middle-class dream as our white neighbors.

Personally, as a kid, I preferred *The Mary Tyler Moore Show,* which I absorbed with fascination. Mary had a job, a snappy wardrobe, and really great hair. She was independent and funny, and unlike those of the other ladies on TV, her problems were interesting. She had conversations that weren't about children or homemaking. She didn't let Lou Grant boss her around, and she wasn't fixated on finding a husband. She was youthful and at the same time grown-up. In the pre-pre-pre-internet landscape, when the world came packaged almost exclusively through three channels of network TV, this stuff mattered. If you were a girl with a brain and a dawning sense that you wanted to grow into something more than a wife, Mary Tyler Moore was your goddess.

And here I was now, twenty-nine years old, sitting in the very same apartment where I'd watched all that TV and consumed all those meals dished up by the patient and selfless Marian Robinson. I had so much—an education, a healthy sense of self, a deep arsenal of ambition—and I was wise enough to credit my mother, in particular, with instilling it in me. She'd taught me how to read before I started kindergarten, helping me sound out words as I sat curled like a kitten in her lap, studying a library copy of *Dick and Jane*. She'd cooked for us with care, putting broccoli and Brussels sprouts on our plates and requiring that we eat them. She'd hand sewn my prom dress, for God's sake. The point was, she'd given diligently and she'd given everything. She'd let our family define her. I was old enough now to realize that all the hours she gave to me and Craig were hours she didn't spend on herself.

My considerable blessings in life were now causing a kind of psychic whiplash. I'd been raised to be confident and see no limits, to believe I could go after and get absolutely anything I wanted. And I wanted everything. Because, as Suzanne would say, *why not?* I wanted to live with the hat-tossing, independent-career-woman zest of Mary Tyler Moore, and at the same time I gravitated toward the stabilizing, self-sacrificing, seemingly bland normalcy of being a wife and mother. I wanted to have a work life and a home life, but with some promise that one would never fully squelch the other. I hoped to be exactly like my own mother and at the same time nothing like her at all. It was an odd and confounding thing to ponder. Could I have everything? Would I have everything? I had no idea.

Barack, meanwhile, came home from Bali looking tanned and carrying a satchel stuffed with legal pads, having converted his isolation into a literary victory. The book was basically finished. Within a matter of months, his agent had resold it to a new publisher, paying off his debt and securing a plan for publication. More important to me was the fact that within a matter of hours we'd returned to the easy rhythm of our newlywed life. Barack was here, done with his solitude, landed back in my world. *My husband.* He was smiling at the jokes I made, wanting to hear about my day, kissing me to sleep at night.

As the months went by, we cooked, worked, laughed, and planned. Later that spring, we had our finances in order enough to buy a condo, moving out of 7436 South Euclid Avenue and into a pretty, railroad-style apartment in Hyde Park with hardwood floors and a tiled fireplace, a new launchpad for our life. With Barack's encouragement, I took another risk and switched jobs again, this time saying good-bye to Valerie and Susan at city hall in order to finally explore the kind of nonprofit work that had always intrigued me, finding a leadership role that would give me a chance to grow. There was still plenty I hadn't figured out about my life— the riddle of how to be both a Mary and a Marian remained unsolved— but for now all those deeper questions drifted out to the margins of my mind, where they'd sit dormant and unattended for the time being. Any worries could wait, I figured, because we were an *us* now, and we were happy. And happy seemed like a starting place for everything.

M Y NEW JOB MADE ME NERVOUS. I'D BEEN HIRED TO be the executive director for the brand-new Chicago chapter of an organization called Public Allies, which itself was basically brand-new. It was something like a start-up inside a start-up, and in a field in which I had no professional experience to speak of. Public Allies had been founded only a year earlier in Washington, D.C., and was the brain-child of Vanessa Kirsch and Katrina Browne, who were both just out of college and interested in helping more people find their way into careers in public service and nonprofit work. Barack had met the two of them at a conference and become a member of their board, eventually suggesting they get in touch with me regarding the job.

The model was similar to what was being used at Teach for America, which itself was relatively new at the time: Public Allies recruited talented young people, gave them intensive training and committed mentorship, and placed them in paid ten-month apprentice positions inside commu-nity organizations and public agencies, the hope being that they'd flour-ish and contribute in meaningful ways. The broader aim was that these opportunities would give the recruits—Allies, we called them—both the experience and the drive to continue working in the nonprofit or public sector for years to come, thereby helping to build a new generation of community leaders.

For me, the idea resonated in a big way. I still remembered how during my senior year at Princeton so many of us had marched into MCAT and LSAT exams or suited up to interview for corporate training programs without once (at least in my case) considering or maybe even realizing that a wealth of more civic-minded job options existed. Public Allies was meant as a corrective to this, a means of widening the horizon for young people thinking about careers. But what I especially liked was that its founders were focused less on parachuting Ivy Leaguers into urban communities and more on finding and cultivating talent that was already there. You didn't need a college degree to become an Ally. You needed only a high school diploma or GED, to be older than seventeen and younger than thirty, and to have shown some leadership capability, even if thus far in life it had gone largely untapped.

Public Allies was all about promise—finding it, nurturing it, and putting it to use. It was a mandate to seek out young people whose best qualities might otherwise be overlooked and to give them a chance to do something meaningful. To me, the job felt almost like destiny. For every moment I'd spent looking wistfully at the South Side from my forty-seventh-floor window at Sidley, here was an invitation, finally, to use what I knew. I had a sense of how much latent promise sat undiscovered in neighborhoods like my own, and I was pretty sure I'd know how to find it.

As I contemplated the new job, my mind often traveled back to childhood, and in particular to the month or so I'd spent in the pencil-flying pandemonium of that second-grade class at Bryn Mawr Elementary, before my mother had the wherewithal to have me plucked out. In the moment, I'd felt nothing but relieved by my own good fortune. But as my luck in life seemed only to snowball from there, I thought more about the twenty or so kids who'd been marooned in that classroom, stuck with an uncaring and unmotivated teacher. I knew I was no smarter than any of them. I just had the advantage of an advocate. I thought about this more often now that I was an adult, especially when people applauded me for my achievements, as if there weren't a strange and cruel randomness to it all. Through no fault of their own, those second graders had lost a year of learning. I'd seen enough at this point to understand how quickly even small deficits can snowball, too.

Back in Washington, D.C., the Public Allies founders had mustered a fledgling class of fifteen Allies who were working in various organizations around the city. They'd also raised enough money to launch a new chapter in Chicago, becoming one of the first organizations to receive federal funding through the AmeriCorps service program created under President Clinton. Which is where I came into the picture, thrilled and anxious in equal parts. Negotiating the terms of the job, though, I'd had what maybe should have been an obvious revelation about nonprofit work: It doesn't pay. I was initially offered a salary so small, so far below what I was making working for the city of Chicago, which was already half of what I'd been earning as a lawyer, that I literally couldn't afford to say yes. Which led to a second revelation about certain nonprofits, especially young-person-driven start-ups like Public Allies, and many of the bighearted, tirelessly passionate people who work in them: Unlike me, it seemed they could actually afford to be there, their virtue discreetly underwritten by privilege, whether it was that they didn't have student loans to pay off or perhaps had an inheritance to someday look forward to and thus weren't worried about saving for the future.

It became clear that if I wanted to join the tribe, I'd have to negotiate my way in, asking for exactly what I needed in terms of salary, which was significantly more than Public Allies had expected to pay. This was simply my reality. I couldn't be shy or embarrassed about my needs. I still had roughly $600 of student debt to pay off each month on top of my regular expenses, and I was married to a man with his own load of law school loans to cover. The organization's leaders were almost disbelieving when I informed them how much I'd borrowed in order to get through school and what that translated to in terms of monthly debt, but they gamely went out and secured new funding that enabled me to come on board.

And with that, I was off and running, eager to make good on the opportunity I'd been handed. This was my first chance ever, really, to build something basically from the ground up: Success or failure would depend almost entirely on my efforts, not those of my boss or anyone else. I spent the spring of 1993 working furiously to set up an office and hire a small staff so that we could have a class of Allies in place by the fall. We'd found cheap office space in a building on Michigan Avenue and managed to get a load of donated secondhand chairs and tables from a corporate consulting firm that was redecorating its offices.

Meanwhile, I leveraged more or less every connection Barack and I'd ever made in Chicago, seeking donors and people who could help us secure longer-term foundation support, not to mention anyone in the public service field who'd be willing to host an Ally in their organization for the coming year. Valerie Jarrett helped me arrange placements in the mayor's office and the city health department, where Allies would work on a neighborhood-based childhood immunization project. Barack activated his network of community organizers to connect us with legal aid, advocacy, and teaching opportunities. Various Sidley partners wrote checks and helped introduce me to key donors.

The most exciting part for me was finding the Allies themselves. With help from the national organization, we advertised for applicants on college campuses across the country while also looking for talent closer to home. My team and I visited community colleges and some of the big urban high schools around Chicago. We knocked on doors in the Cabrini-Green housing project, went to community meetings, and canvassed programs that worked with single mothers. We quizzed everyone we met, from pastors to professors to the manager of the neighborhood McDonald's, asking them to identify the most interesting young people they knew. Who were the leaders? Who was ready for something bigger than what he or she had? These were the people we wanted to encourage to apply, urging them to forget for a minute whatever obstacles normally made such things impossible, promising that as an organization we'd do what we could—whether it was supplying a bus pass or a stipend for child care—to help cover their needs.

By fall, we had a cohort of twenty-seven Allies working all over Chicago, holding internships everywhere from city hall to a South Side community assistance agency to Latino Youth, an alternative high school in

Pilsen. The Allies together were an eclectic, spirited group, loaded with idealism and aspirations and representing a broad swath of backgrounds. Among them we had a former gang member, a Latina woman who'd grown up in the southwest part of Chicago and had gone to Harvard, another woman in her early twenties who lived in the Robert Taylor Homes and was raising a child while also trying to save money for college, and a twenty-six-year-old from Grand Boulevard who'd left high school but had kept up his education with library books and later gone back to earn his diploma.

Each Friday, the whole group of Allies gathered at one of our host agency's offices, taking a full day to debrief, connect, and go through a series of professional development workshops. I loved these days more than anything. I loved how the room got noisy as the Allies piled in, dumping their backpacks in the corner and peeling off layers of winter wear as they settled into a circle. I loved helping them sort through their issues, whether it was mastering Excel, figuring out how to dress for an office job, or finding the courage to voice their ideas in a roomful of better-educated, more confident people. I sometimes had to give an Ally less-than-pleasant feedback. If I'd heard reports of Allies being late to work or not taking their duties seriously, I was stern in letting them know that we expected better. When Allies grew frustrated with poorly organized community meetings or problematic clients at their agencies, I counseled them to keep perspective, reminding them of their own relative good fortune.

Above all, though, we celebrated each new bit of learning or progress. And there was lots of it. Not all the Allies would go on to work in the nonprofit or public sectors and not everyone would manage to overcome the hurdles of coming from a less privileged background, but I've been amazed over time to see how many of our recruits did, in fact, succeed and commit themselves long term to serving a larger public good. Some became Public Allies staff themselves; some are now even leaders in government agencies and inside national nonprofit organizations. Twenty-five years after its inception, Public Allies is still going strong, with chapters in Chicago and two dozen other cities and thousands of alumni around the country. To know that I played some small part in that, helping to create something that's endured, is one of the most gratifying feelings I've had in my professional life.

I tended to Public Allies with the half-exhausted pride of a new parent. I went to sleep each night thinking about what still needed to be done and opened my eyes every morning with my mental checklists for the day, the week, and the month ahead already made. After graduating our first class of twenty-seven Allies in the spring, we welcomed a new set of forty in the fall and continued to grow from there. In hindsight, I think of it as the best job I ever had, for how wonderfully on the edge I felt while I was doing it and for how even a small victory—whether it was finding a good placement for a native Spanish speaker or sorting through someone's fears about working in an unfamiliar neighborhood—had to be thoroughly earned.

For the first time in my life, really, I felt I was doing something immediately meaningful, directly impacting the lives of others while also staying connected to both my city and my culture. It gave me a better understanding, too, of how Barack had felt when he'd worked as an organizer or on Project VOTE!, caught up in the all-consuming primacy of an uphill battle—the only kind of battle Barack loved, the kind he would always love—knowing how it can drain you while at the same time giving you everything you'll ever need.

WHILE I WAS focused on Public Allies, Barack had settled into what was—by his standard, anyway—a period of relative tameness and predictability. He was teaching a class on racism and the law at the University of Chicago Law School and working by day at his law firm, mostly on cases involving voting rights and employment discrimination. He still sometimes ran community-organizing workshops as well, leading a couple of Friday sessions with my cohort at Public Allies. Outwardly, it seemed like a perfect existence for an intellectual, civic-minded guy in his thirties who'd flatly turned down any number of more lucrative and prestigious options in favor of his principles. He'd done it, as far as I was concerned. He'd found a noble balance. He was a lawyer, a teacher, and also an organizer. And he was soon to be a published author, too.

After returning from Bali, Barack had spent more than a year writing a second draft of his book during the hours he wasn't at one of his jobs. He worked late at night in a small room we'd converted to a study at the rear of our apartment—a crowded, book-strewn bunker I referred to lovingly as the Hole. I'd sometimes go in, stepping over his piles of paper to sit on the ottoman in front of his chair while he worked, trying to lasso him with a joke and a smile, to tease him back from whatever far-off fields he'd been galloping through. He was good-humored about my intrusions, but only if I didn't stay too long.

Barack, I've come to understand, is the sort of person who needs a hole, a closed-off little warren where he can read and write undisturbed. It's like a hatch that opens directly onto the spacious skies of his brain. Time spent there seems to fuel him. In deference to this, we've managed to create some version of a hole inside every home we've ever lived in— any quiet corner or alcove will do. To this day, when we arrive at a rental house in Hawaii or on Martha's Vineyard, Barack goes off looking for an empty room that can serve as the vacation hole. There, he can flip between the six or seven books he's reading simultaneously and toss his newspapers on the floor. For him, the Hole is a kind of sacred high place, where insights are birthed and clarity comes to visit. For me, it's an off-putting and disorderly mess. One requirement has always been that the Hole, wherever it is, have a door so that I can shut it. For obvious reasons.

Dreams from My Father was published, finally, in the summer of 1995. It got good reviews yet sold only modestly, but that was okay. The important thing was that Barack had managed to process his life story, snapping together the disparate pieces of his Afro-Kansan-Indonesian-Hawaiian-Chicagoan identity, writing himself into a sort of wholeness this way. I was proud of him. Through the narrative, he'd made a kind of literary peace with his phantom father. The work to get there had been one-sided, of course, with Barack alone trying to fill every gap and understand every mystery the senior Obama had ever created. But this was also in keeping with how he'd always done it anyway. Since the time he was a boy, I realized, he'd tried to carry everything all on his own.

· · ·

WITH THE BOOK FINISHED, there was new space in his life, and—also in keeping with who he'd always been—Barack felt compelled to fill it immediately. On the personal side, he'd been coping with difficult news: His mother, Ann, had been diagnosed with ovarian cancer and had moved from Jakarta back to Honolulu for treatment. As far as we knew, she was getting good medical care, and the chemotherapy seemed to be working. Both Maya and Toot were helping look after her in Hawaii, and Barack checked in often. But her diagnosis had come late, after the cancer had advanced, and it was difficult to know what would happen. I knew this weighed heavily on Barack's mind.

In Chicago, meanwhile, the political chatter was starting to kick up again. Mayor Daley had been elected to a third term in the spring of 1995, and now everyone was gearing up for the 1996 election, in which Illinois would select a new U.S. senator and President Clinton would make his bid for a second term. More scandalously, we had a sitting U.S. congressman under investigation for sex crimes, leaving an opening for a new Democratic contender in the state's Second District, which included much of Chicago's South Side. A popular state senator named Alice Palmer, who represented Hyde Park and South Shore and whom Barack had gotten to know while working on Project VOTE!, had begun saying privately that she intended to run for it. Which, in turn, would leave her state senate seat vacant, opening up the possibility that Barack could run for it.

Was he interested? Would he run?

I couldn't have known it then, but these questions would come to dominate the next decade of our lives, pulsing like a drumbeat behind almost everything we did. *Would he? Could he? Was he? Should he?* But ahead of these always came another question, posed by Barack himself, preliminary and supposedly preemptive when it came to running for office of any sort. The first time he asked it was on the day he'd let me know about Alice Palmer and her open seat and this notion he had that maybe he could be not just a lawyer/professor/organizer/author but all those things plus a state legislator as well: "What do you think about it, Miche?"

For me, the answer was never actually all that tough to come up with.

I didn't think it was a great idea for Barack to run for office. My specific reasoning might have varied slightly each time the question came back around, but my larger stance would hold, like a sequoia rooted in the ground, though clearly you can see that it stopped absolutely nothing.

In the case of the Illinois senate in 1996, my reasoning went like this: I didn't much appreciate politicians and therefore didn't relish the idea of my husband becoming one. Most of what I knew about state politics came from what I read in the newspaper, and none of it seemed especially good or productive. My friendship with Santita Jackson had given me a sense that politicians were often required to be away from home. In general, I thought of lawmakers almost like armored tortoises, leather-skinned, slow moving, thick with self-interest. Barack was too earnest, too full of valiant plans, in my opinion, to abide by the hardscrabble, drag-it-out rancor that went on inside the domed capitol downstate in Springfield.

In my heart, I just believed there were better ways for a good person to have an impact. Quite honestly, I thought he'd get eaten alive.

Already, however, there was a counterargument brewing in the recesses of my own conscience. If Barack believed he could do something in politics, who was I to get in his way? Who was I to stomp on the idea before he'd even tried it? After all, he was the lone person who had waved me forward when I wanted to leave my law career, who'd had his concerns about my going to city hall but supported me nonetheless, and who right now was working multiple jobs, partly to compensate for the pay cut I'd taken to become a full-time do-gooder at Public Allies. In our six years together, he hadn't once doubted my instincts or my capabilities. The refrain had always been the same: *Don't worry. You can do this. We'll figure it out.*

And so I gave my approval to his first run for office, larding it with a bit of wifely caution. "I think you'll be frustrated," I warned. "If you end up getting elected, you're gonna go down there and nothing will get accomplished, no matter how hard you try. It'll drive you crazy."

"Maybe," Barack said, with a bemused shrug. "But maybe I can do some good. Who knows?"

"That's right," I said, shrugging back. It wasn't my job to interfere with his optimism. "Who knows?"

. . .

THIS WON'T BE news to anyone, but my husband did become a politician. He was a good person who wanted to have an impact in the world, and despite my skepticism he decided this was the best way to go about it. Such is the nature of his faith.

Barack was elected to the Illinois senate in November 1996 and sworn in two months later, at the start of the following year. To my surprise, I'd enjoyed watching the campaign unfold. I'd helped collect signatures to put him on the ballot, knocking on doors in my old neighborhood on Saturdays, listening to what residents had to say about the state and its government, all the things they thought needed fixing. For me, it was reminiscent of the weekends I'd spent as a child trailing my dad as he climbed up all those porch steps, going about his duties as a precinct captain. Beyond this, I wasn't much needed, and that suited me perfectly. I could treat campaigning like a hobby, picking it up when it was convenient, having some fun with it, and then getting back to my own work.

Barack's mother had passed away in Honolulu shortly after he announced his candidacy. Her decline had been so swift that he hadn't made it there to say good-bye. This crushed him. It was Ann Dunham who'd introduced him to the richness of literature and the power of a well-reasoned argument. Without her, he wouldn't have felt the monsoon downpours in Jakarta or seen the water temples of Bali. He might never have learned to appreciate how easy and thrilling it was to jump from one continent to another, or how to embrace the unfamiliar. She was an explorer, an intrepid follower of her own heart. I saw her spirit in Barack in big and small ways. The pain of losing her sat lodged like a blade in both of us, right alongside the blade that had been embedded when we'd lost my dad.

Now that it was winter and the legislature was in session, we were separated for a good part of every week. Barack drove four hours to Springfield on Monday nights and checked into a cheap hotel where a lot of the other legislators stayed, usually returning late on Thursday. He had a small office in the statehouse and a part-time staffer in Chicago. He'd scaled back his work at the law firm but as a way of keeping pace with our debts, he'd added more courses to his teaching load at the law school, scheduling classes for days he wasn't in Springfield and teaching more when the senate wasn't in session. We spoke on the phone every night he was downstate, comparing notes and swapping tales about our respective days. On Fridays, back in Chicago, we had a standing date night, usually meeting downtown at a restaurant called Zinfandel after we'd both finished up work.

I remember these nights with a deep fondness now, for the low, warm lights of the restaurant and how it had become predictable that with my devotion to punctuality I'd always be the first to show up. I'd wait for Barack, and because it was the end of the workweek, and because I was accustomed to it at this point, it didn't bother me that he was late. I knew he'd get there eventually and that my heart would leap as it always did, seeing him walk through the door and hand his winter coat off to the hostess before threading his way through the tables, grinning when his eyes finally landed on mine. He'd kiss me and then take off his suit jacket, draping it on the back of his chair before sitting down. *My husband.* The routine settled me. We ordered the same thing pretty much every Friday—pot roast, Brussels sprouts, and mashed potatoes—and when it came, we ate every bite.

This was a golden time for us, for the balance of our marriage, him with his purpose and me with mine. During a single, early week of senate business in Springfield, Barack had introduced seventeen new bills—possibly a record, and at the very least a measure of his eagerness to get something done. Some would ultimately pass, but most would get quickly picked off in the Republican-controlled chamber, downed by partisanship and a cynicism passed off as practicality among his new colleagues. I saw in those early months how, just as I'd predicted, politics would be a fight, and the fight would be wearying, involving standoffs and betrayals, dirty-deal makers and compromises that sometimes felt painful. But I saw, too, that Barack's own forecast had been correct as well. He was strangely suited to the tussle of lawmaking, calm inside the maelstrom, accustomed to being an outsider, taking defeats in his easy Hawaiian stride. He stayed hopeful, insistently so, convinced that some part of his vision would someday, somehow, manage to prevail.

He was getting battered already, but it wasn't bothering him. It did seem he was built for this. He'd get dinged up and stay shiny, like an old copper pot.

I, too, was in the midst of a transition. I'd taken a new job, surprising myself somewhat by deciding to leave Public Allies, the organization I'd put together and grown with such care. For three years, I'd given myself to it with zeal, taking responsibility for the largest and the smallest of operational tasks, right down to restocking paper in the photocopier. With Public Allies thriving, and its longevity all but assured thanks to multiyear federal grants and foundation support, I felt that I could now step away in good faith. And it just so happened that in the fall of 1996 a new opportunity had cropped up almost out of nowhere. Art Sussman, the lawyer at the University of Chicago who'd met with me a few years earlier, called to let me know about a position that had just been created there.

The school was looking for an associate dean to focus on community relations, committing at long last to do a better job of integrating with the city, and most especially the South Side neighborhood that surrounded it, including through the creation of a community service program to connect students to volunteer opportunities in the neighborhood. Like the position at Public Allies, this new job spoke to a reality I'd lived personally. As I'd told Art years earlier, the University of Chicago had always felt less attainable and less interested in me than the fancy East Coast schools I'd ultimately attended, a place with its back turned to the neighborhood. The chance to try to lower those walls, to get more students involved with the city and more city residents with the university, was one I found inspiring.

All inspiration aside, there were underlying reasons for making the transition. The university offered the kind of institutional stability that a still-newish nonprofit could not. My pay was better, my hours would be more reasonable, and there were other people designated to keep paper in the copier and fix the laser printer when it broke. I was thirty-two years old now and starting to think more about what kind of load I wanted to carry. On our date nights at Zinfandel, Barack and I often continued a conversation we'd been having in one form or another for years—about impact, about how and where each one of us could make a difference, how best to apportion our time and energy.

For me, some of the old questions about who I was and what I wanted to be in life were starting to drift in again, fixing themselves at the forefront of my mind. I'd taken the new job in part to create a little more room in our life, and also because the health-care benefits were better than anything I'd ever had. And this would end up being important. As Barack and I sat holding hands across the table in the candle glow of another Friday night at Zinfandel, with the pot roast polished off and dessert on its way, there was one big wrinkle in our happiness. We were trying to get pregnant and it wasn't going well.

I T TURNS OUT that even two committed go-getters with a deep love and a robust work ethic can't will themselves into being pregnant. Fertility is not something you conquer. Rather maddeningly, there's no straight line between effort and reward. For me and Barack, this was as surprising as it was disappointing. No matter how hard we tried, we couldn't seem to come up with a pregnancy. For a while, I told myself it was simply an issue of access, the result of Barack's comings and goings from Springfield. Our attempts at procreation took place not in service of important monthly hormonal markers but rather in concert with the Illinois legislative schedule. This, I figured, was one thing we could try to fix.

But our adjustments didn't work, even with Barack flooring it up the interstate after a late vote so that he could hit my ovulation window and even after the senate went into its summer recess and he was home and available full-time. After many years of taking careful precautions to avoid pregnancy, I was now singularly dedicated to the opposite endeavor. I treated it like a mission. We had one pregnancy test come back positive, which caused us both to forget every worry and swoon with joy, but a couple of weeks later I had a miscarriage, which left me physically uncomfortable and cratered any optimism we'd felt. Seeing women and their children walking happily along a street, I'd feel a pang of longing followed by a bruising wallop of inadequacy. The only comfort was that Barack and I were living only about a block from Craig and his wife, who now had two beautiful children, Leslie and Avery. I found solace in dropping by to play and read stories with them.

If I were to start a file on things nobody tells you about until you're right in the thick of them, I might begin with miscarriages. A miscarriage is lonely, painful, and demoralizing almost on a cellular level. When you have one, you will likely mistake it for a personal failure, which it is not. Or a tragedy, which, regardless of how utterly devastating it feels in the moment, it also is not. What nobody tells you is that miscarriage happens all the time, to more women than you'd ever guess, given the relative silence around it. I learned this only after I mentioned that I'd miscarried to a couple of friends, who responded by heaping me with love and support and also their own miscarriage stories. It didn't take away the pain, but in unburying their own struggles, they steadied me during mine, helping me see that what I'd been through was no more than a normal biological hiccup, a fertilized egg that, for what was probably a very good reason, had needed to bail out.

One of these friends also steered me toward a fertility doctor whom she and her husband had used. Barack and I went in for exams, and when we later sat down with the doctor, he told us there was no discernible issue with either of us. The mystery of why we weren't getting pregnant would remain just that. He suggested that I try taking Clomid, a drug meant to stimulate egg production, for a couple of months. When that didn't work, he recommended we move to in vitro fertilization. We were inordinately lucky that my university health insurance would cover most of the bill.

It felt like having a high-stakes lottery ticket, only with science involved. By the time the preliminary medical work was finished, rather unfortunately, the state legislature had returned to its fall session, swallowing up my sweet, attentive husband and leaving me largely on my own to manipulate my reproductive system into peak efficiency. This would involve giving myself a regimen of daily shots over the course of several weeks. The plan was I'd administer first one drug to suppress my ovaries and then later a new drug to stimulate them, the idea being that they'd then produce a cascade of viable eggs.

All the work and uncertainty involved made me anxious, but I wanted a baby. It was a need that had been there forever. As a girl, when I'd grown tired of kissing the vinyl skin of my baby dolls, I'd begged my mother to have another baby, a real one, just for me. I promised I'd do all the work. When she wouldn't go along with the plan, I'd hunted through her underwear drawer, searching for her birth control pills, figuring that if I confiscated them, maybe it would yield some results. It didn't, obviously, but the point is I'd been waiting a long time for this. I wanted a family and Barack wanted a family, too, and now here I was alone in the bathroom of our apartment, trying, in the name of all that want, to screw up the courage to plunge a syringe into my thigh.

It was maybe then that I felt a first flicker of resentment involving politics and Barack's unshakable commitment to the work. Or maybe I was just feeling the acute burden of being female. Either way, he was gone and I was here, carrying the responsibility. I sensed already that the sacrifices would be more mine than his. In the weeks to come, he'd go about his regular business while I went in for daily ultrasounds to monitor my eggs. He wouldn't have his blood drawn. He wouldn't have to cancel any meetings to have a cervix inspection. He was doting and invested, my husband, doing what he could do. He read all the IVF literature and would talk to me all night about it, but his only actual duty was to show up at the doctor's office and provide some sperm. And then, if he chose, he could go have a martini afterward. None of this was his fault, but it wasn't equal, either, and for any woman who lives by the mantra that equality is important, this can be a little confusing. It was me who'd alter everything, putting my passions and career dreams on hold, to fulfill this piece of our dream. I found myself in a small moment of reckoning. Did I want it? Yes, I wanted it so much. And with this, I hoisted the needle and sank it into my flesh.

ABOUT EIGHT WEEKS LATER, I heard a sound that erased all traces of resentment: a swishing, watery heartbeat picked up on ultrasound, emanating from the warm cave of my body. We were pregnant. It was for real. Suddenly the responsibility and relative sacrifice meant something completely different, like a landscape taking on new colors, or all the furniture in a house being rearranged so that now everything appeared perfectly in place. I walked around with a secret inside me. This was my privilege, the gift of being female. I felt bright with the promise of what I carried.

I would feel this way right through, even as first-trimester fatigue left me drained, as my job stayed busy and Barack continued making his weekly treks to the state capital. We had our outward lives, but now there was something inward happening, a baby growing, a tiny girl. (Because Barack's a fact guy and I'm a planner, finding out her gender was obligatory.) We couldn't see her, but she was there, gaining in size and spirit as fall became winter and then became spring. That thing I'd felt—my envy for Barack's separateness from the process—had now utterly reversed itself. He was on the outside, while I got to live the process. I *was* the process, indivisible from this small, burgeoning life that was now throwing elbows and poking my bladder with her heel. I was never alone, never lonely. She was there, always, while I was driving to work, or chopping vegetables for a salad, or lying in bed at night, poring over the pages of *What to Expect When You're Expecting* for the nine hundredth time.

Summers in Chicago are special to me. I love how the sky stays light right into evening, how Lake Michigan gets busy with sailboats and the heat ratchets up to the point that it's almost impossible to recall the struggles of winter. I love how in summer the business of politics slowly starts to go quiet and life tilts more toward fun.

Though really we'd had no control over anything, somehow in the end it felt as if we'd timed it all perfectly. Very early in the morning on July 4, 1998, I felt the first twinges of labor. Barack and I checked into the University of Chicago hospital, bringing both Maya—who'd flown in from Hawaii to be there the week I was due—and my mom for support. It was still hours before the barbecue coals would start to blaze across the city and people would spread their blankets on the grass along the lakeshore, waving flags and waiting for the spectacle of the city fireworks to bloom over the water. We'd miss all of it that year anyway, lost in a whole new blaze and bloom. We were thinking not about country but about family as Malia Ann Obama, one of the two most perfect babies ever to be born to anyone, anywhere, dropped into our world.

14

MOTHERHOOD BECAME MY MOTIVATOR. IT DIC-tated my movements, my decisions, the rhythm of every day. It took no time, no thought at all, for me to be fully consumed by my new role as a mother. I'm a detail-oriented person, and a baby is nothing if not a reservoir of details. Barack and I studied little Malia, taking in the mystery of her rosebud lips, her dark fuzzy head and unfocused gaze, the herky-jerky way she moved her tiny limbs. We bathed and swaddled her and kept her pressed to our chests. We tracked her eating, her hours of sleep, her every gurgle. We analyzed the contents of each soiled diaper as if it might tell us all her secrets.

She was a tiny person, a person entrusted to us. I was heady with the responsibility of it, fully in her thrall. I could lose an hour just watching her breathe. When there's a baby in the house, time stretches and contracts, abiding by none of the regular rules. A single day can feel endless, and then suddenly six months have blown right past. Barack and I laughed about what parenthood had done to us. If we'd once spent the dinner hour parsing the intricacies of the juvenile justice system, comparing what I'd learned during my stint at Public Allies with some of the ideas he was trying to fit into a reform bill in the legislature, we now, with no less fervor, debated whether Malia was too dependent on her pacifier and compared our respective methods for getting her to sleep. We were, as most new parents are, obsessive and a little boring, and nothing made us happier. We hauled little Malia in her baby carrier with us to Zinfandel for our Friday night dates, figuring out how to streamline our order so we could be in and out quickly, before she got too restless.

Several months after Malia was born, I'd returned to work at the University of Chicago. I negotiated to come back only half-time, figuring this would be a win-win sort of arrangement—that I could now be both career woman and perfect mother, striking the Mary Tyler Moore/ Marian Robinson balance I'd always hoped for. We'd found a babysitter, Glorina Casabal, a doting, expert caregiver about ten years older than I was. Born in the Philippines, she was trained as a nurse and had raised two kids of her own. Glorina—"Glo"—was a short, bustling woman with a short, practical haircut and gold wire-rimmed glasses who could change a diaper in twelve seconds flat. She had a nurse's hypercompetent, do-anything energy and would become a vital and cherished member of our family for the next few years. Her most important quality was that she loved my baby passionately.

What I didn't realize—and this would also go into my file of things many of us learn too late—is that a part-time job, especially when it's meant to be a scaled-down version of your previously full-time job, can be something of a trap. Or at least that's how it played out for me. At work, I was still attending all the meetings I always had while also grappling with most of the same responsibilities. The only real difference was that I now made half my original salary and was trying to cram everything into a twenty-hour week. If a meeting ran late, I'd end up tearing home at breakneck speed to fetch Malia so that we could arrive on time (Malia eager and happy, me sweaty and hyperventilating) to the afternoon Wiggleworms class at a music studio on the North Side. To me, it felt like a sanity-warping double bind. I battled guilt when I had to take work calls at home. I battled a different sort of guilt when I sat at my office distracted by the idea that Malia might be allergic to peanuts. Part-time work was meant to give me more freedom, but mostly it left me feeling as if I were only half doing everything, that all the lines in my life had been blurred.

Meanwhile, it seemed that Barack had hardly missed a stride. A few months after Malia's birth, he'd been reelected to a four-year term in the state senate, winning with 89 percent of the vote. He was popular and successful, and plate spinner that he was, he was also starting to think about bigger things—namely, running for the U.S. Congress, hoping to unseat a four-term Democrat named Bobby Rush. Did I think it was a good idea for him to run for Congress? No, I did not. It struck me as unlikely that he'd win, given that Rush was well-known and Barack was still a virtual nobody. But he was a politician now and had traction inside the state Democratic Party. He had advisers and supporters, some of whom were urging him to give it a shot. Somebody had conducted a preliminary poll that seemed to suggest maybe he could win. And this I know for sure about my husband: You don't dangle an opportunity in front of him, something that could give him a wider field of impact, and expect him just to walk away. Because he doesn't. He won't.

A T THE END OF 1999, when Malia was almost eighteen months old, we took her to Hawaii at Christmastime to visit her great grandmother Toot, who was now seventy-seven years old and living in the same small high-rise apartment she'd been in for decades. It was meant to be a family visit—the one time each year Toot could see her grandson and great-granddaughter. Winter had once again clapped itself over Chicago, siphoning the warmth from the air and the blue from the sky. Feeling antsy both at home and at work, we'd booked a modest hotel room near Waikiki Beach and started counting down the days. Barack's teaching duties at the law school had wrapped up for the semester, and I'd put in for time off at my job. But then politics got in the way.

The Illinois senate was hung up in a marathon debate, trying to settle on the provisions of a major crime bill. Instead of breaking for the holidays, it went into a special session with the aim of pushing through to a vote before Christmas. Barack called me from Springfield, saying we'd need to delay our trip by a few days. This wasn't great news, but I understood it was out of his hands. All I cared was that we eventually got there. I didn't want Toot spending Christmas alone, and beyond that Barack and I needed the downtime. The trip to Hawaii, I was figuring, would separate both of us from our work and give us a chance to simply breathe.

He was now officially running for Congress, which meant that he rarely switched off. He would later give an interview to a local paper, estimating that during the six or so months he campaigned for Congress, he spent less than four full days at home with me and Malia. This was the painful reality of campaigning. On top of his other responsibilities, Barack lived with a ticking clock, one that incessantly reminded him of the minutes and hours remaining before the March primary. How he spent each of those minutes and hours could, at least in theory, affect the eventual outcome. What I was learning, too, was that in the eyes of a campaign operation, any minutes or hours a candidate spends privately with family are viewed basically as a waste of that valuable time.

I was enough of a veteran now to try to keep myself largely disengaged from the daily ups and downs of the race. I'd given Barack's decision to run a wan blessing, adopting a let's-just-get-this-out-of-the-way attitude about the whole thing. I thought maybe he'd try and fail to get into national politics and that this would then motivate him to want to try something entirely different. In an ideal world (my ideal world, anyway), Barack would do something like become the head of a foundation, where he could have an impact on issues that mattered and also make it home for dinner at night.

We flew to Hawaii on December 23, after the legislature finally hit pause for the holiday, though it still hadn't managed to find a resolution. But to my relief, we'd made it. Waikiki Beach was a revelation for young Malia. She tootled up and down the shoreline, kicking at the waves and exhausting herself with joy. We spent a merry, uneventful Christmas with Toot in her apartment, opening gifts and marveling at her devotion to the five-thousand-piece jigsaw puzzle she had going on a card table. As it always had, Oahu's languid green waters and cheery populace helped unhitch us from our everyday concerns, leaving us blissful and caught up in little more than the feeling of warm air on our skin and our daughter's delight at absolutely everything. As the headlines kept reminding us, we were fast approaching the dawn of a new millennium. And we were in a lovely place to spend the final days of 1999.

All was going fine until Barack got a call from someone back in Illinois, letting him know that the senate was somewhat abruptly going back into session to finish work on the crime bill. If he intended to vote, he had something like forty-eight hours to get back to Springfield. Another clock was now ticking. With a sinking heart, I watched as Barack jumped into action, rebooking our flights to leave the following day, pulling the plug on our vacation. We had to go. We had no choice. I suppose I could've stayed on alone with Malia, but what would be the fun in that? I wasn't happy with the idea of leaving, but I understood, again, this was the way of politics. The vote was an important one—the bill included new gun-control measures, which Barack had fervently supported—and it had also proven divisive enough that a single absent senator could potentially prevent the bill from passing. We were going home.

But then something unexpected happened. Overnight, Malia spiked a high fever. She'd ended the day as an exuberant surf kicker but was now, not even twelve hours later, a hot and listless heap of toddler-shaped misery, glassy-eyed and wailing in pain, but still too young to tell us anything specific about it. We gave her Tylenol, but it didn't help much. She was tugging at one ear, which made me suspect it was infected. The reality of what this meant started to set in. We sat on the bed, watching Malia drift into a restless, uncomfortable sleep. We were only a matter of hours now from our flight home. I saw the worry deepening on Barack's face, caught as he was in the crosscurrents of his opposing obligations. What we were about to decide went far beyond the moment at hand.

"She can't fly," I said, "obviously."

"I know."

"We have to switch the flights again."

"I know."

Unspoken was the fact that he could just go. He could walk out the door and catch a cab to the airport and still make it to Springfield in time to vote. He could leave his sick daughter and fretting wife halfway across the Pacific and go join his colleagues. It was an option. But I wasn't going to martyr myself by suggesting it. I was vulnerable, I'll admit, swimming in the uncertainty of what was going on with Malia. What if the fever got worse? What if she needed a hospital? Meanwhile, around the world, there were more paranoid people than us readying fallout shelters, hoarding cash and jugs of water just in case the worst of the Y2K predictions came true and the power and communication grids went on the fritz due to buggy computer networks unable to register the new millennium. It wasn't going to happen, but still. Was he really thinking about leaving?

It turns out he wasn't. He didn't. He would never.

I didn't listen to the call he made to his legislative aide that day, explaining that he'd miss the crime-bill vote. I didn't care. I was just focused on our girl. And as soon as Barack got off that call, he was, too. She was our little human. We owed everything to her first.

In the end, the year 2000 arrived without incident. After a couple of days of rest and some antibiotics, what indeed had turned out to be a nasty ear infection for Malia cleared up, returning our toddler to her normal bouncy state. Life would go on. It always did. On another perfect blue-sky day in Honolulu, we boarded a plane and flew home to Chicago, back into the chill of winter and into what for Barack was shaping up to be a political disaster.

THE CRIME BILL had failed to pass the state legislature, losing by five votes. For me, there was no math to do: Even if Barack had made it back from Hawaii in time, his vote almost certainly wouldn't have changed the outcome. Still, he took a beating for his absence. His opponents in the congressional primary pounced on the opportunity to depict Barack as some kind of bon vivant lawmaker who'd been on vacation—in Hawaii, no less—and hadn't deigned to come back to vote on something as significant as gun control.

Bobby Rush, the incumbent congressman, had tragically lost a family member to gun violence in Chicago only a few months earlier, which cast Barack in an even poorer light. Nobody seemed to register that he was from Hawaii, that he'd been visiting his widowed grandmother, or that his daughter had fallen ill. All that mattered was the vote. The press hammered on it for weeks. The *Chicago Tribune*'s editorial page criticized the group of senators who hadn't managed to vote that day, calling them "a bunch of gutless sheep." Barack's other opponent, a fellow state senator named Donne Trotter, took his own shots, telling a reporter that "to use your child as an excuse for not going to work also shows poorly on the individual's character."

I wasn't accustomed to any of this. I wasn't used to having opponents or seeing my family life scrutinized in the news. Never before had I heard my husband's character questioned like that. It hurt to think that a good decision—the right decision, as far as I was concerned—seemed to be costing him so much. In a column he wrote for our neighborhood's weekly newspaper, Barack calmly defended his choice to stay with me and Malia in Hawaii. "We hear a lot of talk from politicians about the importance of family values," he wrote. "Hopefully, you will understand when your state senator tries to live up to those values as best he can."

It seemed that with the fickleness of a child's earache, Barack's three years of work in the state senate had been all but wiped away. He'd led an overhaul of state campaign finance laws that ushered in stricter ethics rules for elected officials. He'd fought for tax cuts and credits for the working poor and was focused on cutting prescription drug costs for senior citizens. He'd earned the trust of legislators from all parts of the state, Republican and Democrat alike. But none of the real stuff seemed to matter now. The race had devolved into a series of low blows.

From the start of the campaign, Barack's opponents and their supporters had been propagating unseemly ideas meant to gin up fear and mistrust among African American voters, suggesting that Barack was part of an agenda cooked up by the white residents of Hyde Park—read, white Jews—to foist their preferred candidate on the South Side. "Barack is viewed in part to be the white man in blackface in our community," Donne Trotter told the *Chicago Reader*. Speaking to the same publication, Bobby Rush said, "He went to Harvard and became an educated fool. We're not impressed with these folks with these eastern elite degrees." He's not one of us, in other words. Barack wasn't a real Black man, like them—someone who spoke like that, looked like that, and read that many books could never be.

What bothered me most was that Barack exemplified everything parents on the South Side often said they wanted for their kids. He was everything people like Bobby Rush and Jesse Jackson and so many Black leaders had talked about for years: He'd gotten an education, and rather than abandoning the African American community, he was now trying to serve it. This was a heated election, sure, but Barack was being attacked for all the wrong things. I was astonished to see how our leaders treated him only as a threat to their power, inciting mistrust by playing on backward, anti-intellectual ideas about race and class.

It made me sick.

Barack, for his part, took it more in stride than I did, having already seen in Springfield how nasty politics could get and how the truth was so often distorted to serve people's political aims. Bruised but unwilling to give up, he continued to campaign through the winter, making his weekly trips back and forth to Springfield while trying earnestly to beat back the storm, even as donations began to dwindle and more and more endorsements went to Bobby Rush. With the clock ticking down to the primary, Malia and I hardly saw him at all, though he called us every evening to say good night.

I was more grateful than ever for those few stolen days we'd had on the beach. I knew that in his heart Barack was, too. What never got lost inside all the noise, inside all those nights he spent away from us, was that he cared. He took none of it lightly. I caught a trace of agony in his voice nearly every time he hung up the phone. It was almost as if every day he were forced to cast another vote, between family and politics, politics and family.

In March, Barack lost the Democratic primary in what ended up being a resounding victory for Bobby Rush.

All the while, I just kept hugging our girl.

.   .   .

A ND THEN CAME our second girl. Natasha Marian Obama was born on June 10, 2001, at the University of Chicago Medical Center, after a single round of IVF, a fantastically simple pregnancy, and a straightforward delivery, while Malia, now almost three, waited at home with my mom. Our new baby was beautiful, a little lamb-child with a full head of dark hair and alert brown eyes—the fourth corner to our square. Barack and I were over the moon.

Sasha, we planned to call her. I'd chosen the name because I thought it had a sassy ring. A girl named Sasha would brook no fools. Like all parents, I found myself wanting so much for our children, praying that nothing would ever hurt them. My hope was that they'd grow up to be bright and energetic, optimistic like their father and hard-driving like their mom. More than anything, I wanted them to be strong, to have a certain steeliness, the kind that would keep them upright and forward moving, no matter what. I didn't know a thing about what was coming our way, how our family's life would unfold—whether everything would go well or everything would go poorly, or whether, like most people, we'd get a solid mix of both. My job was just to make sure they were ready for it.

My stint at the university had left me feeling worn out, putting me in a far-from-perfect juggle while also straining our finances with the expense of child care. After Sasha was born, I debated whether I even wanted to return to my job at all, thinking that maybe our family would be better served if I stayed home full-time. Glo, our beloved babysitter, had been offered a higher-paying nursing job and had reluctantly decided she needed to move on. I couldn't blame her, of course, but losing Glo rearranged everything in my working mother's heart. Her investment in my family had allowed me to maintain my investment in my job. She loved our kids as if they were her own. I'd wept and wept the night she gave her notice, knowing how hard it would be for us to balance without her. I knew how fortunate we were to have the resources to hire her in the first place. But now that she was gone, it felt like losing an arm.

I loved being with my little daughters. I recognized the value of every minute and hour put in at home, especially with Barack's schedule being so irregular. I thought once again of my mother's decision to stay home with me and Craig. Surely, I was guilty of romanticizing her life—imagining it had actually been fun for her to Pine-Sol the windowsills and make all our clothes—but compared with the way I'd been living, it seemed quaint and manageable, and possibly worth trying. I liked the idea of being in charge of one thing rather than two, of not having my brain scrambled by the competing narratives of home and work. And it did seem that we could swing it financially. Barack had moved from an adjunct position to a senior lecturer at the law school, which gave us a tuition break at the university's Lab School, where Malia was soon to start preschool.

But then came a call from Susan Sher, my former mentor and colleague at city hall who was now general counsel and a vice president at the University of Chicago Medical Center, where we'd just had Sasha. The center had a brand-new president whom everyone was raving about, and one of his top priorities was improving community outreach. He was looking to hire an executive director for community affairs, a job that seemed almost custom-made for me. Was I interested in interviewing?

I debated whether to even send in my résumé. It sounded like a great opportunity, but I'd just basically talked myself into the idea that I was—that we all were—better off with my staying home. In any event, this was not a moment of high glamour for me, not a time I could really imagine blow-drying my hair and putting on a business suit. I was up several times a night to nurse Sasha, which put me behind on sleep and therefore sanity. Even as I was still rather fanatically devoted to neatness, I was losing the battle. Our condo was strewn with baby toys, toddler books, and packages of diaper wipes. Any trip outside the house involved a giant stroller and an unfashionable diaper bag full of the essentials: a Ziploc of Cheerios, a few everyday toys, and an extra change of clothes—for everyone.

But motherhood had also brought with it a set of wonderful friendships. I'd managed to connect with a group of professional women and form a kind of chatty, hands-on social cluster. Most of us were deep into our thirties and working in all sorts of careers, from banking and government to nonprofits. Many of us were having children at the same time. The more children we had, the tighter we grew. We saw one another nearly every weekend. We looked after each other's babies, went on group outings to the zoo, and bought bulk tickets for Disney on Ice. Sometimes on a Saturday afternoon, we just set the whole pack of kids loose in somebody's playroom and cracked open a bottle of wine.

Each one of these women was educated, ambitious, dedicated to her kids, and generally as bewildered as I was about how to put it all together. When it came to working and parenting, we were doing it every sort of way. Some of us worked full-time, some part-time, some stayed at home with their kids. Some allowed their toddlers to eat hot dogs and corn chips; others served whole-grain everything. A few had super-involved husbands; others had husbands like mine, who were oversubscribed and away a lot. Some of my friends were incredibly happy; others were trying to make changes, to attempt a different sort of balance. Most of us lived in a state of constant calibration, tweaking one area of life in hopes of bringing more steadiness to another.

Our afternoons together taught me that there was no formula for motherhood. No single approach could be deemed right or wrong. This was useful to see. Regardless of who was living which way and why, every small child in that playroom was cherished and growing just fine. I felt it every time we gathered, the collective force of all these women trying to do right by their kids: In the end, no matter what, I knew we'd help one another out and we'd all be okay.

After talking it through with both Barack and my friends, I decided to interview for the university hospital job, to at least see what it was about. My feeling was I'd be perfect for the job. I knew I had the right skills and plenty of passion. But if I were to take it, I'd also need to operate from a position of strength, on terms that worked for my family. I could nail it, I thought, if I wasn't overburdened with superfluous meetings and could be given the leeway to manage my own time, working from home when I needed to, dashing out of the office for day-care pickup or a pediatrician's visit when necessary.

Also, I didn't want to work part-time anymore. I was done with that. I wanted a full-time job, with a competitive salary to match so that we could better afford child care and housekeeping help—so that I could lay off the Pine-Sol and spend my free time playing with the girls. In the meantime, I wasn't going to try to hide the messiness of my existence, from the breast-feeding baby and the three-year-old in preschool to the fact that with my husband's topsy-turvy political schedule I was in charge of more or less every aspect of life at home.

Somewhat brazenly, I suppose, I laid all this out in my interview with Michael Riordan, the hospital's new president. I even brought three-month-old Sasha along with me, too. I can't remember the circumstances exactly, whether I couldn't find a babysitter that day or whether I'd even bothered to try. Sasha was little, though, and still needed a lot from me. She was a fact of my life—a cute, burbling, impossible-to-ignore fact— and something compelled me almost literally to put her on the table for this discussion. *Here is me,* I was saying, *and here also is my baby.*

It seemed a miracle that my would-be boss appeared to get it. If he had any reservations listening to me explain how flextime was a necessity while I bounced Sasha on my lap, hoping all the while that her diaper wouldn't leak, he didn't express them. I walked out of the interview feeling pleased and fairly certain I'd be offered the job. But no matter how it panned out, I knew I'd at least done something good for myself in speaking up about my needs. There was power, I felt, in just saying it out loud. With a clear mind and a baby who was starting to fuss, I rushed us both back home.

THIS WAS THE new math in our family: We had two kids, three jobs, two cars, one condo, and what felt like no free time. I accepted the new position at the hospital; Barack continued teaching and legislating. We both served on the boards of several nonprofits, and as much as he'd been stung by his defeat in the congressional primary, Barack still had ideas about trying for a higher office. George W. Bush was now president. As a country, we'd endured the shock and tragedy of the terror attacks of 9/11. There was a war going on in Afghanistan, a new color-coded threat advisory system being used in the United States, and Osama bin Laden was apparently hiding somewhere in a cave. As always, Barack was absorbing every bit of news carefully, going about his regular business while quietly developing his own thoughts about it all.

I don't recall exactly when it was that he first raised the possibility of running for a seat in the U.S. Senate. The idea was still nascent and an actual decision many months away, but clearly it was taking hold in Barack's mind. What I do remember is my response, which was just to look at him incredulously, as if to say, *Don't you think we're busy enough?*

My distaste for politics was only intensifying, less because of what went on in either Springfield or D.C. and more because five years into his tenure as state senator Barack's overloaded schedule was starting to really grate on me. As Sasha and Malia grew, I found that the pace only quickened and the to-do lists only got longer, leaving me operating in what felt like a never-ending state of overdrive. Barack and I did all we could to keep the girls' lives calm and manageable. We had a new baby-sitter helping out at home. Malia was happy at her University of Chicago Laboratory School, making friends and loading up her own little calendar with birthday parties and swim classes on weekends. Sasha was now about a year old, wobbling on two feet and beginning to say words and crack us up with her megawatt smiles. She was madly inquisitive and utterly bent on keeping up with Malia and her four-year-old buddies. My hospital job was going well, though the best way to stay on top of it, I was discovering, was to hoist myself from bed at 5:00 a.m. and put in a couple of hours on the computer before anyone else woke up.

This left me a little ragged in the evenings and sometimes put me in direct conflict with my night-owl husband, who turned up on Thursday nights from Springfield relatively chipper and wanting to dive headfirst into family life, making up for all the time he'd lost. But time was now officially an issue for us. If Barack's disregard for punctuality had once been something I'd gently teased him about, it was now a straight-up aggravation. I knew that Thursdays made him happy. I'd hear his excitement when he called to report that he was done with work and finally headed home. I understood it was nothing but good intentions that would lead him to say "I'm on my way!" or "Almost home!" And for a while, I believed those words. I'd give the girls their nightly bath but delay bedtime so that they could wait up to give their dad a hug. Or I'd feed them dinner and put them to bed but hold off on eating myself, lighting a few candles and looking forward to sharing a meal with Barack.

And then I'd wait. I'd wait so long that Sasha's and Malia's eyelids would start to droop and I'd have to carry them to bed. Or I'd wait alone, hungry, and increasingly bitter as my own eyes got heavy and candle wax pooled on the table. *On my way,* I was learning, was the product of Barack's eternal optimism, an indication of his eagerness to be home that did nothing to signify when he would actually arrive. *Almost home* was not a geo-locator but rather a state of mind. Sometimes he was on his way but needed to stop in to have one last forty-five-minute conversation with a colleague before he got into the car. Other times, he was almost home but forgot to mention that he was first going to fit in a quick workout at the gym.

In our life before children, such frustrations might have seemed petty, but as a working full-time mother with a half-time spouse and a predawn wake-up time, I felt my patience slipping away until finally, at some point, it just fell off a cliff. When Barack made it home, he'd either find me raging or unavailable, having flipped off every light in the house and gone sullenly to sleep.

W E LIVE BY the paradigms we know. In Barack's childhood, his father disappeared and his mother came and went. She was devoted to him but never tethered to him, and as far as he was concerned, there was nothing wrong in this approach. He'd had hills, beaches, and his own mind to keep him company. Independence mattered in Barack's world. It always had and always would. I, meanwhile, had been raised inside the tight weave of my own family, in our boxed-in apartment, in our boxed-in South Side neighborhood, with my grandparents and aunts and uncles all around, everyone jammed at one table for our regular Sunday night meals. After thirteen years in love, we needed to think through what this meant.

When it came down to it, I felt vulnerable when he was away. Not because he wasn't fully devoted to our marriage—this is and has always been a meaningful certainty in my life—but because having been brought up in a family where everyone always showed up, I could be extra let down when someone didn't show. I was prone to loneliness and now also felt fierce about sticking up for the girls' needs, too. We wanted him close. We missed him when he was gone. I worried that he didn't understand what that felt like for us. I feared that the path he'd chosen for himself— and still seemed so clearly committed to pursuing—would end up steam-rolling our every need. When he'd first approached me about running for state senate years earlier, there had been only two of us to think about. I had no conception of what saying yes to politics might mean for us later, once we'd added two children to the mix. But I now knew enough to understand that politics was never especially kind to families. I'd had a glimpse of it back in high school, through my friendship with Santita Jackson, and had seen it again when Barack's political opponents had exploited his decision to stay with Malia in Hawaii when she was sick.

Sometimes, watching the news or reading the paper, I found myself staring at images of the people who'd given themselves over to political life—the Clintons, the Gores, the Bushes, old photos of the Kennedys— and wondering what the backstories were. Was everyone normal? Happy? Were those smiles real?

At home, our frustrations began to rear up often and intensely. Barack and I loved each other deeply, but it was as if at the center of our relationship there were suddenly a knot we couldn't loosen. I was thirty-eight years old and had seen other marriages come undone in a way that made me feel protective of ours. I'd had close friends go through devastating breakups, brought on by small problems left unattended or lapses in communication that led eventually to irreparable rifts. A couple of years earlier, my brother, Craig, had moved temporarily back into the upstairs apartment we'd grown up in, living above our mother after his own marriage had slowly and painfully fallen apart.

Barack was reluctant at first to try couples counseling. He was ac-customed to throwing his mind at complicated problems and reasoning them out on his own. Sitting down in front of a stranger struck him as uncomfortable, if not a tad dramatic. Couldn't he just run over to Bor-ders and buy some relationship books? Weren't there discussions we could have on our own? But I wanted to really talk, and to really listen, and not to do it late at night or during hours we could be together with the girls. The few people I knew who'd tried couples counseling and were open enough to talk about it said that it had done them some good. And so I booked us an appointment with a downtown psychologist who came recommended by a friend, and Barack and I went to see him a handful of times.

Our counselor—Dr. Woodchurch, let's call him—was a soft-spoken white man who'd gone to good universities and always wore khakis. My assumption was that he would hear what Barack and I had to say and then instantly validate all my grievances. Because every last one of those grievances was, as I saw it, absolutely valid. I'm going to guess that Barack might have felt the same way about his own grievances.

This turned out to be the big revelation for me about counseling: No validating went on. No sides were taken. When it came to our disagreements, Dr. Woodchurch would never be the deciding vote. Instead, he was an empathic and patient listener, coaxing each of us through the maze of our feelings, separating out our weapons from our wounds. He cautioned us when we got too lawyerly and posited careful questions intended to get us to think hard about why we felt the way we felt. Slowly, over hours of talking, the knot began to loosen. Each time Barack and I left his office, we felt a bit more connected.

I began to see that there were ways I could be happier and that they didn't necessarily need to come from Barack's quitting politics in order to take some nine-to-six foundation job. (If anything, our counseling sessions had shown me that this was an unrealistic expectation.) I began to see how I'd been stoking the most negative parts of myself, caught up in the notion that everything was unfair and then assiduously, like a Harvard-trained lawyer, collecting evidence to feed that hypothesis. I now tried out a new hypothesis: It was possible that I was more in charge of my happiness than I was allowing myself to be. I was too busy resenting Barack for managing to fit workouts into his schedule, for example, to even begin figuring out how to exercise regularly myself. I spent so much energy stewing over whether or not he'd make it home for dinner that dinners, with or without him, were no longer fun.

This was my pivot point, my moment of self-arrest. Like a climber about to slip off an icy peak, I drove my ax into the ground. That isn't to say that Barack didn't make his own adjustments—counseling helped him to see the gaps in how we communicated, and he worked to be better at it—but I made mine, and they helped me, which then helped us. For starters, I recommitted myself to being healthy. Barack and I belonged to the same gym, run by a jovial and motivating athletic trainer named Cornell McClellan. I'd worked out with Cornell for a couple of years, but having children had changed my regular routine. My fix for this came in the form of my ever-giving mother, who still worked full-time but volunteered to start coming over to our house at 4:45 in the morning several days a week so that I could run out to Cornell's and join a girlfriend for a 5:00 a.m. workout and then be home by 6:30 to get the girls up and ready for their days. This new regimen changed everything: Calmness and strength, two things I feared I was losing, were now back.

When it came to the home-for-dinner dilemma, I installed new boundaries, ones that worked better for me and the girls. We made our schedule and stuck to it. Dinner each night was at 6:30. Baths were at 7:00, followed by books, cuddling, and lights-out at 8:00 sharp. The routine was ironclad, which put the weight of responsibility on Barack to either make it on time or not. For me, this made so much more sense than holding off dinner or having the girls wait up sleepily for a hug. It went back to my wishes for them to grow up strong and centered and also unaccommodating to any form of old-school patriarchy: I didn't want them ever to believe that life began when the man of the house arrived home. We didn't wait for Dad. It was his job now to catch up with us.

15

O N CLYBOURN AVENUE IN CHICAGO, JUST NORTH OF downtown, there was a strange paradise, seemingly built for the working parent, seemingly built for me: a standard, supremely American, got-it-all strip mall. It had a BabyGap, a Best Buy, a Gymboree, and a CVS, plus a handful of other chains, small and large, meant to take care of any urgent consumer need, be it a toilet plunger, or a ripe avocado, or a child-sized bathing cap. There was also a nearby Container Store and a Chipotle, which made things even better. This was my place. I could park the car, whip through two or three stores as needed, pick up a burrito bowl, and be back at my desk inside sixty minutes. I excelled at the lunchtime blitz—the replacing of lost socks, the purchasing of gifts for whatever five-year-old was having a birthday party on Saturday, the stocking and restocking of juice boxes and single-serving applesauce cups.

Sasha and Malia were three and six years old now, feisty, smart, and growing fast. Their energy left me breathless. Which only added to the occasional allure of the shopping plaza. There were times when I'd sit in the parked car and eat my fast food alone with the car radio playing, overcome with relief, impressed with my efficiency. This was life with little kids. This was what sometimes passed for achievement. I had the applesauce. I was eating a meal. Everyone was still alive.

Look how I'm managing, I wanted to say in those moments, to my audience of no one. *Does everyone see that I'm pulling this off?*

This was me at the age of forty, a little bit June Cleaver, a little bit Mary Tyler Moore. On my better days, I gave myself credit for making it happen. The balance of my life was elegant only from a distance, and only if you squinted, but there was at least something there that resembled balance. The hospital job had turned out to be a good one, challenging and satisfying and in line with my beliefs. It astonished me, actually, to see how a big esteemed institution like a university medical center with ninety-five hundred employees traditionally operated, run primarily by academics who did medical research and wrote papers and who also, in general, seemed to find the neighborhood around them so scary that they wouldn't even cross an off-campus street. For me, that fear was galvanizing. It got me out of bed in the morning.

I'd spent most of my life living alongside those barriers—noting the nervousness of white people in my neighborhood, registering all the subtle ways people with any sort of influence seemed to gravitate away from my home community and into clusters of affluence that seemed increasingly far removed. Here was an invitation to undo some of that, to knock down barriers where I could—mostly by encouraging people to get to know one another. I was well supported by my new boss, given the freedom to build my own program, creating a stronger relationship between the hospital and its neighboring community. I started with one person working for me but eventually led a team of twenty-two. I instituted programs to take hospital staff and trustees out into neighborhoods around the South Side, having them visit community centers and schools, signing them up to be tutors, mentors, and science-fair judges, getting them to try the local barbecue joints. We brought local kids in to job shadow hospital employees, set up a program to increase the number of neighborhood people volunteering in the hospital, and worked with a summer academic institute through the medical school, encouraging students in the community to consider medicine as a career. After realizing that the hospital system could be better about hiring minority- and women-owned businesses for its contracted work, I helped set up the Office of Business Diversity as well.

Finally, there was the issue of people desperately needing care. The South Side had just over a million residents and a dearth of medical providers, not to mention a population that was disproportionately affected by the kinds of chronic conditions that tend to afflict the poor—asthma, diabetes, hypertension, heart disease. With huge numbers of people uninsured and many others dependent on Medicaid, patients regularly jammed the university hospital's emergency room, often seeking what amounted to routine nonemergency treatment or having gone so long without preventive care that they were now in dire need of help. The problem was glaring, expensive, inefficient, and stressful for everyone involved. ER visits did little to improve anyone's long-term health, either. Trying to address this problem became an important focus for me. Among other things, we began hiring and training patient advocates— friendly, helpful local people, generally—who could sit with patients in the ER, helping them set up follow-up appointments at community health centers and educating them on where they could go to get decent and affordable regular care.

My work was interesting and rewarding, but still I had to be careful not to let it consume me. I felt I owed that to my girls. Our decision to let Barack's career proceed as it had—to give him the freedom to shape and pursue his dreams—led me to tamp down my own efforts at work. Almost deliberately, I'd numbed myself somewhat to my ambition, stepping back in moments when I'd normally step forward. I'm not sure anyone around me would have said I wasn't doing enough, but I was always aware of everything I could have followed through on and didn't. There were certain small-scale projects I chose not to take on. There were young employees whom I could have mentored better than I did. You hear all the time about the trade-offs of being a working mother. These were mine. If I'd once been someone who threw herself completely into every task, I was now more cautious, protective of my time, knowing I had to maintain enough energy for life at home.

. . .

M Y GOALS MOSTLY involved maintaining normalcy and stability, but those would never be Barack's. We'd grown better about recognizing this and letting it be. One yin, one yang. I craved routine and order, and he did not. He could live in the ocean; I needed the boat. When he was present at home, he was at least impressively present, playing on the floor with the girls, reading *Harry Potter* out loud with Malia at night, laughing at my jokes and hugging me, reminding us of his love and steadiness before vanishing again for another half a week or more. We made the most of the gaps in his schedule, having meals and seeing friends. He indulged me (sometimes) by watching *Sex and the City*. I indulged him (sometimes) by watching *The Sopranos*. I'd given myself over to the idea that being away was just part of his job. I didn't like it, but for the most part I'd stopped fighting it. Barack could happily end a day in a faraway hotel with all sorts of political battles brewing and loose ends floating. I, meanwhile, lived for the shelter of home—for the sense of completeness I felt each night with Sasha and Malia tucked into their beds and the dishwasher humming in the kitchen.

I had no choice but to adjust to Barack's absences anyway, because they weren't slated to end. On top of his regular work, he was once again campaigning, this time for a seat in the U.S. Senate, ahead of the fall 2004 elections.

He'd been slowly growing restless in Springfield, frustrated by the meandering pace of state government, convinced he could accomplish more and better in Washington. Knowing that I had plenty of reasons to be against the idea of a Senate run, and knowing also that he had a counterargument to present, midway through 2002 we'd convened an informal meeting of maybe a dozen of our closest friends, held over brunch at Valerie Jarrett's house, thinking we would kind of air the whole thing out and see what people thought.

Valerie lived in a high-rise not far from us in Hyde Park. Her condo was clean and modern, with white walls and white furniture and sprays

of exquisite bright orchids adding color. At the time, she was the executive vice president at a real-estate firm and a trustee at the University
of Chicago Medical Center. She'd supported my efforts at Public Allies
when I was there and helped raise funds for Barack's various campaigns,
marshaling her wide network of connections to boost our every endeavor. Because of this, and because of her warm, wise demeanor, Valerie
had come to occupy a curious position in our lives. Our friendship was
equally personal and professional. And she was equally my friend and
Barack's, which in my experience is a rare thing inside a couple. I had
my high-powered mom posse, and Barack spent what little leisure time
he had playing basketball with a group of buddies. We had some great
friends who were couples, their children friends with our children, families we liked to vacation with. But Valerie was something different, a big
sister to each of us individually and someone who helped us stand back
and take measure of our dilemmas when they arose. She saw us clearly,
saw our goals clearly, and was protective of us both.

She'd also told me privately ahead of time that she wasn't convinced
Barack should run for the Senate, so I'd walked into brunch that morning figuring I had the argument sewn up.

But I'd been wrong.

This Senate race presented a unique opportunity, Barack explained
that day. He felt he had a real shot. The incumbent, Peter Fitzgerald, was
a conservative Republican in an increasingly Democratic state and was
having trouble maintaining the support of his own party. It was likely
that multiple candidates would run in the primary, which meant that
Barack would only need to command a plurality of the vote to win the
Democratic nomination. As for money, he assured me that he wouldn't
need to touch our personal finances. When I asked how we'd afford living expenses if we were going to have homes in both D.C. and Chicago,
he'd said, "Well, I'll write another book and it'll be a big book, one that
makes money."

This made me laugh. Barack was the only person I knew who had
this kind of faith, thinking that a book could solve any problem. He was
like the little boy from "Jack and the Beanstalk," I teased, who trades his

family's livelihood for a handful of magic beans, believing with his whole heart that they will yield something, even if no one else does.

On all other fronts, Barack's logic was dismayingly solid. I watched Valerie's face as he spoke, realizing that he was quickly racking up points with her, that he had an answer for every "but what about?" question we could throw his way. I knew he was making sense, even as I fought off the urge to tally up all the additional hours he'd spend away from us now, not to mention the specter of a move to D.C. Though we'd argued over the drain of his political career on our family for years now, I did love and trust Barack. He was already a man with two families, his attention divided between me and the girls and his 200,000 or so South Side constituents. Would sharing him with the state of Illinois really be all that different? I couldn't know one way or another, but I also couldn't bring myself to stand in the way of his aspiration, that thing always tugging at him to try for more.

And so that day, we'd made a deal. Valerie agreed to be the finance chair for Barack's Senate campaign. A number of our friends agreed to donate time and money to the effort. I signed off on all of it, with one important caveat, repeated out loud so that everyone could hear it: If he lost, he'd move on from politics altogether and find a different sort of job. If it didn't work out on Election Day, this would be the end.

Really and for real, this would be the end.

What came next for Barack, though, was a series of lucky twists. First, Peter Fitzgerald decided not to run for reelection, clearing the field for challengers and relative newcomers like my husband. Then, somewhat oddly, both the Democratic front-runner in the primary and the ensuing Republican nominee became embroiled in scandals involving their ex-wives. With just a few months remaining before the election, Barack didn't even have a Republican opponent.

To be sure, he'd been running an excellent campaign, having learned plenty from his failed congressional run. He'd beaten out seven primary opponents and earned more than half the vote to win the nomination. Traveling the state and interacting with potential constituents, he was the same man I knew at home—funny and charming, smart and prepared.

His overly verbose answers to questions at town-hall forums and campaign debates seemed only to drive home the point that he belonged on the Senate floor. But still, effort notwithstanding, Barack's path to the Senate seemed paved in four-leaf clover.

All this, too, was before John Kerry invited him to give the keynote address at the 2004 Democratic National Convention being held in Boston. Kerry, then a senator from Massachusetts, was locked in a back-and-forth fight for the presidency with George W. Bush.

My husband was, in all of this, a complete nobody—a humble state legislator who'd never stood before a crowd like the one of fifteen thousand or more that would be gathered in Boston. He'd never used a teleprompter, never been live on prime-time television. He was a newcomer, a Black man in what was historically a white man's business, surfacing from obscurity with a weird name and odd backstory, hoping to strike a chord with the common Democrat. As the network pundits would later acknowledge, choosing Barack Obama to speak to an audience of millions had been a mighty gamble.

And yet, in his curious and roundabout way, he seemed destined for exactly this moment. I knew because I'd seen up close how his mind churned nonstop. Over years, I'd watched him inhale books, newspapers, and ideas, sparking to life anytime he spoke with someone who offered a shard of new experience or knowledge. He'd stowed every piece of it. What he was building, I see now, was a vision—and not a small one, either. It was the very thing I'd had to create room for in our shared life, to coexist with, even if reluctantly. It aggravated me sometimes to no end, but it was also what I could never disavow in Barack. He'd been working at this thing, quietly and meticulously, as long as I'd known him. And now maybe the size of the audience would finally match the scope of what he believed to be possible. He'd been ready for that call. All he had to do was speak.

MUST'VE BEEN A good speech" became my refrain afterward. It was a joke between me and Barack, one I repeated often and with irony following that night—July 27, 2004.

I'd left the girls at home with my mother and flown to be with him in Boston for the speech, standing in the wings at the convention center as Barack stepped into the hot glare of the stage lights and into view of all those millions of people. He was a little nervous and so was I, though we were both determined not to show it. This was how Barack operated anyway. The more pressure he was under, the calmer he seemed to get. He'd written his remarks over the course of a couple of weeks, working on them in between Illinois senate votes. He memorized his words and rehearsed them carefully, to the point where he wouldn't actually need the teleprompter unless his nerves got triggered and his mind went blank. But that wasn't at all what happened. Barack looked out at the audience and into the TV cameras, and as if kick-starting some internal engine, he just smiled and began to roll.

He spoke for seventeen minutes that night, explaining who he was and where he came from—his grandfather a GI who'd joined Patton's Army, his grandmother who'd worked on an assembly line during the war, his father who'd grown up herding goats in Kenya, his parents' improbable love, their faith in what a good education could do for a son who wasn't born rich or well connected. Earnestly and expertly, he cast himself not as an outsider but rather as a literal embodiment of the American story. He reminded the audience that a country couldn't be carved up simply into red and blue, that we were united by a common humanity, compelled to care for the whole of society. He called for hope over cynicism. He spoke with hope, projected hope, almost sang with it, really.

It was seventeen minutes of Barack's deft and easy way with words, seventeen minutes of his deep, dazzling optimism on display. By the time he finished, with a last plug for John Kerry and his running mate, John Edwards, the crowd was on its feet and roaring, the applause booming in the rafters. I walked out onto the stage, stepping into the blinding lights wearing high heels and a white suit, to give Barack a congratulatory hug before turning to wave with him at the whipped-up audience.

The energy was electric, the sound absolutely deafening. That Barack was a good person with a big mind and serious faith in democracy was no longer any sort of secret. I was proud of what he'd done, though it didn't surprise me. This was the guy I'd married. I'd known his capabilities all along. Looking back, I think it was then that I quietly began to let go of the idea that there was any reversing his course, that he'd ever belong solely to me and the girls. I could hear it almost in the pulse of the applause. *More of this, more of this, more of this.*

The media response to Barack's speech was hyperbolic. "I've just seen the first Black president," Chris Matthews declared to his fellow commentators on NBC. A front-page headline in the *Chicago Tribune* the next day read simply, "The Phenom." Barack's cell phone began to ring nonstop. Cable pundits were dubbing him a "rock star" and an "overnight success," as if he hadn't spent years working up to that moment onstage, as if the speech had created him instead of the other way around. Still, the speech was the beginning of something new, not just for him, but for us, our whole family. We were swept into another level of exposure and into the swift current of other people's expectations.

It was surreal, the whole thing. All I could do, really, was joke about it.

"Must've been a good speech," I'd say with a shrug as people began stopping Barack on the street to ask for his autograph or to tell him they'd loved what he'd said. "Must've been a good speech," I said when we walked out of a restaurant in Chicago to find that a crowd had gathered on the sidewalk to wait for him. I said the same thing when journalists started asking for Barack's thoughts on important national issues, when big-time political strategists started to hover around him, and when nine years after publication the formerly obscure *Dreams from My Father* got a paperback reissue and landed on the *New York Times* bestseller list.

"Must've been a good speech," I said when a beaming, bustling Oprah Winfrey showed up at our house to spend a day interviewing us for her magazine.

What was happening to us? I almost couldn't track it. In November, Barack was elected to the U.S. Senate, winning 70 percent of the vote statewide, the largest margin in Illinois history and the biggest landslide of any Senate race in the country that year. He'd won significant majorities among Blacks, whites, and Latinos; men and women; rich and poor; urban, suburban, and rural. At one point, we went to Arizona for a quick getaway, and he was mobbed by well-wishers there. This for me felt like a true and odd measure of his fame: Even white people were recognizing him now.

I TOOK WHAT WAS left of my normalcy and wrapped myself in it. When we were at home, everything was the same. When we were with our friends and family, everything was the same. With our kids, it was always the same. But outside, things were different. Barack was flying back and forth to D.C. all the time now. He had a Senate office and an apartment in a shabby building on Capitol Hill, a little one-bedroom that was already cluttered with books and papers, his Hole away from home. Anytime the girls and I came to visit, we didn't even pretend to want to stay there, booking a hotel room for the four of us instead.

I stuck to my routine in Chicago. Gym, work, home, repeat. Dishes in the dishwasher. Swim lessons, soccer, ballet. I kept pace as I always had. Barack had a life in Washington now, operating with some of the gravitas that came with being a senator, but I was still me, living my same normal life. I was sitting one day in my parked car at the shopping plaza on Clybourn Avenue, having some Chipotle and a little me-time after a dash through BabyGap, when my secretary at work called on my cell phone to ask if she could patch through a call. It was from a woman in D.C.—someone I'd never met, the wife of a fellow senator—who'd tried a few times already to reach me.

"Sure, put her through," I said.

And on came the voice of this senator's wife, pleasant and warm. "Well, hello!" she said. "I'm so glad to finally talk to you!"

I told her that I was excited to talk to her, too.

"I'm just calling to welcome you," she said, "and to let you know that we'd like to invite you to join something very special."

She'd called to ask me to be in some sort of private organization, a club that, from what I gathered, was made up primarily of the wives of important people in Washington. They got together regularly for luncheons and to discuss issues of the day. "It's a nice way to meet people, and I know that's not always easy when you're new to town," she said.

In my whole life, I'd never been asked to join a club. I'd watched friends in high school go off on ski trips with their Jack and Jill groups. At Princeton, I'd waited up sometimes for Suzanne to come home, buzzed and tittering, from her eating-club parties. Half the lawyers at Sidley, it seemed, belonged to country clubs. I'd visited plenty of those clubs over time, raising money for Public Allies, raising money for Barack's campaigns. You learned early on that clubs, in general, were saturated with money. Belonging signified more than just belonging.

It was a kind offer she was making, coming from a genuine place, and yet I was all too happy to turn it down.

"Thank you," I said. "It's so nice of you to think of me. But actually, we've made the decision I won't be moving to Washington." I let her know that we had two little girls in school in Chicago and that I was pretty attached to my job. I explained that Barack was settling into life in D.C., commuting home when he could. I didn't mention that we were so committed to Chicago that we were looking to buy a new house, thanks to the royalty money that was starting to come in from the renewed sales of his book and the fact that he now had a generous offer on a second book—the surprise harvest of Barack's magic beans.

The senator's wife paused, letting a delicate beat pass. When she spoke again, her voice was gentle. "That can be very hard on a marriage, you know," she said. "Families fall apart."

I felt her judgment then. She herself had been in Washington for many years. The implication was she'd seen things go poorly when a spouse stayed back. The implication was that I was making a dangerous choice, that there was only one correct way to be a senator's wife and I was choosing wrong.

I thanked her again, hung up, and sighed. None of this had been my choice in the first place. None of this was my choice at all. I was now, like her, the wife of a U.S. senator—Mrs. Obama, she'd called me throughout the conversation—but that didn't mean I had to drop everything to support him. Truly, I didn't want to drop a thing.

I knew there were other senators with spouses who chose to live in their hometowns rather than in D.C. I knew that the Senate, with fourteen of its one hundred members being female, was not quite as antiquated as it had once been. But still, I found it presumptuous that another woman would tell me I was wrong to want to keep my kids in school and remain in my job. A few weeks after the election, I'd gone with Barack to Washington for a daylong orientation offered to newly elected senators and their spouses. There'd been only a few of us attending that year, and after a quick introduction the politicians went one way, while spouses were ushered into another room. I'd come with questions, knowing that politicians and their families were expected to adhere to strict federal ethics policies dictating everything from whom they could receive gifts from to how they paid for travel to and from Washington. I thought maybe we'd discuss how to navigate social situations with lobbyists or the legalities of raising money for a future campaign.

What we got, however, was an elaborate disquisition on the history and architecture of the Capitol and a look at the official china patterns produced for the Senate, followed by a polite and chitchatty lunch. The whole thing had gone on for hours. It would have been funny, maybe, if I hadn't taken a day off from work and left our kids with my mother in order to be there. If I was going to be a political spouse, I wanted to treat it seriously. I didn't care about the politics per se, but I also didn't want to screw anything up.

The truth was that Washington confused me, with its decorous traditions and sober self-regard, its whiteness and maleness, its ladies having lunch off to one side. At the heart of my confusion was a kind of fear, because as much as I hadn't chosen to be involved, I was getting sucked in. I'd been Mrs. Obama for the last twelve years, but it was starting to mean something different. At least in some spheres, I was now Mrs. Obama in a way that could feel diminishing, a missus defined by her mister. I was the wife of Barack Obama, the political rock star, the only Black person in the Senate—the man who'd spoken of hope and tolerance so poignantly and forcefully that he now had a hornet buzz of expectation following him.

My husband was a senator, but somehow people seemed to want to vault right over that. Instead, everyone was keen to know whether he would make a run for president in 2008. There was no shaking the question. Every reporter asked it. Nearly every person who approached him on the street asked it. My colleagues at the hospital would stand in my doorway and casually drop the question, probing for some bit of early news. Even Malia, who was six and a half on the day she put on a pink velvet dress and stood next to Barack as he was sworn in to the Senate by Dick Cheney, wanted to know. Unlike many of the others, though, our first grader was wise enough to sense how premature it all seemed.

"Daddy, are you gonna try to be president?" she'd asked. "Don't you think maybe you should be vice president or something first?"

I was with Malia on this matter. As a lifelong pragmatist, I would always counsel a slow approach, the methodical checking of boxes. I was a natural-born fan of the long and judicious wait. In this regard, I felt better anytime I heard Barack pushing back at his inquisitors with an aw-shucks kind of modesty, batting away questions about the presidency, saying that the only thing he was planning was to put his head down and work hard in the Senate. He often reminded people that he was just a low-ranking member of the minority party, a backbench player if there ever was one. And, he would sometimes add, he had two kids he needed to raise.

But the drum was already beating. It was hard to make it stop. Barack was writing what would become *The Audacity of Hope*—thinking through his beliefs and his vision for the country, threshing them into words on his legal pads late at night. He really was content, he told me, to stay where he was, building his influence over time, awaiting his turn to speak inside the deliberative cacophony of the Senate, but then a storm arrived.

Hurricane Katrina blasted the Gulf Coast of the United States late in August 2005, overwhelming the levees in New Orleans, swamping low-lying regions, stranding people—Black people, mostly—on the rooftops of their destroyed homes. The aftermath was horrific, with media reports showing hospitals without backup power, distraught families herded into the Superdome, emergency workers hamstrung by a lack of supplies. In the end, some eighteen hundred people died, and more than half a million others were displaced, a tragedy exacerbated by the ineptitude of the federal government's response. It was a wrenching exposure of our country's structural divides, most especially the intense, lopsided vulnerability of African Americans and poor people of all races when things got rough.

Where was hope now?

I watched the Katrina coverage with a knot in my stomach, knowing that if a disaster hit Chicago, many of my aunts and uncles, cousins and neighbors, would have suffered a similar fate. Barack's reaction was no less emotional. A week after the hurricane, he flew to Houston to join former president George H. W. Bush, along with Bill and Hillary Clinton, who was then a colleague of his in the Senate, spending time with the tens of thousands of New Orleans evacuees who'd sought shelter in the Astrodome there. The experience kindled something in him, that nagging sense he wasn't yet doing enough.

THIS WAS THE THOUGHT I returned to a year or so later, when the drumbeat truly got loud, when the pressure on both of us felt immense. We went about our regular business, but the question of whether Barack would run for president unsettled the air around us. *Could he? Will he? Should he?* In the summer of 2006, poll respondents filling out open-ended questionnaires were naming him as a presidential possibility, though Hillary Clinton was decidedly the number one pick. By fall, though, Barack's stock had begun to rise in part thanks to the publication of *The Audacity of Hope* and a slew of media opportunities afforded by the book tour. His poll numbers were suddenly even with or ahead of those of Al Gore and John Kerry, the Democrats' previous two nominees—evidence of his potential. I was aware that he'd been having private conversations with friends, advisers, and prospective donors, signaling to everyone that he was mulling over the idea. But there was one conversation he avoided having, and that was with me.

He knew, of course, how I felt. We'd discussed it obliquely, around the edges of other topics. We'd lived with other people's expectations so long that they were almost embedded in every conversation we had. Barack's potential sat with our family at the dinner table. Barack's potential rode along to school with the girls and to work with me. It was there even when we didn't want it to be there, adding a strange energy to everything. From my point of view, my husband was doing plenty already. If he was going to even think about running for president, I hoped he'd take the prudent path, preparing slowly, biding his time in the Senate, and waiting until the girls were older—until 2016, maybe.

Since I'd known him, it seemed to me that Barack had always had his eyes on some far-off horizon, on his notion of the world as it should be. Just for once, I wanted him to be content with life as it was. I didn't understand how he could look at Sasha and Malia, now five and eight, with their pigtailed hair and giggly exuberance, and feel any other way. It hurt me sometimes to think that he did.

We were riding a seesaw, the two of us, the mister on one side and the missus on the other. We lived in a nice house now, a Georgian brick home on a quiet street in the Kenwood neighborhood, with a wide porch and tall trees in the yard—exactly the kind of place Craig and I used to gape at during Sunday drives in my dad's Buick. I thought often of my father and all he'd invested in us. I wished desperately for him to be alive, to see how things were playing out. Craig was profoundly happy now, having finally made a swerve, leaving his career in investment banking and pivoting back to his first love—basketball. After a few years as an assistant at Northwestern, he was now head coach at Brown University in Rhode Island, and he was getting married again, to Kelly McCrum, a beautiful, down-to-earth college dean of admissions from the East Coast. His two children had grown tall and confident, vibrant advertisements for what the next generation could do.

I was a senator's wife, but beyond that, and more important, I had a career that mattered to me. Back in the spring, I'd been promoted to become a vice president at the University of Chicago Medical Center. I'd spent the past couple of years leading the development of a program called the South Side Healthcare Collaborative, which had already connected more than fifteen hundred patients who'd turned up in our Emergency Department with care providers they could see regularly, regardless of whether they could pay or not. My work felt personal. I saw Black folks streaming into the ER with issues that had long been neglected—diabetic patients whose circulation issues had gone untended and who now needed a leg amputated, for example—and couldn't help but think of every medical appointment my own father had failed to make for himself, every symptom of his MS he'd downplayed in order not to make a fuss, or cost anyone money, or generate paperwork, or to spare himself the feeling of being belittled by a wealthy white doctor.

I liked my job, and while it wasn't perfect, I also liked my life. With Sasha about to move into elementary school, I felt as though I was at the start of a new phase, on the brink of being able to fire up my ambition again and consider a new set of goals. What would a presidential campaign do? It would hijack all that. I knew enough to understand this ahead of time. Barack and I had been through five campaigns in eleven years already, and each one had forced me to fight a bit harder to hang on to my own priorities. Each one had put a little dent in my soul and also in our marriage. A presidential run, I feared, would really bang us up. Barack would be gone far more than he was while serving in Springfield or Washington—not for half weeks, but full weeks; not for four- to eight-week stretches with recesses in between, but for months at a time. What would that do to our family? What would the publicity do to our girls?

I did what I could to ignore the whirlwind around Barack, even if it showed no sign of dying down. Cable news pundits were debating his prospects. David Brooks, the conservative columnist at the *New York Times,* published a surprising sort of just-do-it plea titled "Run, Barack, Run." He was recognized nearly everywhere he went now, but I still had the blessing of invisibility. Standing in line at a convenience store one day in October, I spotted the cover of *Time* magazine and had to turn my head away: It was an extreme close-up of my husband's face, next to the headline "Why Barack Obama Could Be the Next President."

What I hoped was that at some point Barack himself would put an end to the speculation, declaring himself out of contention and directing the media gaze elsewhere. But he didn't do this. He wouldn't do this. He wanted to run. He wanted it and I didn't.

Anytime a reporter asked whether he'd join the race for president,

Barack would demur, saying simply, "I'm still thinking about it. It's a family decision." Which was code for "Only if Michelle says I can."

On nights when Barack was in Washington, I lay alone in bed, feeling as if it were me against the world. I wanted Barack for our family. Everyone else seemed to want him for our country. He had his council of advisers—David Axelrod and Robert Gibbs, the two campaign strategists who'd been critical in getting him elected to the Senate; David Plouffe, another consultant from Axelrod's firm; his chief of staff, Pete Rouse; and Valerie—all of whom were cautiously supportive. But they'd also made clear that there was no half doing a presidential campaign. Barack and I both would need to be fully on board. The demands on him would be unimaginable. Without missing a beat in his Senate duties, he'd have to build and maintain a coast-to-coast campaign operation, develop a policy platform, and also raise an astonishing amount of money. My job would be not just to give tacit support to the campaign but to participate in it. I'd be expected to make myself and our children available for viewing, to smile approvingly and shake a lot of hands. Everything would be about him now, I realized, in support of this larger cause.

Even Craig, who'd so avidly protected me since the day I was born, had gotten swept up in the excitement of a potential run. He called me one evening explicitly to make a plug. "Listen, Miche," he said, speaking as he often did, in basketball terms. "I know you're worried about this, but if Barack's got a shot, he's got to take it. You can see that, right?"

It was on me. It was all on me. Was I afraid or just tired?

For better or worse, I'd fallen in love with a man with a vision who was optimistic without being naive, undaunted by conflict, and intrigued by how complicated the world was. He was strangely unintimidated by how much work there was to be done. He was dreading the thought of leaving me and the girls for long stretches, he said, but he also kept reminding me of how secure our love was. "We can handle this, right?" he said, holding my hand one night as we sat in his upstairs study and finally began to really talk about it. "We're strong and we're smart, and so are our kids. We'll be just fine. We can afford this."

What he meant was yes, a campaign would be costly. There were things we'd give up—time, togetherness, our privacy. It was too early to predict exactly how much would be required, but surely it would be a lot. For me, it was like spending money without knowing your bank balance. How much resilience did we have? What was our limit? What would be left in the end? The uncertainty alone felt like a threat, a thing that could drown us. I'd been raised, after all, in a family that believed in forethought—that ran fire drills at home and showed up early to everything. Growing up in a working-class community and with a disabled parent, I'd learned that planning and vigilance mattered a lot. It could mean the difference between stability and poverty. The margins always felt narrow. One missed paycheck could leave you without electricity; one missed homework assignment could put you behind and possibly out of college.

Having lost a fifth-grade classmate to a house fire, having watched Suzanne die before she'd had a chance to really be an adult, I'd learned that the world could be brutal and random, that hard work didn't always assure positive outcomes. My sense of this would only grow in the future, but even now, sitting in our quiet brick home on our quiet street, I couldn't help but want to protect what we had—to look after our girls and forget the rest, at least until they'd grown up a bit more.

And yet there was a flip side to this, and Barack and I both knew it well. We'd watched the devastation of Katrina from our privileged remove. We'd seen parents hoisting their babies above floodwaters and African American families trying to hold themselves together in the dehumanizing depravity that existed in the Superdome. My various jobs—from city hall to Public Allies to the university—had helped me see how hard it could be for some people to secure things like basic health care and housing. I'd seen the flimsy line that separated getting by and going under. Barack, for his part, had spent plenty of time listening to laid-off factory workers, young military veterans trying to manage lifelong disabilities, mothers fed up with sending their kids to poorly functioning schools. We understood, in other words, how ridiculously fortunate we were, and we both felt an obligation not to be complacent.

Knowing that I really had no choice but to consider it, I finally opened the door and allowed the possibility of this thing inside. Barack and I talked the idea through, not once, but many times, right up to and through our Christmas trip to visit Toot in Hawaii. Some of our conversations were angry and tearful, some of them earnest and positive. It was the extension of a dialogue we'd been having over seventeen years already. *Who were we? What mattered to us? What could we do?*

In the end, it boiled down to this: I said yes because I believed that Barack could be a great president. He was self-assured in ways that few people are. He had the intellect and discipline to do the job, the temperament to endure everything that would make it hard, and the rare degree of empathy that would keep him tuned carefully to the country's needs. He was also surrounded by good, smart people who were ready to help. Who was I to stop him? How could I put my own needs, and even those of our girls, in front of the possibility that Barack could be the kind of president who helped make life better for millions of people?

I said yes because I loved him and had faith in what he could do.

I said yes, though I was at the same time harboring a painful thought, one I wasn't ready to share: I supported him in campaigning, but I also felt certain he wouldn't make it all the way. He spoke so often and so passionately of healing our country's divisions, appealing to a set of higher ideals he believed were innate in most people. But I'd seen enough of the divisions to temper my own hopes. Barack was a Black man in America, after all. I didn't really think he could win.

16

A LMOST FROM THE MINUTE WE AGREED IT WOULD be okay for him to run, Barack became a kind of human blur, a pixelated version of the guy I knew—a man who quite suddenly had to be everywhere all at once, driven by and beholden to the force of the larger effort. There was not quite a year until the primary contests got started, beginning in Iowa. Barack had to quickly hire staff, woo the types of donors who could write big checks, and figure out how to introduce his candidacy in the most resonant way possible. The goal was to get on people's radar and stay there right through Election Day. Campaigns could be won and lost on their earliest moves.

The whole operation would be overseen by the two deeply invested Davids—Axelrod and Plouffe. Axe, as everyone called him, had a soft voice, a courtly manner, and a brushy mustache that ran the length of his top lip. He'd worked as a reporter for the *Chicago Tribune* before turning to political consulting and would lead the messaging and media for Barack. Plouffe, who at thirty-nine had a boyish smile and a deep love of numbers and strategy, would manage the overall campaign. The team was growing rapidly, with experienced people recruited to look after the finances and handle advance planning on events.

Someone had the wisdom to suggest that Barack might want to formally announce his candidacy in Springfield. Everyone agreed that it would be a fitting, middle-of-America backdrop for what we hoped would be a different kind of campaign—one led from the ground up, largely by people new to the political process. This was the cornerstone of Barack's hope. His years as a community organizer had shown him how many people felt unheard and disenfranchised within our democracy. Project VOTE! had helped him see what was possible if those people were empowered to participate. His run for president would be an even bigger test of that idea. Would his message work on a larger scale? Would enough people come out to help? Barack knew he was an unusual candidate. He wanted to run an unusual campaign.

The plan became for Barack to make his announcement from the steps of the Old State Capitol, a historic landmark that would of course be more visually appealing than any convention center or arena. But it also put him outdoors, in the middle of Illinois, in the middle of February, when temperatures were often below freezing. The decision struck me as well-intentioned but generally impractical, and it did little to build my confidence in the campaign team that now more or less ran our lives. I was unhappy about it, imagining the girls and me trying to smile through blowing snow or frigid winds, Barack trying to appear invigorated instead of chilled. I thought about all the people who would decide to stay home that day rather than stand out in the cold for hours. I was a midwesterner: I knew the weather could ruin everything. I knew also that Barack couldn't afford an early flop.

About a month earlier, Hillary Clinton had declared her own candidacy, brimming with confidence. John Edwards, Kerry's former running mate from North Carolina, had launched his campaign a month prior to that, speaking in front of a New Orleans home that had been ravaged by Hurricane Katrina. In all, a total of nine Democrats would throw their hats into the ring. The field would be crowded and the competition fierce.

Barack's team was gambling with an outdoor announcement, but it wasn't my place to second-guess. I insisted that the advance team at least equip Barack's podium with a heater to keep him from appearing too uncomfortable on the national news. Otherwise, I held my tongue. I had little control anymore. Rallies were being planned, strategies mapped, volunteers mustered. The campaign was under way, and there was no parachuting out of it.

In what was probably a subconscious act of self-preservation, my focus shifted toward something I could control, which was finding acceptable headwear for Malia and Sasha for the announcement. I'd found new winter coats for them, but I'd forgotten all about hats until it was nearly too late.

As the announcement day neared, I began making harried afterwork trips to the department stores at Water Tower Place, rifling through the dwindling midseason supply of winter wear, hunting the clearance racks in vain. It wasn't long before I became less concerned with making sure Malia and Sasha looked like the daughters of a future president than making sure they looked like they at least had a mother. Finally, on what was probably my third outing, I found some—two knit hats, white for Malia and pink for Sasha, both in a women's size small, which ended up fitting snugly on Malia's head but drooping loosely around Sasha's little five-year-old face. They weren't high fashion, but they looked cute enough, and more important they'd keep the girls warm regardless of what the Illinois winter had in store. It was a small triumph, but a triumph nonetheless, and it was mine.

A NNOUNCEMENT DAY—February 10, 2007—turned out to be a bright, cloudless morning, the kind of sparkling midwinter Saturday that looks a lot better than it actually feels. The air temperature sat at about twelve degrees, with a light breeze blowing. Our family had arrived in Springfield the previous day, staying in a three-room suite at a downtown hotel, on a floor that had been rented out entirely by the campaign to house a couple dozen of our family and friends who'd traveled down from Chicago as well.

Already, we were beginning to experience the pressures of a national campaign. Barack's announcement had inadvertently been scheduled for the same day as the State of the Black Union, a forum organized each year by the public-broadcasting personality Tavis Smiley, who was evidently angry about it. He'd made his displeasure clear to the campaign staff, suggesting that the move showed a disregard for the African American community and would end up hurting Barack's candidacy. I was surprised that the first shots fired at us came from within the Black community. Then, just a day ahead of the announcement, *Rolling Stone* published a piece on Barack that included the reporter making a visit to Trinity Church in Chicago. We were still members there, though our attendance had dropped off significantly after the girls were born. The piece quoted from an angry and inflammatory sermon the Reverend Jeremiah Wright had delivered many years earlier regarding the treatment of Blacks in our country, intimating that Americans cared more about maintaining white supremacy than they did about God.

While the profile itself was largely positive, the cover line of the magazine read, "The Radical Roots of Barack Obama," which we knew would quickly get weaponized by the conservative media. It was a disaster in the making, especially on the eve of the campaign launch and especially because Reverend Wright was scheduled to lead the invocation ahead of Barack's speech. Barack had to make a difficult call, phoning the pastor and asking whether he'd be willing to step back from the spotlight, giving us a private backstage blessing instead. Reverend Wright's feelings were hurt, Barack said, but he also seemed to understand the stakes, leading us to believe that he'd be supportive without dwelling on his disappointment.

That morning, it hit me that we'd reached the no-turning-back moment. We were literally now putting our family in front of the American people. The day was meant to be a massive kickoff party for the campaign, one for which everyone had spent weeks preparing. And like every paranoid host, I couldn't shake the fear that when the time finally came, no one would show up. Unlike Barack, I could be a doubter. I still held on to the worries I'd had since childhood. What if we're not good enough? Maybe everything we'd been told was an exaggeration. Maybe Barack was less popular than his people believed. Maybe it just wasn't yet his time. I tried to shove all doubts aside as we arrived through a side entrance to a staging area inside the old capitol, still unable to see what was going on out front. So that I could get a briefing from the staff, I handed Sasha and Malia off to my mother and Kaye Wilson—"Mama Kaye"—a former mentor of Barack's who had in recent years stepped into the role of second grandmother to our girls.

The crowd was looking good, I was told. People had started gathering before dawn. The plan was for Barack to walk out first, and then the girls and I would join him a few moments later on the platform, climbing a few stairs before turning to wave at the crowd. I'd made it clear already that we would not stay onstage for his twenty-minute address. It was too much to ask two little kids to sit still and pretend to be interested. If they looked at all bored, if either one sneezed or started fidgeting, it would do nothing for Barack's cause. The same went for me. I knew the stereotype I was meant to inhabit, the immaculately groomed doll-wife with the painted-on smile, gazing bright-eyed at her husband, as if hanging on every word. This was not me and never would be. I could be supportive, but I couldn't be a robot.

Following the briefing and a moment of prayer with Reverend Wright, Barack walked out to greet the audience, his appearance met with a roar I could hear from inside the capitol. I went back to find Sasha and Malia, beginning to feel truly nervous. "Are you girls ready?" I said.

"Mommy, I'm hot," Sasha said, tearing off her pink hat.

"Oh, sweetie, you've got to keep that on. It's freezing outside." I grabbed the hat and fitted it back on her head.

"But we're not outside, we're inside," she said.

This was Sasha, our round-faced little truth teller. I couldn't argue with her logic. Instead, I glanced at one of the staffers nearby, trying to telegraph a message to a young person who almost certainly didn't have kids of her own: *Dear God, if we don't get this thing started now, we're going to lose these two.*

In an act of mercy, she nodded and motioned us toward the entrance. It was time.

I'd been to a fair number of Barack's political events by now and had seen him interact many times with big groups of constituents. I'd been at campaign kickoffs, fund-raisers, and election-night parties. I'd seen audiences filled with old friends and longtime supporters. But Springfield was something else entirely.

My nerves left me the moment we stepped onstage. I was focused completely on Sasha, making sure she was smiling and not about to trip over her own booted feet. "Look up, sweetie," I said, holding her hand. "Smile!" Malia was out ahead of us already, her chin high and her smile giant as she caught up with her father and waved. It wasn't until we ascended the stairs that I was finally able to take in the crowd, or at least try to. The rush was enormous. More than fifteen thousand people, it turned out, had come that day. They were spread out in a three-hundred-degree panorama, spilling out from the capitol, enveloping us with their enthusiasm.

I'd never been one who'd choose to spend a Saturday at a political rally. The appeal of standing in an open gym or high school auditorium to hear lofty promises and platitudes never made much sense to me. Why, I wondered, were all these people here? Why would they layer on extra socks and stand for hours in the cold? I could imagine people bundling up and waiting to hear a band whose every lyric they could sing or enduring a snowy Super Bowl for a team they'd followed since childhood. But politics? This was unlike anything I'd experienced before.

It began dawning on me that we were the band. We were the team about to take the field. What I felt more than anything was a sudden sense of responsibility. We owed something to each one of these people. We were asking for an investment of their faith, and now we had to deliver on what they'd brought us, carrying that enthusiasm through twenty months and fifty states and right into the White House. I hadn't believed it was possible, but maybe now I did. This was the call-and-response of democracy, I realized, a contract forged person by person. *You show up for us, and we'll show up for you.* I had fifteen thousand more reasons to want Barack to win.

I was fully committed now. Our whole family was committed, even if it felt a little scary. I couldn't yet begin to imagine what lay ahead. But there we were—out there—the four of us standing before the crowd and the cameras, naked but for the coats on our backs and a slightly too big pink hat on a tiny head.

. . .

HILLARY CLINTON WAS a serious and formidable opponent. In poll after poll, she held a commanding lead among the country's potential Democratic primary voters, with Barack lagging ten or twenty points behind, and Edwards sitting a few points behind Barack. Democratic voters knew the Clintons, and they were hungry for a win. Far fewer people could even pronounce my husband's name. All of us— Barack and I as well as the campaign team—understood long before his announcement that regardless of his political gifts a Black man named Barack Hussein Obama would always be a long shot.

It was a hurdle we faced within the Black community, too. Similar to how I'd initially felt about Barack's candidacy, plenty of Black folks couldn't bring themselves to believe that my husband had a real chance of winning. Many had yet to believe that a Black man could win in predominantly white areas, which meant they'd often go for the safer bet, the next-best thing. One facet of the challenge for Barack was to shift Black voters away from their long-standing allegiance to Bill Clinton, who'd shown unusual ease with the African American community and formed many connections there as a result. Barack had already built goodwill with a diverse range of constituents throughout Illinois, including in the rural white farm areas in the southern part of the state. He'd already proven that he could reach all demographics, but many people didn't yet understand this about him.

The scrutiny of Barack would be extra intense, the lens always magnified. We knew that as a Black candidate he couldn't afford any sort of stumble. He'd have to do everything twice as well. For Barack, and for every candidate not named Clinton, the only hope for winning the nomination was to raise a lot of money and start spending it fast, hoping that a strong performance in the earliest primaries would give the campaign enough momentum to slingshot past the Clinton machine.

Our hopes were pinned on Iowa. We had to win it or otherwise stand down. Mostly rural and more than 90 percent white, it was a curious state to serve as the nation's political bellwether and was maybe not the most obvious place for a Black guy based in Chicago to try to define himself, but this was the reality. Iowa went first in presidential primaries and had since 1972. Members of both parties cast their votes at precinct-level meetings—caucuses—in the middle of winter, and the whole nation paid attention. If you got yourself noticed in Des Moines and Dubuque, your candidacy automatically mattered in Orlando and L.A. We knew, too, that if we made a good showing in Iowa, it would send the message to Black voters nationally that it was okay to start believing. The fact that Barack was a senator in neighboring Illinois, giving him some name recognition and a familiarity with the area's broader issues, had convinced David Plouffe that we had at least a small advantage in Iowa—one upon which we would now try to capitalize.

This meant that I would be going to Iowa almost weekly, catching early-morning United Airlines flights out of O'Hare, making three or four campaign stops in a day. I told Plouffe early on that while I was happy to campaign, part of the deal had to be that they'd get me back to Chicago in time to put the girls to bed at night. My mother had agreed to cut down her hours at work so that she could be around for the kids more when I was traveling. Barack, too, would be logging many hours in Iowa, though we'd rarely show up there—or anywhere—together. I was now what they call a surrogate for the candidate, a stand-in who could meet with voters at a community center in Iowa City while he campaigned in Cedar Falls or raised money in New York. Only when it really seemed important would the campaign staff put the two of us in the same room.

Barack now traveled with a swarm of attentive aides, and I was allotted funds to hire a two-person staff of my own, which given that I planned to volunteer only two or three days per week to the campaign seemed like plenty to me. I had no idea what I needed in terms of support. Melissa Winter, who was my first hire and would later become my chief of staff, had been recommended by Barack's scheduler. She'd worked in Senator Joe Lieberman's office on Capitol Hill and had been involved in his 2000 vice presidential campaign. I interviewed Melissa—blond, bespectacled, and in her late thirties—in our living room in Chicago and was impressed by her irreverent wit and almost obsessive devotion to detail, which I knew would be important as I tried to integrate campaigning into my already-busy schedule at the hospital. She was sharp, highly efficient, and quick moving. She'd also been around politics enough to be unfazed by its intensity and pace. Just a few years younger than I was, Melissa also felt more like a peer and an ally than the much younger campaign workers I'd encountered. She would become someone I trusted—as I do still, to this day—with literally every part of my life.

Katie McCormick Lelyveld rounded out our little trio by coming on board as my communications director. Not yet thirty, she'd already worked on a presidential campaign and also for Hillary Clinton when she was First Lady, which made her experience doubly relevant. Spunky, intelligent, and always perfectly dressed, Katie would be in charge of wrangling reporters and TV crews, making sure our events were well covered and also—thanks to the leather briefcase she kept packed with stain remover, breath mints, a sewing kit, and an extra pair of nylons—that I didn't make a mess of myself as we sprinted between airplanes and events.

O VER THE YEARS, I'd seen news coverage of presidential candidates making their way around Iowa, awkwardly interrupting tables full of unassuming citizens having coffee at diners, or posing goofily in front of a full-sized cow carved out of butter or eating fried whatevers-on-a-stick at the state fair. What was meaningful to voters and what was just grandstanding, though, I wasn't quite sure.

Barack's advisers had tried to demystify Iowa for me, explaining that my mission was primarily to spend time with Democrats in every corner of the state, addressing small groups, energizing volunteers, and trying to win over leaders in the community. Iowans, they said, took their role as political trendsetters seriously. They did their homework on candidates and asked serious policy questions. Accustomed as they were to months of careful courtship, they were not likely to be won over with a smile and a handshake, either. Some would hold out for months, I was told, expecting a face-to-face conversation with every candidate before finally committing to one. What they didn't tell me was what my message in

Iowa was supposed to be. I was given no script, no talking points, no advice. I figured I'd just work it out for myself.

My first solo campaign event took place in early April inside a modest home in Des Moines. A few dozen people had collected in the living room, sitting on couches and folding chairs that had been brought in for the occasion, while others sat cross-legged on the floor. As I scanned the room, preparing to speak, what I observed probably shouldn't have surprised me, but it did, at least a little. Laid out on the end tables were the same sorts of white crocheted doilies that my grandmother Shields used to have at her house. I spotted porcelain figurines that looked just like the ones Robbie had kept on her shelves downstairs from us on Euclid Avenue. A man in the front row was smiling at me warmly. I was in Iowa, but I had the distinct feeling of being at home. Iowans, I was realizing, were like Shieldses and Robinsons. They didn't suffer fools. They didn't trust people who put on airs. They could sniff out a phony a mile away.

My job, I realized, was to be myself, to speak as myself. And so I did.

"Let me tell you about me. I'm Michelle Obama, raised on the South Side of Chicago, in a little apartment on the top floor of a two-story house that felt a lot like this one. My dad was a water-pump operator for the city. My mom stayed at home to raise my brother and me."

I talked about everything—about my brother and the values we were raised with, about this hotshot lawyer I met at work, the guy who'd stolen my heart with his groundedness and his vision for the world, the man who'd left his socks lying around the house that morning and sometimes snored in his sleep. I told them about how I was keeping my job at the hospital, about how my mother was picking our girls up from school that day.

I didn't sugarcoat my feelings about politics. The political world was no place for good people, I said, explaining how I'd been conflicted about whether Barack should run at all, worried about what the spotlight might do to our family. But I was standing before them because I believed in my husband and what he could do. I knew how much he read and how deeply he thought about things. I said that he was exactly the kind of smart, decent president I would choose for this country, even if selfishly I'd have rather kept him closer to home all these years.

As weeks went by, I'd tell the same story—in Davenport, Cedar Rapids, Council Bluffs; in Sioux City, Marshalltown, Muscatine—in bookstores, union halls, a home for aging military veterans, and, as the weather warmed up, on front porches and in public parks. The more I told my story, the more my voice settled into itself. I liked my story. I was comfortable telling it. And I was telling it to people who despite the difference in skin color reminded me of my family—postal workers who had bigger dreams just as Dandy once had; civic-minded piano teachers like Robbie; stay-at-home moms who were active in the PTA like my mother; blue-collar workers who'd do anything for their families, just like my dad. I didn't need to practice or use notes. I said only what I sincerely felt.

Along the way, reporters and even some acquaintances began asking me some form of the same question: What was it like to be a five-foot-eleven, Ivy League–educated Black woman speaking to roomfuls of mostly white Iowans? How odd did that feel?

I never liked this question. It always seemed to be accompanied by a sheepish half smile and the don't-take-this-the-wrong-way inflection that people often use when approaching the subject of race. It was an idea, I felt, that sold us all short, assuming that the differences were all anyone saw.

Mainly I bristled because the question was so antithetical to what I was experiencing and what the people I was meeting seemed to be experiencing, too—the man with a seed-corn logo on his breast pocket, the college student in a black-and-gold pullover, the retiree who'd brought an ice cream bucket full of sugar cookies she'd frosted with our rising-sun campaign logo. These people found me after my talks, seeming eager to talk about what we shared—to say that their dad had lived with MS, too, or that they'd had grandparents just like mine. Many said they'd never gotten involved with politics before but something about our campaign made them feel it would be worth it. They were planning to volunteer at the local office, they said, and they'd try persuading a spouse or neighbor to come along, too.

These interactions felt natural, genuine. I found myself hugging people instinctively and getting hugged tightly back.

I T WAS AROUND this time that I took Malia to our pediatrician for a well-child visit, which we did every three to six months to keep tabs on the asthma she'd had since she was a baby. The asthma was under control, but the doctor alerted me to something else—Malia's body mass index, a measure of health that factors together height, weight, and age, was beginning to creep up. It wasn't a crisis, he said, but it was a trend to take seriously. If we didn't change some habits, it could become a real problem over time, increasing her risk for high blood pressure and type 2 diabetes. Seeing the stricken look on my face, he assured me that the problem was both common and solvable. The rate of childhood obesity was rising all around the country. He'd seen many examples in his practice, which was made up mostly of working-class African Americans.

The news landed like a rock through a stained-glass window. I'd worked so hard to make sure my daughters were happy and whole. What had I done wrong? What kind of mother was I if I hadn't even noticed a change?

Talking further with the doctor, I began to see the pattern we were in. With Barack gone all the time, convenience had become the single most important factor in my choices at home. We'd been eating out more. With less time to cook, I often picked up takeout on my way home from work. In the mornings, I packed the girls' lunch boxes with Lunchables and Capri Suns. Weekends usually meant a trip to the McDonald's drive-through window after ballet and before soccer. None of this, our doctor said, was out of the ordinary, or even all that terrible in isolation. Too much of it, though, was a real problem.

Clearly, something had to change, but I was at a loss about how to make that happen. Every solution seemed to demand more time—time at the grocery store, time in the kitchen, time spent chopping vegetables or slicing the skin off a chicken breast—all this coming right when time felt as if it were already on the verge of extinction in my world.

I then remembered a conversation I'd had a few weeks earlier with an old friend I'd bumped into on a plane, who'd mentioned that she and her husband had hired a young man named Sam Kass to cook regular healthy meals at her house. By coincidence, it turned out Barack and I had met Sam years earlier through a different set of friends.

I never expected to be the sort of person who hired someone to come into my house and prepare meals for my family. It felt a little bougie, the kind of thing that would elicit a skeptical side eye from my South Side relatives. Barack, he of the Datsun with the hole in the floor, wasn't hot on the idea, either; it didn't fit with his ingrained community-organizer frugality, nor the image he wanted to promote as a presidential candidate. But to me, it felt like the only sane choice. Something had to give. No one else could run my programs at the hospital. No one else could campaign as Barack Obama's wife. No one could fill in as Malia and Sasha's mother at bedtime. But maybe Sam Kass could cook some dinners for us.

I hired Sam to come to our house a couple of times a week, making a meal we could eat that night and another that I could pull from the refrigerator to heat up the next evening. He was a bit of an outlier in the Obama household—a white twenty-six-year-old with a shiny shaved head and a perpetual five o'clock shadow—but the girls took to his corny jokes as quickly as they took to his cooking. He showed them how to chop carrots and blanch greens, shifting our family away from the fluorescent sameness of the grocery store and toward the rhythm of the seasons. He could be reverent about the arrival of fresh peas in springtime or the moment raspberries came ripe in June. He waited until peaches were rich and plump before serving them to the girls, knowing that then they might actually compete with candy. Sam also had an educated perspective on food and health issues, namely how the food industry marketed processed foods to families in the name of convenience and how that was having severe public health consequences. I was intrigued, realizing that it tied in to some of what I'd seen while working for the hospital system, and to the compromises I'd made myself as a working mother trying to feed her family.

One evening Sam and I spent a couple of hours talking in my kitchen, the two of us batting around ideas about how, if Barack ever managed to win the presidency, I might use my role as First Lady to try to address some of these issues. One idea bloomed into another. What if we grew vegetables at the White House and helped advocate for fresh food? What if we then used that as a cornerstone for something bigger, a whole children's health initiative that might help parents avoid some of the pitfalls I'd experienced?

We talked until it was late. I looked at Sam and let out a sigh. "The only problem is our guy is down by thirty points in the polls," I said as the two of us began to crack up. "He's never gonna win."

It was a dream, but I liked it.

W HEN IT CAME to campaigning, each day was another race to be run. I was still trying to cling to some form of normalcy and stability, not just for the girls, but for me. I carried two BlackBerrys—one for work, the other for my personal life and political obligations, which were now, for better or worse, deeply entwined. My daily phone calls with Barack tended to be short and newsy—*Where are you? How's it going? How are the kids?*—both of us accustomed now to not speaking of fatigue or our personal needs. There was no point, because we couldn't attend to them anyway. Life was all about the ticking clock.

At work, I was doing what I could to keep up, sometimes checking in with my staff at the hospital from the cluttered backseat of a Toyota Corolla belonging to an anthropology student volunteering for the campaign in Iowa or from the quiet corner of a Burger King in Plymouth, New Hampshire. Several months after Barack's announcement in Springfield and with the support of my colleagues, I'd decided to scale back to part-time hours, knowing it was the only sustainable way to keep going. On the road two or three days a week together, Melissa, Katie, and I had become an efficient family, meeting up at the airport in the mornings and hustling through security, where the guards all knew my name. I was recognized more often now, mostly by African American women who'd call out "Michelle! Michelle!" as I walked past them to the gate.

Something was changing, so gradually that at first it was hard to register. I sometimes felt as if I were floating through a strange universe, waving at strangers who acted as if they knew me, boarding planes that lifted me out of my normal world. I was becoming *known*. And I was becoming known for being someone's wife and as someone involved with politics, which made it doubly and triply weird.

Working a rope line during campaign events had become like trying to stay upright inside a hurricane, I'd found, with well-meaning, deeply enthusiastic strangers reaching for my hands and touching my hair, people trying to thrust pens, cameras, and babies at me without warning. I'd smile, shake hands, and hear stories, all the while trying to move forward down the line. Ultimately, I'd emerge, with other people's lipstick on my cheeks and handprints on my blouse, looking as if I'd just stepped out of a wind tunnel.

I had little time to think much about it, but quietly I worried that as my visibility as Barack Obama's wife rose, the other parts of me were dissolving from view. When I spoke to reporters, they rarely asked about my work. They inserted "Harvard-educated" in their description of me, but generally left it at that. A couple of news outlets had published stories speculating that I'd been promoted at the hospital not due to my own hard work and merit but because of my husband's growing political stature, which was painful to read. In April, Melissa called me one day at home to let me know about a snarky column written by Maureen Dowd of the *New York Times*. In it, she referred to me as a "princess of South Chicago," suggesting that I was emasculating Barack when I spoke publicly about how he didn't pick up his socks or put the butter back in the fridge. For me, it had always been important that people see Barack as human and not as some otherworldly savior. Maureen Dowd would have preferred, apparently, that I adopt the painted-on smile and the adoring gaze. I found it odd and sad that such a harsh critique would come from another professional woman, someone who had not bothered to get to know me but was now trying to shape my story in a cynical way.

I tried not to take this stuff personally, but sometimes it was hard not to.

With every campaign event, every article published, every sign we might be gaining ground, we became slightly more exposed, more open to attack. Crazy rumors swirled about Barack: that he'd been schooled in a radical Muslim madrassa and sworn into the Senate on a Koran. That he refused to recite the Pledge of Allegiance. That he wouldn't put his hand over his heart during the national anthem. That he had a close friend who was a domestic terrorist from the 1970s. The falsehoods were routinely debunked by reputable news sources but still blazed through anonymous email chains, forwarded not just by basement conspiracy theorists but also by uncles and colleagues and neighbors who couldn't separate fact from fiction online.

Barack's safety was something I didn't want to think about, let alone discuss. So many of us had been brought up with assassinations on the news at night. The Kennedys had been shot. Martin Luther King Jr. had been shot. Ronald Reagan had been shot. John Lennon had been shot. If you drew too much heat, you bore a certain risk. But then again, Barack was a Black man. The risk, for him, was nothing new. "He could get shot just going to the gas station," I sometimes tried to remind people when they brought it up.

Beginning in May, Barack had been assigned Secret Service protection. It was the earliest a presidential candidate had been given a protective detail ever, a full year and a half before he could even become president-elect, which said something about the nature and the seriousness of the threats against him. Barack now traveled in sleek black SUVs provided by the government and was trailed by a team of suited, earpieced men and women with guns. At home, an agent stood guard on our front porch.

For my part, I rarely felt unsafe. As I continued to travel, I was managing to pull in bigger crowds. If I'd once met with twenty people at a time at low-key house parties, I was now speaking to hundreds in a high school gym. The Iowa staff reported that my talks tended to yield a lot of pledges of support (measured in signed "supporter cards," which the campaign collected and followed up with meticulously). At some point, the campaign began referring to me as "the Closer" for the way I helped make up minds.

Each day brought a new lesson about how to move more efficiently, how not to get slowed down by illness or mess of any kind. After being served some questionable food at otherwise charming roadside diners, I learned to value the bland certainty of a McDonald's cheeseburger. On bumpy drives between small towns, I learned how to protect my clothing from spills by seeking out snacks that would crumble rather than drip, knowing that I couldn't be photographed with a dollop of hummus on my dress. I trained myself to limit my water intake, understanding there was rarely time for bathroom breaks on the road. I learned to sleep through the sound of long-haul trucks barreling down the Iowa interstate after midnight and (as happened at one particularly thin-walled hotel) to ignore a happy couple enjoying their wedding night in the next room.

As up and down as I sometimes felt, that first year of campaigning was filled primarily with warm memories and bursts of laughter. As often as I could, I brought Sasha and Malia along with me out on the trail. They were hardy, happy travelers. On a busy day at an outdoor fair in New Hampshire, I'd gone off to give remarks and shake hands with voters, leaving the girls with a campaign staffer to explore the booths and rides before we regrouped for a magazine photo shoot. An hour or so later, I spotted Sasha and panicked. Her cheeks, nose, and forehead had been covered, meticulously and comprehensively, in black and white face paint. She'd been transformed into a panda bear, and she was thrilled about it. My mind went instantly to the magazine crew waiting for us, the schedule that would now be thrown off. But then I looked back at her little panda face and exhaled. My daughter was cute and content. All I could do was laugh and find the nearest restroom to scrub off the paint.

From time to time, we'd travel together as a family, all four of us. The campaign rented an RV for a few days in Iowa, so that we could do barnstorming tours of small towns, punctuated by rousing games of Uno between stops. We passed an afternoon at the Iowa State Fair, riding bumper cars and shooting water soakers to win stuffed animals, as photographers jostled for position, shoving their lenses in our faces. The real fun started after Barack got swept off to his next destination, leaving the girls and me free from the tornado of press, security, and staff that now moved with him, stirring up everything in its wake. Once he'd left, we got to explore the midway on our own, the air rushing past us as we rocketed down a giant yellow slide on burlap sacks.

Week after week, I returned to Iowa, watching through the plane window as the seasons changed, as the earth slowly greened and the soybean and corn crops grew in ruler-straight lines. I loved the tidy geometry of those fields, the pops of color that turned out to be barns, the flat county highways that ran straight to the horizon. I had come to love the state, even if despite all our work it was looking like we might not be able to win there.

For the better part of a year now, Barack and his team had poured resources into Iowa, but according to most polls he was still running second or third behind Hillary and John Edwards. The race looked to be close, but Barack was losing. Nationally, the picture appeared worse: Barack consistently trailed Hillary by a full fifteen or twenty points—a reality I was hit with anytime I passed by the cable news blaring in airports or at campaign-stop restaurants.

Months earlier, I'd become so fed up with the relentless, carnival-barker commentary on CNN, MSNBC, and Fox News that I'd permanently blacklisted those channels during my evenings at home, treating myself instead to a more steadying diet of E! and HGTV. At the end of a busy day, I will tell you, there is nothing better than watching a young couple find their dream home in Nashville or some young bride-to-be saying yes to the dress.

Quite honestly, I didn't believe the pundits, and I wasn't sure about the polls, either. In my heart, I was convinced they were wrong. The climate described from inside sterile urban studios was not the one I was encountering in the church halls and rec centers of Iowa. The pundits weren't meeting teams of high school "Barack Stars," who volunteered after football practice or drama club. They weren't holding hands with a white grandmother who imagined a better future for her mixed-race grandchildren. Nor did they seem aware of the proliferating giant that was our field organization. We were in the process of building a massive grassroots campaign network—ultimately two hundred staffers in thirty-seven offices—the largest in the history of the Iowa caucuses.

We had youth on our side. Our organization was powered by the idealism and energy of twenty-two- to twenty-five-year-olds who had dropped everything and driven themselves to Iowa to join the campaign, each one carrying some permutation of the gene that had compelled Barack to take the organizing job in Chicago all those years ago. They had a spirit and skill that hadn't yet been accounted for in the polls. I felt it every time I visited, a surge of hope that came from interacting with true believers who were spending four or five hours every evening knocking on doors and calling voters, building networks of supporters in even the tiniest and most conservative towns, while learning by heart the intricacies of my husband's stance on hog confinements or his plan to fix the immigration system.

To me, the young people managing our field offices represented the promise of the coming generation of leaders. They weren't jaded, and now they'd been galvanized and united. They were connecting voters more directly to their democracy, whether through the field office down the street or a website through which they could organize their own meetings and phone banks. As Barack often said, what we were doing wasn't just about a single election. It was about making politics better for the future—less money-driven, more accessible, and ultimately more hopeful. Even if we didn't end up winning, we were making progress that mattered. One way or another, their work would count.

A S THE WEATHER began to turn cold again, Barack knew he had basically one last chance to change up the race in Iowa, and that was by making a strong showing at the Jefferson-Jackson dinner, an annual Democratic ritual in every state. In Iowa, during a presidential election, it was held in early November, about eight weeks ahead of the January caucuses, and covered by the national media. The premise was that every candidate gave a speech—with no notes and no teleprompter—and also tried to bring along as many supporters as possible. It was, in essence, a giant and competitive pep rally.

For months, the cable news commentators had doubted that Iowans would stand up for Barack at caucus time, insinuating that as dynamic and unusual a candidate as he was, he still wouldn't manage to convert the enthusiasm into votes. The crowd at the Jefferson-Jackson dinner was our answer to this. About three thousand of our supporters had driven in from all over the state, showing that we were both organized and active— stronger than anyone thought.

Onstage that night, John Edwards took a shot at Clinton, speaking in veiled terms about sincerity and trustworthiness being important. Grinning, Joe Biden acknowledged the impressive and noisy turnout of Obama supporters with a sardonic "Hello, Chicago!" Hillary, who was fighting a cold, also used the opportunity to go after Barack. "'Change' is just a word," she said, "if you don't have the strength and experience to make it happen."

Barack was the last to speak that night, delivering a rousing defense of his central message—that our country had arrived at a defining moment, a chance to step beyond not just the fear and failures of the Bush administration but the polarized way politics had been waged long before, including, of course, during the Clinton administration. "I don't want to spend the next year or the next four years refighting the same fights that we had in the 1990s," he said. "I don't want to pit Red America against Blue America, I want to be the president of the United States of America."

The auditorium thundered. I watched from the floor with huge pride. "America, our moment is now," Barack said. "Our moment is now."

His performance that night gave the campaign exactly what it needed, catapulting him forward in the race. He took the lead in about half the Iowa polls and was only gaining steam as the caucuses approached.

In the days after Christmas, with just a week or so left in the Iowa campaign, it seemed as if half of the South Side had migrated to the deep freeze of Des Moines. My mother and Mama Kaye showed up. My brother and Kelly came, bringing their kids. Sam Kass was there. Valerie, who'd joined the campaign earlier in the fall as one of Barack's advisers, was there, along with Susan and my posse of girlfriends and their husbands and children. I was touched when colleagues from the hospital showed up, friends of ours from Sidley & Austin, law professors who'd taught with Barack. And, in step with the use-every-moment ethic of the campaign, they all signed on to help make the final push, reporting to a local field office, knocking on doors in zero-degree weather, talking up Barack, and reminding people to caucus. The campaign was further reinforced by hundreds of others who'd traveled to Iowa from around the country for the final week, staying in the spare bedrooms of local supporters, heading out each day into even the smallest towns and down the most tucked away of gravel roads.

I myself was barely present in Des Moines, doing five or six events a day that kept me moving back and forth across the state, traveling in a rented van with Melissa and Katie, driven by a rotating crew of volunteers. Barack was out doing the same, his voice beginning to grow hoarse.

Regardless of how many miles we had to cover, I made sure to be back at the Residence Inn in West Des Moines, our home-base hotel, each night in time for Malia and Sasha's eight o'clock bedtime. They, of course, barely seemed to notice I wasn't around, having been surrounded by cousins and friends and babysitters all day long, playing games in the hotel room and going on excursions around town. One night, I opened the door, hoping to flop on the bed for a few moments of silence, only to find our room strewn with kitchen utensils. There were rolling pins on the bedspread, dirty cutting boards on the small table, kitchen shears on the floor. The lamp shades and the television screen were covered with a light dusting of . . . was that *flour*?

"Sam taught us to make pasta!" Malia announced. "We got a little carried away."

I laughed. I'd been worried about how the girls would handle their first Christmas break away from their great-grandmother in Hawaii. But blessedly, a bag of flour in Des Moines appeared to be a fine substitute for a beach towel in Waikiki.

Several days later, a Thursday, the caucuses arrived. Barack and I dropped into a downtown Des Moines food court over lunch and later made visits to various caucus sites to greet as many voters as we could. Late that evening, we joined a group of friends and family at dinner, thanking them for their support during what had been a nutty eleven months since the announcement in Springfield. I left the meal early to return to my hotel room in time to prepare, win or lose, for Barack's speech later that night. Within moments, Katie and Melissa burst in with fresh news from the campaign's war room: "We won!"

We were wild with joy, shouting so loudly that the Secret Service rapped on our door to make sure something wasn't wrong.

On one of the coldest nights of the year, a record number of Iowans had fanned out to their local caucuses, almost double the turnout from four years earlier. Barack had won among whites, Blacks, and young people. More than half of the attendees had never participated in a caucus before, and that group likely helped secure Barack's victory. The cable news anchors had finally made their way to Iowa and were now singing the praises of this political wunderkind who'd comfortably bested the Clinton machine as well as a former vice presidential nominee.

That night at Barack's victory speech, as the four of us—Barack, me, Malia, Sasha—stood onstage at Hy-Vee Hall, I felt great, even a little chastened. Maybe, I thought to myself, everything Barack had been talking about for all those years really was possible. All those drives to Springfield, all his frustrations about not making a big enough impact, all his idealism, his unusual and earnest belief that people were capable of moving past the things that divided them, that in the end politics could work—maybe he'd been right all along.

We'd accomplished something historic, something monumental— not just Barack, not just me, but Melissa and Katie, and Plouffe, Axelrod, and Valerie, and every young staffer, every volunteer, every teacher and farmer and retiree and high schooler who stood up that night for something new.

It was after midnight when Barack and I went to the airport to leave Iowa, knowing we wouldn't be back for months. The girls and I were headed home to Chicago, returning to work and school. Barack was flying to New Hampshire, where the primary was less than a week away.

Iowa had changed us all. Iowa had given me, in particular, real faith. Our mandate now was to share it with the rest of the country. In the coming days, our Iowa field organizers would fan out to other states—to Nevada and South Carolina, to New Mexico, Minnesota, and California—to continue spreading the message that had now been proven, that change was really possible.

17

W HEN I WAS IN FIRST GRADE, A BOY IN MY CLASS
punched me in the face one day, his fist coming like a comet, full force and out of nowhere. We'd been lining up to go to lunch, all of us discussing whatever felt urgent just then to six- and seven-year-olds—who was the fastest runner or why crayon colors had such weird names—when *blam,* I got whacked. I don't know why. I've forgotten the boy's name, but I remember staring at him dumbfounded and in pain, my lower lip already swelling, my eyes hot with tears. Too shocked to be angry, I ran home to my mom.

The boy got a talking-to from our teacher. My mother went over to school to personally lay eyes on the kid, wanting to assess what kind of threat he posed. Southside, who must have been over at our house that day, got his grandfatherly hackles up and insisted on going over with her as well. I was not privy to it, but some sort of conversation between adults took place. Some type of punishment was meted out. I received a shamefaced apology from the boy and was instructed not to worry about him further.

"That boy was just scared and angry about things that had nothing to do with you," my mother told me later in our kitchen as she stirred dinner on the stove. She shook her head as if to suggest she knew more than she was willing to share. "He's dealing with a whole lot of problems of his own."

This was how we talked about bullies. When I was a kid, it was easy to grasp: Bullies were scared people hiding inside scary people. I'd see it in DeeDee, the tough girl on my neighborhood block, and even in Dandy, my own grandfather, who could be rude and pushy even with his own wife. They lashed out because they felt overwhelmed. You avoided them if you could and stood up to them if you had to. According to my mother, who would probably want some sort of live-and-let-live slogan carved on her headstone, the key was never to let a bully's insults or aggression get to you personally.

If you did—well, then, you could really get hurt.

Only later in life would this become a real challenge for me. Only when I was in my early forties and trying to help get my husband elected president would I think back to that day in the lunch line in first grade, remembering how confusing it was to be ambushed, how much it hurt to get socked in the face with no warning at all.

I spent much of 2008 trying not to worry about the punches.

I'LL BEGIN BY jumping ahead to a happy memory from that year, because I do have many of them. We visited Butte, Montana, on the Fourth of July, which happened to be Malia's tenth birthday and about four months ahead of the general election. Butte is a hardy, historic copper-mining town set down in the brushy southwestern corner of Montana, with the dark ridgeline of the Rocky Mountains visible in the distance. Butte was a toss-up town in what our campaign hoped could be a toss-up state. Montana had gone for George W. Bush in the last election but had also elected a Democratic governor. It seemed like a good place for Barack to visit.

More than ever, there were calculations involved in how Barack spent every minute of every day. He was being watched, measured, evaluated. People took note of which states he visited, which diner he showed up at for breakfast, what kind of meat he ordered to go with his eggs. About twenty-five members of the press traveled with him continuously now, filling the back of the campaign plane, filling the corridors and breakfast rooms of small-town hotels, trailing him from stop to stop, their pens immortalizing everything. If a presidential candidate caught a cold, it got reported. If someone got an expensive haircut or asked for Dijon mustard at a TGI Fridays (as Barack had naively done years earlier, meriting an eventual headline in the *New York Times*), it would get reported and then parsed a hundred ways on the internet. Was the candidate weak? Was he a snob? A phony? A true American?

This was part of the process, we understood—a test to see who had the mettle to hold up as both a leader and a symbol for the country itself. It was like having your soul X-rayed every day, scanned and rescanned for any sign of fallibility. You didn't get elected if you didn't first submit to the full-bore scrutiny of the American gaze, which ran itself over your entire history, including your social associations, professional choices, and tax returns. And that gaze was arguably more intense and open to manipulation than ever. We were just coming into an age where clicks were being measured and monetized. Facebook had only recently gone mainstream. Twitter was relatively new. Most American adults owned a cell phone, and most cell phones had a camera. We were standing at the edge of something I'm not sure any of us yet fully understood.

Barack was no longer just trying to win the support of Democratic voters; he was now courting all of America. Following the Iowa caucuses, in a process that was at times as punishing and ugly as it was heartening and defining, Barack and Hillary Clinton had spent the winter and spring of 2008 slogging it out in every state and territory, battling vote by hard-earned vote for the privilege of becoming a boundary-breaking candidate. (John Edwards, Joe Biden, and the other contenders had all dropped out by the end of January.) The two candidates had tested each other mightily, with Barack opening up a small but ultimately decisive lead midway through February. "Is he president now?" Malia would ask me sometimes over the months that followed as we stood on one stage or another, with celebratory music blasting around us, her young mind unable to grasp anything but the larger purpose.

"Okay, *now* is he president?"

"No, honey, not yet."

It wasn't until June that Hillary acknowledged that she lacked the delegate count to win. Her delay in conceding had wasted precious campaign resources, preventing Barack from being able to reorient the battle toward his Republican opponent, John McCain. The longtime Arizona senator had become the Republican Party's presumptive nominee all the way back in March and was running as a maverick war hero with a history of bipartisanship and deep experience in national security, the implication being that he'd lead differently than George W. Bush.

We were in Butte on the Fourth of July with twin purposes, because nearly everything had a twin purpose now. Barack had spent the previous four days campaigning in Missouri, Ohio, Colorado, and North Dakota. There was little time to waste by having him come off the campaign trail to celebrate Malia's birthday, and he couldn't slip out of voters' view on what was the country's most symbolic holiday. So instead we flew to him, for what would be a sort of attempt to have it both ways—a family day spent mostly in full view of the public. Barack's half sister Maya and her husband, Konrad, came with us, along with their daughter Suhaila, a cute little four-year-old.

Any parent of a child born on a major holiday knows that there's already a certain line to be walked between an individual celebration and more universal festivities. The good people of Butte seemed to get it. There were "Happy Birthday Malia!" signs taped inside the windows of storefronts along Main Street. Bystanders shouted out their good wishes to her over the pounding of bass drums and flutes piping "Yankee Doodle" as our family watched the town's Fourth of July parade from a set of bleachers. The people we met were kind to the girls and respectful to us, even when confessing that voting for any Democrat would be a half-crazy departure from tradition.

Later that day, the campaign hosted a picnic in an open field with views of the spiny mountains marking the Continental Divide. The gathering was meant to be a rally for several hundred of our local supporters as well as a kind of casual birthday celebration for Malia. I was moved by all the people who'd turned out to meet us, but at the same time I was feeling something more intimate and urgent that had nothing to do with where we were. I was struck that day by the gobsmacked tenderness that comes with being a parent, the weird telescoping of time that happens when you notice suddenly that your babies are half-grown, their limbs going from pudgy to lean, their eyes getting wise.

For me, the Fourth of July 2008 was the most significant threshold we'd crossed: Ten years ago, Barack and I had shown up on the labor and delivery floor believing that we knew a lot about the world when, truly, we hadn't yet known a thing.

So much of the last decade had been about trying to strike a balance between my family and my work, figuring out how to be loving and present for Malia and Sasha while also trying to be decent at my job. But the axis had shifted: I was now trying to balance parenting with something altogether different and more confusing—politics, America, Barack's quest to do something important. The magnitude of what was happening in Barack's life, the demands of the campaign, the spotlight on our family, all seemed to be growing quickly. After the Iowa caucuses, I'd decided to take a leave of absence from my position at the hospital, knowing that it would be impossible, really, to stay on and be effective. The campaign was slowly consuming everything. I'd been too busy after Iowa to even go over and box up the things in my office or say any sort of proper goodbye. I was a full-time mother and wife now, albeit a wife with a cause and a mother who wanted to guard her kids against getting swallowed by that cause. It had been painful to step away from my work, but there was no choice: My family needed me, and that mattered more.

And so here I was at a campaign picnic in Montana, leading a group of mostly strangers in singing "Happy Birthday" to Malia, who sat smiling on the grass with a hamburger on her plate. Voters saw our daughters as sweet, I knew, and our family's closeness as endearing. But I did think often of how all this appeared to our daughters, what their view was looking outward. I tried to tamp down any guilt. We had a real birthday party planned for the following weekend, one involving a heap of Malia's friends sleeping over at our house in Chicago and no politics whatsoever. And that evening, we'd hold a more private gathering back at our hotel. Still, as the afternoon went on and our girls ran around the picnic grounds while Barack and I shook hands and hugged potential voters, I found myself wondering if the two of them would remember this outing as fun.

I watched Sasha and Malia these days with a new fierceness in my heart. Like me, they now had strangers calling their names, people wanting to touch them and take their pictures. Over the winter, the government had deemed me and the girls exposed enough to assign us Secret Service protection, which meant that when Sasha and Malia went to school or their summer day camp, usually driven by my mother, it was with the Secret Service tailing them in a second car.

At the picnic, each one of us had our own agent flanking us, canvassing the gathering for any sign of threat, subtly intervening if a well-wisher got overenthused and grabby. Thankfully, the girls seemed to see the agents less as guards and more as grown-up friends, new additions to the growing knot of friendly people with whom we traveled, distinguishable only by their earpieces and quiet vigilance. Sasha generally referred to them as "the secret people."

The girls made campaigning more relaxing, if only because they weren't much invested in the outcome. For both me and Barack, they were a relief to be around—a reminder that in the end our family meant more than any tallying of supporters or bump in the polls. Neither daughter cared much about the hubbub surrounding their dad. They weren't focused on building a better democracy or getting to the White House. All they really wanted (really, really wanted) was a puppy. They loved playing tag or card games with campaign staff during the quieter moments and made a point of finding an ice cream shop in every new place they went. Everything else was just noise.

To this day, Malia and I still crack up about the fact that she'd been eight years old when Barack, clearly feeling some sense of responsibility, posed the question one night while he was tucking her into bed. "How would you feel if Daddy ran for president?" he'd asked. "Do you think that's a good idea?"

"Sure, Daddy!" she'd replied, pecking him on the cheek. His decision to run would alter nearly everything about her life after that, but how was she to know? She'd just rolled over then and drifted off to sleep.

That day in Butte, we visited the local mining museum, had a water-pistol battle, and kicked a soccer ball around in the grass. Barack gave his stump speech and shook the usual number of hands, but he also got to anchor himself back inside the unit of us. Sasha and Malia climbed all over him, giggling and regaling him with their thoughts. I saw the lightness in his smile, admiring him for his ability to block out the peripheral distractions and just be a dad when he had the chance. He chatted with Maya and Konrad and kept an arm hooked around my shoulder as we walked from place to place.

We were never alone. We had staff around us, agents guarding us, members of the press waiting for interviews, onlookers snapping pictures from a distance. But this was now our normal. Over the course of the campaign, our days had become so programmed that we'd watched our privacy and autonomy slowly slip away, both Barack and I handing nearly every aspect of our lives over to a bunch of twentysomethings who were highly intelligent and capable but still couldn't know how painful it could feel to give up control over my own life. If I needed something at the store, I had to ask someone to get it for me. If I wanted to speak to Barack, I usually had to send a request through one of his young staffers. Events and activities I didn't know about would sometimes show up on my calendar.

But slowly, as a matter of survival, we were learning to live our lives more publicly, accepting the reality for what it was.

Before the afternoon ended in Butte, we gave a TV interview, all four of us—me, Barack, and the girls—which was something we'd never done before. Usually, we insisted on keeping the press corps at a distance from our kids, limiting them to photos and then only at public campaign events. I'm not sure what prompted us to say yes this time. As I recall, the campaign staff thought it would be nice to give the public a closer glimpse of Barack as a parent, and in the moment I saw no harm in this. He loved our children, after all. He loved all children. It was precisely why he'd make a great president.

We sat down for about fifteen minutes with Maria Menounos of *Access Hollywood*, the four of us speaking to her while sitting together on a park bench that had been draped with some sort of cloth to make it look more festive. Malia had her hair braided and Sasha wore a red tank dress. As always, they were disarmingly cute. Menounos was gracious and kept the conversation light as Malia, the family's junior professor, earnestly pondered every question. She said that her dad embarrassed her sometimes when he tried to shake hands with her friends and also that he bothered all of us when he left his campaign luggage blocking the door at home. Sasha did her best to sit still and stay focused, interrupting the interview only once, turning to me to ask, "Hey, when are we getting ice cream?" Otherwise, she listened to her sister, interjecting periodically with whatever semirelevant detail popped into her head. "Daddy had an Afro once!" she squealed at one point toward the end, and we all started to laugh.

Days later, the interview aired in four parts on ABC and was met with an enthused fervor, covered by other news outlets with cloying tag-lines like "Curtain Rises on Obama's Girls in TV Interview" and "The Obamas' Two Little Girls Tell All." Suddenly Malia's and Sasha's little-kid comments were being picked up in newspapers around the world.

Immediately, Barack and I regretted what we'd done. There was nothing salacious about the interview. There was no exploitative question asked, no especially revealing detail offered. Still, we felt like we'd made a wrong choice, putting their voices into the public sphere long before they could really understand what any of it meant. Nothing in the video would hurt Sasha or Malia. But it was out in the world now and would live forever on the internet. We'd taken two young girls who hadn't chosen this life, and without thinking it through, we'd fed them into the maw.

B Y NOW, I knew something about the maw. We lived with the gaze upon us. It added a strange energy to everything. I had Oprah Winfrey sending me encouraging texts. Stevie Wonder, my childhood idol, was showing up to play at campaign events, joking and calling me by my first name as if we'd known each other forever. The amount of attention was disorienting, especially because I felt as if we hadn't really done much to deserve it. We were being lifted by the strength of the message Barack was putting forward, but also, I knew, by the promise and the symbolism of the moment. If America elected its first Black president, it would say something not just about Barack but also about the country. For so many people, and for so many reasons, this mattered a lot.

Barack, of course, got the most of it—the public adulation as well as the scrutiny that rode inevitably on its back. The more popular you became, the more haters you acquired. It seemed almost like an unwritten rule, especially in politics, where adversaries put money into opposition research—hiring investigators to crawl through every piece of a candidate's background, looking for anything resembling dirt.

We are built differently, my husband and I, which is why one of us chose politics and the other did not. He was aware of rumors and misperceptions that got pumped like toxic vapor into the campaign, but rarely did any of it bother him. Barack had lived through other campaigns. He'd studied political history and girded himself with the context it provided. And in general, he's just not someone who's easily rattled or thrown off course by anything as abstract as doubt or hurt.

I, on the other hand, was still learning about public life. I considered myself a confident, successful woman, but I was also the same kid who used to tell people she planned to be a pediatrician and devoted herself to setting perfect attendance records at school. In other words, I cared what people thought. I'd spent my young life seeking approval, dutifully collecting gold stars and avoiding messy social situations. Over time, I'd gotten better about not measuring my self-worth strictly in terms of standard, by-the-book achievement, but I did tend to believe that if I worked diligently and honestly, I'd avoid the bullies and always be seen as myself.

This belief, though, was about to come undone.

After Barack's victory in Iowa, my message on the campaign trail grew only more impassioned, almost proportional to the size of the crowds that were turning out at rallies. I'd gone from meeting hundreds of people at a gathering to a thousand or more. I remember pulling up to an event in Delaware with Melissa and Katie and seeing a line of people five-deep and stretching around the block, waiting to get inside an already-jammed auditorium. It stunned me in the happiest of ways. I relayed this to every crowd: I was floored by what people were bringing to Barack's campaign in terms of enthusiasm and involvement. I was humbled by their investment, the work I saw everyday people doing to help get him elected.

When it came to my stump speech, building on the theory of campaigning that had worked so well for me in Iowa, I'd developed a loose structure for it, though I didn't use a teleprompter or worry if I went off on a slight tangent. My words weren't polished, and I'd never be as eloquent as my husband, but I spoke from the heart. I described how my initial doubts about the political process had slowly diminished week by week, replaced by something more encouraging and hopeful. So many of us, I was realizing, had the same struggles, the same concerns for our kids and worries about the future. And so many believed as I did that Barack was the only candidate capable of delivering real change.

Barack wanted to get American troops out of Iraq. He wanted to roll back the tax cuts George W. Bush had pushed through for the super-wealthy. He wanted affordable health care for all Americans. It was an ambitious platform, but every time I walked into an auditorium of revved-up supporters, it seemed as if maybe as a nation we were ready to look past our differences and make it happen. There was pride in those rooms, a united spirit that went well past the color of anyone's skin. The optimism was big and it was energizing. I surfed it like a wave. "Hope is making a comeback!" I would declare at every stop.

I'd been in Wisconsin one day in February when Katie got a call from someone on Barack's communications team, saying that there seemed to be a problem. I'd evidently said something controversial in a speech I'd given at a theater in Milwaukee a few hours earlier. Katie was confused, as was I. What I'd said in Milwaukee was really no different from what I'd just finished saying to a crowd in Madison, which was no different from what I'd been saying to every crowd for months. There'd never been an issue before. Why would there be one now?

Later that day, we saw the issue for ourselves. Someone had taken film from my roughly forty-minute talk and edited it down to a single ten-second clip, stripping away the context, putting the emphasis on a few words.

There were clips suddenly circulating from both the Milwaukee and the Madison speeches, focused on the part where I talked about feeling encouraged. The fuller version of what I'd said that day went like this: "What we've learned over this year is that hope is making a comeback! And let me tell you something, for the first time in my adult lifetime, I'm really proud of my country. Not just because Barack has done well, but because I think people are hungry for change. I have been desperate to see our country moving in that direction, and just not feeling so alone in my frustration and disappointment. I've seen people who are hungry to be unified around some basic common issues, and it's made me proud. I feel privileged to be a part of even witnessing this."

But nearly all of that had been peeled back, including my references to hope and unity and how moved I was. The nuance was gone; the gaze directed toward one thing. What was in the clips—and now sliding into heavy rotation on conservative radio and TV talk shows, we were told— was this: "For the first time in my adult lifetime, I'm really proud of my country."

I didn't need to watch the news to know how it was being spun. *She's not a patriot. She's always hated America. This is who she really is. The rest is just a show.*

Here was the first punch. And I'd seemingly brought it on myself. In trying to speak casually, I'd forgotten how weighted each little phrase could be. Unwittingly, I'd given the haters a fourteen-word feast. Just like in first grade, I hadn't seen it coming.

I flew home to Chicago that night, feeling guilty and dispirited. I knew that Melissa and Katie were quietly tracking the negative news stories via BlackBerry, though they were careful not to share them with me, understanding it would only make things worse. The three of us had worked together for the better part of a year at this point, logging more miles than any of us could count, perpetually racing the clock so I could get back home to my kids at night. We'd trekked through auditoriums all over the country, eaten more fast food than we ever wanted to, and shown up for fancy fund-raisers at homes so opulent we'd had to actively keep ourselves from gawking. While Barack and his campaign team traveled in chartered planes and cushy tour buses, we were still taking off our shoes in slow-moving airport security lines, sitting in coach on United and Southwest, relying on the goodwill of volunteers to shuttle us to and from events that were sometimes a hundred miles apart.

I felt as if overall we'd been doing a pretty excellent job. I'd seen Katie stand on a chair to shout marching orders at photographers twice her age and dress down reporters who asked out-of-line questions. I'd watched Melissa mastermind every detail of my schedule, expertly co-ordinating multiple campaign events in a day, pounding her BlackBerry to squelch potential problems, while also making sure I never missed a school play, an old friend's birthday, or a chance to get myself to the gym. The two of them had given everything over to this effort, sacrificing their own personal lives so that I could try to preserve some semblance of mine.

I sat under the dome light of the airplane, worried that I'd somehow blown it with those fourteen stupid words.

At home, after I'd put the girls to bed and sent my mom back to Euclid Avenue to get some rest, I called Barack on his cell. It was the eve of the Wisconsin primaries, and polls there were showing a tight race. Barack had a thin but growing lead when it came to delegates for the national convention, but Hillary had been running ads criticizing Barack on everything from his health-care plan to his not agreeing to debate her more frequently. The stakes seemed high. Barack's campaign couldn't afford a letdown. I apologized for what was happening with my speech. "I had no idea I was doing something wrong," I said. "I've been saying the same thing for months."

Barack was traveling that night between Wisconsin and Texas. I could almost hear him shrugging on the other end of the line. "Look, it's because your crowds are so big," he said. "You've become a force in the campaign, which means people are going to come after you a little. This is just the nature of things."

As he did pretty much every time we spoke, he thanked me for the time I was putting in, adding that he was sorry I had to deal with any fallout at all. "I love you, honey," he told me, before hanging up. "I know this stuff is rough, but it'll blow over. It always does."

. . .

H E WAS BOTH right and wrong about this. On February 19, 2008, Barack won the Wisconsin primary by a good margin, which seemed to suggest I'd done him no damage there. That same day, Cindy McCain took a potshot at me while speaking at a rally, saying, "I am proud of my country. I don't know about you, if you heard those words earlier—I am very proud of my country." CNN deemed us to be in a "patriotism flap," and the bloggers did what bloggers do. But within about a week, it seemed that most of the commotion had died down. Barack and I both made comments to the press, clarifying that I felt a pride in seeing so many Americans making phone calls for the campaign, talking to their neighbors, and gaining confidence about their power inside our democracy, which to me did feel like a first. And then we moved on. In my campaign speeches, I tried to be more careful about how the words came out of my mouth, but my message remained the same. I was still proud and still encouraged. Nothing there had changed.

And yet a pernicious seed had been planted—a perception of me as disgruntled and vaguely hostile, lacking some expected level of grace. Whether it was originating from Barack's political opponents or elsewhere, we couldn't tell, but the rumors and slanted commentary almost always carried less-than-subtle messaging about race, meant to stir up the deepest and ugliest kind of fear within the voting public. *Don't let the Black folks take over. They're not like you. Their vision is not yours.*

This wasn't helped by the fact that ABC News had combed through twenty-nine hours of the Reverend Jeremiah Wright's sermons, splicing together a jarring highlight reel that showed the preacher careening through callous and inappropriate fits of rage and resentment at white America, as if white people were to blame for every woe. Barack and I were dismayed to see this, a reflection of the worst and most paranoid parts of the man who'd married us and baptized our children. Both of us had grown up with family members who viewed race through a lens of cranky mistrust. I'd experienced Dandy's simmering resentment over the decades he'd spent being passed by professionally because of his skin color, as well as Southside's worries that his grandkids weren't safe in white neighborhoods. Barack, meanwhile, had listened to Toot, his white grandmother, make offhanded ethnic generalizations and even confess to her Black grandson that she sometimes felt afraid when running into a Black man on the street. We had lived for years with the narrow-mindedness of some of our elders, having accepted that no one is perfect, particularly those who'd come of age in a time of segregation. Perhaps this had caused us to overlook the more absurd parts of Reverend Wright's spitfire preaching, even if we hadn't been present for any of the sermons in question. Seeing an extreme version of his vitriol broadcast in the news, though, we were appalled. The whole affair was a reminder of how our country's distortions about race could be two-sided—that the suspicion and stereotyping ran both ways.

Someone, meanwhile, had dug up my senior thesis from Princeton, written more than two decades earlier—a survey that looked at how African American alumni felt about race and identity after being at Princeton. For reasons I'll never understand, the conservative media was treating my paper as if it were some secret Black-power manifesto, a threat that had been unburied. It was as if at the age of twenty-one, instead of trying to get an A in sociology and a spot at Harvard Law School, I'd been hatching a Nat Turner plan to overthrow the white majority and was now finally, through my husband, getting a chance to put it in motion. "Is Michelle Obama Responsible for the Jeremiah Wright Fiasco?" was the subtitle of an online column written by the author Christopher Hitchens. He tore into the college-age me, suggesting that I'd been unduly influenced by Black radical thinkers and furthermore was a crappy writer. "To describe it as hard to read would be a mistake," he wrote. "The thesis cannot be 'read' at all, in the strict sense of the verb. This is because it wasn't written in any known language."

I was being painted not simply as an outsider but as fully "other," so foreign that even my language couldn't be recognized. It was a small-minded and ludicrous insult, sure, but his mocking of my intellect, his marginalizing of my young self, carried with it a larger dismissiveness. Barack and I were now too well-known to be rendered invisible, but if people saw us as alien and trespassing, then maybe our potency could be drained. The message seemed often to get telegraphed, if never said directly: *These people don't belong.* A photo of Barack wearing a turban and traditional Somali clothing that had been bestowed on him during an official visit he'd made to Kenya as a senator had shown up on the *Drudge Report,* reviving old theories that he was secretly Muslim. A few months later, the internet would burp up another anonymous and unfounded rumor, this one questioning Barack's citizenship, floating the idea that he'd been born not in Hawaii but in Kenya, which would make him ineligible to become president.

As we carried on through primaries in Ohio and Texas, in Vermont and Mississippi, I had continued to speak about optimism and unity, feeling the positivity of people at campaign events coalescing around the idea of change. All along, though, the unflattering counternarrative about me seemed only to gain traction. On Fox News, there'd be discussions of my "militant anger." The internet would produce more rumors that a videotape existed of me referring to white people as "whitey," which was outlandish and just plainly untrue. In June, when Barack finally clinched the Democratic nomination, I'd greet him with a playful fist bump onstage at an event in Minnesota, which would then make headlines, interpreted by one Fox commentator as a "terrorist fist jab," again suggesting that we were dangerous. A news chyron on the same network had referred to me as "Obama's Baby Mama," conjuring clichéd notions of Black-ghetto America, implying an otherness that put me outside even my own marriage.

I was getting worn out, not physically, but emotionally. The punches hurt, even if I understood that they had little to do with who I really was as a person. It was as if there were some cartoon version of me out there wreaking havoc, a woman I kept hearing about but didn't know—a too-tall, too-forceful, ready-to-emasculate Godzilla of a political wife named Michelle Obama. Painfully, too, my friends would sometimes call and unload their worries on me, heaping me with advice they thought I should pass on to Barack's campaign manager or wanting me to reassure them after they'd heard a negative news report about me, or Barack, or the state of the campaign. When rumors about the so-called whitey tape surfaced, a friend who knows me well called up, clearly worried that the lie was true. I had to spend a good thirty minutes convincing her that I hadn't turned into a racist, and when the conversation ended, I hung up, thoroughly demoralized.

In general, I felt as if I couldn't win, that no amount of faith or hard work would push me past my detractors and their attempts to invalidate me. I was female, Black, and strong, which to certain people, maintaining a certain mind-set, translated only to "angry." It was another damaging cliché, one that's been forever used to sweep minority women to the perimeter of every room, an unconscious signal not to listen to what we've got to say.

I was now starting to actually feel a bit angry, which then made me feel worse, as if I were fulfilling some prophecy laid out for me by the haters, as if I'd given in. It's remarkable how a stereotype functions as an actual trap. How many "angry Black women" have been caught in the circular logic of that phrase? When you aren't being listened to, why wouldn't you get louder? If you're written off as angry or emotional, doesn't that just cause more of the same?

I was exhausted by the meanness, thrown off by how personal it had become, and feeling, too, as if there were no way I could quit. Sometime in May, the Tennessee Republican Party released an online video, replaying my remarks in Wisconsin against clips of voters saying things like "Boy, I've been proud to be an American since I was a kid." NPR's website carried a story with the headline: "Is Michelle Obama an Asset or Liability?" Below it, in boldface, came what were apparently points of debate about me: "Refreshingly Honest or Too Direct?" and "Her Looks: Regal or Intimidating?"

I am telling you, this stuff hurt.

I sometimes blamed Barack's campaign for the position I was in. I understood that I was more active than many candidates' spouses, which made me more of a target for attacks. My instinct was to hit back, to speak up against the lies and unfair generalizations or to have Barack make some comment, but his campaign team kept telling me it was better not to respond, to march forward and simply take the hits. "This is just politics" was always the mantra, as if we could do nothing about it, as if we'd all moved to a new city on a new planet called Politics, where none of the normal rules applied.

Anytime my spirits started to dip, I'd punish myself further with a slew of disparaging thoughts: I hadn't chosen this. I'd never liked politics. I'd left my job and given my identity over to this campaign and now I was a liability? Where had my power gone?

Sitting in our kitchen in Chicago on a Sunday evening when Barack was home for a one-night stopover, I'd let all my frustrations pour out.

"I don't need to do this," I told him. "If I'm hurting the campaign, why on earth am I out there?"

I explained that Melissa, Katie, and I were feeling overmatched by the volume of media requests and the work it took to travel on the tight budget we were on. I didn't want to foul anything up and I wanted to be supportive, but we lacked the time and resources to do any more than react to the moment at hand. And when it came to the mounting scrutiny of me, I was tired of being defenseless, tired of being seen as someone altogether different from the person I was. "I can just stay home and be with the kids if that's better," I told Barack. "I'll just be a regular wife who shows up only at the big events and smiles. Maybe that'd be a lot easier on everybody."

Barack listened sympathetically. I could tell he was tired, eager to head upstairs and get some needed sleep. I hated sometimes how the lines had blurred between family life and political life for us. His days were filled with split-second problem solving and hundreds of interactions. I didn't want to be another issue he needed to contend with, but then again, my existence had been fully folded into his.

"You're so much more of an asset than a liability, Michelle, you have to know that," he said, looking stricken. "But if you want to stop or slow down, I completely understand. You can do whatever you want here."

He told me I should never feel beholden to him or to the machinery of the campaign. And if I wanted to keep going but needed more support and resources to do it, he'd figure out how to get them.

I was comforted by this, though only a little. I still felt like the first grader in the lunch line who'd just been walloped.

This is my family, sometime around 1965, dressed up for a celebration. Note my brother Craig's protective expression and careful hold on my wrist.

We grew up living in the apartment above my great-aunt Robbie Shields, pictured here holding me. During the years she gave me piano lessons, we had many stubborn standoffs, but she always brought out the best in me.

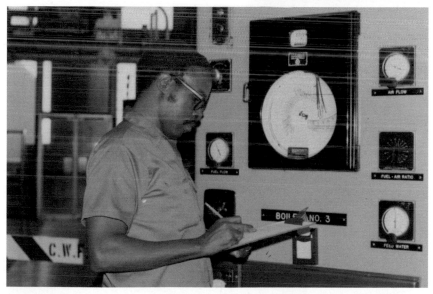

My father, Fraser Robinson, worked for more than twenty years for the city of Chicago, tending boilers at a water filtration plant on the lakeshore. Even as his multiple sclerosis made it increasingly difficult for him to walk, he never missed a day of work.

My dad's Buick Electra 225—the Deuce and a Quarter, we called it—was his pride and joy and the source of many happy memories. Each summer we drove to Dukes Happy Holiday Resort in Michigan for vacation, which is where this picture was taken.

When I began kindergarten in 1969, my neighborhood on the South Side of Chicago was made up of a racially diverse mix of middle-class families. But as many better-off families moved to the suburbs—a phenomenon commonly known as "white flight"— the demographics changed fast. By fifth grade, the diversity was gone. ABOVE: My kindergarten class; I'm third row, second from right. BELOW: My fifth-grade class; I'm third row, center.

Here I am at Princeton (LEFT). I was nervous about heading off to college but found many close friends there, including Suzanne Alele (ABOVE), who taught me a lot about living joyfully.

For a while, Barack and I lived in the second-floor apartment on Euclid Avenue where I'd been raised. We were both young lawyers then. I was just beginning to question my professional path, wondering how to do meaningful work and stay true to my values.

Our wedding on October 3, 1992, was one of the happiest days of my life. Standing in for my father, who had passed away a year and a half earlier, Craig walked me down the aisle.

I knew early on in our relationship that Barack would be a great father. He's always loved and devoted himself to children. When Malia arrived in 1998, the two of us were smitten. Our lives had changed forever.

Sasha was born about three years after Malia, completing our family with her chubby cheeks and indomitable spirit. Our Christmastime trips to Barack's home state of Hawaii became an important tradition for us, a time to catch up with his side of the family and enjoy some warm weather.

Malia and Sasha's bond has always been tight. And their cuteness still melts my heart.

I spent three years as executive director for the Chicago chapter of Public Allies, an organization devoted to helping young people build careers in public service. Here I'm pictured (on right) with a group of young community leaders at an event with Chicago mayor Richard M. Daley.

I later transitioned to working at the University of Chicago Medical Center, where I strove to improve community relations and established a service that helped thousands of South Side residents find affordable health care.

As a full-time working mom with a spouse who was often away from home, I became well acquainted with the juggle many women know—trying to balance the needs of my family with the demands of my job.

I first met Valerie Jarrett (left) in 1991, when she was deputy chief of staff at the Chicago mayor's office. She quickly became a trusted friend and adviser to both me and Barack. Here we are during his U.S. Senate campaign in 2004.

From time to time our kids came out to visit Barack on the campaign trail. Here's Malia, watching through the campaign bus window in 2004 as her dad gives yet another speech.

Barack announced his candidacy for president in Springfield, Illinois, on a freezing-cold day in February 2007. I'd bought Sasha a too-big pink hat for the occasion and kept worrying it was going to slip off her head, but miraculously she managed to keep it on.

Here we are on the campaign trail, accompanied as always by a dozen or more members of the press.

I liked campaigning, energized by the connections I made with voters across America. And yet the pace could be grueling. I stole moments of rest when I could.

In the months leading up to the general election, I was given access to a campaign plane, which boosted my overall efficiency and made traveling a lot more fun. Pictured here with me (from left) is my tight-knit team: Kristen Jarvis, Katie McCormick Lelyveld, Chawn Ritz (our flight attendant that day), and Melissa Winter.

Joe Biden was a great running mate for Barack for many reasons, including that our two families instantly hit it off. Jill and I began talking early on about how we wanted to be of service to military families. Here we are in 2008, taking a break from campaigning in Pennsylvania.

After a difficult spring and summer on the campaign trail, I spoke at the 2008 Democratic National Convention in Denver, which allowed me to share my story for the first time before a massive prime-time audience. Afterward, Sasha and Malia joined me onstage to say hello to Barack via video.

On November 4, 2008—election night—my mom, Marian Robinson, sat next to Barack, the two of them quietly watching as the results came in.

Malia was ten years old and Sasha just seven in January 2009 when their dad was sworn in as president. Sasha was so small, she had to stand on a special platform in order to be visible during the ceremony.

Officially POTUS and FLOTUS, Barack and I hit ten inaugural balls that night, dancing onstage at each one. I was wiped out after the day's festivities, but this gorgeous gown designed by Jason Wu gave me fresh energy, and my husband—my best friend, my partner in all things—has a way of making every moment we have together feel intimate.

This image of Sasha's little face peering through ballistic-proof glass as she headed to her first day of school stays with me to this day. At the time, I couldn't help but worry about what this experience would do to our kids.

Laura Bush kindly hosted me and the girls for an early visit to the White House. Her own daughters, Jenna and Barbara, were there to show Sasha and Malia the more fun parts of the place, including how to use this sloping hallway as a slide.

It took some adjustment to get used to the constant presence of U.S. Secret Service agents in our lives, but over time many of them became dear friends.

Wilson Jerman (shown here) first came to work at the White House in 1957. Like many of the butlers and residence staff, he served with dignity under several different presidents.

The White House garden was designed to be a symbol of nutrition and healthy living, a springboard from which I could launch a larger initiative like Let's Move! But I also loved it because it's where I could get my hands dirty with kids as we rooted around in the soil.

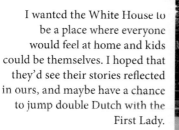

I wanted the White House to be a place where everyone would feel at home and kids could be themselves. I hoped that they'd see their stories reflected in ours, and maybe have a chance to jump double Dutch with the First Lady.

Barack and I developed a special fondness for Queen Elizabeth, who reminded Barack of his no-nonsense grandmother. Over the course of many visits she showed me that humanity is more important than protocol or formality.

Meeting Nelson Mandela gave me the perspective I needed a couple of years into our White House journey—that real change happens slowly, not just over months and years but over decades and lifetimes.

A hug, for me, is a way to melt away pretenses and simply connect. Here I'm at Oxford University with the girls from London's Elizabeth Garrett Anderson School.

I'll never forget the spirit of optimism and resilience that lived in the service members and military families I met during visits to Walter Reed Medical Center.

Hadiya Pendleton's mother, Cleopatra Cowley-Pendleton, did everything right but still couldn't protect her child from the awful randomness of gun violence. Meeting her before Hadiya's funeral in Chicago, I was overwhelmed by how unfair it was.

I tried as often as possible to be home to greet the girls when they came back from school. It was one benefit of living above the office.

Barack always maintained a healthy separation between work and family time, making it upstairs for dinner nearly every night and managing to be fully present with us at home. In 2009, the girls and I broke down the barrier and surprised him in the Oval Office on his birthday.

We made good on our promise to Malia and Sasha that if Barack became president, we'd get a dog. In fact, we eventually got two. Bo (pictured here) and Sunny brought a sense of lightness to everything.

Each spring I hoped to use my commencement speeches to inspire graduates and help them see the power of their own stories. Here I am preparing to speak at Virginia Tech in 2012. In the background, Tina Tchen, my tireless chief of staff for five years, can be seen as she often was: multitasking on her phone.

The dogs were free to roam throughout much of the White House. They especially loved hanging out in the garden and also in the kitchen. Here they are in the pantry with butler Jorge Davila, probably hoping to get slipped some food.

We're deeply grateful to all of the staff who kept our lives running smoothly for eight years. We came to know about their kids and grandkids and also celebrated milestones with them, as we did here with assistant usher Reggie Dickson on his birthday in 2012.

Being the First Family came with unusual privileges and some unusual challenges. Barack and I sought to maintain a sense of normalcy for our girls.

ABOVE LEFT: Malia, Barack, and I cheer on Sasha's basketball team, the Vipers.

ABOVE RIGHT: The girls relax on Bright Star, the call sign for the First Lady's plane.

We made sure our girls had the opportunity to do standard teenage things, like learning to drive a car, even if it meant having driving lessons with the Secret Service.

The Fourth of July always gives us a lot to celebrate, since it's also Malia's birthday.

If there's one thing I've learned in life, it's the power of using your voice. I tried my best to speak the truth and shed light on the stories of people who are often brushed aside.

In 2015, my family joined Congressman John Lewis and other icons of the civil rights movement in commemorating the fiftieth anniversary of the march across the Edmund Pettus Bridge in Selma, Alabama. I was reminded that day of how far our country has come—and how far we still have to go.

But with this, we dropped the politics and took our weary selves to bed.

N OT LONG AFTER THAT, I went to David Axelrod's office in Chicago and sat down with him and Valerie to watch video of some of my public appearances. It was, I realize now, something of an intervention, an attempt to show me which small parts of this process I could control. The two of them praised me for how hard I'd been working and how effectively I was able to rally Barack's supporters. But then Axe muted the volume as he replayed my stump speech, removing my voice so that we could look more closely at my body language, specifically my facial expressions.

What did I see? I saw myself speaking with intensity and conviction and never letting up. I always addressed the tough times many Americans were facing, as well as the inequities within our schools and our health-care system. My face reflected the seriousness of what I believed was at stake, how important the choice that lay before our nation really was.

But it was too serious, too severe—at least given what people were conditioned to expect from a woman. I saw my expression as a stranger might perceive it, especially if it was framed with an unflattering message. I could see how the opposition had managed to dice up these images and feed me to the public as some sort of pissed-off harpy. It was, of course, another stereotype, another trap. The easiest way to disregard a woman's voice is to package her as a scold.

No one seemed to criticize Barack for appearing too serious or not smiling enough. I was a wife and not a candidate, obviously, so perhaps the expectation was for me to provide more lightness, more fluff. And yet, if there was any question about how women in general fared on Planet Politics, one needed only to look at how Nancy Pelosi, the smart and hard-driving Speaker of the House of Representatives, was often depicted as a shrew or what Hillary Clinton was enduring as cable pundits and opinion writers hashed and rehashed each development in the campaign.

Hillary's gender was used against her relentlessly, drawing from all the worst stereotypes. She was called domineering, a nag, a bitch. Her voice was interpreted as screechy; her laugh was a cackle. Hillary was Barack's opponent, which meant that I wasn't inclined to feel especially warmly toward her just then, but I couldn't help but admire her ability to stand up and keep fighting amid the misogyny.

Reviewing videotape with Axe and Valerie that day, I felt tears pricking at my eyes. I was upset. I could see now that there was a performative piece to politics that I hadn't yet fully mastered. And I'd been out there giving speeches already for more than a year. I'd communicated best, I realized now, in smaller venues like the ones I'd done in Iowa. It was harder to convey warmth in larger auditoriums. Bigger crowds required clearer facial cues, which was something I needed to work on. I was worried now that it was almost too late.

Valerie, my dear friend of more than fifteen years, reached out to squeeze my hand.

"Why didn't you guys talk to me about this sooner?" I asked. "Why didn't anyone try to help?"

The answer was that no one had been paying all that much attention. The perception inside Barack's campaign seemed to be that I was doing fine until I wasn't. Only now, when I was a problem, was I summoned to Axe's office.

For me, this was a turnaround point. The campaign apparatus existed exclusively to serve the candidate, not the spouse or the family. And as much as Barack's staffers respected me and valued my contribution, they'd never given me much in the way of guidance. Until that point, no one from the campaign had bothered to travel with me or show up for my events. I'd never received media training or speech prep. No one, I realized, was going to look out for me unless I pushed for it.

Knowing that the gaze was only going to intensify as we moved into the last six or so months of the campaign, we agreed, finally, that I needed real help. If I was going to continue to campaign like a candidate, I needed to be supported like a candidate. I'd protect myself by being better organized, by insisting on having the resources I needed to do the job well. In the final weeks of the primaries, Barack's campaign began expanding my team to include a scheduler and a personal aide—Kristen Jarvis, a warmhearted former staffer from Barack's U.S. Senate office whose steady demeanor would keep me grounded in high-stress moments—plus a no-nonsense, politically savvy communications specialist named Stephanie Cutter. Working with Katie and Melissa, Stephanie helped me sharpen my message and my presentation, building toward a major speech I'd deliver late that summer at the Democratic National Convention. We were also finally granted access to a campaign plane, which allowed me to move more efficiently. I could now give media interviews during flights, get my hair and makeup done en route to an event, or bring Sasha and Malia along with me at no extra cost.

It was a relief. All of it was a relief. And I do think that it allowed me to smile more, to feel less on guard.

As we planned my public appearances, Stephanie counseled me to play to my strengths and to remember the things I most enjoyed talking about, which was my love for my husband and kids, my connection with working mothers, and my proud Chicago roots. She recognized that I liked to joke around and told me not to hold back with my humor. It was okay, in other words, to be myself. Shortly after the primaries wrapped up, I signed on to co-host *The View*, spending a happy and spirited hour with Whoopi Goldberg, Barbara Walters, and the other hosts in front of a live audience, talking about the attacks against me, but also laughing about the girls and the fist bumps and the nuisance of panty hose. I felt a new ease, a new ownership of my voice. The show aired to generally positive commentary. I'd worn a $148 black-and-white dress that women were suddenly scrambling to buy.

I was having an impact and beginning to enjoy myself at the same time, feeling more and more open and optimistic. I also was trying to learn from the Americans I was meeting around the country, holding roundtables designed to focus on work-family balance, an issue in which I had a keen interest. For me, the most humbling lessons came when I visited military communities and met with soldiers' spouses—groups of mostly women, though sometimes with a few men mixed in.

"Tell me about your lives," I'd say. And then I'd listen as women with babies on their laps, some of them still teenagers themselves, told me stories. Some described being transferred between bases eight or more times in as many years, in each instance needing to start over in settling their children into things like music lessons or enrichment programs. They explained, too, how difficult it could be to maintain a career over the course of all those moves: A teacher, for instance, wasn't able to find a job because her new state didn't recognize the old state's teaching certificate; nail technicians and physical therapists faced similar problems with licensing. Many young parents had trouble finding affordable child care. All of it, of course, was shaded by the logistical and emotional burdens of having a loved one deployed for twelve months or more at a time to a place like Kabul or Mosul or on an aircraft carrier in the South China Sea. Meeting these spouses instantly put whatever hurt I was feeling into perspective. Their sacrifices were far greater than mine. I sat in these meetings, engrossed and somewhat taken aback by the fact that I knew so little about military life. I vowed to myself that if Barack was fortunate enough to be elected, I'd find some way to better support these families.

All this left me more energized to help make the final push for Barack and Joe Biden, the affable senator from Delaware who'd soon be announced as his running mate. I felt emboldened to follow my instincts again, surrounded by people who had my back. At public events, I focused on making personal connections with the people I met, in small groups and in crowds of thousands, in backstage chats and harried rope lines. When voters got to see me as a person, they understood that the caricatures were untrue. I've learned that it's harder to hate up close.

I would go on to spend the summer of 2008 moving faster and working harder, convinced that I could make a positive difference for Barack. With the convention drawing close, I worked with a speechwriter for the first time, a gifted young woman named Sarah Hurwitz who helped shape my ideas into a tight seventeen-minute speech. After weeks of careful preparation, I walked onstage at the Pepsi Center in Denver in late August and stood before an audience of some twenty thousand people and a TV audience of millions more, ready to articulate to the world who I really was.

That night, my brother, Craig, introduced me. My mother sat in the front row of a skybox, looking a little stunned by how giant the platform for our lives had become. I spoke of my father—his humility, his resilience, and how all that had shaped me and Craig. I tried to give Americans the most intimate view possible of Barack and his noble heart. When I finished, people applauded and applauded, and I felt a powerful blast of relief, knowing that maybe I'd done something, finally, to change people's perception of me.

It was a big moment, for sure—grand and public and to this day readily findable on YouTube. But the truth is, for those exact reasons, it was also strangely kind of a small moment. My view of things was starting to reverse itself, like a sweater slowly being turned inside out. Stages, audiences, lights, applause. These were becoming more normal than I'd ever thought they could be. What I lived for now were the unrehearsed, unphotographed, in-between moments where nobody was performing and no one was judging and real surprise was still possible—where sometimes without warning you might feel a tiny latch spring open on your heart.

For this, we need to go back to Butte, Montana, on the Fourth of July. It was the end of our day there, the summer sun finally dropping behind the western mountains, the sound of firecrackers beginning to pop in the distance. We were holing up for the night at a Holiday Inn Express next to the interstate, with Barack leaving for Missouri the next day and the girls and I headed home to Chicago. We were tired, all of us. We'd done the parade and the picnic. We'd engaged with what felt like every last resident in the town of Butte. And now, finally, we were going to have a little gathering just for Malia.

If you asked me at the time, I'd have said that we came up short for her in the end—that her birthday felt like an afterthought in the maelstrom of the campaign. We got together in a fluorescent-lit, low-ceilinged conference room in the basement of the hotel, with Konrad, Maya, and Suhaila, plus a handful of staffers who were close with Malia, and of course the Secret Service agents, who were always close no matter what. We had some balloons, a grocery-store cake, ten candles, and a tub of ice cream. There were a few gifts bought and wrapped on the fly by someone who was not me. The mood was not exactly desultory, but it wasn't festive, either. It had simply been too long of a day. Barack and I shared a dark look, knowing we'd failed.

Ultimately, though, like so many things, it was a matter of perception— how we decided to look at what was in front of us. Barack and I were focused on only our faults and insufficiencies, seeing them reflected in that drab room and thrown-together party. But Malia was looking for something different. And she saw it. She saw kind faces, people who loved her, a thickly frosted cake, a little sister and cousin by her side, a new year ahead. She'd spent the day outdoors. She'd seen a parade. Tomorrow there would be an airplane ride.

She marched over to where Barack sat and threw herself into his lap. "This," she declared, "is the best birthday *ever!*"

She didn't notice that both her mom and her dad got teary or that half the people in the room were now choked up as well. Because she was right. And suddenly we all saw it. She was ten years old that day, and everything was the best.

18

FOUR MONTHS LATER, ON NOVEMBER 4, 2008, I CAST my vote for Barack. The two of us went early that morning to our polling place, which was in the gym at Beulah Shoesmith Elementary School, just a few blocks away from our house in Chicago. We brought Sasha and Malia along, both of them dressed and ready for school. Even on Election Day—maybe especially on Election Day—I thought school would be a good idea. School was routine. School was comfort. As we walked past banks of photographers and TV cameras to get into the gym, as people around us talked about the historic nature of everything, I was happy to have the lunch boxes packed.

What kind of day would this be? It would be a long day. Beyond that, none of us knew.

Barack, as he always is on high-pressure days, was more easygoing than ever. He greeted the poll workers, picked up his ballot, and shook hands with anyone he encountered, appearing relaxed. It made sense, I guess. This whole endeavor was about to be out of his hands.

We stood shoulder to shoulder at our voting stations while the girls leaned in closely to watch what each of us was doing.

I'd voted for Barack many times before, in primaries and general elections, in state-level and national races, and this trip to the polls felt no different. Voting, for me, was a habit, a healthy ritual to be done conscientiously and at every opportunity. My parents had taken me to the polls as a kid, and I'd made a practice of bringing Sasha and Malia with me anytime I could, hoping to reinforce both the ease and the importance of the act.

My husband's career had allowed me to witness the machinations of politics and power up close. I'd seen how just a handful of votes in every precinct could mean the difference not just between one candidate and another but between one value system and the next. If a few people stayed home in each neighborhood, it could determine what our kids learned in schools, which health-care options we had available, or whether or not we sent our troops to war. Voting was both simple and incredibly effective.

That day, I stared for a few extra seconds at the little oblong bubble next to my husband's name for president of the United States. After almost twenty-one months of campaigning, attacks, and exhaustion, this was it—the last thing I needed to do.

Barack glanced my way and laughed. "You still trying to make up your mind?" he said. "Need a little more time?"

Were it not for the anxiety, an Election Day might qualify as a kind of mini-vacation, a surreal pause between everything that's happened and whatever lies ahead. You've leaped but you haven't landed. You can't know yet how the future's going to feel. After months of everything going too fast, time slows to an agonizing crawl. Back at home, I played hostess to family and friends who stopped by our house to make small talk and help pass the hours.

At some point that morning, Barack went off to play basketball with Craig and some friends at a nearby gym, which had become a kind of Election Day custom. Barack loved nothing more than a strenuous thrash-or-be-thrashed game of basketball to settle his nerves.

"Just don't let anyone break his nose," I said to Craig as the two of them walked out the door. "He's gotta be on TV later, you know."

"Way to make me responsible for everything," Craig said back, as only a brother can. And then they were gone.

If you believed the polls, it appeared that Barack was poised to win, but I also knew he'd been working on two possible speeches for the night ahead—one for a victory, another for a concession. By now we understood enough about politics and polling to take nothing for granted. We knew of the phenomenon called the Bradley effect, named for an African American candidate, Tom Bradley, who'd run for governor in California in the early 1980s. While the polls had consistently shown Bradley leading, he'd lost on Election Day, surprising everyone and supplying the world with a bigger lesson about bigotry, as the pattern repeated itself for years to come in different high-profile races involving Black candidates around the country. The theory was that when it came to minority candidates, voters often hid their prejudice from pollsters, expressing it only from the privacy of the voting booth.

Throughout the campaign, I'd asked myself over and over whether America was really ready to elect a Black president, whether the country was in a strong enough place to see beyond race and move past prejudice. Finally, we were about to find out.

As a whole, the general election had been less grueling than the pitched battle of the primaries. John McCain had done himself no favors by choosing Alaska's governor, Sarah Palin, as his running mate. Inexperienced and unprepared, she'd quickly become a national punch line. And then, in mid-September, the news had turned disastrous. The U.S. economy began to spiral out of control when Lehman Brothers, one of the country's largest investment banks, abruptly went belly-up. The titans of Wall Street, the world now realized, had spent years racking up profits on the backs of junk home loans. Stocks plummeted. Credit markets froze. Retirement funds vanished.

Barack was the right person for this moment in history, for a job that was never going to be easy but that had grown, thanks to the financial crisis, exponentially more difficult. I'd been trumpeting it for more than a year and a half now, all over America: My husband was calm and prepared. Complexity didn't scare him. He had a brain capable of sorting through every intricacy. I was biased, of course, and personally I still would've been content to lose the election and reclaim some version of our old lives, but I also was feeling that as a country we truly needed his help. It was time to stop thinking about something as arbitrary as skin color. We'd be foolish at this point not to put him in office. Still, he would inherit a mess.

As evening drew closer, I felt my fingers getting numb, a nervous tingle running through my body. I couldn't really eat. I lost interest in making small talk with my mom or the friends who'd stopped in. At some point, I went upstairs just to catch a moment to myself.

Barack, it turned out, had retreated up there as well, clearly needing a moment of his own.

I found him sitting at his desk, looking over the text of his victory speech in the little book-strewn office adjacent to our bedroom—his Hole. I walked over and began rubbing his shoulders.

"You doing okay?" I said.

"Yep."

"Tired?"

"Nope." He smiled up at me, as if trying to prove it was true. Only a day earlier, we'd received news that Toot, Barack's eighty-six-year-old grandmother, had passed away in Hawaii after being sick for months with cancer. Knowing he'd missed saying good-bye to his mother, Barack had made a point of seeing Toot. We'd taken the kids to visit her late that summer, and he'd gone again on his own ten days earlier, stepping off the campaign trail for a day to sit and hold her hand. It occurred to me what a sad thing this was. Barack had lost his mother at the very genesis of his political career, two months after announcing his run for state senate. Now, as he reached its apex, his grandmother wouldn't be around to witness it. The people who'd raised him were gone.

"I'm proud of you, no matter what happens," I said. "You've done so much good."

He lifted himself out of his seat and put his arms around me. "So have you," he said, pulling me close. "We've both done all right."

All I could think about was everything he still had to carry.

AFTER A FAMILY dinner at home, we got dressed up and rode downtown to watch election returns with a small group of friends and family in a suite the campaign had rented for us at the Hyatt Regency. The campaign staff had cloistered itself in a different area of the hotel, trying to give us some privacy. Joe and Jill Biden had their own suite for friends and family across the hall.

The first results came in around 6:00 p.m. central time, with Kentucky going for McCain and Vermont for Barack. Then West Virginia went for McCain, and after that so did South Carolina. My confidence lurched a little, though none of this was a surprise. According to Axe and Plouffe, who were buzzing in and out of the room, announcing what felt like every sliver of information they received, everything was unfolding as predicted. Though the updates were generally positive, the political chatter was the last thing I wanted to hear. We had no control over anything anyway, so what was the point? We'd leaped and now, one way or another, we'd land. We could see on TV that thousands of people were already amassing at Grant Park, a mile or so away on the lake front, where election coverage was being broadcast on Jumbotron screens and where Barack would later show up to deliver one of his two speeches. There were police officers stationed on practically every corner, Coast Guard boats patrolling the lake, helicopters overhead. All of Chicago, it seemed, was holding its breath, waiting for news.

Connecticut went for Barack. Then New Hampshire went for Barack. So did Massachusetts, Maine, Delaware, and D.C. When Illinois was called for Barack, we could hear cars honking and shouts of excitement from the streets below. I found a chair near the door to the suite and sat alone, surveying the scene in front of me. The room had gone mostly quiet now, the political team's nervous updates having given way to an expectant, almost sober kind of calm. To my right, the girls sat in their red and black dresses on a couch, and to my left, Barack, his suit coat draped elsewhere in the room, had taken a seat on another couch next to my mother, who was dressed that evening in an elegant black suit and silver earrings.

"Are you ready for this, Grandma?" I heard Barack say to her.

Never one to overemote, my mom just gave him a sideways look and shrugged, causing them both to smile. Later, though, she'd describe to me how overcome she'd felt right then, struck just as I'd been by his vulnerability. America had come to see Barack as self-assured and powerful, but my mother also recognized the gravity of the passage, the loneliness of the job ahead. Here was this man who no longer had a father or a mother, about to be elected the leader of the free world.

The next time I looked over, I saw that she and Barack were holding hands.

IT WAS EXACTLY ten o'clock when the networks began to flash pictures of my smiling husband, declaring that Barack Hussein Obama would become the forty-fourth president of the United States. We all leaped to our feet and started instinctively to yell. Our campaign staff streamed into the room, as did the Bidens, everyone hurling themselves from one hug to the next. It was surreal. I felt as if I'd been lifted out of my own body, only watching myself react.

He had done it. We'd all done it. It hardly seemed possible, but the victory was sound.

Here is where I felt like our family got launched out of a cannon and into some strange underwater universe. Things felt slow and aqueous and slightly distorted, even if we were moving quickly and with precise guidance, waved by Secret Service agents into a freight elevator, hustled out a back exit at the hotel and into a waiting SUV. Did I breathe the air as we stepped outside? Did I thank the person who held open the door as we passed by? Was I smiling? I don't know. It was as if I were still trying to frog-kick my way back to reality. Some of this, I assumed, had to be fatigue. It had been, as predicted, a very long day. I could see the grogginess in the girls' faces. I'd prepared them for this next part of the night, explaining that whether Dad won or lost, we were going to have a big noisy celebration in a park.

We were gliding now in a police-escorted motorcade along Lake Shore Drive, speeding south toward Grant Park. I'd traveled this same road hundreds of times in my life, from my bus rides home from Whitney Young to the predawn drives to the gym. This was my city, as familiar to me as a place could be, and yet that night it felt different, transformed into something strangely quiet. It was as if we were suspended in time and space, a little like a dream.

Malia had been peering out the window of the SUV, taking it all in.

"Daddy," she said, sounding almost apologetic. "There's no one on the road. I don't think anyone's coming to your celebration."

Barack and I looked at each other and started to laugh. It was then that we realized that ours were the only cars on the street. Barack was now president-elect. The Secret Service had cleared everything out, shutting down an entire section of Lake Shore Drive, blocking every intersection along the route—a standard precaution for a president, we'd soon learn. But for us, it was new.

Everything was new.

I put an arm around Malia. "The people are already there, sweetie," I said. "Don't worry, they're waiting for us."

And they were. More than 200,000 people had crammed into the park to see us. We could hear an expectant hum as we exited the vehicle and were ushered into a set of white tents that had been put up at the front of the park, forming a tunnel that led to the stage. A group of friends and family had gathered there to greet us, only now, due to Secret Service protocol, they were cordoned off behind a rope. Barack put his arm around me, almost as if to make sure I was still there.

We walked out onto the stage a few minutes later, the four of us, me holding Malia's hand and Barack holding Sasha's. I saw a lot of things at once. I saw that a wall of thick, bulletproof glass had been erected around the stage. I saw an ocean of people, many of them waving little American flags. My brain could process none of it. It all felt too big.

I remember little of Barack's speech that night. Sasha, Malia, and I watched him from the wings as he said his words, surrounded by those glass shields and by our city and by the comfort of more than sixty-nine million votes. What stays with me is that sense of comfort, the unusual calmness of that unusually warm November night by the lake in Chicago. After so many months of going to high-energy campaign rallies with crowds deliberately whipped up into a shouting, chanting frenzy, the atmosphere in Grant Park was different. We were standing before a giant, jubilant mass of Americans who were also palpably reflective. What I heard was relative silence. It seemed almost as if I could make out every face in the crowd. There were tears in many eyes.

Maybe the calmness was something I imagined, or maybe for all of us, it was just a product of the late hour. It was almost midnight, after all. And everyone had been waiting. We'd been waiting a long, long time.

Becoming More

19

T HERE IS NO HANDBOOK FOR INCOMING FIRST LA-
dies of the United States. It's not technically a job, nor is it an official government title. It comes with no salary and no spelled-out set of
obligations. It's a strange kind of sidecar to the presidency, a seat that by
the time I came to it had already been occupied by more than forty-three
different women, each of whom had done it in her own way.

I knew only a little about previous First Ladies and how they'd approached the position. I knew that Jackie Kennedy had dedicated herself
to redecorating the White House. I recalled that Rosalynn Carter had sat
in on cabinet meetings, Nancy Reagan had gotten into some trouble accepting free designer dresses, and Hillary Clinton had been derided for
taking on a policy role in her husband's administration. Once, a couple
of years earlier at a luncheon for U.S. Senate spouses, I'd watched—half
in shock, half in awe—as Laura Bush posed, serene and smiling, for ceremonial photos with about a hundred different people, never once losing
her composure or needing a break. First Ladies showed up in the news,
having tea with the spouses of foreign dignitaries; they sent out official
greetings on holidays and wore pretty gowns to state dinners. I knew that
they normally picked a cause or two to champion as well.

I understood already that I'd be measured by a different yardstick. As the only African American First Lady to set foot in the White House, I was "other" almost by default. If there was a presumed grace assigned to my white predecessors, I knew it wasn't likely to be the same for me. I'd learned through the campaign stumbles that I had to be better, faster, smarter, and stronger than ever. My grace would need to be earned. I worried that many Americans wouldn't see themselves reflected in me, or that they wouldn't relate to my journey. I wouldn't have the luxury of settling into my new role slowly before being judged. And when it came to judgment, I was as vulnerable as ever to the unfounded fears and racial stereotypes that lay just beneath the surface of the public consciousness, ready to be stirred up by rumor and innuendo.

I was humbled and excited to be First Lady, but not for one second did I think I'd be sliding into some glamorous, easy role. Nobody who has the words "first" and "Black" attached to them ever would. I stood at the foot of the mountain, knowing I'd need to climb my way into favor.

For me, it revived an old internal call-and-response, one that tracked all the way back to high school, when I'd shown up at Whitney Young and found myself suddenly gripped by doubt. Confidence, I'd learned then, sometimes needs to be called from within. I've repeated the same words to myself many times now, through many climbs.

Am I good enough? Yes I am.

The seventy-six days between election and inauguration felt like a critical time to start setting the tone for the kind of First Lady I wanted to be. After all I'd done to lever myself out of corporate law and into more meaningful community-minded work, I knew I'd be happiest if I could engage actively and work toward achieving measurable results. I intended to make good on the promises I'd made to the military spouses I'd met while campaigning—to help share their stories and find ways to support them. And then there were my ideas for planting a garden and looking to improve children's health and nutrition on a larger scale.

I didn't want to go about any of it casually. I intended to arrive at the White House with a carefully thought-out strategy and a strong team backing me. If I'd learned anything from the ugliness of the campaign, from the myriad ways people had sought to write me off as angry or un-becoming, it was that public judgment sweeps in to fill any void. If you don't get out there and define yourself, you'll be quickly and inaccurately defined by others. I wasn't interested in slotting myself into a passive role, waiting for Barack's team to give me direction. After coming through the crucible of the last year, I knew that I would never allow myself to get that banged up again.

M Y MIND RACED with all that needed to get done. There had been no way to plan for this transition. Doing anything ahead of time would have been viewed as presumptuous. For a planner like me, it had been hard to sit back. So now we went into overdrive. My top prior-ity was looking out for Sasha and Malia. I wanted to get them settled as quickly and comfortably as possible, which meant nailing down the de-tails of our move and finding them a new school in Washington, a place where they'd be happy.

Six days after the election, I flew to D.C., having set up meetings with administrators at a couple of different schools. Under normal circum-stances, I'd have focused solely on the academics and culture of each place, but we were far past the possibility of normal now. There were all sorts of cumbersome new factors to be considered and discussed—Secret Service protocols, emergency evacuation setups, strategies for protecting our kids' privacy now that they had the eyes of a nation upon them. The variables had become exponentially more complex. More people were in-volved; more conversations needed to be had before even a small decision could be made.

Thankfully, I was able to keep my key campaign staffers—Melissa, Katie, and Kristen—working with me during the transition. We imme-diately set about figuring out the logistics of our family's move while also beginning to hire staff—schedulers, policy experts, communications pros—for my future East Wing offices, as well as interviewing people for jobs in the family residence. One of my first hires was Jocelyn Frye, an old friend from law school who had a fantastic analytic mind and agreed to come on as my policy director, helping to oversee the initiatives I planned to launch.

Barack, meanwhile, was working on filling positions for his cabinet and huddling with various experts on ways to rescue the economy. By now, more than ten million Americans were unemployed, and the auto industry was in a perilous free fall. I could tell by the hard set of my husband's jaw following these sessions that the situation was worse than most Americans even understood. He was also receiving daily written intelligence briefings, suddenly privy to the nation's heavier secrets—the classified threats, quiet alliances, and covert operations about which the public remained largely unaware.

Now that the Secret Service would be protecting us for years to come, the agency selected official code names for us. Barack was "Renegade," and I was "Renaissance." The girls were allowed to choose their own names from a preapproved list of alliterative options. Malia became "Radiance," and Sasha picked "Rosebud." (My mother would later get her own informal code name, "Raindance.")

When speaking to me directly, the Secret Service agents almost always called me "ma'am." As in, "This way, ma'am. Please step back, ma'am." And, "Ma'am, your car will be here shortly."

Who's "Ma'am"? I'd wanted to ask at first. Ma'am sounded to me like an older woman with a proper purse, good posture, and sensible shoes who was maybe sitting somewhere nearby.

But I was Ma'am. Ma'am was me. It was part of this larger shift, this crazy transition we were in.

All this was on my mind the day I traveled to Washington to visit schools. After one of my meetings, I went back to Reagan National Airport to meet Barack, who was due in on a chartered flight from Chicago. As was protocol for the president-elect, we'd been invited by President and Mrs. Bush to drop by for a visit to the White House and had scheduled it to coincide with my trip to look at schools. I stood waiting at the private terminal as Barack's plane touched down. Next to me was Cornelius Southall, one of the agents heading my security detail.

Cornelius was a square-shouldered former college football player who'd previously worked as a part of President Bush's security team. Like all of my detail leaders, he was smart, trained to be hyperaware at every moment, a human sensor. Even then, as the two of us watched Barack's plane taxi and come to a stop maybe twenty yards away on the tarmac, he was picking up on something before I did.

"Ma'am," he said as some new piece of information arrived via his earpiece, "your life is about to change forever."

When I looked at him quizzically, he added, "Just wait."

He then pointed to the right, and I turned to look. Exactly on cue, something massive came around the corner: a snaking, vehicular army that included a phalanx of police cars and motorcycles, a number of black SUVs, two armored limousines with American flags mounted on their hoods, a hazmat mitigation truck, a counterassault team riding with machine guns visible, an ambulance, a signals truck equipped to detect incoming projectiles, several passenger vans, and another group of police escorts. The presidential motorcade. It was at least twenty vehicles long, moving in orchestrated formation, car after car after car, before finally the whole fleet rolled to a quiet halt, and the limos stopped directly in front of Barack's parked plane.

I turned to Cornelius. "Is there a clown car?" I said. "Seriously, this is what he's going to travel with now?"

He smiled. "Every day for his entire presidency, yes," he said. "It's going to look like this all the time."

I took in the spectacle: thousands and thousands of pounds of metal, a squad of commandos, bulletproof everything. I had yet to grasp that Barack's protection was still only half-visible. I didn't know that he'd also, at all times, have a nearby helicopter ready to evacuate him, that sharpshooters would position themselves on rooftops along the routes he traveled, that a personal physician would always be with him in case of a medical problem, or that the vehicle he rode in contained a store of blood of the appropriate type in case he ever needed a transfusion. In a matter of weeks, just ahead of Barack's inauguration, the presidential limo would be upgraded to a newer model—aptly named the Beast— a seven-ton tank disguised as a luxury vehicle, tricked out with hidden tear-gas cannons, rupture-proof tires, and a sealed ventilation system meant to get him through a biological or chemical attack.

I was now married to one of the most heavily guarded human beings on earth. It was simultaneously relieving and distressing.

I looked to Cornelius, who waved me forward in the direction of the limo.

"You can head over now, ma'am," he said.

I'D BEEN INSIDE the White House just once before, a couple of years earlier. Through Barack's office at the Senate, I'd signed myself and Malia and Sasha up for a special tour being offered during one of our visits to Washington, figuring it'd be a fun thing to do. White House tours are generally self-guided, but this one involved being taken around by a White House curator, who walked a small group of us through its grand hallways and various public rooms.

We stared at the cut-glass chandeliers that dangled from the high ceiling of the East Room, where opulent balls and receptions were historically held, and inspected George Washington's red cheeks and sober expression in the massive, gilt-framed portrait that hung on one wall. We learned, courtesy of our guide, that in the late eighteenth century First Lady Abigail Adams had used the giant space to hang her laundry and that decades later, during the Civil War, Union troops had temporarily been quartered there. A number of First Daughters' weddings had taken place in the East Room. Abraham Lincoln's and John F. Kennedy's caskets had also lain there for viewing.

I could feel my mind sifting through all the various presidents that day, trying to match what I remembered from history classes with visions of the families who'd walked these actual halls. Malia, who was about eight at the time, seemed mostly awestruck by the size of the place, while Sasha, at five, was doing her best not to touch the many things that weren't supposed to be touched. She gamely held it together as we moved from the East Room to the Green Room, which had delicate emerald-silk walls and came with a story about James Madison and the War of 1812, and the Blue Room, which had French furniture and came with a story about Grover Cleveland's wedding, but when our guide asked if we'd now please follow him to the Red Room, Sasha looked up at me and blurted, in the unquiet voice of an aggrieved kindergartner, "Oh nooo, not another *ROOM!*" I quickly shushed her and gave her the mother-look that said, "Do not embarrass me."

But who, honestly, could blame her? It's a huge place, the White House, with 132 rooms, 35 bathrooms, and 28 fireplaces spread out over six floors, all of it stuffed with more history than any single tour could begin to cover. It was frankly hard to imagine real life happening there. Somewhere on the level below, government employees flowed in and out of the building, while somewhere above, the president and First Lady lived with their Scottish terriers in the family residence. But we were standing then in a different area of the house, the frozen-in-time, museum-like part of the place, where symbolism lived and mattered, where the country's old bones were on display.

Two years later, I was arriving all over again, this time through a different door and with Barack. We were now going to see the place as our soon-to-be home.

President and Mrs. Bush greeted us at the Diplomatic Reception Room, just off the South Lawn. The First Lady clasped my hand warmly. "Please call me Laura," she said. Her husband was just as welcoming, possessing a magnanimous Texas spirit that seemed to override any political hard feelings. Throughout the campaign, Barack had criticized the president's leadership frequently and in detail, promising voters he would fix the many things he viewed as mistakes. Bush, as a Republican, had naturally supported John McCain's candidacy. But he'd also vowed to make this the smoothest presidential transition in history, instructing every department in the executive branch to prepare briefing binders for the incoming administration. Even on the First Lady's side, staffers were putting together contact lists, calendars, and sample correspondence to help me find my footing when it came to the social obligations that came with the title. There was kindness running beneath all of it, a genuine love of country that I will always appreciate and admire.

Though President Bush mentioned nothing directly, I swore I could see the first traces of relief on his face, knowing that his tenure was almost finished, that he'd run the race and could soon head home to Texas. It was time to let the next president through the door.

While our husbands walked off to the Oval Office to have a talk, Laura led me to the private wood-paneled elevator reserved for the First Family, which was operated by a gentlemanly African American in a tuxedo.

As we rode two floors up to the family residence, Laura asked how Sasha and Malia were doing. She was sixty-two years old then and had parented two older daughters while in the White House. A former schoolteacher and librarian, she'd used her platform as First Lady to promote education and advocate for teachers. She inspected me with warm blue eyes.

"How are you feeling?" she asked.

"A little overwhelmed," I admitted.

She smiled with what felt like real compassion. "I know. Trust me, I do."

In the moment, I wasn't able to fully apprehend the significance of what she was saying, but later I would think of it often: Barack and I were joining a strange and very small society made up of the Clintons, the Carters, two sets of Bushes, Nancy Reagan, and Betty Ford. These were the only people on earth who knew what Barack and I were facing, who'd experienced firsthand the unique delights and hardships of life in the White House. As different as we all were, we'd always share this bond.

Laura walked me through the residence, showing me room upon room upon room. The private area of the White House occupies about twenty thousand square feet on the top two stories of the main historical structure—the one you'd recognize from photos with its iconic white pillars. I saw the dining room where First Families ate their meals and popped my head into the tidy kitchen, where a culinary staff was already at work on dinner. I saw the guest quarters on the top floor, scouting them out as a possible place my mother could live, if we could manage to talk her into moving in with us. (There was a small gym up there as well, which was the place both Barack and President Bush got most excited about during the guys' version of the tour.) I was most interested in checking out the two bedrooms that I thought would work best for Sasha and Malia, just down the hall from the master bedroom.

For me, the girls' sense of comfort and home was key. If we pared back all the pomp and circumstance—the fairy-tale unreality of moving into a big house that came with chefs, a bowling alley, and a swimming pool— what Barack and I were doing was something no parent really wants to do: yanking our kids midyear out of a school they loved, taking them away from their friends, and plopping them into a new home and new school without a whole lot of notice. I was preoccupied by this thought, though I was also comforted by the knowledge that other mothers and children had successfully done this before.

Laura took me into a pretty, light-filled room off the master bedroom that was traditionally used as the First Lady's dressing room. She pointed out the view of the Rose Garden and the Oval Office through the window, adding that it gave her comfort to be able to look out and sometimes get a sense of what her husband was doing. Hillary Clinton, she said, had shown her this same view when she'd first come to visit the White House eight years earlier. And eight years before that, her mother-in-law, Barbara Bush, had pointed out the view to Hillary. I looked out the window, reminded that I was part of a humble continuum.

In the coming months, I'd feel the power of connection to these other women. Hillary graciously shared wisdom over the phone, walking me through her experience picking out a school for Chelsea. I had a meeting with Rosalynn Carter and a phone call with Nancy Reagan, both women warm and offering support. And Laura kindly invited me to return with Sasha and Malia a couple of weeks after that first visit, on a day when her own girls, Jenna and Barbara, could be there to introduce my kids to the "fun parts" of the White House, showing them everything from the plush seats of the in-house movie theater to how to slide down a sloping hallway on the top floor.

This was all heartening. I already looked forward to the day I could pass whatever wisdom I picked up to the next First Lady in line.

WE ENDED UP moving to Washington right after our traditional Christmas holiday in Hawaii so that Sasha and Malia could start school just as their new classmates were coming back from winter break.

It was still about three weeks ahead of the inauguration, which meant that we had to make temporary arrangements, renting rooms on the top floor of the Hay-Adams hotel in the center of the city. Our rooms over-looked Lafayette Square and the North Lawn of the White House, where we could see the grandstand and metal bleachers being set up in prepara-tion for the inaugural parade. On a building across from the hotel, some-one had hung a massive banner that read, "Welcome Malia and Sasha." I choked up a little at the sight.

After a lot of research, two visits, and many conversations, we'd opted to enroll our daughters at Sidwell Friends, a private Quaker school with an excellent reputation. Sasha would be a second grader in the lower school, which was located in suburban Bethesda, Maryland, and Malia would attend fifth grade on the main campus, which sat on a quiet block just a few miles north of the White House. Both kids would need to com-mute by motorcade, escorted by a group of armed Secret Service agents, some of whom would also remain posted outside their classroom doors and follow them to every recess, playdate, and sports practice.

We lived in a kind of bubble now, sealed off at least partially from the everyday world. I couldn't remember the last time I'd run an errand by myself or walked in a park just for fun. All movements first required a discussion about both security and schedule. The bubble had formed around us slowly over the course of the campaign as Barack's notoriety grew and as it became more necessary to put boundaries up between us and the general public—and, in some instances, between us and our friends and family members. It was odd, being in the bubble, and not a feeling I particularly enjoyed, but I also understood it was for the best. With a regular police escort, our vehicles no longer stopped at traffic lights. We rarely walked in or out of a building's front door when we could be rushed through a service entrance or loading dock on a side street. From the Secret Service's point of view, the less visible we could be, the better.

I held on to a hope that Sasha and Malia's bubble might be different, that they could remain safe but not contained, that their range would be greater than ours. I wanted them to make friends, real friends—to find kids who liked them for reasons other than that they were Barack

Obama's daughters. I wanted them to learn, to have adventures, to make mistakes and bounce back. I hoped that school for them would be a kind of shelter, a place to be themselves. Sidwell Friends appealed to us for a lot of reasons, including the fact that it was the school Chelsea Clinton had attended when her father was president. The staff knew how to safeguard the privacy of high-profile students and had already made the sorts of security accommodations that would now be needed for Malia and Sasha, which meant we wouldn't be too big a drain on the school's resources. Above all, I liked the feel of the place. The Quaker philosophy was all about community, built around the idea that no one individual should be prized over another, which seemed to me like a healthy counterbalance to the big fuss that now surrounded their father.

On the first day of school, Barack and I ate an early breakfast in our hotel suite with Malia and Sasha before helping them into their winter coats. Barack couldn't help but to offer bits of advice about surviving a first day at a new school (keep smiling, be kind, listen to your teachers), adding finally, as the two girls donned their purple backpacks, "And definitely don't pick your noses!"

My mother joined us in the hallway, and we took an elevator downstairs.

Outside the hotel, the Secret Service had erected a security tent, meant to keep us out of sight of the photographers and television crews who'd posted themselves by the entrance, hungry for images of our family in transition. Having arrived only the night before from Chicago, Barack was hoping to ride all the way to school with the girls, but he knew it would create too much of a scene. His motorcade was too big. He'd become too heavy. I could read the pain of this in his face as Sasha and Malia hugged him good-bye.

My mom and I then accompanied the girls in what would become their new form of school bus—a black SUV with smoked windows made of bulletproof glass. I tried that morning to model confidence, smiling and joking with the kids. Inside, however, I felt a thrumming nervousness, that sense of inching perpetually farther out on a limb. We arrived first at the upper school campus, where Malia and I hustled past a gauntlet of news cameras and into the building, the two of us flanked by Secret

Service agents. After I delivered Malia to her new teacher, the motorcade took us to Bethesda, where I repeated the routine with little Sasha, releasing her into a sweet classroom with low tables and wide windows—what I prayed would be a safe and happy place.

I returned to the motorcade and rode back to the Hay-Adams, ensconced in my bubble. I had a busy day ahead, every minute of it scheduled with meetings, but my mind would stay locked on our daughters. What kind of day were they having? What were they eating? Were they being gawked at or made to feel at home? I'd later see a media photo of Sasha taken during the morning trip to school, one that brought me to tears. I believe it was snapped as I was dropping off Malia, while Sasha waited in the car with my mom. She had her round little face pressed up against the window of the SUV and was staring outward, wide-eyed and pensive, taking in the sight of photographers and onlookers, her thoughts unreadable but her expression sober.

We were asking so much of them. I sat with that thought not just for that entire day but for months and years to come.

T HE PACE OF the transition never slowed. I was bombarded with hundreds of decisions, all of them evidently urgent. I was supposed to pick out everything from bath towels and toothpaste to dish soap and beer for the White House residence, choose my outfits for the inauguration ceremony and fancy balls that would follow it, and figure out logistics for the 150 or so of our close friends and relatives who'd be coming from out of town as our guests. I delegated what I could to Melissa and other members of my transition team. We also hired Michael Smith, a talented interior designer we'd found through a Chicago friend, to help us with furnishing and redecorating the residence and the Oval Office.

The president-elect, I learned, is given access to $100,000 in federal funds to help with moving and redecorating, but Barack insisted that we pay for everything ourselves, using what we'd saved from his book royalties. As long as I've known him, he's been this way: extra-vigilant when it comes to matters of money and ethics, holding himself to a higher standard than even what's dictated by law. There's an age-old maxim in the Black community: *You've got to be twice as good to get half as far.* As the first African American family in the White House, we were being viewed as representatives of our race. Any error or lapse in judgment, we knew, would be magnified, read as something more than what it was.

In general, I was less interested in the redecorating and inauguration planning than I was in figuring out what I could do with my new role. As I saw it, I didn't actually *have* to do anything. No job description meant no job requirements, and this gave me the freedom to choose my agenda. I wanted to ensure any effort I made helped advance the new administration's larger goals.

To my great relief, both our kids came home happy after the first day of school, and the second, and the third. Sasha brought back homework, which she'd never had before. Malia was already signed up to sing in a middle school choral concert. They reported that kids in other grades sometimes did a double take when they saw them, but everyone was nice. Each day afterward, the motorcade ride to Sidwell Friends felt a little more routine. After about a week, the girls felt comfortable enough to start traveling to school without me, swapping my mother in as their regular escort, which automatically made drop-offs and pickups a bit less of a production, involving fewer agents, vehicles, and guns.

My mother hadn't wanted to come with us to Washington, but I'd forced the issue. The girls needed her. I needed her. I liked to believe that she needed us, too. For the last few years, she'd been a nearly every-day presence in our lives, her practicality a salve to everyone's worries. At seventy-one, though, she'd never lived anywhere but Chicago. She was reluctant to leave the South Side and her home on Euclid Avenue. ("I love those people, but I love my own house," she told a reporter after the election, not mincing any words. "The White House reminds me of a museum and it's like, how do you sleep in a museum?")

I tried to explain that if she moved to Washington, she'd meet all sorts of interesting people, wouldn't have to cook or clean for herself anymore, and would have more room on the top floor of the White House than she'd ever had at home. None of this was meaningful to her. My mother was impervious to all manner of glamour and hype.

I'd finally called Craig. "You've got to talk to Mom for me," I said. "Please get her on board with this."

Somehow that worked. Craig was good at strong-arming when he needed to be.

My mother would end up staying with us in Washington for the next eight years, but at the time she claimed the move was temporary, that she'd stay only until the girls got settled. She also refused to get put into any bubble. She declined Secret Service protection and avoided the media in order to keep her profile low and her footprint light. She'd charm the White House housekeeping staff by insisting on doing her own laundry, and for years to come, she'd slip in and out of the residence as she pleased, walking out the gates and over to the nearest CVS or Filene's Basement when she needed something, making new friends and meeting them out regularly for lunch. Anytime a stranger commented that she looked exactly like Michelle Obama's mother, she'd just give a polite shrug and say, "Yeah, I get that a lot," before carrying on with her business. As she always had, my mother did things her own way.

M Y WHOLE FAMILY came for the inauguration. My aunts, uncles, and cousins came. Our friends from Hyde Park came, along with my girlfriends and their spouses. Everyone brought their kids. We'd planned twin festivities for the big and small people over inauguration week, including a kids' concert, a separate lunch for kids to take place during the traditional luncheon at the Capitol right after the swearing in, and a scavenger hunt and children's party at the White House that would go on while the rest of us went to inaugural balls.

One of the surprise blessings of the final few months of campaigning had been an organic and harmonious merging of our family with Joe Biden's. Though they'd been political rivals only months earlier, Barack and Joe had a natural rapport, both of them able to slide with ease between the seriousness of their work and the lightness of family.

I liked Jill, Joe's wife, right away, admiring her gentle fortitude and her work ethic. She'd married Joe and become stepmother to his two sons in 1977, five years after his first wife and baby daughter were tragically killed in a car accident. Later, they'd had a daughter of their own. Jill had recently earned her doctorate in education and had managed to teach English at a community college in Delaware not just through Joe's years as a senator but also through his two presidential campaigns. Like me, she was interested in finding new ways to support military families. Unlike me, she had a direct emotional connection to the issue: Beau Biden, Joe's older son, was serving in Iraq with the National Guard. He'd been granted a short leave to travel to Washington and see his dad get sworn in as vice president.

And then there were the Biden grandkids, five altogether, all of them as outgoing and unassuming as Joe and Jill themselves. They'd shown up at the Democratic National Convention in Denver and swept Sasha and Malia right into their boisterous fold, hosting our girls for a sleepover in Joe's hotel suite, all too happy to ignore the politics happening around them in favor of making new friends. We were grateful, always, to have the Biden kids around.

Inauguration Day was bitingly cold, with temperatures never going above freezing and the wind making it feel more like fifteen degrees. That morning, Barack and I went to church with the girls, my mom, Craig and Kelly, Maya and Konrad, and Mama Kaye. All the while, we were hearing that people had begun forming lines at the National Mall before dawn, bundled up as they waited for the inaugural activities to begin. As cold as I would eventually get that day, I'd forever remember how many people stood outside for many more hours than I did, convinced it was worth it to endure the chill. We'd learn later that nearly two million people had flooded the Mall, arriving from all parts of the country, a sea of diversity, energy, and hope stretching for more than a mile from the U.S. Capitol past the Washington Monument.

After church, Barack and I headed to the White House to join up with Joe and Jill, along with President Bush, Vice President Dick Cheney, and their wives, all of us gathering for coffee and tea before motorcading together to the Capitol for the swearing in. At some point earlier, Barack had received the authorization codes that would allow him to access the country's nuclear arsenal and a briefing on the protocols for using them. From now on, wherever he went, he'd be closely trailed by a military aide carrying a forty-five-pound briefcase containing launch authentication codes and sophisticated communications devices, often referred to as the nuclear football. That, too, was heavy.

For me, the ceremony itself would become another one of those strange, slowed-down experiences where the scope was so enormous I couldn't fully process what was going on. We were ushered to a private room in the Capitol ahead of the ceremony so that the girls could have a snack and Barack could take a few minutes with me to practice putting his hand on the small red Bible that had belonged 150 years earlier to Abraham Lincoln. At that same moment, many of our friends, relatives, and colleagues were finding their seats on the platform outside. It occurred to me later that this was probably the first time in history that so many people of color had sat before the public and a global television audience, acknowledged as VIPs at an American inauguration.

Barack and I both knew what this day represented to many Americans, especially those who'd been a part of the civil rights movement. He'd made a point of including the Tuskegee Airmen, the history-making African American pilots and ground crews who fought in World War II, among his guests. He'd also invited the group known as the Little Rock Nine, the nine Black students who in 1957 had been among the first to test the Supreme Court's *Brown v. Board of Education* decision by enrolling at an all-white high school in Arkansas, enduring many months of cruelty and abuse in the name of a higher principle. All of them were senior citizens now, their hair graying and shoulders curving, a sign of the decades and maybe also the weight they'd carried for future generations. Barack had often said that he aspired to climb the steps of the White House because the Little Rock Nine had dared to climb the steps of Central High School. Of every continuum we belonged to, this was perhaps the most important.

Almost exactly at noon that day, we stood before the country with our two girls. I remember really only the smallest things—how brightly the sun fell across Barack's forehead just then, how a respectful hush came over the crowd as the Supreme Court chief justice, John Roberts, began the proceedings. I remember how Sasha, too small for her presence to register amid a sea of adults, stood proudly on a footstool in order to stay visible. I remember the crispness of the air. I lifted Lincoln's Bible, and Barack placed his left hand on it, vowing to protect the U.S. Constitution—with a couple of short sentences, solemnly agreeing to take on the country's every concern. It was weighty and at the same time it was joyful, a feeling mirrored in the inaugural speech Barack would then deliver.

"On this day," he said, "we gather because we have chosen hope over fear, unity of purpose over conflict and discord."

I saw that truth mirrored again and again in the faces of the people who stood shivering in the cold to witness it. There were people in every direction, as far back as I could see. They filled every inch of the National Mall and the parade route. I felt as if our family were almost falling into their arms now. We were making a pact, all of us. You've got us; we've got you.

M ALIA AND SASHA were quickly learning what it meant to be watched publicly. I realized this once we climbed into the presidential limo and began our slow crawl to the White House, leading the inaugural parade. By then, Barack and I had said good-bye to George and Laura Bush, waving as they lifted off from the Capitol in a Marine helicopter. We'd also had lunch. Barack and I were served duck breast in a formal marbled hall inside the Capitol with a couple hundred guests, including his new cabinet, members of Congress, and the justices of the Supreme Court, while the girls feasted on their favorite delicacies— chicken fingers and mac and cheese—with the Biden kids and a handful of cousins in a nearby room.

I marveled at how our daughters had managed themselves perfectly throughout the inauguration, never fidgeting, slouching, or forgetting to smile. We still had many thousands of people watching from the sides of the road and on television as the motorcade made its way up Pennsylvania Avenue, though the darkened windows made it difficult for anyone to see inside. When Barack and I stepped out to walk a short stretch of the parade route and wave to the public, Malia and Sasha stayed behind inside the warm cocoon of the moving limo. It seemed to hit them then that they were finally relatively alone and out of sight.

By the time Barack and I climbed back in, the two girls were breathless and laughing, having released themselves from all ceremonial dignity. They'd shucked off their hats and messed up each other's hair and were thrashing around, engaged in a sisterly tickle fight. Tired out, finally, they sprawled across the seats and rode the rest of the way with their feet kicked up, blasting Beyoncé on the car stereo as if it were just any old day.

Barack and I both felt a kind of sweet relief just then. We were the First Family now, but we were also still ourselves.

As the sun began to set on Inauguration Day, the air temperature dropped further. Barack and I, along with the indefatigable Joe Biden, spent the next two hours in an outdoor reviewing stand in front of the White House, watching bands and floats from all fifty states pass by us on Pennsylvania Avenue. At some point, I stopped feeling my toes, even after someone passed me a blanket to wrap around my legs and feet. One by one, our guests in the stand excused themselves to go get ready for the evening balls.

It was nearly 7:00 p.m. when the last marching band finished and Barack and I walked through the dark and into the White House, arriving for the first time as residents. Over the course of the afternoon, the staff had pulled off an extraordinary top-to-bottom flip of the residence, whisking the Bushes' belongings out and our belongings in. In the span of about five hours, the carpets had been steamed to help keep Malia's allergies from being activated by traces of the former president's dogs. Furniture was brought in and arranged, floral decorations set out. By the time we rode the elevator upstairs, our clothes were organized neatly in the closets; the kitchen pantry had been stocked with our favorite foods. The White House butlers who staffed the residence, mostly African American men who were our age or older, stood poised to help us with anything we needed.

I was almost too cold to take anything in. We were due at the first of ten inaugural balls in less than an hour. I remember seeing very few people upstairs beyond the butlers, who were strangers to me. I remember, in fact, feeling a little lonely as I moved down a long hallway, past a bunch of closed doors. For the last two years, I'd been constantly surrounded by people, with Melissa, Katie, and Kristen always right by my side. Now, suddenly, I felt very much on my own. The kids had already headed to another part of the house for their evening of fun. My mom, Craig, and Maya were staying with us in the residence but had been packed into cars and shuttled off already to the night's festivities. A hairdresser waited to style me; my gown hung on a rack. Barack had disappeared to take a shower and put on his tux.

It had been an incredible, symbolic day for our family and I hoped for the country, but it was also a kind of ultramarathon. I had only about five minutes alone to soak in a warm bath and reboot myself for what came next. Afterward, I'd have a few bites of steak and potatoes that Sam Kass had prepared. I'd have my hair touched up and makeup redone, and then I'd slip into the ivory silk chiffon gown I'd picked for the night ahead, specially made for me by a young designer named Jason Wu. The dress had a single shoulder strap and delicate organza flowers sewn across it, each one with a tiny crystal at its center, and a full skirt that cascaded richly to the floor.

In my life so far, I'd worn very few gowns, but Jason Wu's creation performed a potent little miracle, making me feel soft and beautiful and open again, just as I began to think I had nothing of myself left to show. The dress resurrected the dreaminess of my family's metamorphosis, the promise of this entire experience, transforming me if not into a full-blown ballroom princess, then at least into a woman capable of climbing onto another stage. I was now FLOTUS—First Lady of the United States—to Barack's POTUS. It was time to celebrate.

That night, Barack and I went to the Neighborhood Ball, the first inaugural ball ever to be broadly accessible and affordable to the general public and where Beyoncé—real-life Beyoncé—sang a stunning, full-throated rendition of the R&B classic "At Last," which we'd chosen as our "first dance" song. From there, we moved on to a Home States Ball and after that to the Commander in Chief Ball, then onward to the Youth Ball, and six more beyond that. Our stay at each one was relatively brief and pretty much exactly the same: A band played "Hail to the Chief," Barack made a few remarks, we tried to beam our appreciation to those who'd come, and as everyone stood and watched, we slow danced yet another time to "At Last."

I held on to my husband each time, my eyes finding the calm in his. We were still the same seesawing, yin-and-yang duo we'd been for twenty years now and still connected by a visceral and grounding love. This was one thing I was always content to show.

As the hour got late, however, I could feel myself starting to sag.

The best part of the evening was supposed to be what came last— a private party being held for a couple hundred of our friends back at the White House. It was there that we'd finally be able to let down, have some champagne, and stop worrying about how we appeared. For sure, I'd be taking off my shoes.

It was close to 2:00 a.m. by the time we got ourselves there. Barack and I walked across the marble floors leading to the East Room to find the party in full swing, drinks flowing and elegantly dressed people swirling beneath the sparkling chandeliers. Wynton Marsalis and his band were playing jazz on a small stage at the back of the room. I saw friends from nearly every phase of my life—Princeton friends, Harvard friends, Chicago friends, Robinsons and Shieldses galore. These were the people I wanted to laugh with, to say, *How in holy hell did we all get here?*

But I was done. I'd hit a final fence line. I was also thinking ahead, knowing that the next morning—really just a matter of hours from now—we'd be going to the National Prayer Service and after that we'd stand and greet two hundred members of the public who were coming to visit the White House. Barack looked at me, reading my thoughts. "You don't need to do this," he said. "It's okay."

Partygoers were moving toward me now, eager to interact. Here came a donor. Here was the mayor of a big city. "Michelle! Michelle!" people were calling. I was so exhausted I thought I might cry.

As Barack stepped over the threshold and got promptly sucked into the room, I froze for a split second, then pivoted and fled. I had no energy left to verbalize some First Lady–like excuse or even wave to my friends. I just walked quickly away over the thick red carpet, ignoring the agents who trailed behind me, ignoring everything as I found the elevator to the residence and took myself there—down an unfamiliar hallway and into an unfamiliar room, out of my shoes and out of my gown and into our strange new bed.

20

PEOPLE ASK WHAT IT'S LIKE TO LIVE IN THE WHITE House. I sometimes say that it's a bit like what I imagine living in a fancy hotel might be like, only the fancy hotel has no other guests in it—just you and your family. There are fresh flowers everywhere, with new ones brought in almost every day. The building itself feels old and a little intimidating. The walls are so thick and the planking on the floors so solid that sound in the residence seems to get absorbed quickly. The windows are grand and tall and also fitted with bomb-resistant glass, kept shut at all times for security reasons, which further adds to the stillness. The place is kept immaculately clean. There's a staff made up of ushers, chefs, housekeepers, florists, and also electricians, painters, and plumbers, everyone coming and going politely and quietly, doing their best to keep a low profile, waiting until you've moved out of a room before slipping in to change the towels or put a fresh gardenia in the little vase at the side of your bed.

The rooms are big, all of them. Even the bathrooms and closets are built on a scale different from anything I'd ever encountered. Barack and I were surprised by how much furniture we had to pick out in order to make each room feel homey. Our bedroom had not just a king-sized bed—a beautiful four-poster with a wheat-colored cloth canopy overhead—but also a fireplace and a sitting area, with a couch, a coffee table, and a couple of upholstered chairs. There were five bathrooms for the five of us living in the residence, plus another ten spare bathrooms to go with them. I had not just a closet but a spacious dressing room adjoining it—the same room from which Laura Bush had shown me the Rose Garden view. Over time, this became my de facto private office, the place where I could sit quietly and read, work, or watch TV, dressed in a T-shirt and a pair of sweatpants, blessedly out of sight of everyone.

I understood how lucky we were to be living this way. The master suite in the residence was bigger than the entirety of the upstairs apartment my family had shared when I was growing up on Euclid Avenue. There was a Monet painting hanging outside my bedroom door and a bronze Degas sculpture in our dining room. I was a child of the South Side, now raising daughters who slept in rooms designed by a high-end interior decorator and who could custom order their breakfast from a chef.

I had these thoughts sometimes, and it gave me a kind of vertigo.

I tried, in my way, to loosen the protocol of the place. I made it clear to the housekeeping staff that our girls, as they had in Chicago, would make their own beds every morning. I also instructed Malia and Sasha to act as they'd always acted—to be polite and gracious and to not ask for anything more than what they absolutely needed or couldn't get for themselves. But it was important to me, too, that our daughters feel released from some of the ingrown formalities of the place. *Yes, you can throw balls in the hallway,* I told them. *Yes, you can rummage through the pantry looking for snacks.* I made sure they knew they didn't have to ask permission to go outside and play. I was heartened one afternoon during a snowstorm when I caught sight of the two of them through the window, sledding on the slope of the South Lawn, using plastic trays lent to them by the kitchen staff.

The truth was that in all of this the girls and I were supporting players, beneficiaries of the various luxuries afforded to Barack—important because our happiness was tied to his; protected for one reason, which was that if our safety was compromised, so too would be his ability to think clearly and lead the nation. The White House, one learns, operates with the express purpose of optimizing the well-being, efficiency, and overall power of one person—and that's the president. Barack was now surrounded by people whose job was to treat him like a precious gem. It sometimes felt like a throwback to some lost era, when a household revolved solely around the man's needs, and it was the opposite of what I wanted our daughters to think was normal. Barack, too, was uncomfortable with the attention, though he had little control over all the fuss.

He now had about fifty staffers reading and answering his mail. He had Marine helicopter pilots standing by to fly him anywhere he needed to go, and a six-person team that organized thick briefing books so he could stay current on the issues and make educated decisions. He had a crew of chefs looking after his nutrition, and a handful of grocery shoppers who safeguarded us from any sort of food sabotage by making anonymous runs to different stores, picking up supplies without ever revealing whom they worked for.

As long as I've known him, Barack has never derived pleasure from shopping, cooking, or home maintenance of any kind. He's not someone who keeps power tools in the basement or shakes off work stress by making a risotto or trimming hedges. For him, the removal of all obligations and worries concerning the home made him nothing but happy, if only because it freed his brain, allowing it to roam unfettered over larger concerns, of which there were many.

Most amusing to me was the fact that he now had three personal military valets whose duties included standing watch over his closet, making sure his shoes were shined, his shirts pressed, his gym clothes always fresh and folded. Life in the White House was very different from life in the Hole.

"You see how neat I am now?" Barack said to me one day as we sat at breakfast, his eyes mirthful. "Have you looked in my closet?"

"I have," I said, smiling back. "And you get no credit for any of it."

IN HIS FIRST month in office, Barack signed the Lilly Ledbetter Fair Pay Act, which helped protect workers from wage discrimination based on factors like gender, race, or age. He ordered the end of the use of torture in interrogations and began an effort (ultimately unsuccessful) to close the detention facility at Guantánamo Bay within a year. He overhauled ethics rules governing White House employees' interactions with lobbyists and, most important, managed to push a major economic stimulus bill through Congress, even though not a single House Republican voted in its favor. From where I sat, he seemed to be on a roll. The change he'd promised was becoming real.

As an added bonus, he was showing up for dinner on time.

For me and the girls, this was the startling, happy shift that came from living in the White House with the president of the United States as opposed to living in Chicago with a father who served in some faraway senate and was often out campaigning for higher office. We had access, at long last, to Dad. His life was more orderly now. He worked a ridiculous number of hours, as he always had, but at 6:30 p.m. sharp he'd get on the elevator and ride upstairs to have a family meal, even if he often had to go right back down to the Oval Office afterward. My mother sometimes joined us for dinner, too, though she'd fallen into her own sort of routine, coming down to say hello before accompanying Malia and Sasha to school but mostly choosing to leave us in the evenings, instead eating dinner upstairs in the solarium adjacent to her bedroom while *Jeopardy!* was on. Even when we asked her to stay, she'd usually wave us off. "You all need your time," she'd say.

For the first few months in the White House, I felt the need to be watchful over everything. One of my earliest lessons was that it could be relatively costly to live there. While we stayed rent-free in the residence and had our utilities and staffing paid for, we nonetheless covered all other living expenses, which seemed to add up quickly, especially given the fancy-hotel quality of everything. We got an itemized bill each month for every food item and roll of toilet paper. We paid for every guest who came for an overnight stay or joined us for a meal. And with a culinary staff that had Michelin-level standards and a deep eagerness to please the president, I had to keep an eye on what got served. When Barack offhandedly remarked that he liked the taste of some exotic fruit at breakfast or the sushi on his dinner plate, the kitchen staff took note and put them into regular rotation on the menu. Only later, inspecting the bill, would we realize that some of these items were being flown in at great expense from overseas.

Most of my watchfulness in those early months, though, was reserved for Malia and Sasha. I monitored their moods, quizzing them on their feelings and their interactions with other children. I tried not to over-react anytime they reported making a new friend, though inwardly I was jubilant. I understood by now that there was no straightforward way to arrange playdates at the White House or outings for the kids, but slowly we were figuring out a system.

I was allowed to use a personal BlackBerry but had been advised to limit my contacts to only about ten of my most intimate friends—the people who loved and supported me without any sort of agenda. Most of my communications were mediated by Melissa, who was now my deputy chief of staff and knew the contours of my life better than anyone. She kept track of all my cousins, all my college friends. We gave out her phone number and email address instead of mine, directing all requests to her. Part of the issue was that old acquaintances and distant relatives were surfacing from nowhere and with a flood of inquiries. Could Barack speak at somebody's graduation? Could I please give a speech for somebody's nonprofit? Would we come to this party or that fund-raiser? Most of it was good-hearted, but it was too much for me to absorb all at once.

When it came to the day-to-day lives of our girls, I often had to rely on young staffers to help with logistics. My team met early on with teachers and administrators at Sidwell, recording important dates for school events, ironing out processes for media inquiries, and answering questions from teachers about handling classroom topics involving politics or news of the day. As the girls began making social plans outside school, my personal assistant (or "body person," as it's called in political parlance) became the point of contact, collecting the phone numbers of other parents, orchestrating pickups and drop-offs for playdates. Just as I always had in Chicago, I made a point of trying to get to know the parents of the girls' new friends, inviting a few moms over for lunch and introducing myself to others during school events. Admittedly, these interactions could be awkward. I knew it sometimes took a minute for new acquaintances to move past whatever ideas they held about me and Barack, whatever they thought they knew of me from TV or the news, and to see me simply, if possible, as Malia's or Sasha's mom.

It was awkward to explain to people that before Sasha could come to little Julia's birthday party, the Secret Service would need to stop by and do a security sweep. It was awkward to require Social Security numbers from any parent or caregiver who was going to drive a kid over to our house to play. It was all awkward, but it was all necessary. I didn't like that there was this strange little divide to be crossed anytime I met someone new, but I was relieved to see that it was far different for Sasha and Malia, who went dashing outside to greet their school friends as they got dropped off at the Diplomatic Reception Room—or Dip Room, as we came to call it—grabbing them by the hand and running giggling inside. Kids care about fame, it turns out, for only a few minutes. After that, they just want to have fun.

I LEARNED EARLY ON that I was meant to work with my staff to plan and execute a series of traditional parties and dinners, beginning most immediately with the Governors' Ball, a black-tie gala held every February in the East Room. The same went for the annual Easter Egg Roll, an outdoor family celebration that had been started in 1878 and involved thousands of people. There were also springtime luncheons I would attend in honor of congressional and Senate spouses—similar to the one where I'd seen Laura Bush smiling so unflappably while having an official photo taken with every single guest.

For me, these social events could feel like distractions from what I hoped would be more impactful work, but I also started thinking about ways I might add to or at least modernize some of them, to bend the bar of tradition ever so slightly. In general, I was thinking that life in the White House could be forward leaning without losing any of its established history and tradition. Over time, Barack and I would take steps in this direction, hanging more abstract art and works by African American artists on the walls, for example, and mixing contemporary furniture in with the antiques. In the Oval Office, Barack swapped out a bust of Winston Churchill and replaced it with a bust of Martin Luther King Jr. And we gave the tuxedoed White House butlers the option of dressing more casually on days when there were no public events, introducing a khaki and golf shirt option.

Barack and I knew we wanted to do a better job of democratizing the White House, making it feel less elitist and more open. When we hosted an event, I wanted everyday people to show up, not just those accustomed to black-tie attire. And I wanted more kids around, because kids made everything better. I hoped to make the Easter Egg Roll accessible to more people—adding more slots for city schoolchildren and military families to go with the tickets guaranteed to the children and grandchildren of members of Congress and other VIPs. Lastly, if I was going to sit and lunch with the (mostly) wives of the House and the Senate, couldn't I also invite them to join me out in the city for a community service project?

I knew what mattered to me. I didn't want to be some sort of well-dressed ornament who showed up at parties and ribbon cuttings. I wanted to do things that were purposeful and lasting. My first real effort, I decided, would be the garden.

I was not a gardener and never had been in my life, but thanks to Sam Kass and our family's efforts to eat better at home, I now knew that strawberries were at their most succulent in June, that darker-leaf lettuces had the most nutrients, and that it wasn't so hard to make kale chips in the oven. I saw my daughters eating things like spring pea salad and cauliflower mac and cheese and understood that until recently most of what we knew about food had come through food-industry advertising of everything boxed, frozen, or otherwise processed for convenience, whether it was in snap-crackle TV jingles or clever packaging aimed at the harried parent dashing through the grocery store. Nobody, really, was out there advertising the fresh, healthy stuff—the gratifying crunch of a fresh carrot or the unparalleled sweetness of a tomato plucked right off the vine.

Planting a garden at the White House was my response to this problem, and I hoped it would signal the start of something bigger. Barack's administration was focused on improving access to affordable health care, and for me the garden was a way to offer a parallel message about healthy living. I saw it as an early test, a trial run that could help me determine what I might be able to accomplish as First Lady, a literal way to root myself in this new job. I conceived of it as a kind of outdoor classroom, a place kids could visit to learn about growing food. On the surface, a garden felt elemental and apolitical, a harmless and innocent undertaking by a lady with a spade—pleasing to Barack's West Wing advisers who were constantly concerned about "optics," worrying about how everything appeared to the public.

But there was more to it than that. I planned to use the work we did in the garden to spark a public conversation about nutrition, especially at schools and among parents, which ideally would lead to discussions about how food was produced, labeled, and marketed and the ways that was affecting public health. And in speaking on these topics from the White House, I'd be offering an implicit challenge to the behemoth corporations in the food and beverage industry and the way they'd been doing business for decades.

The truth was, I really didn't know how any of it would go over. But as I directed Sam, who'd joined the White House staff, to begin taking steps to create the garden, I knew I was ready to find out.

My optimism in those first months was primarily tempered by one thing, and that was politics. We lived in Washington now, right up close to the ugly red-versus-blue dynamic I'd tried for years to avoid, even as Barack had chosen to work inside it. Now that he was president, these forces all but ruled his every day. Weeks earlier, before the inauguration, the conservative radio host Rush Limbaugh baldly announced, "I hope Obama fails." I'd watched with dismay as Republicans in Congress followed suit, fighting Barack's every effort to stanch the economic crisis, refusing to support measures that would cut taxes and save or create millions of jobs. On the day he took office, according to some indicators, the American economy was collapsing as fast as or faster than it had at the onset of the Great Depression. Nearly 750,000 jobs had been lost that January alone. And while Barack had campaigned on the idea that it was possible to build consensus between parties, that Americans were at heart more united than divided, the Republican Party was making a deliberate effort, in a time of dire national emergency no less, to prove him wrong.

This was on my mind during the evening of February 24, when Barack addressed a joint session of Congress. The event is basically meant to be a substitute State of the Union for any newly inaugurated president, a chance to outline the goals for the coming year in a speech televised live during prime time, delivered in the hall of the House of Representatives with Supreme Court justices, cabinet members, military generals, and members of Congress present. It's also a tradition of high pageantry, in which lawmakers dramatically express their approval or disapproval of the president's ideas by either leaping to their feet in repeat standing ovations or remaining seated and sullen.

I took my seat that evening in the balcony between a fourteen-year-old who'd written a heartfelt letter to her president and a gracious veteran of the Iraq war, all of us waiting for my husband to arrive. From where I sat, I could see most of the chamber below. It was an unusual, bird's-eye view of our country's leaders, an ocean of whiteness and maleness dressed in dark suits. The absence of diversity was glaring—honestly, it was embarrassing—for a modern, multicultural country. It was most dramatic among the Republicans. At the time, there were just seven non-white Republicans in Congress—none of them African American and only one was a woman. Overall, four out of five members of Congress were male.

A few minutes later, the spectacle began with a thunderclap—the beating of a gavel and the call of the sergeant at arms. The crowd stood, applauding for more than five minutes straight as elected leaders jostled for position on the aisles. At the center of the storm, surrounded by a knot of security agents and a backward-walking videographer, was Barack, shaking hands and beaming as he slowly made his way through the room and toward the podium.

I'd observed this ritual many times before on television, during other times with other presidents. But something about seeing my husband down there amid the crush made the magnitude of the job and the fact he'd need to win over more than half of Congress to get anything done suddenly very real.

Barack's speech that night was detailed and sober-minded, acknowledging the grim state of the economy, the wars going on, the ongoing threat of terror attacks, and the anger of many Americans who felt the government's bailout of the banks was unfairly helping those responsible for the financial crisis. He was careful to be realistic but also to sound notes of hope, reminding his listeners of our resilience as a nation, our ability to rebound after tough times.

I watched from the balcony as Republican members of Congress stayed seated through most of it, appearing obstinate and angry, their arms folded and their frowns deliberate, looking like children who hadn't gotten their way. They would fight everything Barack did, I realized, whether it was good for the country or not. It was as if they'd forgotten that it was a Republican president who'd governed us into this mess in the first place. More than anything, it seemed they just wanted Barack to fail. I confess that in that moment, with that particular view, I did wonder whether there was any path forward.

WHEN I WAS A GIRL, I had vague ideas about how my life could be better. I'd go over to play at the Gore sisters' house and envy their space—the fact that their family had a whole house to themselves. I thought that it would mean something if my family could afford a nicer car. I couldn't help but notice who among my friends had more bracelets or Barbies than I did, or who got to buy their clothes at the mall instead of having a mom who sewed everything on the cheap using Butterick patterns at home. As a kid, you learn to measure long before you understand the size or value of anything. Eventually, if you're lucky, you learn that you've been measuring all wrong.

We lived in the White House now. Very slowly, it was starting to feel familiar—not because I'd ever grow accustomed to the vastness of the space or the opulence of the lifestyle, but because this was where my family slept, ate, laughed, and lived. In the girls' rooms we'd put on display the growing collections of trinkets that Barack made a habit of bringing home from his various travels—snow globes for Sasha, key chains for Malia. We began to make subtle changes to the residence, adding modern lighting to go with the traditional chandeliers and scented candles that made the place feel more like home. I would never take our good fortune or comfort for granted, though what I began to appreciate more was the humanity of the place.

Even my mother, who'd fretted about the museum-like formality of the White House, soon learned that there was more there to be measured. The place was full of people not all that different from us. A number of the butlers had worked for many years in the White House, tending to every family that came through. Their quiet dignity reminded me of my great-uncle Terry, who'd lived downstairs when I was growing up on Euclid Avenue, mowing our lawn dressed in wingtips and suspenders. I tried to make sure that our interactions with staff were respectful and affirming. I wanted to make sure they never felt invisible. If the butlers cared about politics, if they had private allegiances to one party or another, they kept it to themselves. They were careful to respect our privacy, but also were always open and welcoming, and gradually we became close. They instinctively sensed when to give me some space or when I could stand some gentle ribbing. Often they were talking trash about their favorite sports teams in the kitchen, where they liked to fill me in on the latest staff gossip or the exploits of their grandchildren as I looked over the morning headlines. If there was a college basketball game playing on the TV in the evening, Barack came in sometimes to join them for a little while to watch. Sasha and Malia came to love the convivial spirit of the kitchen, slipping in to make smoothies or pop popcorn after school. Many of the staff took a special shine to my mother, stopping in to catch up with her upstairs in the solarium.

It took some time for me to be able to recognize the voices of the different White House phone operators who gave me wake-up calls in the morning or connected me with the East Wing offices downstairs, but soon they, too, became familiar and friendly. We'd chat about the weather, or I'd joke about how I often had to be roused hours earlier than

Barack to have my hair done ahead of official events. These interactions were quick, but in some small way they made life feel a little more normal.

One of the more experienced butlers, a white-haired African American man named James Ramsey, had served since the Carter administration. Every so often, he'd hand me the latest copy of *Jet* magazine, smiling proudly and saying, "I got you covered, Mrs. Obama."

Life was better, always, when we could measure the warmth.

I'D BEEN WALKING around thinking that our new house was big and grand to the point of being over the top, but then in April I went to England and met Her Majesty the Queen.

This was the first international trip Barack and I made together since the election, flying to London on Air Force One so that he could attend a meeting of the Group of 20, or G20, made up of leaders representing the world's largest economies. It was a critical moment for such a gathering. The economic crisis in the United States had created devastating ripples across the globe, sending world financial markets into a tailspin. The G20 summit also marked Barack's debut as president on the world stage. And as was often the case during those first months in office, his main job was to clean up a mess, in this case absorbing the frustration of other world leaders who felt the United States had missed important opportunities to regulate reckless bankers and prevent the disaster with which all of them were now dealing.

Beginning to feel more confident that Sasha and Malia were comfortable in their routines at school, I'd left my mother in charge for the few days I'd be abroad, knowing that she'd immediately relax all my regular rules about getting to bed early and eating every vegetable served at dinner. My mom relished being a grandmother, most especially the part where she got to throw over all my rigidity in favor of her own looser and lighter style, which was markedly more lax than when Craig and I had been the kids under her care. The girls were always thrilled to have Grandma in charge.

Gordon Brown, Britain's prime minister, was hosting the G20 summit, which included a full day of economic meetings at a conference center in the city, but as often happened when world leaders showed up in London for official events, the Queen would also have everyone over to Buckingham Palace for a ceremonial hello. Because of America and Great Britain's close relationship and also, I suppose, because we were new on the scene, Barack and I were invited to arrive at the palace early for a private audience with the Queen ahead of the larger reception.

Needless to say, I had no experience meeting royalty. I was given to understand that I could either curtsy or shake the Queen's hand. I knew that we were to refer to her as "Your Majesty," while her husband, Prince Philip, the Duke of Edinburgh, went by "Your Royal Highness." Other than that, I wasn't sure what to expect as our motorcade rolled through the tall iron gates at the entrance to the palace, past onlookers pressed at the fences, past a collection of guards and a royal horn player, through an interior arch and up to the courtyard, where the official master of the household waited outside to greet us.

It turns out that Buckingham Palace is big—so big that it almost defies description. It has 775 rooms and is fifteen times the size of the White House. In the years to come, Barack and I would be lucky enough to return there a few times as invited guests. On our later trips, we'd sleep in a sumptuous bedroom suite on the ground floor of the palace, looked after by liveried footmen and ladies-in-waiting. We'd attend a formal banquet in the ballroom, eating with forks and knives coated in gold. At one point, as we were given a tour, we were told things like "This is our Blue Room," our guide gesturing into a vast hall that was five times the size of our Blue Room back home. The Queen's head usher one day would take me, my mother, and the girls through the palace Rose Garden, which contained thousands of flawlessly blooming flowers and occupied nearly an acre of land, making the few rosebushes we so proudly kept outside the Oval Office suddenly seem a tad less impressive. I found Buckingham Palace breathtaking and incomprehensible at the same time.

On that first visit, we were escorted to the Queen's private apartment and shown into a sitting room where she and Prince Philip stood waiting to receive us. Queen Elizabeth II was eighty-two years old then, diminutive and graceful with a delicate smile and her white hair curled regally away from her forehead. She wore a pale pink dress and a set of pearls and kept a black purse draped properly over one arm. We shook hands and posed for a photo. The Queen politely inquired about our jet lag and invited us to sit down. I don't remember exactly what we talked about after that—a little bit about the economy and the state of affairs in England, the various meetings Barack had been having.

There's an awkwardness that comes with just about any formally arranged meeting, but in my experience it's something you need to consciously work your way past. Sitting with the Queen, I had to will myself out of my own head—to stop processing the splendor of the setting and the paralysis I felt coming face-to-face with an honest-to-goodness icon. I'd seen Her Majesty's face dozens of times before, in history books, on television, and on currency, but here she was in the flesh, looking at me intently and asking questions. She was warm and personable, and I tried to be the same. The Queen was a living symbol and well practiced at managing it, but she was as human as the rest of us. I liked her immediately.

Later that afternoon, Barack and I floated around at the palace reception, eating canapés with the other G20 leaders and their spouses. I chatted with Angela Merkel of Germany and Nicolas Sarkozy of France. I met the king of Saudi Arabia, the president of Argentina, the prime ministers of Japan and Ethiopia. I did my best to remember who came from which nation and which spouse went with whom, careful not to say too much for fear of getting anything wrong. Overall, it was a dignified, friendly affair and a reminder that even heads of state are capable of talking about their children and joking about the British weather.

At some point toward the end of the party, I turned my head to find that Queen Elizabeth had surfaced at my elbow, the two of us suddenly alone together in the otherwise crowded room. She was wearing a pair of pristine white gloves and appeared just as fresh as she'd been hours earlier when we first met. She smiled up at me.

"You're so tall," she remarked, cocking her head.

"Well," I said, chuckling, "the shoes give me a couple of inches. But yes, I'm tall."

The Queen then glanced down at the pair of black Jimmy Choos I was wearing. She shook her head.

"These shoes are unpleasant, are they not?" she said. She gestured with some frustration at her own black pumps.

I confessed then to the Queen that my feet were hurting. She confessed that hers hurt, too. We looked at each other then with identical expressions, like, *When is all this standing around with world leaders going to finally wrap up?* And with this, she busted out with a fully charming laugh.

Forget that she sometimes wore a diamond crown and that I'd flown to London on the presidential jet; we were just two tired ladies oppressed by our shoes. I then did what's instinctive to me anytime I feel connected to a new person, which is to express my feelings outwardly. I laid a hand affectionately across her shoulder.

I couldn't have known it in the moment, but I was committing what would be deemed an epic faux pas. I'd touched the Queen of England, which I'd soon learn was apparently *not done.* Our interaction at the reception was caught on camera, and in the coming days it would be reproduced in media reports all over the world: "A Breach in Protocol!" "Michelle Obama Dares to Hug the Queen!" It revived some of the campaign-era speculation that I was generally uncouth and lacking the standard elegance of a First Lady, and worried me somewhat, too, thinking I'd possibly distracted from Barack's efforts abroad. But I tried not to let the criticism rattle me. If I hadn't done the proper thing at Buckingham Palace, I had at least done the human thing. I daresay that the Queen was okay with it, too, because when I touched her, she only pulled closer, resting a gloved hand lightly on the small of my back.

The following day, while Barack went off for a marathon session of meetings on the economy, I went to visit a school for girls. It was a government-funded, inner-city secondary school in the Islington neighborhood, not far from a set of council estates, which is what public-housing projects are called in England. More than 90 percent of the school's nine hundred students were Black or from an ethnic minority; a fifth of them were the children of immigrants or asylum seekers. I was drawn to it because it was a diverse school with limited financial resources and yet had been deemed academically outstanding. I also wanted to make sure that when I visited a new place as First Lady, I really visited it—meaning that I'd have a chance to meet the people who actually lived there, not just those who governed them. Traveling abroad, I had opportunities that Barack didn't. I could escape the stage-managed multilateral meetings and sit-downs with leaders and find new ways to bring a little extra warmth to those otherwise staid visits. I aimed to do it with every foreign trip, beginning in England.

I wasn't fully prepared, though, to feel what I did when I set foot inside the Elizabeth Garrett Anderson School and was ushered to an auditorium where about two hundred students had gathered to watch some of their peers perform and then hear me speak. The school was named after a pioneering doctor who also became the first female mayor elected in England. The building itself was nothing special—a boxy brick building on a nondescript street. But as I settled into a folding chair onstage and started watching the performance—which included a Shakespeare scene, a modern dance, and a chorus singing a beautiful rendition of a Whitney Houston song—something inside me began to quake. I almost felt myself falling backward into my own past.

You had only to look around at the faces in the room to know that despite their strengths these girls would need to work hard to be seen. There were girls in *hijab,* girls for whom English was a second language, girls whose skin made up every shade of brown. I knew they'd have to push back against the stereotypes that would get put on them, all the ways they'd be defined before they'd had a chance to define themselves. They'd need to fight the invisibility that comes with being poor, female, and of color. They'd have to work to find their voices and not be diminished, to keep themselves from getting beaten down. They would have to work just to learn.

But their faces were hopeful, and now so was I. For me it was a strange, quiet revelation: They were me, as I'd once been. And I was them, as they could be. The energy I felt thrumming in that school had nothing to do with obstacles. It was the power of nine hundred girls striving.

When the performance was done and I went to the lectern to speak, I could barely contain my emotion. I glanced down at my prepared notes but suddenly had little interest in them. Looking up at the girls, I just began to talk, explaining that though I had come from far away, carrying this strange title of First Lady of the United States, I was more like them than they knew. That I, too, was from a working-class neighborhood, raised by a family of modest means and loving spirit, that I'd realized early on that school was where I could start defining myself—that an education was a thing worth working for, that it would help spring them forward in the world.

At this point, I'd been First Lady for just over two months. In different moments, I'd felt overwhelmed by the pace, unworthy of the glamour, anxious about our children, and uncertain of my purpose. There are pieces of public life, of giving up one's privacy to become a walking, talking symbol of a nation, that can seem specifically designed to strip away part of your identity. But here, finally, speaking to those girls, I felt something completely different and pure—an alignment of my old self with this new role. *Are you good enough? Yes, you are, all of you.* I told the students of Elizabeth Garrett Anderson that they'd touched my heart. I told them that they were precious, because they truly were. And when my talk was over, I did what was instinctive. I hugged absolutely every single girl I could reach.

BACK HOME IN WASHINGTON, spring had arrived. The sun came up earlier and stayed out a little longer each day. I watched as the slope of the South Lawn gradually turned a lush and vibrant green. From the windows of the residence, I could see the red tulips and lavender grape hyacinth that surrounded the fountain at the base of the hill. My staff and I had spent the past two months working to turn my idea for a garden into reality, which hadn't been easy. For one thing, we'd had to persuade the National Park Service and the White House grounds team to tear up a patch of one of the most iconic lawns in the world. The very suggestion had been met with resistance, initially. It had been decades since a White House Victory Garden had been planted, on Eleanor Roosevelt's watch, and no one seemed much interested in a reprise. "They think we're insane," Sam Kass told me at one point.

Eventually, though, we got our way. We were at first allotted a tiny plot of land tucked away behind the tennis courts, next to a toolshed.

To his credit, Sam fought for better real estate, finally securing an L-shaped eleven-hundred-square-foot plot in a sun-splashed part of the South Lawn, not far from the Oval Office and the swing set we'd recently installed for the girls. We coordinated with the Secret Service to make sure our tilling wouldn't disrupt any of the sensors or sight lines they needed to protect the grounds. We ran tests to determine whether the soil had enough nutrients and didn't contain any toxic elements like lead or mercury.

And then we were good to go.

Several days after I returned from Europe, I hosted a group of students from Bancroft Elementary School, a bilingual school in the northwestern part of the city. Weeks earlier, we'd used shovels and hoes to prepare the soil. Now the same kids were back to help me do the planting. Our patch of dirt sat not far from the southern fence along E Street, where tourists often congregated to gaze up at the White House. I was glad that this would now be a part of their view.

Or at least I hoped to be glad at some point. Because with a garden you never know for sure what will or won't happen—whether anything, in fact, will grow. We'd invited the media to cover the planting. We'd invited all the White House chefs to help us, along with Tom Vilsack, Barack's secretary of agriculture. We'd asked everyone to watch what we were doing. Now we had to wait for the results. "Honestly," I'd said to Sam before anyone arrived that morning, "this better work."

That day, I knelt with a bunch of fifth graders as we carefully put seedlings into the ground, patting the dirt into place around the fragile stalks. After being in Europe and having my every outfit dissected in the press (I'd worn a cardigan sweater to meet the Queen, which was almost as scandalous as touching her had been), I was relieved to be kneeling in the dirt in a light jacket and a pair of casual pants. The kids asked me questions, some about vegetables and the tasks at hand, but also things like "Where's the president?" and "How come he's not helping?" It took only a little while, though, before most of them seemed to lose track of me, their focus centered instead on the fit of their garden gloves and the worms in the soil. I loved being with children. It was, and would be throughout the entirety of my time in the White House, a balm for my spirit, a way to momentarily escape my First Lady worries, my self-consciousness about constantly being judged. Kids made me feel like myself again. To them, I wasn't a spectacle. I was just a nice, kinda-tall lady.

As the morning went on, we planted lettuce and spinach, fennel and broccoli. We put in carrots and collard greens and onions and shell peas. We planted berry bushes and a lot of herbs. What would come from it? I didn't know, the same way I didn't know what lay ahead for us in the White House, nor what lay ahead for the country or for any of these sweet children surrounding me. All we could do then was put our faith into the effort, trusting that with sun and rain and time, something half-decent would push up through the dirt.

21

ONE SATURDAY EVENING AT THE END OF MAY, Barack took me out on a date. In the four months since becoming president, he'd been spending his days working on ways to fulfill the various promises made to voters during the campaign; now he was making good on a promise to me. We were going to New York, to have dinner and see a show.

For years in Chicago, our date nights had been a sacred part of every week, an indulgence we built into our lives and protected no matter what. I love talking to my husband across a small table in a low-lit room. I always have, and I expect I always will. Barack is a good listener, patient and thoughtful. I love how he tips his head back when he laughs. I love the lightness in his eyes, the kindness at his core. Having a drink and an unrushed meal together has always been our pathway back to the start, to that first hot summer when everything between us carried an electric charge.

I dressed up for our New York date, putting on a black cocktail dress and lipstick, styling my hair in an elegant updo. I felt a fluttering excitement at the prospect of a getaway, of time alone with my husband. In the last few months, we'd hosted dinners and gone to Kennedy Center performances together, but it was almost always in an official capacity and with lots of other people. This was to be a true night off.

Barack had dressed in a dark suit with no tie. We kissed the girls and my mom good-bye in the late afternoon and walked hand in hand across the South Lawn and climbed onto Marine One, the presidential helicopter, which took us to Andrews Air Force Base. We next boarded a small Air Force plane, flew to JFK Airport, and were then helicoptered into Manhattan. Our movements had been planned meticulously in advance by our scheduling teams and the Secret Service, meant as always to maximize efficiency and security.

Barack (with the help of Sam Kass) had chosen a restaurant near Washington Square Park that he knew I'd love for its emphasis on locally grown foods, a small, tucked-away eatery called Blue Hill. As we motorcaded the last stretch of the journey from the helipad in lower Manhattan to Greenwich Village, I noted the lights of the cop cars being used to barricade the cross streets, feeling a twinge of guilt at how our mere presence in the city was mucking up the Saturday evening flow. New York always awakened a sense of awe in me, big and busy enough to dwarf anyone's ego. I remembered how wide-eyed I'd been on my first trip there decades earlier with Czerny, my mentor from Princeton. Barack, I knew, felt something even deeper. The wild energy and diversity of the city had proven the perfect hatching place for his intellect and imagination years back when he was a student at Columbia.

At the restaurant, we were shown to a table in a discreet corner of the room as around us people tried not to gawk. But there was no hiding our arrival. Anyone who came in after we did would have to get swept with a magnetometer wand by a Secret Service team, a process that was usually quick but still an inconvenience. For this, I felt another twinge.

We ordered martinis. Our conversation stayed light. Four months into our lives as POTUS and FLOTUS, we were still retrofitting—figuring out how one identity worked with the other and what this meant inside our marriage. These days, there was almost no part of Barack's complicated life that didn't in some way impact mine, which meant there was plenty of shared business we could have discussed—his team's decision to schedule a foreign trip during the girls' summer vacation, for example, or whether my chief of staff was being listened to at morning staff meetings in the West Wing—but I tried in general to avoid it, not just this night, but every night. If I had an issue with something going on in the West Wing, I usually relied on my staff to convey it to Barack's, doing what I could to keep White House business out of our personal time.

Sometimes Barack wanted to talk about work, though more often than not he avoided it. So much of his job was just plain grueling, the challenges huge and often seemingly intractable. General Motors was days away from filing for bankruptcy. North Korea had just conducted a nuclear test, and Barack was soon to leave for Egypt to deliver a major address meant to extend an open hand to Muslims around the world. The ground around him never seemed to stop shaking. Anytime old friends came to visit us at the White House, they were amused by the intensity with which both Barack and I quizzed them about their jobs, their kids, their hobbies, anything. The two of us were always less interested in talking about the intricacies of our new existence and more interested in sponging up bits of gossip and everyday news from home. Both of us, it seemed, craved glimpses of regular life.

That evening in New York, we ate, drank, and conversed in the candlelight, reveling in the feeling, however illusory, that we'd stolen away. The White House is a remarkably beautiful and comfortable place, a kind of fortress disguised as a home, and from the point of view of the Secret Service agents tasked with protecting us, it would probably be ideal if we never left its grounds. Even inside it, the agents seemed happiest if we took the elevator instead of the stairs, to minimize the risk of a stumble. If Barack or I had a meeting in Blair House, located just across an already closed-off part of Pennsylvania Avenue, they'd sometimes request that we take the motorcade instead of walking in the fresh air. We respected the watchfulness, but it could feel like a form of confinement. I struggled sometimes, trying to balance my needs with what was convenient for others. If anyone in our family wanted to step outside onto the Truman Balcony—the lovely arcing terrace that overlooked the South Lawn, and the only semiprivate outdoor space we had at the White House—we needed to first alert the Secret Service so that they could shut down the section of E Street that was in view of the balcony, clearing out the flocks of tourists who gathered outside the gates there at all hours of the day and night. There were many times when I thought I'd go out to sit on the balcony, but then reconsidered, realizing the hassle I would cause, the vacations I'd be interrupting, all because I thought it would be nice to have a cup of tea outdoors.

With our movements so controlled, the number of steps Barack and I took in a day had plummeted. As a result, both of us had grown fiercely dependent on the small gym on the top floor of the residence. Barack ran on the treadmill about an hour every day, trying to beat back his physical restlessness. I was working out every morning as well, often with Cornell, who'd been our trainer in Chicago and now lived part-time in Washington on our behalf, coming over at least a few times a week to push us with plyometrics and weights.

Setting aside the business of the country, Barack and I never lacked for things to discuss. We talked that night over dinner about Malia's flute lessons; Sasha's ongoing devotion to her perilously frayed Blankie, which she kept draped over her head as she slept at night. When I told a funny story about how a makeup artist recently tried and failed to put false eyelashes on my mom before a photo shoot, Barack tipped his head and laughed, exactly the way I knew he would. And we had a new and entertaining baby in the house to talk about as well—a seven-month-old, completely rambunctious Portuguese water dog we'd named Bo, a gift to our family from Senator Ted Kennedy and a fulfillment of the promise we'd made to the girls during the campaign. The girls had taken to playing a hide-and-seek game with him on the South Lawn, crouching behind trees and shouting his name as he scampered across the open grass, following their voices. All of us loved Bo.

When we finally finished our meal and stood up to leave, the diners around us rose to their feet and applauded, which struck me as both kind and unnecessary. It's possible that some of them were glad to see us go.

We were a nuisance, Barack and I, a disruption to any normal scene. There was no getting around that fact. We felt it acutely as our motorcade zipped us up Sixth Avenue and over toward Times Square, where hours earlier police had cordoned off an entire block in front of the theater, where our fellow theatergoers were now waiting in line to pass through metal detectors that normally weren't there and the performers would need to wait an extra forty-five minutes to start the show due to the security checks.

The play, when it finally began, was marvelous—a drama by August Wilson set inside a Pittsburgh boardinghouse during the Great Migration, when millions of African Americans left the South and flooded into the Midwest, just as my relatives on both sides had done. Sitting in the dark next to Barack, I was riveted, a little emotional, and for a short while able to get lost in the performance and the sense of quiet contentment that came with just being off duty and out in the world.

As we flew back to Washington late that night, I already knew it would be a long time before we did anything like this again. Barack's political opponents would criticize him for taking me to New York to see a show. The Republican Party would put out a press release before we'd even gotten home, saying that our date had been extravagant and costly to taxpayers, a message that would get picked up and debated on cable news. Barack's team would quietly reinforce the point, urging us to be more mindful of the politics, making me feel guilty and selfish for having stolen a rare moment out and alone with my husband.

But that wasn't even it. The critics would always be there. The Republicans would never let up. Optics would always rule our lives.

It was as if with our date Barack and I had tested a theory and proven both the best and the worst parts of what we'd suspected all along. The nice part was that we *could* step away for a romantic evening the way we used to, years earlier, before his political life took over. We could, as First Couple, feel close and connected, enjoying a meal and a show in a city we both loved. The harder part was seeing the selfishness inherent in making that choice, knowing that it had required hours of advance meetings between security teams and local police. It had involved extra work for our staffers, for the theater, for the waiters at the restaurant, for the people whose cars had been diverted off Sixth Avenue, for the police on the street. It was part of the new heaviness we lived with. There were just too many people involved, too many affected, for anything to feel light.

. . .

FROM THE TRUMAN BALCONY, I could see the fullness of the garden taking shape on the southwest corner of the lawn. For me, it was a gratifying sight—a miniature Eden in progress, made up of spiraling young tendrils and half-grown shoots, carrot and onion stalks just beginning to rise, the patches of spinach dense and green, with bright red and yellow flowers blooming around the edges. We were growing food.

In late June, our original garden-helper crew from Bancroft Elementary joined me for our first harvest, kneeling together in the dirt to tear off lettuce leaves and strip pea pods from their stems. This time they were also entertained by Bo, our puppy, who proved to be a great lover of the garden himself, bounding in circles around the trees before sprawling belly-up in the sun between the raised beds.

After our harvest that day, Sam and the schoolkids made salads with their fresh-picked lettuce and peas in the kitchen, which we then ate with baked chicken, followed by cupcakes topped with garden berries. In ten weeks, the garden had generated over ninety pounds of produce—from only about $200 worth of seeds and mulch.

The garden was popular and the garden was wholesome, but I also knew that for some people it wouldn't feel like enough. I understood that I was being watched with a certain kind of anticipation, especially by women, maybe especially by professional working women, who wondered whether I'd bury my education and management experience to fold myself into some prescribed First Lady pigeonhole, a place lined with tea leaves and pink linen. People seemed worried that I wasn't going to show my full self.

Regardless of what I chose to do, I knew I was bound to disappoint someone. The campaign had taught me that my every move and facial expression would be read a dozen different ways. I was either hard-driving and angry or, with my garden and messages about healthy eating, I was a disappointment to feminists, lacking a certain stridency. Several months before Barack was elected, I'd told a magazine interviewer that my primary focus in the White House would be to continue my role as "mom in chief" in our family. I'd said it casually, but the phrase caught hold and was amplified across the press. Some Americans seemed to embrace it, understanding all too well the amount of organization and drive it takes to raise children. Others, meanwhile, seemed vaguely appalled, presuming it to mean that as First Lady I'd do nothing but pipe-cleaner craft projects with my kids.

The truth was, I intended to do everything—to work with purpose and parent with care—same as I always had. The only difference now was that a lot of people were watching.

My preferred way to work, at least at first, was quietly. I wanted to be methodical in putting together a larger plan, waiting until I had full confidence in what I was presenting before going public with any of it. As I told my staff, I'd rather go deep than broad when it came to taking on issues. I felt sometimes like a swan on a lake, knowing that my job was in part to glide and appear serene, while underwater I never stopped pedaling my legs. The interest and enthusiasm we'd generated with the garden—the positive news coverage, the letters pouring in from around the country—only confirmed for me that I could generate buzz around a good idea. Now I wanted to highlight a larger issue and push for larger solutions.

At the time Barack took office, nearly a third of American children were overweight or obese. Over the previous three decades, rates of childhood obesity had tripled. Kids were being diagnosed with high blood pressure and type 2 diabetes at record rates. Even military leaders were reporting that obesity was one of the most common disqualifiers for service.

The problem was woven into every aspect of family life, from the high price of fresh fruits to widespread cuts in funding for sports and rec programs in public schools. TV, computers, and video games competed for kids' time, and in some neighborhoods staying indoors felt like a safer choice than going outside to play, as Craig and I had done when we were kids. Many families in underserved sections of big cities didn't have grocery stores in their neighborhoods. Rural shoppers across large swaths of the country were similarly out of luck when it came to accessing fresh produce. Meanwhile, portion sizes at restaurants were increasing. Advertising slogans for sugary cereal, microwavable convenience foods, and supersized everything were downloaded directly into the minds of children watching cartoons.

Attempting to improve even one part of the food system, though, could set off adversarial ripples. If I were to try to declare war on sugary drinks marketed to kids, it would likely be opposed not just by the big beverage companies but also by farmers who supplied the corn used in many sweeteners. If I were to advocate for healthier school lunches, I'd put myself on a collision course with the big corporate lobbies that often dictated what food ended up on a fourth grader's tray at the cafeteria. For years, public health experts and advocates had been outmatched by the better-organized, better-funded food and beverage industrial complex. School lunches in the United States were a six-billion-dollar-a-year business.

Still, it felt to me like the right time to push for change. I was neither the first nor the only person to be drawn to these issues. Across America, a nascent healthy food movement was gaining strength. Urban farmers were experimenting in cities across the country. Republicans and Democrats alike had tackled the problem at state and local levels, investing in healthy living, building more sidewalks and community gardens— a proof point that there was common political ground to be explored.

Midway through 2009, my small team and I began coordinating with West Wing policy people and meeting with experts inside and outside government to formulate a plan. We decided to keep our work focused on children. It's tough and politically difficult to get grown-ups to change their habits. We felt certain we'd stand a better chance if we tried to help kids think differently about food and exercise from an early age. And who could take issue with us if we were genuinely looking out for kids?

My own kids were by then out of school for the summer. I'd committed myself to spending three days a week working in my capacity as First Lady while reserving the rest of my time for family. Rather than put the girls in day camps, I decided to run what I called Camp Obama, where we'd invite a few friends and make local excursions, getting to know the area in which we now lived. We went to Monticello and Mount Vernon and explored caves in the Shenandoah Valley. We visited the Bureau of Engraving and Printing to see how dollars got made and toured Frederick Douglass's house in the southeast part of Washington, learning how an enslaved person could become a scholar and a hero. For a while, I required the girls to write up a little report after each visit, summarizing what they had learned, though eventually they started protesting and I let the idea go.

As often as we could, we scheduled these outings for first thing in the morning or late in the day so that the Secret Service could clear the site or rope off an area ahead of our arrival without causing too much of a hassle. We were still a nuisance, I knew, though without Barack along we were at least somewhat less of a nuisance. And when it came to the girls, anyway, I tried to let go of any guilt. I wanted our kids to be able to move with the same kind of freedom that other kids had.

One day, earlier in the year, I'd had a dustup with the Secret Service when Malia had been invited to join a group of school friends who were making a spur-of-the-moment trip to get some ice cream. Because for security reasons she wasn't allowed to ride in another family's car, and because Barack and I had our daily schedules diced down to the minute and set weeks in advance, Malia was told she'd have to wait an hour while the leader of her security detail was summoned from the suburbs, which of course then merited a bunch of apologetic phone calls and delayed everyone involved.

This was exactly the kind of heaviness I didn't want for my daughters. I couldn't contain my irritation. To me, it made no sense. We had agents standing in practically every hallway of the White House. I could look out the window and see Secret Service vehicles parked in the circular drive. But for some reason, she couldn't just get my permission and head off to join her friends. Nothing could be done without her detail leader.

"This isn't how families work or how ice cream runs work," I said. "If you're going to protect a kid, you've got to be able to move like a kid." I went on to insist that the agents revise their protocols so that in the future Malia and Sasha could leave the White House safely and without some massive advance planning effort. For me, it was another small test of the boundaries. Barack and I had by now let go of the idea that we could be spontaneous. We'd surrendered to the idea that there was no longer room for impulsiveness and whimsy in our own lives. But for our girls, we'd fight to keep that possibility alive.

SOMETIME DURING BARACK'S CAMPAIGN, people had begun paying attention to my clothes. Or at least the media paid attention, which led fashion bloggers to pay attention, which seemed then to provoke all manner of commentary across the internet. I don't know why this was, exactly—possibly because I'm tall and unafraid of bold patterns—but so it seemed to be.

When I wore flats instead of heels, it got reported in the news. My pearls, my belts, my cardigans, my off-the-rack dresses from J.Crew, my apparently brave choice of white for an inaugural gown—all seemed to trigger a slew of opinions and instant feedback. I wore a sleeveless aubergine dress to Barack's address to the joint session of Congress and a sleeveless black sheath dress for my official White House photo, and suddenly my arms were making headlines. Late in the summer of 2009, we went on a family trip in the Grand Canyon, and I was lambasted for an apparent lack of dignity when I was photographed getting off Air Force One (in 106-degree heat, I might add) dressed in a pair of shorts.

It seemed that my clothes mattered more to people than anything I had to say. In London, I'd stepped offstage after having been moved to tears while speaking to the girls at the Elizabeth Garrett Anderson School, only to learn that the first question directed to one of my staffers by a reporter covering the event had been "Who made her dress?"

This stuff got me down, but I tried to reframe it as an opportunity to learn, to use what power I could find inside a situation I'd never have chosen for myself. If people flipped through a magazine primarily to see the clothes I was wearing, I hoped they'd also see the military spouse standing next to me or read what I had to say about children's health. When *Vogue* proposed putting me on the cover of the magazine shortly after Barack was elected, my team had debated whether it would make me seem frivolous or elitist during a time of economic worry, but in the end we'd decided to go ahead with it. It mattered every time a woman of color showed up on the cover of a magazine. Also, I insisted on choosing my own outfits, wearing dresses by Jason Wu and Narciso Rodriguez, a gifted Latino designer, for the photo shoot.

I knew a little about fashion, but not a lot. As a working mother, I'd really been too busy to put much thought into what I wore. During the campaign, I'd done most of my shopping at a boutique in Chicago where I'd had the good fortune of meeting a young sales associate named Meredith Koop. Meredith, who'd been raised in St. Louis, was sharp and knowledgeable about different designers and had a playful sense of color and texture. After Barack's election, I was able to persuade her to move to Washington and work with me as a personal aide and wardrobe stylist. Very quickly, she also became a trusted friend.

A couple of times a month, Meredith would roll several big racks of clothing into my dressing room in the residence, and we'd spend an hour or two trying things on, pairing outfits with whatever was on my schedule in the coming weeks. I paid for all my own clothes and accessories—with the exception of some items like the couture-level gowns I wore to formal events, which were lent to me by the designers and would later be donated to the National Archives, thus adhering to White House ethics guidelines. When it came to my choices, I tried to be somewhat unpredictable, to prevent anyone from ascribing any sort of message to what I wore. It was a thin line to walk. I was supposed to stand out without overshadowing others, to blend in but not fade away. As a Black woman, too, I knew I'd be criticized if I was perceived as being showy and high end, and I'd be criticized also if I was too casual. So I mixed it up. I'd match a high-end Michael Kors skirt with a T-shirt from Gap. I wore something from Target one day and Diane von Furstenberg the next. I wanted to draw attention to and celebrate American designers, most especially those who were less established, even if it sometimes frustrated old-guard designers, including Oscar de la Renta, who was reportedly displeased that I wasn't wearing his creations. For me, my choices were simply a way to use my curious relationship with the public gaze to boost a diverse set of up-and-comers.

Optics governed more or less everything in the political world, and I factored this into every outfit. It required time, thought, and money—more money than I'd spent on clothing ever before. It also required careful research by Meredith, particularly on foreign trips. She'd often spend hours making sure the designers, colors, and styles we chose paid proper respect to the people and countries we visited. Meredith also shopped for Sasha and Malia ahead of public events, which added to the overall expense, but they, too, had the gaze upon them. I sighed sometimes, watching Barack pull the same dark suit out of his closet and head off to work without even needing a comb. His biggest fashion consideration for a public moment was whether to have his suit jacket on or off. Tie or no tie?

We were careful, Meredith and I, to always be prepared. In my dressing room, I'd put on a new dress and then squat, lunge, and pinwheel my arms, just to be sure I could move. Anything too restrictive, I put back on the rack. When I traveled, I brought backup outfits, anticipating shifts in weather and schedule, not to mention nightmare scenarios involving spilled wine or broken zippers. I learned, too, that it was important to always, no matter what, pack a dress suitable for a funeral, because Barack sometimes got called with little notice to be there as soldiers, senators, and world leaders were laid to rest.

I came to depend heavily on Meredith but also equally on Johnny Wright, my fast-talking, hard-laughing hurricane of a hairdresser, and Carl Ray, my soft-spoken and meticulous makeup artist. Together, the three of them (dubbed by my larger team "the trifecta") gave me the confidence I needed to step out in public each day, all of us knowing that a slipup would lead to a flurry of ridicule and nasty comments. I never expected to be someone who hired others to maintain my image, and at first the idea was discomfiting. But I quickly found out a truth that no one talks about: Today, virtually every woman in public life—politicians, celebrities, you name it—has some version of Meredith, Johnny, and Carl. It's all but a requirement, a built-in fee for our societal double standard.

How had other First Ladies managed their hair, makeup, and wardrobe challenges? I had no idea. Several times over the course of that first year in the White House, I found myself picking up books either by or about previous First Ladies, but each time I'd lay them down again. I almost didn't want to know what was the same and what was different about any of us.

I did, in September, have a pleasant overdue lunch with Hillary Clinton, the two of us sitting in the residence dining room. After his election and a little to my surprise, Barack had chosen Hillary as his secretary of state, both of them managing to set aside the battle wounds of the primary campaign and build a productive working relationship. She was candid with me about how she'd misjudged the country's readiness to have a proactive professional woman in the role of First Lady. As First Lady of Arkansas, Hillary had kept her job as a law partner while also helping with her husband's efforts to improve health care and education. Arriving in Washington with the same sort of desire and energy to contribute, though, she'd been roundly spurned, pilloried for taking on a policy role in the White House's work on health care reform. The message had been delivered with a resounding, brutal frankness: Voters had elected her husband and not her. First Ladies had no place in the West Wing. She'd tried to do too much too quickly, it seemed, and had run straight into a wall.

I myself tried to be mindful of that wall, learning from other First Ladies' experience, taking care not to directly or overtly insert myself into West Wing business. I relied instead on my staff to communicate daily with Barack's, exchanging advice, syncing our schedules, and reviewing every plan. The president's advisers in my opinion could be overly fretful about appearances. At one point several years later, when I decided to get bangs cut into my hair, my staff would feel the need to first run the idea past Barack's staff, just to make sure there wouldn't be a problem.

With the economy in rough shape, Barack's team was constantly guarding against any image coming out of the White House that might be seen as frivolous or light, given the somberness of the times. This didn't always sit well with me. I knew from experience that even during hard times, maybe especially during hard times, it was still okay to laugh. For the sake of children, in particular, you had to find ways to have fun. On this front, my team had been wrangling with Barack's communications staff over an idea I'd had to host a Halloween party for kids at the White House. The West Wing—particularly David Axelrod, now a senior adviser in the administration, and Press Secretary Robert Gibbs—thought it would be perceived as too showy, too costly, and could potentially alienate Barack from the public. "The optics are just bad" was how they put it. I disagreed, arguing that a Halloween party for local kids and military families who'd never seen the White House before was a perfectly appropriate use for a tiny slice of the Social Office's entertaining budget.

Axe and Gibbs never fully consented, but at some point they stopped fighting us on it. At the end of October, to my great delight, a thousand-pound pumpkin sat on the White House lawn. A brass band of skeletons played jazz music, while a giant black spider descended from the North Portico. I stood in front of the White House, dressed as a leopard—in black pants, a spotted top, and a pair of cat ears on a headband—as Barack, who was never much of a costume guy even before optics mattered, stood next to me in a humdrum sweater. (Gibbs, to his credit, showed up dressed as Darth Vader, ready to have fun.) That night, we handed out bags of cookies, dried fruits, and M&M's in a box emblazoned with the presidential seal as more than two thousand little princesses, grim reapers, pirates, superheroes, ghosts, and football players traipsed up the lawn to meet us. As far as I was concerned, the optics were just right.

THE GARDEN CHURNED through the seasons, teaching us all sorts of things. We grew cantaloupes that turned out pale and tasteless. We endured pelting rainstorms that washed away our topsoil. Birds snacked on our blueberries; beetles went after the cucumbers. Each time something went a little awry, with the help of Jim Adams, the National Park Service horticulturist who served as our head gardener, and Dale Haney, the White House grounds superintendent, we made small adjustments and carried on, savoring the overall abundance. Our dinners in the residence now often included broccoli, carrots, and kale grown on the South Lawn. We started donating a portion of every harvest to Miriam's Kitchen, a local nonprofit that served the homeless. We began, too, to pickle vegetables and present them as gifts to visiting dignitaries, along with jars of honey from our new beehives. Among the staff, the garden became a source of pride. Its early skeptics had quickly become fans. For me, the garden was simple, prosperous, and healthy—a symbol of diligence and faith. It was beautiful while also being powerful. And it made people happy.

Over the previous few months, my East Wing staff and I had spoken with children's health experts and advocates to help us develop the pillars on which our larger effort would be built. We'd give parents better information to help them make healthy choices for their families. We'd work to create healthier schools. We'd try to improve access to nutritious food. And we'd find more ways for young people to be physically active. Knowing that the way we introduced our work would matter as much as anything, I again enlisted the help of Stephanie Cutter, who came on as a consultant to help Sam and Jocelyn Frye shape the initiative, while my communications team was tasked with building a fun public face for the campaign. All the while, the West Wing was apparently fretting about my plans, worried I'd come off as a finger-wagging embodiment of the nanny state at a time when controversial bank and car-company bailouts had left Americans extra leery of anything that looked like government intervention.

My goal, though, was to make this about more than government. I hoped to learn from what Hillary had shared with me about her own experiences, to leave the politics to Barack and focus my own efforts elsewhere. When it came to dealing with the CEOs of soft drink companies and school-lunch suppliers, I thought it was worth making a human appeal as opposed to a regulatory one, to collaborate rather than pick a fight. And when it came to the way families actually lived, I wanted to speak directly to moms, dads, and especially kids.

I wasn't interested in following the tenets of the political world or appearing on Sunday morning news shows. Instead, I did interviews with health magazines geared toward parents and kids. I hula-hooped on the South Lawn to show that exercise could be fun and made a guest appearance on *Sesame Street,* talking about vegetables with Elmo and Big Bird.

Anytime I spoke to reporters from the White House garden, I mentioned that many Americans had trouble accessing fresh produce in their communities and tried to remark on the health-care costs connected to rising obesity levels. I wanted to make sure we had buy-in from everyone we'd need to make the initiative a success, to anticipate any objections that might be raised. With this in mind, we spent weeks and weeks quietly holding meetings with business and advocacy groups as well as members of Congress. We conducted focus groups to test-market our branding for the project, enlisting the pro bono help of PR professionals to fine-tune the message.

In February 2010, I was finally ready to share my vision. On a cold Tuesday afternoon and with D.C. still digging out from a historic blizzard, I stood at a lectern in the State Dining Room at the White House, surrounded by kids and cabinet secretaries, sports figures and mayors, along with leaders in medicine, education, and food production, plus a bevy of media, to proudly announce our new initiative, which we'd decided to name Let's Move! It centered on one goal—ending the childhood obesity epidemic within a generation.

What was important to me was that we weren't just announcing some pie-in-the-sky set of wishes. The effort was real, and the work was well under way. Not only had Barack signed a memorandum earlier that day to create a first-of-its-kind federal task force on childhood obesity, but the three major corporate suppliers of school lunches had announced that they would cut the amount of salt, sugar, and fat in the meals they served. The American Beverage Association had promised to improve the clarity of its ingredient labeling. We'd engaged the American Academy of Pediatrics to encourage doctors to make body mass index measurements a standard of care for children, and we'd persuaded Disney, NBC, and Warner Bros. to air public service announcements and invest in special programming that encouraged kids to make healthy lifestyle choices. Leaders from twelve different professional sports leagues, too, had agreed to promote a 60 Minutes of Play a Day campaign to help get kids moving more.

And that was just the start. We had plans to help bring greengrocers into urban neighborhoods and rural areas known as "food deserts," to push for more accurate nutritional information on food packaging, and to redesign the aging food pyramid to be more accessible and in line with current research on nutrition. Along the way, we'd work to hold the business community accountable for its decision making around issues impacting children's health.

It would take commitment and organization to make all this happen, I knew, but that was exactly the kind of work I liked. We were taking on a huge issue, but now I had the benefit of operating from a huge platform. I was beginning to realize that all the things that felt odd to me about my new existence—the strangeness of fame, the hawkeyed attention paid to my image, the vagueness of my job description—could be marshaled in service of real goals. I was energized. Here, finally, was a way to show my full self.

22

ONE SPRING MORNING, BARACK AND THE GIRLS AND I were summoned downstairs from the residence to the South Lawn. A man I'd never seen before stood waiting for us in the driveway. He had a friendly face and a salt-and-pepper mustache that gave him an air of dignity. He introduced himself as Lloyd.

"Mr. President, Mrs. Obama," he said. "We thought you and the girls might like a little change of pace, and so we've arranged a petting zoo for you." He smiled broadly at us. "Never before has a First Family participated in something like this."

The man gestured to his left and we looked. About thirty yards away, lounging in the shade of the cedar trees, were four big, beautiful cats. There was a lion, a tiger, a sleek black panther, and a slender, spotted cheetah. From where I stood, I could see no fences or chains. There seemed to be nothing penning them in. It all felt odd to me. Most certainly a change of pace.

"Thank you. This is so thoughtful," I said, hoping I sounded gracious. "Am I right—Lloyd, is it?—that there's no fence or anything? Isn't that a little dangerous for kids?"

"Well, yes, of course, we thought about that," Lloyd said. "We figured your family would enjoy the animals more if they were roaming free, like they would in the wild. So we've sedated them for your safety. They're no harm to you." He gave a reassuring wave. "Go ahead, get closer. Enjoy!"

Barack and I took Malia's and Sasha's hands and made our way across the still-dewy grass of the South Lawn. The animals were larger than I expected, languid and sinewy, their tails flicking as they monitored our approach. I'd never seen anything like it, four cats in a companionable line. The lion stirred slightly as we drew closer. I saw the panther's eyes tracking us, the tiger's ears flattening just a little. Then, without warning, the cheetah shot out from the shade with blinding speed, rocketing right at us.

I panicked, grabbing Sasha by the arm, sprinting with her back up the lawn toward the house, trusting that Barack and Malia were doing the same. Judging from the noise, I could tell that all the animals had leaped to their feet and were now coming after us.

Lloyd stood in the doorway, looking unfazed.

"I thought you said they were sedated!" I yelled.

"Don't worry, ma'am," he called back. "We've got a contingency plan for exactly this scenario!" He stepped to one side as Secret Service agents swarmed past him through the door, carrying what looked to be guns loaded with tranquilizer darts. Just then, I felt Sasha slip out of my grasp.

I turned back toward the lawn, horrified to see my family being chased by wild animals and the wild animals being chased by agents, who were firing their guns.

"This is your plan?" I screamed. *"Are you kidding me?"*

Just then, the cheetah let out a snarl and launched itself at Sasha, its claws extended, its body seeming to fly. An agent took a shot, missing the animal though scaring it enough that it veered off course and retreated back down the hill. I was relieved for a split second, but then I saw it— a white-and-orange tranquilizer dart lodged in Sasha's right arm.

I lurched upward in bed, heart hammering, my body soaked in sweat, only to find my husband curled in comfortable sleep beside me. I'd had a very bad dream.

.   .   .

I CONTINUED TO FEEL as if we were falling backward, our whole family in a giant trust fall. I had confidence in the apparatus that had been set up to support us in the White House, but still I could feel vulnerable, knowing that everything from the safety of our daughters to the orchestration of my movements lay almost entirely in the hands of other people—many of them at least twenty years younger than I was. Growing up on Euclid Avenue, I'd been taught that self-sufficiency was everything. I'd been raised to handle my own business, but now that seemed almost impossible. Things got handled for me. Before I traveled, staffers drove the routes I'd take to venues, timing my transit down to the minute, scheduling my bathroom breaks in advance. Agents took my girls to playdates. Housekeepers collected our dirty laundry. I no longer drove a car or carried things like cash or house keys. Aides took phone calls, attended meetings, and drafted statements on my behalf.

All of this was marvelous and helpful, freeing me up to focus on the things I felt were most important. But occasionally it left me—a detail person—feeling as if I'd lost control of the details. Which is when the lions and cheetahs started to lurk.

There was also much that couldn't be planned for, a larger unruliness that paced the borders of our every day. When you're married to the president, you come to understand quickly that the world brims with chaos, that disasters unfurl without notice. Forces seen and unseen stand ready to tear into whatever calm you might feel. The news could never be ignored: An earthquake devastates Haiti. A gasket blows five thousand feet underwater beneath an oil rig off the coast of Louisiana, sending millions of barrels of crude oil gushing into the Gulf of Mexico. Revolution stirs in Egypt. A gunman opens fire in the parking lot of an Arizona supermarket, killing six people and maiming a U.S. congresswoman.

Everything was big and everything was relevant. I read a set of news clips sent by my staff each morning and knew that Barack would be obliged to absorb and respond to every new development. He'd be blamed for things he couldn't control, pushed to solve frightening problems in faraway nations, expected to plug a hole at the bottom of the ocean. His job, it seemed, was to take the chaos and metabolize it somehow into calm leadership—every day of the week, every week of the year.

I tried as best I could not to let the roiling uncertainties of the world impact my day-to-day work as First Lady, but sometimes there was no getting around it. How Barack and I comported ourselves in the face of instability mattered. We understood that we represented the nation and were obligated to step forward and be present when there was tragedy, or hardship, or confusion. Part of our role, as we understood it, was to model reason, compassion, and consistency. After the BP oil spill—the worst in U.S. history—had finally been contained, many Americans were still rattled, unwilling to believe it was safe to return to the Gulf of Mexico for vacation, causing local economies to suffer. So we made a family trip to Florida, during which Barack took Sasha for a swim, releasing a photo to the media that showed the two of them splashing happily in the surf. It was a small gesture, but the message was bigger: *If he trusts the water, then so can you.*

When one or both of us traveled somewhere in the wake of a tragedy, it was often to remind Americans not to look too quickly past the pain of others. When I could, I tried to highlight the efforts of relief workers, educators, or community volunteers—anyone who gave more when things got rough. Traveling to Haiti with Jill Biden three months after the 2010 earthquake there, I felt my heart catch, seeing pyramids of rubble where homes had once been, sites where tens of thousands of people— mothers, grandfathers, babies— had been buried alive. We visited a set of converted buses where local artists were doing art therapy with displaced children who, despite their losses and thanks to the adults around them, still bubbled with hope.

Grief and resilience live together. I learned this not just once as First Lady but many times over.

As often as I could, I visited military hospitals where American troops were recovering from the wounds of war. The first time I went to Walter Reed National Military Medical Center, located less than ten miles from the White House, I was scheduled to be there for something like ninety minutes, but instead I ended up staying about four hours.

Walter Reed tended to be the second or third stop for injured service members who were evacuated out of Iraq and Afghanistan. Many were triaged in the war zone and then treated at a military medical facility in Landstuhl, Germany, before being flown to the United States. Some troops stayed only a few days at Walter Reed. Others were there for months. The hospital employed top-notch military surgeons and offered excellent rehabilitation services, geared to handle the most devastating of battlefield injuries. Thanks to modern developments in armor, American service members were now surviving bomb blasts that would once have killed them. That was the good news. The bad news was that nearly a decade into two conflicts characterized by surprise attacks and hidden explosive devices, those injuries were plentiful and grave.

As much as I tried to prepare for everything in life, there was no preparing for the interactions I had at military hospitals and Fisher Houses—lodgings where, thanks to a charitable organization of the same name, military families could stay for free while tending to an injured loved one. As I've said before, I grew up knowing little about the military. My father had spent two years in the Army, but well before I was born. Until Barack started campaigning, I'd had no exposure to the orderly bustle of an Army base or the modest tract homes that housed service members with families. War, for me, had always been terrifying but also abstract, involving landscapes I couldn't imagine and people I didn't know. To view it this way, I see now, had been a luxury.

When I arrived at a hospital, I was usually met by a charge nurse, handed a set of medical scrubs to wear, and instructed to sanitize my hands each time I entered a room. Before opening a new door, I'd get a quick briefing on the service member and his or her situation. Each patient, too, was asked in advance whether he or she would like a visit from me. A few would decline, possibly because they weren't feeling well enough or maybe for political reasons. Either way, I understood. The last thing I wanted to be was a burden.

My visits to each room were as short or long as the service member wanted them to be. Every conversation was private, with no media or staff observing. The mood was sometimes somber, sometimes light. Prompted by a team banner or photographs on the wall, we'd talk about sports, or our home states, or our children. Or Afghanistan and what had happened to them there. We sometimes discussed what they needed and also what they didn't need, which—as they'd often tell me—was anyone's pity.

At one point, I encountered a piece of red poster board taped to a doorway, with a message written in black marker that seemed to say it all:

ATTENTION TO ALL THOSE WHO ENTER HERE:
If you are coming into this room with sorrow or to feel sorry for my wounds, go elsewhere. The wounds I received, I got in a job I love, doing it for people I love, supporting the freedom of a country I deeply love. I am incredibly tough and will make a full recovery.

This was resilience. It was reflective of a larger spirit of self-sufficiency and pride I'd seen in all parts of the military. I sat one day with a man who'd gone off young and healthy to an overseas deployment, leaving behind a pregnant wife, and had come back quadriplegic, unable to move his arms or legs. As we talked, their baby—a tiny newborn with a pink face—lay swaddled in a blanket on his chest. I met another service member who'd had a leg amputated and asked me a lot of questions about the Secret Service. He explained cheerily that he'd once hoped to become an agent after leaving the military, but that given the injury he was now figuring out a new plan.

Then there were the families. I introduced myself to the wives and husbands, mothers and fathers, cousins and friends I found by the bedside, people who had often put the rest of their lives on hold in order to stay close. Sometimes they were the only ones I could talk to, as their loved one lay immobilized nearby, heavily sedated or asleep. These family members carried their own weight. Some came from generations of military service, while others were teenage girlfriends who'd become brides just ahead of a deployment—their futures now having taken a sudden, complicated turn. I can no longer count the number of mothers with whom I've cried, their distress so acute that all we could do was lace our hands together and pray silently through tears.

What I saw of military life left me humbled. As long as I'd been alive, I'd never encountered the kind of fortitude and loyalty that I found in those rooms.

One day in San Antonio, Texas, I noticed a minor commotion in the hallway of the military hospital I was visiting. Nurses shuffled urgently in and out of the room I was about to enter. "He won't stay in bed," I heard someone whisper. Inside, I found a broad-shouldered young man from rural Texas who had multiple injuries and whose body had been severely burned. He was in clear agony, tearing off the bedsheets and trying to slide his feet to the floor.

It took us all a minute to understand what he was doing. Despite his pain, he was trying to stand up and salute the wife of his commander in chief.

SOMETIME EARLY IN 2011, Barack mentioned Osama bin Laden. We'd just finished dinner and Sasha and Malia had run off to do their homework, leaving the two of us alone in the residence dining room.

"We think we know where he is," Barack said. "We may go in and try to take him out, but nothing's sure."

Bin Laden was the world's most wanted man and had eluded detection for years. Capturing or killing him had been one of Barack's top priorities when he took office. I knew it would mean something to the nation, to the many thousands of military service members who'd spent years trying to protect us from al-Qaeda and especially to all those who'd lost loved ones on September 11.

I could tell from Barack's grim tone that there was much still to be resolved. The variables were clearly weighing heavily on him, though I knew better than to ask too many follow-up questions or insist that he walk me through the particulars. He and I were sounding boards for each other professionally and always had been. But I also knew that he now spent his days surrounded by expert advisers. He had access to all manner of top secret information, and as far as I was concerned, most especially on matters of national security, he needed no input from me. In general, I hoped that time with me and the girls would always be a respite, even though work was forever close by. After all, we literally lived above the shop.

Barack, who's always been good at compartmentalizing, managed to be admirably present and undistracted when he was with us. It was something we'd learned together over time as our work lives had grown increasingly busy and intense. Fences needed to go up; boundaries required protecting. Bin Laden was not invited to dinner, nor was the humanitarian crisis in Libya, nor were the Tea Party Republicans. We had kids, and kids need room to speak and grow. Our family time was when big worries and urgent concerns got abruptly and mercilessly shrunk to nothing so that the small could rightly take over. Barack and I would sit at dinner, hearing tales from the Sidwell playground or listening to the details of Malia's research project on endangered animals, feeling as if these were the most important things in the world. Because they were. They deserved to be.

Still, even as we ate, the work piled up. I could see over Barack's shoulder to the hallway outside the dining room, where aides dropped off our nightly briefing books on a small table, usually as we were in the middle of our meal. This was part of the White House ritual: Two binders got delivered every evening, one for me and a much thicker, leather-bound one for Barack. Each contained papers from our respective offices, which we were meant to read overnight.

After we tucked the kids into bed, Barack would normally disappear into the Treaty Room with his binder, while I took mine to the sitting area in my dressing room, where I'd spend an hour or two each night or early in the morning going through what was inside—usually memos from staff, drafts of upcoming speeches, and decisions to be made regarding my initiatives.

A year after launching Let's Move!, we were seeing results. We'd aligned ourselves with different foundations and food suppliers to install six thousand salad bars in school cafeterias and were recruiting local chefs to help schools serve meals that were not just healthy but tasty. Walmart, which was then the nation's largest grocery retailer, had joined our effort by pledging to cut the amount of sugar, salt, and fat in its food products and to reduce prices on produce. And we'd enlisted mayors from five hundred cities and towns across the country to commit to tackling childhood obesity on the local level.

Most important, over the course of 2010, I'd worked hard to help push a new child nutrition bill through Congress, expanding children's access to healthy, high-quality food in public schools and increasing the reimbursement rate for federally subsidized meals for the first time in thirty years. As much as I was generally happy to stay out of politics and policy making, this had been my big fight—the issue for which I was willing to hurl myself into the ring. I'd spent hours making calls to senators and representatives, trying to convince them that our children deserved better than what they were getting. I'd talked about it endlessly with Barack, his advisers, anyone who would listen. The new law added more fresh fruits and vegetables, whole grains, and low-fat dairy to roughly forty-three million meals served daily. It regulated the junk food that got sold to children via vending machines on school property while also giving funding to schools to establish gardens and use locally grown produce. For me, it was a straightforward good thing—a potent, ground-level way to address childhood obesity.

Barack and his advisers pushed hard for the bill, too. After Republicans won control of the House of Representatives in the midterm elections, he made the effort a priority in his dealings with lawmakers, knowing that his ability to make sweeping legislative change was about to diminish. In early December, before the new Congress was seated, the bill managed to clear its final hurdles, and I stood proudly next to Barack eleven days later as he signed it into law, surrounded by children at a local elementary school.

"Had I not been able to get this bill passed," he joked to reporters, "I would be sleeping on the couch."

As with the garden, I was trying to grow something—a network of advocates, a chorus of voices speaking up for children and their health. I saw my work as complementing Barack's success in establishing the 2010 Affordable Care Act, which greatly increased access to health insurance for all Americans. And I was now also focused on getting a new effort called Joining Forces off the ground—this one in collaboration with Jill Biden, whose son Beau had recently returned safely from his deployment in Iraq. This work, too, would serve to support Barack's duties as commander in chief.

Knowing that we owed more to our service members and their families than token thank-yous, Jill and I had been collaborating with a group
of staffers to identify concrete ways to support the military community
and raise its visibility. Barack had kicked things off earlier in the year
with a government-wide audit, asking each agency to find new ways to
support military families. I, meanwhile, reached out to the country's most
powerful CEOs, generating commitments to hire a significant number of
veterans and military spouses. Jill would garner pledges from colleges
and universities to train teachers and professors to better understand the
needs of military children. We also wanted to fight the stigma surrounding the mental health issues that followed some of our troops home, and
planned to lobby writers and producers in Hollywood to include military
stories in their movies and TV shows.

The issues I was working on weren't simple, but still they were manageable in ways that much of what kept my husband at his desk at night
was not. As had been the case since I first met him, nighttime was when
Barack's mind traveled without distraction. It was during these quiet
hours that he could find perspective or inhale new information, adding
data points to the vast mental map he carried around. Ushers often came
to the Treaty Room a few times over the course of an evening to deliver
more folders, containing more papers, freshly generated by staffers who
were working late in the offices downstairs. If Barack got hungry, a valet
would bring him a small dish of figs or nuts. He was no longer smoking, thankfully, though he'd often chew a piece of nicotine gum. Most
nights of the week, he stayed at his desk until 1:00 or 2:00 in the morning, reading memos, rewriting speeches, and responding to email while
ESPN played low on the TV. He always took a break to come kiss me and
the girls good night.

I was used to it by now—his devotion to the never-finished task of
governing. For years, the girls and I had shared Barack with his constituents, and now there were more than 300 million of them. Leaving him
alone in the Treaty Room at night, I wondered sometimes if they had any
sense of how lucky they were.

The last bit of work he did, usually at some hour past midnight, was to read letters from American citizens. Since the start of his presidency, Barack had asked his correspondence staff to include ten letters or messages from constituents inside his briefing book, selected from the roughly fifteen thousand letters and emails that poured in daily. He read each one carefully, jotting responses in the margins so that a staffer could prepare a reply or forward a concern on to a cabinet secretary. He read letters from soldiers. From prison inmates. From cancer patients struggling to pay health-care premiums and from people who'd lost their homes to foreclosure. From gay people who hoped to be able to legally marry and from Republicans who felt he was ruining the country. From moms, grandfathers, and young children. He read letters from people who appreciated what he did and from others who wanted to let him know he was an idiot.

He read all of it, seeing it as part of the responsibility that came with the oath. He had a hard and lonely job—the hardest and loneliest in the world, it often seemed to me—but he knew that he had an obligation to stay open, to shut nothing out. While the rest of us slept, he took down the fences and let everything inside.

O N MONDAY and Wednesday evenings, Sasha, who was now ten, had swim-team practice at the American University fitness center, a few miles from the White House. I went sometimes to watch her do her workouts, trying to slip unnoticed into the small room next to the pool where parents could sit and observe practice through a window.

Navigating a busy athletic facility during peak workout hours posed a challenge for the agents on my security detail, but they managed it well. For my part, I'd become an expert at walking quickly and lowering my gaze when passing through public spaces, which helped keep things efficient. I zipped past university students busy with their weight workouts and Zumba classes in full swing. Sometimes nobody seemed to notice. Other times, I'd feel the disturbance without even needing to look up, aware of the ripple I caused as people murmured or occasionally just shouted, "Hey, that's Michelle Obama!" But it was never more than a ripple and it happened quickly. I was like an apparition, there and gone before the sight had really registered.

On practice nights, the seats by the pool were generally empty, aside from a handful of other parents idly chatting or scrolling through their iPhones as they waited for their kids to be done. I'd find a quiet spot, sit down, and focus on the swimming.

I loved any time I could glimpse my daughters in the context of their own worlds—free from the White House, free from their parents, in the spaces and relationships they'd forged for themselves. Sasha was a strong swimmer, enthusiastic about breaststroke and intent on mastering the butterfly. She wore a navy-blue swim cap and a one-piece bathing suit and diligently motored through her laps, stopping once in a while to take advice from the coaches, chatting merrily with her teammates during the prescribed breaks.

For me, there was nothing more gratifying than being a bystander in these moments, to sit barely noticed by the people around me and witness the miracle of a girl—our girl—growing independent and whole. We had thrust our daughters into all the strangeness and intensity of White House life, not knowing how it would impact them or what they'd take from the experience. I tried to make our daughters' exposure to the wider world as positive as possible, realizing that Barack and I had a unique opportunity to show them history up close. When Barack had foreign trips that coincided with school vacations, we traveled as a family, knowing it would be educational. In the summer of 2009, we'd brought them on a trip that included visits to the Kremlin in Moscow and the Vatican in Rome. In the span of seven days, they'd met the Russian president, toured the Pantheon and the Roman Colosseum, and passed through the "Door of No Return" in Ghana, the departure point for untold numbers of Africans who'd been sold into slavery.

Surely it was a lot for them to process, but I was learning that each child took in what she could and from her own perspective. Sasha had returned home from our summer travels to start third grade. Walking around her classroom at Sidwell's parents' night that fall, I'd come across a short "What I Did on My Summer Vacation" essay she'd authored, hanging alongside those of her classmates on one of the walls. "I went to Rome and I met the Pope," Sasha had written. "He was missing part of his thumb."

I could not tell you what Pope Benedict XVI's thumb looks like, whether some part of it isn't there. But we'd taken an observant, matter-of-fact eight-year-old to Rome, Moscow, and Accra, and this is what she'd brought back. Her view of history was, at that point, waist-high.

As much as we tried to create a buffer between them and the more fraught aspects of Barack's job, I knew that Sasha and Malia still had a lot to take in. They coexisted with world events in a way that few children did, living with the fact that news occasionally unfolded right under our roof, that their father got called away sometimes for national emergencies, and that always and no matter what there'd be some part of the population that openly reviled him. For me, this was another version of the lions and cheetahs feeling sometimes very close by.

Over the course of the winter of 2011, we'd been hearing news that the reality-show host and New York real-estate developer Donald Trump was beginning to make noise about possibly running for the Republican presidential nomination when Barack came up for reelection in 2012. Mostly, though, it seemed he was just making noise in general, surfacing on cable shows to offer yammering, inexpert critiques of Barack's foreign policy decisions and openly questioning whether he was an American citizen. The so-called birthers had tried during the previous campaign to feed a conspiracy theory claiming that Barack's Hawaiian birth certificate was somehow a hoax and that he'd in fact been born in Kenya. Trump was now actively working to revive the argument, making increasingly outlandish claims on television, insisting that the 1961 Honolulu newspaper announcements of Barack's birth were fraudulent and that none of his kindergarten classmates remembered him. All the while, in their quest for clicks and ratings, news outlets—particularly the more conservative ones—were gleefully pumping oxygen into his groundless claims.

The whole thing was crazy and mean-spirited, of course, its underlying bigotry and xenophobia hardly concealed. But it was also dangerous, deliberately meant to stir up the wingnuts and kooks. I feared the reaction. I was briefed from time to time by the Secret Service on the more serious threats that came in and understood that there were people capable of being stirred. I tried not to worry, but sometimes I couldn't help it. What if someone with an unstable mind loaded a gun and drove to Washington? What if that person went looking for our girls? Donald Trump, with his loud and reckless innuendos, was putting my family's safety at risk. And for this, I'd never forgive him.

We had little choice, though, but to push the fears away, continuing to trust the structure set up to protect us and to simply live. The people who tried to define us as "other" had been doing so for years already. We did everything we could to rise above their lies and distortions, trusting that the way Barack and I lived our lives would show people the truth about who we really were. I'd lived with earnest and well-intentioned concerns for our safety since almost the day Barack first decided to run for president. "We're praying nobody hurts you," people used to say, clasping my hand at campaign events. I'd heard it from people of all races, all backgrounds, all ages—a reminder of the goodness and generosity that existed in our country. "We pray for you and your family every day."

I kept their words with me. I felt the protection of those millions of decent people who prayed for our safety. Barack and I both relied on our personal faith as well. We went to church only rarely now, mostly because it had become such a spectacle, involving reporters shouting questions as we walked in to worship. Ever since the scrutiny of the Reverend Jeremiah Wright had become an issue in Barack's first presidential campaign, ever since opponents had tried to use faith as a weapon—suggesting that Barack was a "secret Muslim"—we'd made the choice to exercise our faith privately and at home, including praying each night before dinner and organizing a few sessions of Sunday school at the White House for our daughters. We didn't join a church in Washington, because we didn't want to subject another congregation to the kind of bad-faith attacks that had rained down on Trinity, our church in Chicago. It was a sacrifice, though. I missed the warmth of a spiritual community. Every night, I'd look over and see Barack lying with his eyes closed on the other side of the bed, quietly saying his prayers.

Months after the birther rumors picked up steam, on a Friday night in November, a man parked his car on a closed part of Constitution

Avenue and started firing a semiautomatic rifle out the window, aimed at the top floors of the White House. A bullet hit one of the windows in the Yellow Oval Room, where I sometimes liked to sit and have tea. Another lodged itself in a window frame, and more ricocheted off the roof. Barack and I were out that night, as was Malia, but Sasha and my mom were both at home, though unaware and unharmed. It took weeks to replace the ballistic glass of the window in the Yellow Oval, and I often found myself staring at the thick round crater that had been left by the bullet, reminded of how vulnerable we were.

In general, I understood that it was better for all of us not to acknowledge the hate or dwell on the risk, even when others felt compelled to bring it up. Malia would eventually join the high school tennis team at Sidwell, which practiced on the school courts on Wisconsin Avenue. She was there one day when a woman, the mother of another student, approached her, gesturing at the busy road running past the courts. "Aren't you afraid out here?" she asked.

My daughter, as she grew, was learning to use her voice, discovering her own ways to reinforce the boundaries she needed. "If you're asking me whether I ponder my death every day," she said to the woman, as politely as she could, "the answer is no."

A couple of years later, that same mother would come up to me at a parent event at school and pass me a heartfelt note of apology, saying that she'd understood right away the error in what she'd done—having put worries on a child who could do nothing about them. It meant a lot to me that she'd thought so much about it. She'd heard, in Malia's answer, both the resilience and the vulnerability, an echo of all that we lived with and all we tried to keep at bay. She'd also understood that the only thing our girl could do, that day and every day after it, was get back on the court and hit another ball.

EVERY CHALLENGE, of course, is relative. I knew my kids were growing up with more advantages and more abundance than most families could ever begin to imagine having. Our girls had a beautiful home, food on the table, devoted adults around them, and nothing but encouragement and resources when it came to getting an education. I put everything I had into Malia and Sasha and their development, but as First Lady I was mindful, too, of a larger obligation. I felt that I owed more to children in general, and in particular to girls. Some of this was spawned by the response people tended to have to my life story—the surprise that an urban Black girl had vaulted through Ivy League schools and executive jobs and landed in the White House. I understood that my trajectory was unusual, but there was no good reason why it had to be. There had been so many times in my life when I'd found myself the only woman of color—or even the only woman, period—sitting at a conference table or attending a board meeting or mingling at one VIP gathering or another. If I was the first at some of these things, I wanted to make sure that in the end I wasn't the only—that others were coming up behind me. As my mother, the plainspoken enemy of all hyperbole, still says anytime someone starts gushing about me and Craig and our various accomplishments, "They're not special at all. The South Side is filled with kids like that." We just needed to help get them into those rooms.

The important parts of my story, I was realizing, lay less in the surface value of my accomplishments and more in what undergirded them—the many small ways I'd been buttressed over the years, and the people who'd helped build my confidence over time. I remembered them all, every person who'd ever waved me forward, doing his or her best to inoculate me against the slights and indignities I was certain to encounter in the places I was headed—all those environments built primarily for and by people who were neither Black nor female.

I thought of my great-aunt Robbie and her exacting piano standards, how she'd taught me to lift my chin and play my heart out on a baby grand even if all I'd ever known was an upright with broken keys. I thought of my father, who showed me how to box and throw a football, same as Craig. There were Mr. Martinez and Mr. Bennett, my teachers at Bryn Mawr, who never dismissed my opinions. There was my mom, my staunchest support, whose vigilance had saved me from languishing in a dreary second-grade classroom. At Princeton, I'd had Czerny Brasuell, who encouraged me and fed my intellect in new ways. And as a young professional, I'd had, among others, Susan Sher and Valerie Jarrett—still good friends and colleagues many years later—who showed me what it looked like to be a working mother and consistently opened doors for me, certain I had something to offer.

These were people who mostly didn't know one another and would never have occasion to meet, many of whom I'd fallen out of touch with myself. But for me, they formed a meaningful constellation. These were my boosters, my believers, my own personal gospel choir, singing, *Yes, kid, you got this!* all the way through.

I'd never forgotten it. I'd tried, even as a junior lawyer, to pay it forward, encouraging curiosity when I saw it, drawing younger people into important conversations. If a paralegal asked me a question about her future, I'd open my office door and share my journey or offer some advice. If someone wanted guidance or help making a connection, I did what I could to give it. Later, during my time at Public Allies, I saw the benefits of more formal mentoring firsthand. I knew from my own life experience that when someone shows genuine interest in your learning and development, even if only for ten minutes in a busy day, it matters. It matters especially for women, for minorities, for anyone society is quick to overlook.

With this in mind, I'd started a leadership and mentoring program at the White House, inviting twenty sophomore and junior girls from high schools around Greater D.C. to join us for monthly get-togethers that included informal chats, field trips, and sessions on things like financial literacy and choosing a career. We kept the program largely behind closed doors, rather than thrusting these girls into the media fray.

We paired each teen with a female mentor who would foster a personal relationship with her, sharing her resources and her life story. Valerie was a mentor. Cris Comerford, the White House's first female executive chef, was a mentor. Jill Biden was, too, as were a number of senior women from both the East and the West Wing staffs. The students were nominated by their principals or guidance counselors and would stay with us until they graduated. We had girls from military families, girls from immigrant families, a teen mom, a girl who'd lived in a homeless shelter. They were smart, curious young women, all of them. No different from me. No different from my daughters. I watched over time as the girls formed friendships, finding a rapport with one another and with the adults around them. I spent hours talking with them in a big circle, munching popcorn and trading our thoughts about college applications, body image, and boys. No topic was off-limits. We ended up laughing a lot. More than anything, I hoped this was what they'd carry forward into the future—the ease, the sense of community, the encouragement to speak and be heard.

My wish for them was the same one I had for Sasha and Malia—that in learning to feel comfortable at the White House, they'd go on to feel comfortable and confident in any room, sitting at any table, raising their voices inside any group.

W E'D LIVED INSIDE the bubble of the presidency for more than two years now. I looked for ways to widen its perimeter as I could. Barack and I continued to open the White House up to more people, most especially children, hoping to make its grandeur feel inclusive, mixing some liveliness into the formality and tradition. Anytime foreign dignitaries came for state visits, we invited local schoolkids to come over to take in the pomp of an official welcome ceremony and taste the food that would be served at the state dinner. When musicians were coming for an evening performance, we asked them to show up early to help with a youth workshop. We wanted to highlight the importance of exposing children to the arts, showing that it's not a luxury but a necessity to their overall educational experience. I relished the sight of high schoolers mingling with contemporary artists like John Legend, Justin Timberlake, and Alison Krauss as well as legends like Smokey Robinson and Patti LaBelle. For me, it was a throwback to the way I'd been raised— the jazz at Southside's house, the piano recitals and Operetta Workshops put on by my great-aunt Robbie, my family's trips to downtown museums. I knew how arts and culture contributed to the development of a child. And it made me feel at home. Barack and I swayed to the beat together in the front row of every performance. Even my mother, who generally steered clear of public appearances, always made her way down to the state floor anytime music was playing.

We also added celebrations of dance and other arts to the mix, bringing in emerging artists to showcase new work. In 2009, we'd put on the first-ever White House poetry and spoken-word event, listening as a young composer named Lin-Manuel Miranda stood up and astonished everyone with a piece from a project he was just beginning to put together, describing it as a "concept album about the life of someone I think embodies hip-hop . . . Treasury secretary Alexander Hamilton."

I remember shaking his hand and saying, "Hey, good luck with the Hamilton thing."

In any given day, we were exposed to so much. Glamour, excellence, devastation, hope. Everything lived side by side, and all the while we had two kids trying to lead their own lives apart from what was going on at home. I did what I could to keep myself and the girls integrated into the everyday world. My goal was what it had always been—to find normalcy where I could, to fit myself back into pockets of regular life. During soccer and lacrosse seasons, I went to many of Sasha's and Malia's home games, taking my place on the sidelines alongside other parents, politely turning down anyone who asked to take a photo, though I was always happy to make small talk. After Malia started tennis, I mostly watched her matches through the window of a Secret Service vehicle parked discreetly near the courts, not wanting to create a distraction. Only when it was over would I emerge to give her a hug.

With Barack, we'd all but given up on normalcy or there being any sense of lightness in his movements. He attended school functions and the girls' sporting events as he could, but his opportunities to mingle were limited, and the presence of his security detail was never subtle. The point, in fact, was to be unsubtle—to send a clear message to the world that nobody could harm the president of the United States. For obvious reasons, I was glad for this. But juxtaposed against the norms of family life, it could be a little much.

This same thought would occur to Malia one day as Barack and I were heading with her to one of Sasha's events at Sidwell's lower school. The three of us were crossing an open outdoor courtyard, passing a group of kindergartners in the middle of their recess, swinging from a set of monkey bars and running around the wood-chipped play area. I'm not sure if the little kids had spotted the squad of Secret Service snipers dressed all in black and spread out across the rooftops of the school buildings with their assault rifles visible, but Malia had.

She looked from the snipers to the kindergartners, then back to her father, giving him a teasing look. "Really, Dad?" she said. "Seriously?"

All Barack could do was smile and shrug. There was no ducking the seriousness of his job.

To be sure, none of us ever stepped outside the bubble. The bubble moved with each one of us individually. Following our early negotiations with the Secret Service, Sasha and Malia were doing things like going to friends' bat mitzvahs, washing cars for the school fund-raiser, and even hanging out at the mall, always with agents and often with my mom tagging along, but they were now at least as mobile as their peers. Sasha's agents, including Beth Celestini and Lawrence Tucker—whom everyone called L.T.—had become beloved fixtures at Sidwell. Kids begged L.T. to push them on the swing set during recess. Families often sent in extra cupcakes for the agents when there were classroom birthday celebrations.

All of us grew close to our agents over time. Preston Fairlamb led my detail then, and Allen Taylor, who'd been with me back in the campaign, would later take over. When we were out in public, they were silent and hyperalert, but anytime we were backstage or on plane rides, they'd loosen up, sharing stories and joking around. "Stone-faced softies," I used to call them, teasingly. Over all the hours we spent together and many miles traveled, we became real friends. I grieved their losses with them and celebrated when their kids hit significant milestones. I was always aware of the seriousness of their duties, what they were willing to sacrifice in order to keep me safe, and I never took it for granted.

Like my daughters, I was cultivating a private life to go along with my official one. I'd found there were ways to keep a low profile when I needed to, helped by the Secret Service's willingness to be flexible. Rather than riding in a motorcade, I was sometimes allowed to travel in an unmarked van and with a lighter security escort. I managed to make lightning-strike shopping trips from time to time, coming and going from a place before anyone really registered I was there. After Bo expertly disemboweled or shredded every last dog toy bought for him by the staff who did our regular shopping, I personally escorted him over to PetSmart in Alexandria one morning. And for a short while, I enjoyed glorious anonymity while browsing for better chew toys as Bo—who was as delighted by the novelty of the outing as I was—loafed next to me on a leash.

Anytime I went somewhere without a fuss, it felt like a small victory, an exercise of free will. I was a detail person, after all. I hadn't forgotten how gratifying it could be to tick through the minutiae of a shopping list. Maybe six months after the PetSmart trip, I made a giddy incognito run to the local Target, dressed in a baseball cap and sunglasses. My security detail wore shorts and sneakers and ditched their earpieces, doing their best not to stand out as they trailed me and my assistant Kristin Jones through the store. We wandered every single aisle. I selected some Oil of Olay face cream and new toothbrushes. We got dryer sheets and laundry detergent for Kristin, and I found a couple of games for Sasha and Malia. And for the first time in several years, I was able to pick out a card to give to Barack on our anniversary.

I went home elated. Sometimes, the smallest things felt huge.

As time went by, I added new adventures to my routine. I started to meet friends occasionally out for dinner in restaurants or at their homes. Sometimes I'd go to a park and take long walks along the Potomac River. I'd have agents walking ahead of and behind me on these excursions, but inconspicuously and at a distance. In later years, I'd begin leaving the White House to hit workout classes, dropping in on SoulCycle and Solidcore studios around the city, slipping into the room at the last minute and leaving as soon as class was done to avoid causing a disturbance. The most liberating activity of all turned out to be downhill skiing, a sport with which I had little experience but that quickly became a passion. Capitalizing on the unusually heavy winters we'd had during our first two years in Washington, I made a few day trips with the girls and some friends to a tiny, aptly named ski area called Liberty Mountain, near Gettysburg, where we found we could don helmets, scarves, and goggles and blend into any crowd. Gliding down a ski slope, I was outdoors, in motion, and unrecognized—all at once. For me, it was like flying.

The blending mattered. The blending, in fact, was everything—a way to feel like myself, to remain Michelle Robinson from the South Side inside this larger sweep of history. I knit my old life into my new one, my private concerns into my public work. In D.C., I'd made a handful of new friends—a couple of the mothers of Sasha's and Malia's classmates and a few people I'd met in the course of White House duties. These were women who cared less about my last name or home address and more about who I was as a person. It's funny how quickly you can tell who's there for you and who's just trying to plant some sort of flag. Barack and I sometimes talked about it with Sasha and Malia over dinner, the fact that there were people, children and adults, who hovered at the edges of our friend groups seeming a little too eager—"thirsty," as we called it.

I'd learned many years earlier to hold my true friends close. I was still deeply connected to the group of women who had started gathering for Saturday playdates years earlier, back in our diaper-bag days in Chicago, when our children blithely pitched food from their high chairs and all of us were so tired we wanted to weep. These were the friends who'd held me together, dropping off groceries when I was too busy to shop, picking up the girls for ballet when I was behind on work or just needing a break. A number of them had hopped planes to join me for unglamorous stops on the campaign trail, giving me emotional ballast when I needed it most. Friendships between women, as any woman will tell you, are built of a thousand small kindnesses like these, swapped back and forth and over again.

In 2011, I started making a deliberate effort to invest and reinvest in my friendships, bringing together old friends and new. Every few months, I invited twelve or so of my closest friends to join me for a weekend at Camp David, the woodsy, summer-camp-like presidential retreat that sits about sixty miles outside Washington in the mountains of northern Maryland. I started referring to these gatherings as "Boot Camp," in part because I did admittedly force everyone to work out with me several times a day (I also at one point tried to ban wine and snacks, though this got swiftly shot down) but more importantly because I like the idea of being rigorous about friendship.

My friends tend to be accomplished, overcommitted people, many of them with busy family lives and heavy-duty jobs. I understood it wasn't always easy for them to get away. But this was part of the point. We were all so used to sacrificing for our kids, our spouses, and our work. I had learned through my years of trying to find balance in my life that it was okay to flip those priorities and care only for ourselves once in a while. I was more than happy to wave this banner on behalf of my friends, to create the reason—and the power of a tradition—for a whole bunch of women to turn to kids, spouses, and colleagues and say, *Sorry, folks, I'm doing this for me.*

Boot Camp weekends became a way for us to take shelter, connect, and recharge. We stayed in cozy, wood-paneled cabins surrounded by forest, buzzed around in golf carts, and rode bikes. We played dodgeball and did burpees and downward dogs. I sometimes invited a few young staffers along, and it was trippy over the years to see Susan Sher, in her late sixties, spider crawling across the floor next to MacKenzie Smith, my twentysomething scheduler who'd been a collegiate soccer player. We ate healthy meals cooked by the White House chefs. We ran through drills overseen by my trainer, Cornell, and several baby-faced naval staffers who called us all "ma'am." We got a lot of exercise and talked and talked and talked. We pooled our thoughts and experiences, offering advice or funny stories or sometimes just the assurance that whoever was spilling her guts in a given moment wasn't the only one ever to have a teenager who was acting out or a boss she couldn't stand. Often, we steadied one another just by listening. And saying good-bye at the end of each weekend, we vowed we'd do it all again soon.

My friends made me whole, as they always have and always will. They gave me a lift anytime I felt down or frustrated or had less access to Barack. They grounded me when I felt the pressures of being judged, having everything from my choice of nail-polish color to the size of my hips dissected and discussed publicly. And they helped me ride out the big, unsettling waves that sometimes hit without notice.

On the first Sunday in May 2011, I went to dinner with two friends at a restaurant downtown, leaving Barack and my mother in charge of the girls at home. The weekend had seemed especially busy. Barack had been pulled into a flurry of briefings that afternoon, and we'd spent Saturday evening at the White House Correspondents' Dinner, where in his speech Barack made a few pointed jokes about Donald Trump's *Celebrity Apprentice* career and his birther theories. I couldn't see him from my seat, but Trump had been in attendance. During Barack's monologue, news cameras zeroed in on him, stone-faced and stewing.

For us, Sunday nights tended to be quiet and free. The girls were usually tired after a weekend of sports and socializing. And Barack, if he was lucky, could sometimes squeeze in a daytime round of golf on the course at Andrews Air Force Base, which left him more relaxed.

That night, after catching up with my friends, I arrived home around 10:00, greeted at the door by an usher, as I always was. Already, I could tell something was going on, sensing a different-from-normal level of activity on the ground floor of the White House. I asked the usher if he knew where the president was.

"I believe he's upstairs, ma'am," he said, "getting ready to address the nation."

This is how I realized that it had finally happened. I knew it was coming, but I hadn't known exactly how it would play out. I'd spent the last two days trying to act completely normal, pretending I didn't know that something dangerous and important was about to take place. After months of high-level intelligence gathering and weeks of meticulous preparation, after security briefings and risk assessments and a final tense decision, seven thousand miles from the White House and under cover of darkness, an elite team of U.S. Navy SEALs had stormed a mysterious compound in Abbottabad, Pakistan, looking for Osama bin Laden.

Barack was coming out of our bedroom as I walked down the hall in the residence. He was dressed in a suit and red tie and seemed thoroughly jacked up on adrenaline. He'd been carrying the pressure of this decision for months.

"We got him," he said. "And no one got hurt."

We hugged. Osama bin Laden had been killed. No American lives had been lost. Barack had taken an enormous risk—one that could have cost him his presidency—and it had all gone okay.

The news was already traveling across the world. People were clogging the streets around the White House, spilling out of restaurants, hotels, and apartment buildings, filling the night air with celebratory shouts. The sound of it grew so loud and jubilant it roused Malia from sleep in her bedroom, audible even through the ballistic glass windows meant to shut everything out.

That night, there was no inside or outside, anyway. In cities across the country, people had taken to the streets, clearly drawn by an impulse to be close to others, linked not just by patriotism but by the communal grief that had been born on 9/11 and the years of worries that we'd be attacked again. I thought about every military base I'd ever visited, all those soldiers working to recover from their wounds, the many people who'd sent family members to a faraway place in the name of protecting our country, the thousands of children who'd lost a parent on that horrible, sad day. There was no restoring any one of those losses, I knew. Nobody's death would ever replace a life. I'm not sure anyone's death is reason to celebrate, ever. But what America got that night was a moment of release, a chance to feel its own resilience.

———

23

TIME SEEMED TO LOOP AND LEAP, MAKING IT FEEL impossible to measure or track. Each day was packed. Each week and month and year we spent in the White House was packed. I'd get to Friday and need to work to remember how Monday and Tuesday had gone. I'd sit down to dinner sometimes and wonder where and how lunch had happened. Even now, I still find it hard to process. The velocity was too great, the time for reflection too limited. A single afternoon could hold a couple of official events, several meetings, and a photo shoot. I might visit several states in a day, or speak to twelve thousand people, or have four hundred kids over to do jumping jacks with me on the South Lawn, all before putting on a fancy dress for an evening reception. I used my down days, those free from official business, to tend to Sasha and Malia and their lives, before going back "up" again—back into hair, makeup, and wardrobe. Back into the vortex of the public eye.

As we moved toward Barack's reelection year in 2012, I felt that I couldn't and shouldn't rest. I was still earning my grace. I thought often of what I owed and to whom. I carried a history with me, and it wasn't that of presidents or First Ladies. I'd never related to the story of John Quincy Adams the way I did to that of Sojourner Truth, or been moved by Woodrow Wilson the way I was by Harriet Tubman. The struggles of Rosa Parks and Coretta Scott King were more familiar to me than those of Eleanor Roosevelt or Mamie Eisenhower. I carried their histories, along with those of my mother and grandmothers. None of these women could ever have imagined a life like the one I now had, but they'd trusted that their perseverance would yield something better, eventually, for someone like me. I wanted to show up in the world in a way that honored who they were.

I put this on myself as pressure, a driving need not to screw anything up. Though I was thought of as a popular First Lady, I couldn't help but feel haunted by the ways I'd been criticized, by the people who'd made assumptions about me based on the color of my skin. To this end, I rehearsed my speeches again and again using a teleprompter set up in one corner of my office. I pushed hard on my schedulers and advance teams to make sure every one of our events ran smoothly and on time. I pushed even harder on my policy advisers to continue growing the reach of Let's Move! and Joining Forces. I was focused on not wasting any of the opportunities I now had, but sometimes I had to remind myself just to breathe.

Barack and I both knew that the months of campaigning ahead would involve extra travel, extra strategizing, and extra worry. It was impossible not to worry about reelection. The cost was huge. (Barack and Mitt Romney, the former Massachusetts governor who would eventually become the Republican nominee, would each raise over a billion dollars in the end to keep their campaigns competitive.) And the responsibility was also huge. The election would determine everything from the fate of the new health-care law to whether America would be part of the global effort to combat climate change. Everyone working in the White House lived in the limbo of not knowing whether we'd get a second term. I tried not to even consider the possibility that Barack might lose the election, but it was there—a kernel of fear he and I carried privately, neither of us daring to give it voice.

The summer of 2011 turned out to be especially bruising for Barack. A group of obstinate congressional Republicans refused to authorize the issuing of new government bonds—a relatively routine process known as raising the debt ceiling—unless he made a series of painful cuts to government programs like Social Security, Medicaid, and Medicare, which he opposed because they would hurt the people who were struggling the most. Meanwhile, the monthly jobs reports published by the Labor Department were showing consistent but sluggish growth, suggesting that when it came to recovering from the 2008 crisis, the nation still wasn't where it needed to be. Many people blamed Barack. In the relief following the death of Osama bin Laden, his approval ratings had spiked, hitting a two-year high, but then, just a few months later, following the debt-ceiling brawl and worries about a new recession, they'd plunged to the lowest they'd been.

As this tumult was beginning, I flew to South Africa for a goodwill visit that had been planned months in advance. Sasha and Malia's school year had just ended, so they were able to join me, along with my mother and Craig's kids Leslie and Avory, who were now teenagers. I was headed there to give a keynote address at a U.S.-sponsored forum for young African women leaders from around the continent, but we'd also filled my schedule with community events connected to wellness and education, as well as visits with local leaders and U.S. consulate workers. We'd finish with a short visit to Botswana, meeting with its president and stopping at a community HIV clinic, and then enjoy a quick safari before heading home.

It had taken no time at all for us to get swept up in South Africa's energy. In Johannesburg, we toured the Apartheid Museum and danced and read books with young children at a community center in one of the Black townships north of the city. At a soccer stadium in Cape Town, we met community organizers and health workers who were using youth sports programs to help educate children about HIV/AIDS, and were introduced to Archbishop Desmond Tutu, the legendary theologian and activist who'd helped dismantle apartheid in South Africa. Tutu was seventy-nine years old, a barrel-chested man with bright eyes and an irrepressible laugh. Hearing that I was at the stadium to promote fitness, he insisted on doing push-ups with me in front of a cheering pack of kids.

Over the course of those few days in South Africa, I felt myself floating. This visit was a long way from my first trip to Kenya in 1991, when I'd ridden around with Barack in *matatus* and pushed Auma's broken-down VW along the side of a dusty road. What I felt was one part jet lag, maybe, but two parts something more profound and elating. It was as if we'd stepped into the larger crosscurrents of culture and history, reminded suddenly of our relative smallness in the wider arc of time. Seeing the faces of the seventy-six young women who'd been chosen to attend the leadership forum because they were doing meaningful work in their communities, I fought back tears. They gave me hope. They made me feel old in the best possible way. A full 60 percent of Africa's population at the time was under the age of twenty-five. Here were women, all of them under thirty and some as young as sixteen, who were building nonprofits, training other women to be entrepreneurs, and risking imprisonment to report on government corruption. And now they were being connected, trained, and encouraged. I hoped this would only amplify their might.

The most surreal moment of all, though, had come early, on just the second day of our trip. My family and I had been at the Nelson Mandela Foundation headquarters in Johannesburg, visiting with Graça Machel, a well-known humanitarian and Mandela's wife, when we received word that Mandela himself would be happy to greet us at his home nearby.

We went immediately, of course. Nelson Mandela was ninety-two at the time. He'd been hospitalized with lung issues earlier in the year. I was told he seldom received guests. Barack had met him six years earlier, as a senator, when Mandela had visited Washington. He'd kept a framed photo of their meeting on the wall of his office ever since. Even my kids— Sasha, ten, and Malia, about to turn thirteen—understood what a big deal this was. Even my eternally unfazed mother looked a little stunned.

There was no one alive who'd had a more meaningful impact on the world than Nelson Mandela had, at least by my measure. He'd been a young man in the 1940s when he first joined the African National Congress and began boldly challenging the all-white South African government and its entrenched racist policies. He'd been forty-four years old when he was put in shackles and sent to prison for his activism, and seventy-one when he was finally released in 1990. Surviving twenty-seven years of deprivation and isolation as a prisoner, having had many of his friends tortured and killed under the apartheid regime, Mandela managed to negotiate—rather than fight—with government leaders, brokering a miraculously peaceful transition to a true democracy in South Africa and ultimately becoming its first president.

Mandela lived on a leafy suburban street in a Mediterranean-style home set behind butter-colored concrete walls. Graça Machel ushered us through a courtyard shaded by trees and into the house, where in a wide, sunlit room her husband sat in an armchair. He had sparse, snowy hair and wore a brown batik shirt. Someone had laid a white blanket across his lap. He was surrounded by several generations of relatives, all of whom welcomed us enthusiastically. Something in the brightness of the room, the volubility of the family, and the squinty smile of the patriarch reminded me of going to my grandfather Southside's house when I was a kid. I'd been nervous to come, but now I relaxed.

The truth is I'm not sure that the patriarch himself completely grasped who we were or why we'd stopped in. He was an old man at this point, his attention seeming to drift, his hearing a little weak. "This is *Michelle Obama!*" Graça Machel said, leaning close to his ear. "The wife of the U.S. president!"

"Oh, lovely," murmured Nelson Mandela. "Lovely."

He looked at me with genuine interest, though in truth I could have been anyone. It seemed clear that he bestowed this same degree of warmth upon every person who crossed his path. My interaction with Mandela was both quiet and profound—maybe more profound, even, for its quietness. His life's words had mostly been spoken now, his speeches and letters, his books and protest chants, already etched not just into his story but into humanity's as a whole. I could feel all of it in the brief moment I had with him—the dignity and spirit that had coaxed equality from a place where none had existed.

I was still thinking about Mandela five days later as we flew back to the United States, traveling north and west over Africa and then across the Atlantic over the course of a long dark night. Sasha and Malia lay sprawled beneath blankets next to their cousins; my mother dozed in a seat nearby. Farther back in the plane, staff and Secret Service members were watching movies and catching up on sleep. The engines hummed. I felt alone and not alone. We were headed home—home being the strange-familiar city of Washington, D.C., with its white marble and clashing ideologies, with everything that still needed to be fought and won. I thought about the young African women I'd met at the leadership forum, all of them now headed back to their own communities to pick up their work again, persevering through whatever tumult they faced.

Mandela had gone to jail for his principles. He'd missed seeing his kids grow up, and then he'd missed seeing many of his grandkids grow up, too. All this without bitterness. All this still believing that the better nature of his country would at some point prevail. He'd worked and waited, tolerant and undiscouraged, to see it happen.

I flew home propelled by that spirit. Life was teaching me that progress and change happen slowly. Not in two years, four years, or even a lifetime. We were planting seeds of change, the fruit of which we might never see. We had to be patient.

THREE TIMES OVER the course of the fall of 2011, Barack proposed bills that would create thousands of jobs for Americans, in part by giving states money to hire more teachers and first responders. Three times the Republicans blocked them, never even allowing a vote.

"The single most important thing we want to achieve," the Senate minority leader, Mitch McConnell, had declared to a reporter a year earlier, laying out his party's goals, "is for President Obama to be a one-term president." It was that simple. The Republican Congress was devoted to Barack's failure above all else. It seemed they weren't prioritizing the governance of the country or the fact that people needed jobs. Their own power came first.

I found it demoralizing, infuriating, sometimes crushing. This was politics, yes, but in its most fractious and cynical form, seemingly disconnected from any larger sense of purpose. I felt emotions that perhaps Barack couldn't afford to feel. He stayed locked in his work, for the most part undaunted, riding out the bumps and compromising where he could, clinging to the sober-minded, someone's-gotta-take-this-on brand of optimism that had always guided him. He'd been in politics for fifteen years now. I continued to think of him as being like an old copper pot—seasoned by fire, dinged up but still shiny.

Returning to the campaign trail—as Barack and I began to do in the fall of 2011—became something of a salve. It took us out of Washington and returned us to communities all around the country again, places like Richmond and Reno, where we could hug and shake hands with supporters, listening to their ideas and concerns. It was a chance to feel the grassroots energy that has always been so central to Barack's vision of democracy, and to be reminded that American citizens are for the most part far less cynical than their elected leaders. We just needed them to get out and vote. I'd been disappointed that millions of people had sat out during the 2010 midterm elections, effectively handing Barack a divided Congress that could barely manage to make a law.

Despite the challenges, there was plenty to feel hopeful about, too. By the end of 2011, the last American soldiers had left Iraq; a gradual draw-down of troops was under way in Afghanistan. Major provisions of the Affordable Care Act had also gone into effect, with young people allowed to remain longer on their parents' insurance policies and companies prevented from capping a patient's lifetime coverage. All this was forward motion, I reminded myself, steps taken along the broader path.

Even with an entire political party conspiring to see Barack fail, we had no choice but to stay positive and carry on. It was similar to when the Sidwell mom had asked Malia if she feared for her life at tennis practice. What can you do, really, but go out and hit another ball?

So we worked. Both of us worked. I threw myself into my initiatives. Under the banner of Let's Move! we continued to rack up results. My team and I persuaded Darden Restaurants, the parent company behind chains like Olive Garden and Red Lobster, to make changes to the kinds of food it offered and how it was prepared. They pledged to revamp their menus, cutting calories, reducing sodium, and offering healthier options for kids' meals. We'd appealed to the company's executives—to their conscience as well as their bottom line—convincing them that the culture of eating in America was shifting and it made good business sense to get out ahead of the curve. Darden served 400 million meals to Americans each year. At that scale, even a small shift—like removing tantalizing photos of cool, icy glasses of soda from the kids' menus—could have a real impact.

A First Lady's power is a curious thing—as soft and undefined as the role itself. And yet I was learning to harness it. I had no executive authority. I didn't command troops or engage in formal diplomacy. Tradition called for me to provide a kind of gentle light, flattering the president with my devotion, flattering the nation primarily by not challenging it. I was beginning to see, though, that wielded carefully the light was more powerful than that. I had influence in the form of being something of a curiosity—a Black First Lady, a professional woman, a mother of young kids. People seemed to want to dial into my clothes, my shoes, and my hairstyles, but they also had to see me in the context of where I was and why. I was learning how to connect my message to my image, and in this way I could direct the American gaze. I could put on an interesting outfit, crack a joke, and talk about sodium content in kids' meals without being totally boring. I could publicly applaud a company that was actively hiring members of the military community, or drop to the floor for an on-air push-up contest with Ellen DeGeneres (and win it, earning gloating rights forever) in the name of Let's Move!

I was a child of the mainstream, and this was an asset. Barack sometimes referred to me as "Joe Public," asking me to weigh in on campaign slogans and strategies, knowing that I kept myself happily steeped in popular culture. Though I'd moved through rarefied places like Princeton and Sidley & Austin, and though I now occasionally found myself wearing diamonds and a ball gown, I'd never stopped reading *People* magazine or let go of my love of a good sitcom. I watched Oprah and Ellen far more often than I'd ever tuned in to *Meet the Press* or *Face the Nation*, and to this day nothing pleases me more than the tidy triumph delivered by a home-makeover show.

All of this is to say that I saw ways to connect with Americans that Barack and his West Wing advisers didn't fully recognize, at least initially. Rather than doing interviews with big newspapers or cable news outlets, I began sitting down with influential "mommy bloggers" who reached an enormous and dialed-in audience of women. Watching my young staffers interact with their phones, seeing Malia and Sasha start to take in news and chat with their high school friends via social media, I realized there was opportunity to be tapped there as well. I crafted my first tweet in the fall of 2011 to promote Joining Forces and then watched it zing through the strange, boundless ether where people increasingly spent their time.

It was a revelation. All of it was a revelation. With my soft power, I was finding I could be strong.

If reporters and television cameras wanted to follow me, then I was going to take them places. They could come watch me and Jill Biden paint a wall, for example, at a nondescript row house in the Northwest part of Washington. There was nothing inherently interesting about two ladies with paint rollers, but it baited a certain hook.

It brought everyone to the doorstep of Sergeant Johnny Agbi, who'd been twenty-five years old and a medic in Afghanistan when his transport helicopter was attacked, shattering his spine, injuring his brain, and requiring a long rehabilitation at Walter Reed. His first floor was now being retrofitted to accommodate his wheelchair—its doorways widened, its kitchen sink lowered—part of a joint effort between a nonprofit called Rebuilding Together and the company that owned Sears and Kmart. This was the thousandth such home they'd renovated on behalf of veterans in need. The cameras caught all of it—the soldier, his house, the goodwill and energy being poured in. The reporters interviewed not just me and Jill but Sergeant Agbi and the folks who'd done the real work. For me, this was how it should be. The gaze belonged here.

O N ELECTION DAY—November 6, 2012—my fears sat with me quietly. Barack and the girls and I were back in Chicago, at home on Greenwood Avenue, caught in the purgatory of waiting for an entire nation to accept or reject us. This vote, for me, was more fraught than any other we'd gone through. It felt like a referendum not only on Barack's political performance and the state of the country but also on his character, on our very presence in the White House. Our girls had established a strong community for themselves, and a sense of normalcy that I didn't want to upend yet again. I was so invested now, having given over four years of our family's life, that it was impossible not to feel everything a bit personally.

The campaign had worn us out, maybe even more than I'd anticipated. While working on my initiatives and keeping up with things like parent-teacher conferences and monitoring the girls' homework, I'd been speaking at campaign events at an average of three cities a day, three days a week. And Barack's pace had been even more grueling. Polls consistently showed him with only a tenuous lead over Mitt Romney. Making matters worse, he'd bombed during their first debate in October, triggering a wave of eleventh-hour anxiety among donors and advisers. We could read the exhaustion on the faces of our hardworking staffers. Though they aimed never to show it, they were surely unsettled by the possibility that Barack could be forced out of office in a matter of months.

Throughout it, Barack stayed calm, though I could see what the pressure did to him. During the final weeks, he began to look a little wan and even skinnier than usual, chewing his Nicorette with unusual vigor. I'd watched with wifely concern as he tried to do everything—soothe the worriers, finish out the campaign, and govern the nation all at once, including responding to a terrorist attack on American diplomats in Benghazi, Libya, and managing a massive federal response to Hurricane Sandy, which tore up the Eastern Seaboard just a week before the election.

As polls on the East Coast began to close that evening, I headed up to the third floor of our house, where we'd set up a kind of de facto hair and makeup salon to prepare for the public part of the night ahead. Meredith had steamed and readied clothes for me, my mom, and the girls. Johnny and Carl were doing my hair and makeup. In keeping with tradition, Barack had gone out to play basketball earlier in the day and had since settled into his office to put finishing touches on his remarks.

We had a TV on the third floor, but I deliberately kept it off. If there was news, good or bad, I wanted to hear it directly from Barack or Melissa, or someone else close to me. The babble of news anchors with their interactive electoral maps always jangled my nerves. I didn't want the details: I just wanted to know how to feel.

It was after 8:00 p.m. in the East now, which meant there had to be some early results coming in. I picked up my BlackBerry and sent emails to Valerie, Melissa, and Tina Tchen, who in 2011 had become my new chief of staff, asking them what they knew.

I waited fifteen minutes, then thirty, but nobody responded. The room around me began to feel strangely silent. My mother sat in the kitchen downstairs, reading a magazine. Meredith was getting the girls ready for the evening. Johnny ran a flat iron over my hair. Was I being paranoid, or were people not looking me in the eye? Did they somehow know something I didn't?

As more time passed, my head started to throb. I felt my equilibrium beginning to slip. I didn't dare turn on the news, assuming suddenly that it was bad. I was accustomed at this point to fighting off negative thoughts, sticking to the good until I was absolutely forced to contend with something unpleasant. I kept my confidence in a little citadel, high on a hill inside my own heart. But for every minute my BlackBerry lay dormant in my lap, I felt the walls starting to breach, the doubts beginning to rampage. Maybe we hadn't worked hard enough. Maybe we didn't deserve another term. My hands had started to shake.

I was just about ready to pass out from the anxiety when Barack came trotting up the stairs, wearing his big old confident grin. His worries were well behind him already. "We're kicking butt," he said, looking surprised that I didn't know it already. "It's basically done."

It turned out that downstairs, the mood had been jubilant all along, the basement TV pumping out a consistent stream of good news. The problem for me was that the cell service on my BlackBerry had somehow disconnected, never sending out my messages or downloading updates from others. I'd allowed myself to get trapped in my own head. Nobody had known I was worrying, not even the people in the room with me.

Barack would win all but one of the battleground states that night. He'd win among young people, minorities, and women, just as he had in 2008. Despite everything the Republicans had done to try to thwart him, despite the many attempts to obstruct his presidency, his vision had prevailed. We'd asked Americans for permission to keep working—to finish strong—and now we'd gotten it. The relief was immediate. *Are we good enough? Yes we are.*

At some late hour, Mitt Romney called to concede. Once again, we found ourselves dressed up and waving from a stage, four Obamas and a lot of confetti, glad to have another four years.

The certainty that came with reelection held me steady. We had more time to further our aims. We could be more patient with our push for progress. We had a sense of the future now, which made me happy. We could keep Sasha and Malia enrolled at school; our staff could stay in their jobs; our ideas still mattered. And when these next four years were over, we'd be truly done, which made me happiest of all. No more campaigning, no more sweating out strategy sessions or polls or debates or approval ratings, ever again. The end of our political life was finally in sight.

The truth is that the future would arrive with its own surprises— some joyous, some unspeakably tragic. Four more years in the White House meant four more years of being out front as symbols, absorbing and responding to whatever came our country's way. Barack and I had campaigned on the idea that we still had the energy and discipline for this sort of work, that we had the heart to take it in. And now the future was coming in our direction, maybe faster than we knew.

F IVE WEEKS LATER, a gunman walked into Sandy Hook Elementary School in Newtown, Connecticut, and started killing children.

I had just finished giving a short speech across the street from the White House and was scheduled to then go visit a children's hospital when Tina pulled me aside to tell me what had happened. While I'd been speaking, she and several others had seen the headlines start to come up on their phones. They'd sat there trying to hide their emotions as I wrapped up my remarks.

The news Tina gave me was so horrifying and sad I could barely process what she was saying.

She mentioned she'd been in touch with the West Wing. Barack was in the Oval Office by himself. "He's asking for you to come," she said. "Right away."

My husband needed me. This would be the only time in eight years that he'd request my presence in the middle of a workday, the two of us rearranging our schedules to be alone together for a moment of dim comfort. Usually, work was work and home was home, but for us, as for many people, the tragedy in Newtown shattered every window and blew down every fence. When I walked into the Oval Office, Barack and I embraced silently. There was nothing to say. No words.

What a lot of people don't know is that the president sees almost everything, or is at least privy to basically any available information related to the country's well-being. Being a fact guy, Barack always asked for more rather than less. He tried to gather both the widest and the most close-up view of every situation, even when it was bad, so that he could offer a truly informed response. As he saw it, it was part of his responsibility, what he'd been elected to do—to look rather than look away, to stay upright when the rest of us felt ready to fall down.

Which is to say that by the time I found him, he'd been briefed in detail on the graphic, horrid crime scene at Sandy Hook. He'd heard about blood pooled on the floors of classrooms and the bodies of twenty first graders and six educators torn apart by a semiautomatic rifle. His shock and grief would never compare with that of the first responders who'd rushed in to secure the building and evacuate survivors from the carnage. It was nothing next to that of the parents who endured an interminable wait in the chilly air outside the building, praying that they'd see their child's face again. And it was nothing at all next to those whose wait would be in vain.

But still, those images were seared permanently into his psyche. I could see in his eyes how broken they'd left him, what this had done already to his faith. He started to describe it to me but then stopped, realizing it was better to spare me the extra pain.

Like me, Barack loved children in a deep and genuine way. Beyond being a doting father, he regularly brought kids into the Oval Office to show them around. He asked to hold babies. He lit up anytime he got to visit a school science fair or a youth sporting event. The previous winter, he'd added a whole new level of delight to his existence when he started volunteering as an assistant coach for the Vipers, Sasha's middle school basketball team.

The proximity of children made everything lighter for him. He knew as well as anyone the promise lost with those twenty young lives.

Staying upright after Newtown was probably the hardest thing he'd ever had to do. When Malia and Sasha came home from school later that day, Barack and I met them in the residence and hugged them tight, trying to mask the urgency of our need just to touch them. It was hard to know what to say or not say to our girls about the shooting. Parents all around the country, we knew, were grappling with the same thing.

Later that day, Barack held a press conference downstairs, trying to put together words that might add up to something like solace. He wiped away tears as news cameras clicked furiously around him, understanding that truly there was no solace to be had. The best he could do was to offer his resolve—something he assumed would also get taken up by citizens and lawmakers around the country—to prevent more massacres by passing basic, sensible laws concerning how guns were sold.

I watched him step forward, knowing that I myself wasn't ready. In nearly four years as First Lady, I had consoled often. I'd prayed with people whose homes had been shredded by a tornado in Tuscaloosa, Alabama, huge swaths of the town turned to matchsticks in an instant. I'd put my arms around men, women, and children who'd lost loved ones to war in Afghanistan, to an extremist who'd shot up an Army base in Texas, and to violence on street corners near their own homes. In the previous four months, I'd paid visits to people who'd survived mass shootings at a movie theater in Colorado and inside a Sikh temple in Wisconsin. It was devastating, every time. I'd tried always to bring the most calm and open part of myself to these meetings, to lend my own strength by being caring and present, sitting quietly on the riverbed of other people's pain. But two days after the shooting at Sandy Hook, when Barack traveled to Newtown to speak at a prayer vigil being held for the victims, I couldn't bring myself to join him. I was so shaken by it that I had no strength available to lend. I'd been First Lady for almost four years, and there had been too much killing already—too many senseless preventable deaths and too little action. I wasn't sure what comfort I could ever give to someone whose six-year-old had been gunned down at school.

Instead, like a lot of parents, I clung to my children, my fear and love intertwined. It was nearly Christmas, and Sasha was among a group of local children selected to join the Moscow Ballet for two performances of *The Nutcracker,* both happening on the same day as the vigil in Newtown. Barack managed to slip into a back row and watch the dress rehearsal before leaving for Connecticut. I went to the evening show.

The ballet was as beautiful and otherworldly as any recounting of that story ever is, with its prince in a moonlit forest and its swirling pageantry of sweets. Sasha played a mouse, dressed in a black leotard with fuzzy ears and a tail, performing her part while an ornate sleigh drifted through the swelling orchestral music and showers of glittering fake snow. My eyes never left her. My whole being was grateful for her. Sasha stood bright-eyed onstage, looking at first like she couldn't believe where she was, as if she found the whole scene dazzling and unreal. Which of course it was. But she was young enough still that she could give herself over to it, at least for the moment, allowing herself to move through this heaven where nobody spoke and everyone danced, and a holiday was always just about to arrive.

B EAR WITH ME HERE, because this doesn't necessarily get easier. It would be one thing if America were a simple place with a simple story. If I could narrate my part in it only through the lens of what was orderly and sweet. If there were no steps backward. And if every sadness, when it came, turned out at least to be redemptive in the end.

But that's not America, and it's not me, either. I'm not going to try to bend this into any kind of perfect shape.

Barack's second term would prove to be easier in many ways than his first. We'd learned so much in four years, putting the right people into place around us, building systems that generally worked. We knew enough now to avoid some of the inefficiencies and small mistakes that had been made the first time around, beginning on Inauguration Day in January 2013, when I requested that the viewing stand for the parade be fully heated this time so our feet wouldn't freeze. In an attempt to conserve our energy, we hosted only two inaugural balls that night, as opposed to the ten we'd gone to in 2009. We had four years still to go, and if I'd learned anything, it was to relax and try to pace myself.

Sitting next to Barack at the parade after he'd renewed his vows to the country, I watched the flow of floats and the marching bands moving in and out of snappy formation, already able to savor more than I had our first time around. From my vantage point, I could barely make out the individual faces of the performers. There were thousands of them, each with his or her own story. Thousands of others had come to D.C. to perform in the many other events being held in the days leading up to the inauguration, and tens of thousands more had come to watch.

Later, I'd wish almost frantically that I'd been able to catch sight of one person in particular, a willowy Black girl wearing a sparkling gold headband and a blue majorette's uniform who'd come with the King College Prep marching band from the South Side of Chicago to perform at some of the side events. I wanted to believe that I somehow would have had the occasion to see her inside the great wash of people flowing through the city over those days—Hadiya Pendleton, a girl in ascent, fifteen years old and having a big moment, having ridden a bus all the way to Washington with her bandmates. At home in Chicago, Hadiya lived with her parents and her little brother, about two miles from our house on Greenwood Avenue. She was an honor student at school who liked to tell people she wanted to go to Harvard someday. She'd begun planning her sweet-sixteen birthday party. She loved Chinese food and cheeseburgers and going for ice cream with friends.

I learned these things several weeks later, at her funeral. Eight days after the inauguration, Hadiya Pendleton was shot and killed in a public park in Chicago, not far from her school. She and a group of friends had been standing under a metal shelter next to a playground, waiting for a rainstorm to pass. They'd been mistaken for gang members, sprayed with bullets by an eighteen-year-old belonging to a different gang. Hadiya had been hit in the back as she tried to run for cover. Two of her friends were injured. All this at 2:20 on a Tuesday afternoon.

I wish I'd seen her alive, if only to have a memory to share with her mom, now that the memories of her daughter were suddenly finite, things to be collected and hung on to.

I went to Hadiya's funeral because it felt like the right thing to do. I'd stayed back when Barack went to the Newtown memorial, but now was my time to step up. My hope was that my presence would help turn the gaze toward the many innocent kids being gunned down in city streets almost every day—and that this, coupled with the horror of Newtown, would help prompt Americans to demand reasonable gun laws. Hadiya Pendleton came from a close-knit, working-class South Side family, much like my own. Put simply, I could have known her. I could have been her once, even. And had she taken a different route home from school that day, or even moved six inches left instead of six inches right when the gunfire started, she could have been me.

"I did everything I was supposed to," her mother told me when we met just before the funeral started, her brown eyes leaking tears. Cleopatra Cowley-Pendleton was a warm woman with a soft voice and close-cropped hair who worked in customer service at a credit rating company. On the day of her daughter's funeral, she wore a giant pink flower pinned to her lapel. She and her husband, Nathaniel, had watched over Hadiya carefully, encouraging her to apply to King, a selective public high school, and making sure she had little time to be out on the streets, signing her up for volleyball, cheerleading, and a dance ministry at church. As my parents had once done for me, they'd made sacrifices so that she could be exposed to things outside her neighborhood. She was to have gone to Europe with the marching band that spring, and she'd apparently loved her visit to Washington.

"It's so clean there, Mom," she'd reported to Cleopatra after returning. "I think I'm going to go into politics."

Instead, Hadiya Pendleton became one of three people who died in separate incidents of gun violence in Chicago on that one January day. She was the thirty-sixth person in Chicago killed in gun violence that year, and the year was at that point just twenty-nine days old. It goes without saying that nearly all those victims were Black. For all her hopes and hard work, Hadiya became a symbol of the wrong thing.

Her funeral was filled with people, another broken community jammed into a church, this one working to handle the sight of a teen-age girl in a casket lined with purple silk. Cleopatra stood up and spoke about her daughter. Hadiya's friends stood up and told stories about her, each one punctuated by a larger feeling of outrage and helplessness. These were children, asking not just *why* but *why so often?* There were powerful adults in the room that day—not only me, but the mayor of the city, the governor of the state, Jesse Jackson Sr., and Valerie Jarrett, among others—all of us packed into pews, left to reckon privately with our grief and guilt as the choir sang with such force that it shook the floor of the church.

I T WAS IMPORTANT to me to be more than a consoler. In my life, I'd heard plenty of empty words coming from important people, lip service paid during times of crisis with no action to follow. I was deter-mined to be someone who told the truth, using my voice to lift up the voiceless when I could, and to not disappear on people in need. I under-stood that when I showed up somewhere, it appeared dramatic from the outside—a sudden and swift-descending storm kicked up by the motor-cade, the agents, the aides, and the media, with me at the center. We were there and then gone. I didn't like what this did to my interactions, the way my presence sometimes caused people to stammer or go silent, unsure of how to be themselves. It's why I often tried to introduce myself with a hug, to slow down the moment and shuck some of the pretense, landing us all in the flesh.

I tried to build relationships with the people I met, especially those who didn't normally have access to the world I now inhabited. I wanted to share the brightness as I could. I invited Hadiya Pendleton's parents to sit next to me at Barack's State of the Union speech a few days after the funeral and then hosted the family at the White House for the Easter Egg Roll. Cleopatra, who became a vocal advocate for violence preven-tion, also returned a couple of times to attend different meetings on the issue. I made a point of writing letters to the girls from the Elizabeth Garrett Anderson School in London who had so profoundly moved me, encouraging them to stay hopeful and keep working, despite their lack of privilege. In 2011, I'd taken a group of thirty-seven girls from the school to visit the University of Oxford, bringing not the high achievers but students whose teachers thought they weren't yet reaching their potential. The idea was to give them a glimpse of what was possible, to show them what a reach could yield. In 2012, I'd hosted students from the school at the White House during the British prime minister's state visit. I felt it was important to reach out to kids multiple times and in multiple ways in order for them to feel that it was all real.

My early successes in life were, I knew, a product of the consistent love and high expectations with which I was surrounded as a child, both at home and at school. It was this insight that drove my White House mentoring program, and it lay at the center of a new education initiative my staff and I were now preparing to launch, called Reach Higher. I wanted to encourage kids to strive to get to college and, once there, to stick with it. I knew that in the coming years, a college education would only become more essential for young people entering a global job market. Reach Higher would seek to help them along the way, providing more support for school counselors and easier access to federal financial aid.

I'd been lucky to have parents, teachers, and mentors who'd fed me with a consistent, simple message: *You matter.* As an adult, I wanted to pass those words to a new generation. It was the message I gave my own daughters, who were fortunate to have it reinforced daily by their school and their privileged circumstances, and I was determined to express some version of it to every young person I encountered. I wanted to be the opposite of the guidance counselor I'd had in high school, who'd blithely told me I wasn't Princeton material.

"All of us believe you belong here," I'd said to the Elizabeth Garrett Anderson girls as they sat, many of them looking a little awestruck, in the Gothic old-world dining hall at Oxford, surrounded by university professors and students who'd come out for the day to mentor them. I said something similar anytime we had kids visit the White House—teens we invited from the Standing Rock Sioux Reservation; children from local schools who showed up to work in the garden; high schoolers who came for our career days and workshops in fashion, music, and poetry; even kids I only got to give a quick but emphatic hug to in a rope line. The message was always the same. *You belong. You matter. I think highly of you.*

An economist from a British university would later put out a study that looked at the test performances of Elizabeth Garrett Anderson students, finding that their overall scores jumped significantly after I'd started connecting with them—the equivalent of moving from a C average to an A. Any credit for improvement really belonged to the girls, their teachers, and the daily work they did together, but it also affirmed the idea that kids will invest more when they feel they're being invested in. I understood that there was power in showing children my regard.

TWO MONTHS AFTER Hadiya Pendleton's funeral, I returned to Chicago. I'd directed Tina, my chief of staff and an attorney who herself had spent many years in the city, to throw her energy into rallying support for violence prevention there. Tina was a bighearted policy wonk with an infectious laugh and more hustle than just about anyone I knew. She understood which levers to pull inside and outside government to make an impact at the scale I envisioned. Moreover, her nature and experience wouldn't allow her voice to go unheard, especially at tables dominated by men, where she often found herself. Throughout Barack's second term, she would wrestle with the Pentagon and various state governors to clear away red tape so that veterans and military spouses could more efficiently build their careers, and she'd also help engineer a mammoth new administration-wide effort centered on girls' education worldwide.

In the wake of Hadiya's death, Tina had leveraged her local contacts, encouraging Chicago business leaders and philanthropists to work with Mayor Rahm Emanuel to expand community programs for at-risk youth across the city. Her efforts had helped yield $33 million in pledges in just a matter of weeks. On a cool day in April, Tina and I flew out to attend a meeting of community leaders discussing youth empowerment, and also to meet a new group of kids.

Earlier that winter, the public radio program *This American Life* had devoted two hours to telling the stories of students and staff from

William R. Harper Senior High School in Englewood, a neighborhood on the South Side. In the previous year, twenty-nine of the school's current and recent students had been shot, eight of them fatally. These numbers were astonishing to me and my staff, but the sad fact is that urban schools around the country were contending with epidemic levels of gun violence. Amid all the talk of youth empowerment, it seemed important to actually sit down and hear from the youth.

When I was young, Englewood had been a rough neighborhood but not necessarily as deadly as it was now. In junior high, I'd traveled to Englewood for weekly biology labs at a community college there. Now, years later, as my motorcade made its way past strips of neglected bungalows and shuttered storefronts, past vacant lots and burned-out buildings, it looked to me as if the only thriving businesses left were the liquor stores.

I thought back to my own childhood and my own neighborhood, and how the word "ghetto" got thrown around like a threat. The mere suggestion of it, I understood now, caused stable, middle-class families to bail preemptively for the suburbs, worried their property values would drop. "Ghetto" signaled that a place was both Black and hopeless. It was a label that foretold failure and then hastened its arrival. It closed corner groceries and gas stations and undermined schools and educators trying to instill self-worth in neighborhood kids. It was a word everyone tried to run from, but it could rear up on a community quick.

In the middle of West Englewood sat Harper High School, a large sand-brick building with multiple wings. I met the school's principal, Leonetta Sanders, a quick-moving African American woman who'd been at the school for six years, and two school social workers who immersed themselves in the lives of the 510 kids enrolled at Harper, most of them from low-income families. One of the social workers, Crystal Smith, could often be found pacing Harper's hallways between classes, peppering students with positivity, communicating her high regard for them by calling out, "I'm so proud of you!" and "I see you trying hard!" She'd shout, "I appreciate you in advance!" for every good choice she trusted those students would make.

In the school library that day, I joined a circle of twenty-two Harper students—all African American, mostly juniors and seniors—who were seated in chairs and on couches, dressed in khakis and collared shirts. Most were eager to talk. They described a daily, even hourly, fear of gangs and violence. Some explained that they had absent or addicted parents; a couple had spent time in juvenile detention centers. A junior named Thomas had witnessed a good friend—a sixteen-year-old girl—get shot and killed the previous summer. He'd also been there when his older brother, who had been partially paralyzed due to a gunshot injury, was shot and wounded in the same incident while sitting outside in his wheelchair. Nearly every kid there that day had lost someone—a friend, relative, neighbor—to a bullet. Few, meanwhile, had ever been downtown to see the lakefront or visit Navy Pier.

At one point, one of the social workers interjected, saying to the group, "Eighty degrees and sunny!" Everyone in the circle began nodding, ruefully. I wasn't sure why. "Tell Mrs. Obama," she said. "What goes through your mind when you wake up in the morning and hear the weather forecast is eighty and sunny?"

She clearly knew the answer, but wanted me to hear it.

A day like that, the Harper students all agreed, was no good. When the weather was nice, the gangs got more active and the shooting got worse.

These kids had adapted to the upside-down logic dictated by their environment, staying indoors when the weather was good, varying the routes they took to and from school each day based on shifting gang territories and allegiances. Sometimes, they told me, taking the safest path home meant walking right down the middle of the street as cars sped past them on both sides. Doing so gave them a better view of any escalating fights or possible shooters. And it gave them more time to run.

America is not a simple place. Its contradictions set me spinning. I'd found myself at Democratic fund-raisers held in vast Manhattan penthouses, sipping wine with wealthy women who would claim to be passionate about education and children's issues and then lean in conspiratorially to tell me that their Wall Street husbands would never vote for anyone who even thought about raising their taxes.

And now I was at Harper, listening to children talking about how to stay alive. I admired their resilience, and I wished desperately that they didn't need it so much.

One of them then gave me a candid look. "It's nice that you're here and all," he said with a shrug. "But what're you actually going to do about any of this?"

To them, I represented Washington, D.C., as much as I did the South Side. And when it came to Washington, I felt I owed them the truth.

"Honestly," I began, "I know you're dealing with a lot here, but no one's going to save you anytime soon. Most people in Washington aren't even trying. A lot of them don't even know you exist." I explained to those students that progress is slow, that they couldn't afford to simply sit and wait for change to come. Many Americans didn't want their taxes raised, and Congress couldn't even pass a budget let alone rise above petty partisan bickering, so there weren't going to be billion-dollar investments in education or magical turnarounds for their community. Even after the horror of Newtown, Congress appeared determined to block any measure that could help keep guns out of the wrong hands, with legislators more interested in collecting campaign donations from the National Rifle Association than they were in protecting kids. Politics was a mess, I said. On this front, I had nothing terribly uplifting or encouraging to say.

I went on, though, to make a different pitch, one that came directly from my South Side self. *Use school,* I said.

These kids had just spent an hour telling me stories that were tragic and unsettling, but I reminded them that those same stories also showed their persistence, self-reliance, and ability to overcome. I assured them that they already had what it would take to succeed. Here they were, sitting in a school that was offering them a free education, I said, and there were a whole lot of committed and caring adults inside that school who thought they mattered. About six weeks later, thanks to donations from local businesspeople, a group of Harper students would come to the White House, to visit with me and Barack personally, and also spend time at Howard University, learning what college was about. I hoped that they could see themselves getting there.

I will never pretend that words or hugs from a First Lady alone can turn somebody's life around or that there's any easy path for students trying to navigate everything that those kids at Harper were dealing with. No story is that simple. And of course, every one of us sitting in the library that day knew this. But I was there to push back against the old and damning narrative about being a Black urban kid in America, the one that foretold failure and then hastened its arrival. If I could point out those students' strengths and give them some glimpse of a way forward, then I would always do it. It was a small difference I could make.

24

I N THE SPRING OF 2015, MALIA ANNOUNCED THAT SHE'D been invited to the prom by a boy she kind of liked. She was sixteen then, finishing her junior year at Sidwell. To us, she was still our kid, long-legged and enthusiastic as she'd always been, though every day she seemed to become a little more adult. She was now nearly as tall as I was and starting to think about applying to college. She was a good student, curious and self-possessed, a collector of details much like her dad. She'd become fascinated by films and filmmaking and the previous summer had taken it upon herself to seek out Steven Spielberg one evening when he'd come to the White House for a dinner party, asking him so many questions that he followed up with an offer to let her intern on a TV series he was producing. Our girl was finding her way.

Normally, for security reasons, Malia and Sasha weren't allowed to ride in anyone else's car. Malia had a provisional license by then and was able to drive herself around town, though always with agents following in their own vehicle. But still, since moving to Washington at the age of ten, she'd never once ridden a bus or the Metro or been driven by someone who didn't work for the Secret Service. For prom night, though, we were making an exception.

On the appointed evening, her date arrived in his car, clearing security at the southeast gate of the White House, following the path up and around the South Lawn by which heads of state and other visiting dignitaries normally arrived, and then gamely—bravely—walking into the Dip Room dressed in a black suit.

"Just be cool please, okay?" Malia had said to me and Barack, her embarrassment already beginning to smolder as we rode the elevator downstairs. I was barefoot, and Barack was in flip-flops. Malia wore a long black skirt and an elegant bare-shouldered top. She looked beautiful and about twenty-three years old.

By my reckoning, we did manage to play it cool, though Malia still laughs, remembering it all as a bit excruciating. Barack and I shook the young man's hand, snapped a few pictures, and gave our daughter a hug before sending them on their way. We took what was perhaps unfair comfort in the knowledge that Malia's security detail would basically ride the boy's bumper all the way to the restaurant where they were going for dinner before the dance and would remain on quiet duty throughout the night.

From a parent's point of view, it wasn't a bad way to raise teenagers—knowing that a set of watchful adults was trailing them at all times, tasked with extricating them from any sort of emergency. From a teenager's standpoint, though, this was understandably a complete and total drag. As with many aspects of life in the White House, we were left to sort out what it meant for our family—where and how to draw the lines, how to balance the requirements of the presidency against the needs of two kids learning how to mature on their own.

Once they got to high school, we gave the girls curfews—first 11:00 and eventually midnight—and enforced them, according to Malia and Sasha, with more vigor than many of their friends' parents did. If I was concerned about their safety or whereabouts, I could always check in with the agents, but I tried not to. It was important to me that the kids trusted their security team. Instead, I did what I think a lot of parents do and relied on a network of other parents for information, all of us pooling what we knew about where the flock of them was going and whether there'd be an adult in charge. Of course, our girls carried extra responsibility by virtue of who their father was, knowing that their screwups could make headlines. Barack and I both recognized how unfair this was. Both of us had pushed boundaries and done dumb things as teenagers, and we'd been fortunate to do it all without the eyes of a nation on us.

Malia had been eight when Barack sat on the edge of her bed in Chicago and asked if she thought it was okay for him to run for president. I think now of how little she'd known at the time, how little any of us could have known. It meant one thing to be a child in the White House. It meant something different to try to emerge from it as an adult. How could Malia have guessed that she'd have men with guns following her to prom someday? Or that people would take photos of her sneaking a cigarette and sell them to gossipy websites?

Our kids were coming of age during what felt like a unique time. Apple had begun selling the iPhone in June 2007, about four months after Barack announced his candidacy for president. A million of them sold in less than three months. A billion of them sold before his second term was over. His was the first presidency of a new era, one involving the disruption and dismantling of all norms around privacy—involving selfies, data hacks, Snapchats, and Kardashians. Our daughters lived more deeply inside it than we did, in part because social media governed teen life and in part because their routines put them in closer contact with the public than ours did. As Malia and Sasha moved around Washington with their friends after school or on weekends, they'd catch sight of strangers pointing their phones in their direction, or contend with grown men and women asking— even demanding—to take a selfie with them. "You do know that I'm a child, right?" Malia would sometimes say when turning someone down.

Barack and I did what we could to protect our kids from too much exposure, declining all media requests for them and working to keep their everyday lives largely out of sight. Their Secret Service escorts supported us by trying to be less conspicuous when following the girls around in public, wearing board shorts and T-shirts instead of suits and swapping their earpieces and wrist microphones for earbud headsets, in order to better blend in at the teenage hangouts they now frequented. We strongly disapproved of the publication of any photos of our children that weren't connected to an official event, and the White House press office made this clear to the media. Melissa and others on my team became my enforcers anytime an image of one of the girls surfaced on a gossip site, making haranguing phone calls to get it taken down.

Guarding the girls' privacy meant finding other ways to satiate the public's curiosity about our family. Early in Barack's second term, we'd added a new puppy to the household—Sunny—a free-spirited rambler who seemed to see no point in being house-trained, given how big her new house was. The dogs added a lightness to everything. They were living, loafing proof that the White House was a home. Knowing that Malia and Sasha were basically off-limits, the White House communications teams began requesting the dogs for official appearances. In the evenings, I'd find memos in my briefing book asking me to approve a "Bo and Sunny Drop-By," allowing the dogs to mingle with members of the media or children coming for a tour. The dogs would get deployed when reporters came to learn about the importance of American trade and exports or, later, to hear Barack speak in favor of Merrick Garland, his pick for the Supreme Court. Bo starred in a promotional video for the Easter Egg Roll. He and Sunny posed with me for photos in an online campaign to urge people to sign up for health-care coverage. They made excellent ambassadors, impervious to criticism and unaware of their own fame.

L IKE ALL KIDS, Sasha and Malia outgrew things over time. Since the first year of Barack's presidency, they had joined him in front of reporters each fall while he performed what had to be the most ridiculous ritual of the office—pardoning a live turkey just ahead of the Thanksgiving holiday. For the first five years, they'd smiled and giggled as their dad cracked corny jokes. But by the sixth year, at thirteen and sixteen, they were too old to even pretend it was funny. Within hours of the ceremony, photos of the two of them looking aggrieved appeared all over the internet—Sasha stone-faced, Malia with her arms crossed—as they stood next to the president, his lectern, and the oblivious turkey. A USA Today headline summed it up fairly enough: "Malia and Sasha Obama Are So Done with Their Dad's Turkey Pardon."

Their attendance at the pardon, as well as at virtually every White House event, became entirely optional. These were happy, well-adjusted teens with lives that were accordingly rich with activities and social intrigue having nothing to do with their parents. As a parent, you're only sort of in control, anyway. Our kids had their own agendas, which left them less impressed with even the more fun parts of ours.

"Don't you want to come downstairs tonight and hear Paul McCartney play?"

"Mom, please. No."

There was often music blasting from Malia's room. Sasha and her friends had taken a shine to cable cooking shows and sometimes commandeered the residence kitchen to decorate cookies or whip up elaborate, multicourse meals for themselves. Both our daughters relished the relative anonymity they enjoyed when going on school trips or joining friends' families for vacations (their agents always in tow). Sasha loved nothing more than to pick out her own snacks at Dulles International Airport before boarding a packed commercial flight, for the simple fact that it was so different from the presidential rigmarole that went on at Andrews Air Force Base and had become our family's norm.

Traveling with us did have its advantages. Before Barack's presidency was over, our girls would enjoy a baseball game in Havana, walk along the Great Wall of China, and visit the Christ the Redeemer statue in Rio one evening in magical, misty darkness. But it could also be a pain in the neck, especially when we were trying to tend to things unrelated to the presidency. Earlier in Malia's junior year, the two of us had gone to spend a day visiting colleges in New York City, for instance, setting up tours at New York University and Columbia. It had worked fine for a while. We'd moved through NYU's campus at a brisk pace, our efficiency aided by the fact that it was still early and many students were not yet up for the day. We'd checked out classrooms, poked our heads into a dorm room, and chatted with a dean before heading uptown to grab an early lunch and move on to the next tour.

The problem is that there's no hiding a First Lady–sized motorcade, especially on the island of Manhattan in the middle of a weekday. By the time we finished eating, about a hundred people had gathered on the sidewalk outside the restaurant, the commotion only breeding more commotion. We stepped out to find dozens of cell phones hoisted in our direction as we were engulfed by a chorus of cheers. It was beneficent, this attention—"Come to Columbia, Malia!" people were shouting—but it was not especially useful for a girl who was trying quietly to imagine her own future.

I knew immediately what I needed to do, and that was to bench myself—to let Malia go see the next campus without me, sending Kristin Jones, my personal assistant, as her escort instead. Without me there, Malia's odds of being recognized went down. She could move faster and with a lot fewer agents. Without me, she could maybe, possibly, look like just another kid walking the quad. I at least owed her a shot at that.

Kristin, in her late twenties and a California native, was like a big sister to both my girls anyway. She'd come to my office as a young intern, and along with Kristen Jarvis, who until recently had been my trip director, was instrumental in our family's life, filling some of these strange gaps caused by the intensity of our schedules and the hindering nature of our fame. "The Kristins," as we called them, stood in for us often. They served as liaisons between our family and Sidwell, setting up meetings and interacting with teachers, coaches, and other parents when Barack and I weren't able. With the girls, they were protective, loving, and far hipper than I'd ever be in the eyes of my kids. Malia and Sasha trusted them implicitly, seeking their counsel on everything from wardrobe and social media to the increasing proximity of boys.

While Malia toured Columbia that afternoon, I was put into a secure holding area designated by the Secret Service—what turned out to be the basement of an academic building on campus—where I sat alone and unnoticed until it was time to leave, wishing I'd at least brought a book to read. It hurt a little to be down there, I'll admit. I felt a kind of loneliness that probably had less to do with the fact that I was by myself killing time in a windowless room and more to do with the idea that, like it or not, the future was coming, that our first baby was going to grow up and leave.

. . .

W E WEREN'T AT the end yet, but already I was beginning to take stock. I found myself tallying the gains and losses, what had been sacrificed and what we could count as progress—in our country, in our family. Had we done all we could? Were we going to come out of this intact?

I tried to think back and remember how it was that my life had forked away from the predictable, control-freak fantasy existence I'd envisioned for myself—the one with the steady salary, a house to live in forever, a routine to my days. At what point had I chosen away from that? When had I allowed the chaos inside? Had it been on the summer night when I lowered my ice cream cone and leaned in to kiss Barack for the first time? Was it the day I'd finally walked away from my orderly piles of documents and my partner-track career in law, convinced I'd find something more fulfilling?

My mind sometimes landed back in the church basement in Roseland, on the Far South Side of Chicago, where I'd gone twenty-five years earlier to be with Barack as he spoke to a neighborhood group that was struggling to push back against hopelessness and indifference. Listening to the conversation that evening, I'd heard something familiar articulated in a new way. It was possible, I knew, to live on two planes at once—to have one's feet planted in reality but pointed in the direction of progress. It was what I'd done as a kid on Euclid Avenue, what my family—and marginalized people more generally—had always done. You got somewhere by building that better reality, if at first only in your own mind. Or as Barack had put it that night, you may live in the world as it is, but you can still work to create the world as it should be.

I'd known the guy for only a couple of months then, but in retrospect I see now that this was my swerve. In that moment, without saying a word, I'd signed on for a lifetime of us, and a lifetime of this.

All these years later, I was thankful for the progress I saw. In 2015, I was still making visits to Walter Reed, but each time it seemed there were fewer wounded warriors to visit. The United States had fewer service members at risk overseas, fewer injuries needing care, fewer mothers with their hearts broken. This, to me, was progress.

Progress was the Centers for Disease Control reporting that childhood obesity rates appeared to be leveling off, particularly among children ages two to five. It was two thousand high school students in Detroit showing up to help me celebrate College Signing Day, a holiday we'd helped expand as a part of Reach Higher, to mark the day when young people committed to their colleges. Progress was the Supreme Court's decision to reject a challenge to a key part of the country's new health-care law, all but ensuring that Barack's signature domestic achievement—the security of health insurance for every American—would remain strong and intact once he left office. It was an economy that had been hemorrhaging 800,000 jobs a month when Barack entered the White House having now racked up nearly five straight years of continuous job growth.

I took this all in as evidence that as a country we were capable of building a better reality. But still, we lived in the world as it is.

A year and a half after Newtown, Congress had passed not a single gun-control measure. Bin Laden was gone, but ISIS had arrived. The homicide rate in Chicago was going up rather than down. A Black teen named Michael Brown was shot by a cop in Ferguson, Missouri, his body left in the middle of the road for hours. A Black teen named Laquan McDonald was shot sixteen times by police in Chicago, including nine times in the back. A Black boy named Tamir Rice was shot dead by police in Cleveland while playing with a toy gun. A Black man named Freddie Gray died after being neglected in police custody in Baltimore. A Black man named Eric Garner was killed by police after being put in a choke hold during his arrest on Staten Island. All this was evidence of something pernicious and unchanging in America. When Barack was first elected, various commentators had naively declared that our country was entering a "postracial" era, in which skin color would no longer matter. Here was proof of how wrong they'd been. As Americans obsessed over the threat of terrorism, many were overlooking the racism and tribalism that were tearing our nation apart.

Late in June 2015, Barack and I flew to Charleston, South Carolina, to sit with another grieving community—this time at the funeral of a pastor named Clementa Pinckney, who had been one of nine people killed in a racially motivated shooting earlier in the month at an African Methodist

Episcopal church known simply as Mother Emanuel. The victims, all African Americans, had welcomed an unemployed twenty-one-year-old white man—a stranger to them all—into their Bible study group. He'd sat with them for a while; then, after the group bowed their heads in prayer, he stood up and began shooting. In the middle of it, he was reported to have said, "I have to do this, because you rape our women and you're taking over our country."

After delivering a moving eulogy for Reverend Pinckney and acknowledging the deep tragedy of the moment, Barack surprised everyone by leading the congregation in a slow and soulful rendition of "Amazing Grace." It was a simple invocation of hope, a call to persist. Everyone in the room, it seemed, joined in. For more than six years now, Barack and I had lived with an awareness that we ourselves were a provocation. As minorities across the country were gradually beginning to take on more significant roles in politics, business, and entertainment, our family had become the most prominent example. Our presence in the White House had been celebrated by millions of Americans, but it also contributed to a reactionary sense of fear and resentment among others. The hatred was old and deep and as dangerous as ever.

We lived with it as a family, and we lived with it as a nation. And we carried on, as gracefully as we could.

THE SAME DAY as the funeral service in Charleston—June 26, 2015—the Supreme Court of the United States issued a landmark decision, affirming that same-sex couples had the right to marry in all fifty states. This was the culmination of a legal battle that had been fought methodically over decades, state by state, court by court, and as with any civil rights struggle it had required the persistence and courage of many people. On and off over the course of the day, I'd caught reports of Americans overjoyed by the news. A jubilant crowd chanted, "Love has won!" on the steps of the Supreme Court. Couples were flocking to city halls and county courthouses to exercise what was now a constitutional right. Gay bars were opening early. Rainbow flags waved on street corners around the country.

All this had helped buoy us through a sad day in South Carolina. Returning home to the White House, we'd changed out of our funeral clothes, had a quick dinner with the girls, and then Barack had disappeared into the Treaty Room to flip on ESPN and catch up on work. I was heading to my dressing room when I caught sight of a purplish glow through one of the north-facing windows of the residence, at which point I remembered that our staff had planned to illuminate the White House in the rainbow colors of the pride flag.

Looking out the window, I saw that beyond the gates on Pennsylvania Avenue, a big crowd of people had gathered in the summer dusk to see the lights. The north drive was filled with government staff who'd stayed late to see the White House transformed in celebration of marriage equality. The decision had touched so many people. From where I stood, I could see the exuberance, but I could hear nothing. It was an odd part of our reality. The White House was a silent, sealed fortress, almost all sound blocked by the thickness of its windows and walls. The Marine One helicopter could land on one side of the house, its rotor blades kicking up gale-force winds and slamming tree branches, but inside the residence we'd hear nothing. I usually figured out that Barack had arrived home from a trip not by the sound of his helicopter but rather by the smell of its fuel, which somehow managed to permeate.

Oftentimes, I was happy to withdraw into the protected hush of the residence at the end of a long day. But this night felt different, as paradoxical as the country itself. After a day spent grieving in Charleston, I was looking at a giant party starting just outside my window. Hundreds of people were staring up at our house. I wanted to see it the way they did. I found myself suddenly desperate to join the celebration.

I stuck my head into the Treaty Room. "You want to go out and look at the lights?" I asked Barack. "There are tons of people out there."

He laughed. "You know I can't do tons of people."

Sasha was in her room, engrossed in her iPad. "You want to go see the rainbow lights with me?" I asked.

"Nope."

This left Malia, who surprised me a little by immediately signing on. I'd found my wing-woman. We were going on an adventure—outside, where people were gathered—and we weren't going to ask anyone's permission.

The normal protocol was that we checked in with the Secret Service agents posted by the elevator anytime we wanted to leave the residence, whether it was to go downstairs to watch a movie or to take the dogs out for a walk, but not tonight. Malia and I just busted past the agents on duty, neither one of us making eye contact. We bypassed the elevator, moving quickly down a cramped stairwell. I could hear dress shoes clicking down the stairs behind us, the agents trying to keep up. Malia gave me a devilish smirk. She wasn't used to my flouting the rules.

Reaching the State Floor, we made our way toward the tall set of doors leading to the North Portico, when we heard a voice.

"Hello, ma'am! Can I help you?" It was Claire Faulkner, the usher on night duty. She was a friendly, soft-spoken brunette who I assumed had been tipped off by the agents whispering into their wrist pieces behind us.

I looked over my shoulder at her without breaking my stride. "Oh, we're just going outside," I said, "to see the lights."

Claire's eyebrows lifted. We paid her no heed. Arriving at the door, I grabbed its thick golden handle and pulled. But the door wouldn't budge. Nine months earlier, an intruder wielding a knife had somehow managed to jump a fence and barge through this same door, running through the State Floor before being tackled by a Secret Service officer. In response, security began locking the door.

I turned to the group behind us, which had grown to include a uniformed Secret Service officer in a white shirt and a black tie. "How do you open this thing?" I said, to no one in particular. "There's got to be a key."

"Ma'am?" Claire said. "I'm not sure that's the door you want. Every network news camera is aimed at the north side of the White House right now."

She did have a point. My hair was a mess and I was in flip-flops, shorts, and a T-shirt. Not exactly dressed for a public appearance.

"Okay," I said. "But can't we get out there without being seen?"

Malia and I were now on a crusade. We weren't going to relinquish our goal. We were going to get ourselves outside.

Someone then suggested trying one of the out-of-the-way loading doors on the ground floor, where trucks came to deliver food and office supplies. Our band began moving that way. Malia hooked her arm with mine. We were giddy now.

"We're getting out!" I said.

"Yeah we are!" she said.

We made our way down a marble staircase and over red carpets, around the busts of George Washington and Benjamin Franklin and past the kitchen until suddenly we were outdoors. The humid summer air hit our faces. I could see fireflies blinking on the lawn. And there it was, the hum of the public, people whooping and celebrating outside the iron gates. It had taken us ten minutes to get out of our own home, but we'd done it. We were outside, standing on a patch of lawn off to one side, out of sight of the public but with a beautiful, close-up view of the White House, lit up in pride.

Malia and I leaned into each other, happy to have found our way there.

A S HAPPENS IN politics, new winds were already beginning to gather and blow. By the fall of 2015, the next presidential campaign was in full swing. The Republican side was crowded, including governors like John Kasich and Chris Christie and senators like Ted Cruz and Marco Rubio, plus more than a dozen others. Meanwhile, Democrats were quickly narrowing themselves toward what would become a choice between Hillary Clinton and Bernie Sanders, the liberal, longtime independent senator from Vermont.

Donald Trump had announced his candidacy early in the summer, standing inside Trump Tower in Manhattan and railing on Mexican immigrants—"rapists," he called them—as well as the "losers" he said were running the country. I figured he was just grandstanding, sucking up the media's attention because he could. Nothing in how he conducted himself suggested that he was serious about wanting to govern.

I was following the campaign, but not as intently as in years past. Instead, I'd been busy working on my fourth initiative as First Lady, called

Let Girls Learn, which Barack and I had launched together back in the spring. It was an ambitious, government-wide effort focused on helping adolescent girls around the world obtain better access to education. Over the course of nearly seven years now as First Lady, I'd been struck again and again by both the promise and the vulnerability of young women in our world—from the immigrant girls I'd met at the Elizabeth Garrett Anderson School to Malala Yousafzai, the Pakistani teenager who'd been brutally attacked by the Taliban and who came to the White House to speak with me, Barack, and Malia about her advocacy on behalf of girls' education. I was horrified when, about six months after Malala's visit, 276 Nigerian schoolgirls were kidnapped by the extremist group Boko Haram, seemingly intent on causing other Nigerian families to fear sending their daughters to school. It had prompted me, for the first and only time during the presidency, to sub for Barack during his weekly address to the nation, speaking emotionally about how we needed to work harder at protecting and encouraging girls worldwide.

I felt it all personally. Education had been the primary instrument of change in my own life, my lever upward in the world. I was appalled that many girls—more than 98 million worldwide, in fact, according to UNESCO statistics—didn't have access to it. Some girls weren't able to attend school because their families needed them to work. Sometimes the nearest school was far away or too expensive, or the risk of being assaulted while getting there was too great. In many cases, suffocating gender norms and economic forces combined to keep girls uneducated— effectively locking them out of future opportunities. There seemed to be an idea—astonishingly prevalent in certain parts of the world—that it was simply not worth it to put a girl in school, even as studies consistently showed that educating girls and women and allowing them to enter the workforce did nothing but boost a country's GDP.

Barack and I were committed to changing the perceptions about what made a young woman valuable to a society. He managed to leverage hundreds of millions of dollars in resources from across his administration, through USAID and the Peace Corps, and also through the Departments of State, Labor, and Agriculture. The two of us together lobbied other countries' governments to help fund programming for girls' education while encouraging private companies and think tanks to commit to the cause.

At this point, too, I knew how to make a little noise for a cause. It was natural, I understood, for Americans to feel disconnected from the struggles of people in faraway countries, so I tried to bring it home, calling up celebrities like Stephen Colbert to lend their star power at events and on social media. I'd enlist the help of Janelle Monáe, Zendaya, Kelly Clarkson, and other talents to release a catchy pop song written by Diane Warren called "This Is for My Girls," the proceeds of which would go toward funding girls' education globally.

And lastly, I'd do something that was a little terrifying for me, which was to sing, making an appearance on the late-night host James Corden's hilarious "Carpool Karaoke" series, the two of us circling the South Lawn in a black SUV. We belted out "Signed, Sealed, Delivered I'm Yours," "Single Ladies," and finally—the reason I'd signed on to do it in the first place—"This Is for My Girls," with a guest appearance from Missy Elliott, who slipped into the backseat and rapped along with us. I'd practiced diligently for my karaoke session for weeks, memorizing every beat to every song. The goal was to have it look fun and light, but behind it, as always, was work and a larger purpose—to keep connecting people with the issue. My segment with James had forty-five million views on YouTube within the first three months, making every bit of the effort worth it.

TOWARD THE END OF 2015, Barack, the girls, and I flew to Hawaii to spend Christmas as we always did, renting a big house with wide windows that looked out on the beach, joined by our usual group of family friends. As we had for the last six years, we took time on Christmas Day to visit with service members and their families at a nearby Marine Corps base. And as it had been right through, for Barack the vacation was only a partial vacation—a just-barely vacation, really. He fielded phone calls, sat for daily briefings, and was consulting with a skeleton staff of advisers, aides, and speechwriters who were all staying at a hotel close by. It made me wonder whether he'd remember how to fully relax when the time actually came, whether either one of us would find a way to let down when this was all over. What would it feel like, I wondered, when we finally got to go somewhere without the guy carrying the nuclear football?

Though I was allowing myself to dream a little, I still couldn't picture how any of this would end.

Returning to Washington to begin our final year in the White House, we knew the clock was ticking now in earnest. I began what would become a long series of "lasts." There was the last Governors' Ball, the last Easter Egg Roll, the last White House Correspondents' Dinner. Barack and I also made a last state visit to the United Kingdom together, which included a quick trip to see our friend the Queen.

Barack had always felt a special fondness for Queen Elizabeth, saying that she reminded him of his no-nonsense grandmother, Toot. I personally was awed by her efficiency, a skill clearly forged by necessity over a lifetime in the public eye. One day a few years earlier, Barack and I had stood, hosting a receiving line together with her and Prince Philip. I'd watched, bemused, as the Queen managed to whisk people speedily past with economic, friendly hellos that left no room for follow-up conversation, while Barack projected an amiable looseness, almost inviting chitchat and then ponderously answering people's questions, thereby messing up the flow of the line. All these years after meeting the guy, I was still trying to get him to hurry up.

One afternoon in April 2016, the two of us took a helicopter from the American ambassador's residence in London to Windsor Castle in the countryside west of the city. Our advance team instructed us that the Queen and Prince Philip were planning to meet us when we landed and then personally drive us back to the castle for lunch. As was always the case, we were briefed on the protocol ahead of time: We'd greet the royals formally before getting into their vehicle to make the short drive. I'd sit in the front next to ninety-four-year-old Prince Philip, who would drive, and Barack would sit next to the Queen in the backseat.

It would be the first time in more than eight years that the two of us had been driven by anyone other than a Secret Service agent, or ridden in a car together without agents. This seemed to matter to our security teams, the same way the protocol mattered to the advance teams, who fretted endlessly over our movements and interactions, making sure that every last little thing looked right and went smoothly.

After we'd touched down in a field on the palace grounds and said our hellos, however, the Queen abruptly threw a wrench into everything by gesturing for me to join her in the backseat of the Range Rover. I froze, trying to remember if anyone had prepped me for this scenario, whether it was more polite to go along with it or to insist that Barack take his proper seat by her side.

The Queen immediately picked up on my hesitation. And was having none of it.

"Did they give you some rule about this?" she said, dismissing all the fuss with a wave of her hand. "That's rubbish. Sit wherever you want."

F OR ME, GIVING commencement speeches was an important, almost sacred springtime ritual. Each year I delivered several of them, choosing a mix of high school and college ceremonies, focusing on the sorts of schools that normally didn't land high-profile speakers. (Princeton and Harvard, I'm sorry, but you're fine without me.) In 2015, I'd gone back to the South Side of Chicago to speak at the graduation at King College Prep, the high school from which Hadiya Pendleton would have graduated had she lived long enough. Her spirit was commemorated at the ceremony by an empty chair, which her classmates had decorated with sunflowers and purple fabric.

For my final round of commencements as First Lady, I spoke at Jackson State University in Mississippi, another historically Black school, using the opportunity to talk about striving for excellence. I spoke at the City College of New York, emphasizing the value of diversity and immigration. And on May 26, which happened to be the day Donald Trump clinched the Republican nomination for president, I was in New Mexico, speaking to a class of Native American students who were graduating from a small residential high school, nearly all of them headed next to college. The deeper I got into the experience of being First Lady, the more emboldened I felt to speak honestly and directly about what it meant to be marginalized by race and gender. My intention was to give younger people a context for the hate surfacing in the news and in political discourse and to give them a reason to hope.

I tried to communicate the one message about myself and my station in the world that I felt might really mean something. Which was that I knew invisibility. I'd lived invisibility. I came from a history of invisibility. I liked to mention that I was the great-great-granddaughter of a slave named Jim Robinson, who was probably buried in an unmarked grave somewhere on a South Carolina plantation. And in standing at a lectern in front of students who were thinking about the future, I offered testament to the idea that it was possible, at least in some ways, to overcome invisibility.

The last commencement I attended that spring was personal—Malia's graduation from Sidwell Friends, held on a warm day in June. Our close friend Elizabeth Alexander, the poet who'd written a poem for Barack's first inauguration, spoke to the class, which meant that Barack and I got to sit back and just feel. I was proud of Malia, who was soon to head off to Europe to travel for a few weeks with friends. After taking a gap year, she'd enroll at Harvard. I was proud of Sasha, who turned fifteen that same day and was counting down the hours to the Beyoncé concert she was going to in lieu of a birthday party. She would go on to spend much of the summer on Martha's Vineyard, living with family friends until Barack and I arrived for vacation. She'd make new friends and land her first job, working at a snack bar. I was proud, too, of my mother, who sat nearby in the sunshine, wearing a black dress and heels, having managed to live in the White House and travel the world with us while staying utterly and completely herself.

I was proud of all of us, for almost being done.

Barack sat next to me in a folding chair. I could see the tears brimming behind his sunglasses as he watched Malia cross the stage to pick up her diploma. He was tired, I knew. Three days earlier, he'd given a eulogy for a friend from law school who'd worked for him in the White

House. Two days later, an extremist would open fire inside a gay night-club in Orlando, Florida, killing forty-nine people and wounding fifty-three more. The gravity of his job never let up.

He was a good father, dialed in and consistent in ways his own father had never been, but there were also things he'd sacrificed along the way. He'd entered into parenthood as a politician. His constituents and their needs had been with us all along.

It had to hurt a little bit, realizing he was so close to having more free-dom and more time, just as our daughters were beginning to step away.

But we had to let them go. The future was theirs, just as it should be.

IN LATE JULY, I flew through a violent thunderstorm, the plane dip-ping and diving on its approach to Philadelphia, where I was going to speak for the last time at a Democratic convention. It was perhaps the worst turbulence I'd ever experienced, and while Caroline Adler Mo-rales, my very pregnant communications director, worried that the stress of it would put her into labor and Melissa—a skittish flier under normal circumstances—sat shrieking in her seat, all I could think was *Just get me down in time to practice my speech.* Though I'd long grown comfortable on the biggest stages, I still found huge comfort in preparation.

Back in 2008, during Barack's first run for president, I'd rehearsed and re-rehearsed my convention speech until I could place the commas in my sleep, in part because I'd never given a speech on live television like that, and also because the personal stakes felt so high. I was stepping onto the stage after having been demonized as an angry Black woman who didn't love her country. My speech that night gave me a chance to humanize myself, explaining who I was in my own voice, slaying the caricatures and stereotypes with my own words. Four years later, at the convention in Charlotte, North Carolina, I'd spoken earnestly about what I'd seen in Barack during his first term—how he was still the same principled man I'd married, how I'd realized that "being president doesn't change who you are; it reveals who you are."

This time, I was stumping for Hillary Clinton, Barack's opponent in the brutal 2008 primary who'd gone on to become his loyal and effective secretary of state. I'd never feel as passionately about another candidate as I did about my own husband, which made campaigning for others sometimes difficult for me. I maintained a code for myself, though, when it came to speaking publicly about anything or anyone in the political sphere: I said only what I absolutely believed and what I absolutely felt.

We landed in Philadelphia and I rushed to the convention center, finding just enough time to change clothes and run through my speech twice. Then I stepped out and spoke my truth. I talked about the fears I'd had early on about raising our daughters in the White House and how proud I was of the intelligent young women they'd become. I said that I trusted Hillary because she understood the demands of the presidency and had the temperament to lead, because she was as qualified as any nominee in history. And I acknowledged the stark choice now being put before the country.

Since childhood, I'd believed it was important to speak out against bullies while also not stooping to their level. And to be clear, we were now up against a bully, a man who among other things demeaned minorities and expressed contempt for prisoners of war, challenging the dignity of our country with practically his every utterance. I wanted Americans to understand that words matter—that the hateful language they heard coming from their TVs did not reflect the true spirit of our country and that we could vote against it. It was dignity I wanted to make an appeal for—the idea that as a nation we might hold on to the core thing that had sustained my family, going back generations. Dignity had always gotten us through. It was a choice, and not always the easy one, but the people I respected most in life made it again and again, every single day. There was a motto Barack and I tried to live by, and I offered it that night from the stage: *When they go low, we go high.*

Two months later, just weeks before the election, a tape would surface of Donald Trump in an unguarded moment, bragging to a TV host in 2005 about sexually assaulting women, using language so lewd and vulgar that it put media outlets in a quandary about how to quote it without violating the established standards of decency. In the end, the standards of decency were simply lowered in order to make room for the candidate's voice.

When I heard it, I could hardly believe it. And then again, there was something painfully familiar in the menace and male jocularity of that tape. *I can hurt you and get away with it.* It was an expression of hatred that had generally been kept out of polite company, but still lived in the marrow of our supposedly enlightened society—alive and accepted enough that someone like Donald Trump could afford to be cavalier about it. Every woman I know recognized it. Every person who's ever been made to feel "other" recognized it. It was precisely what so many of us hoped our own children would never need to experience, and yet probably would. Dominance, even the threat of it, is a form of dehumanization. It's the ugliest kind of power.

My body buzzed with fury after hearing that tape. I was scheduled to speak at a campaign rally for Hillary the following week, and rather than delivering a straightforward endorsement of her capabilities, I felt compelled to try to address Trump's words directly—to counter his voice with my own.

I worked on my remarks while sitting in a hospital room at Walter Reed, where my mother was having back surgery, my thoughts flowing fast. I'd been mocked and threatened many times now, cut down for being Black, female, and vocal. I'd felt the derision directed at my body, the literal space I occupied in the world. I'd watched Donald Trump stalk Hillary Clinton during a debate, following her around as she spoke, standing too close, trying to diminish her presence with his. *I can hurt you and get away with it.* Women endure entire lifetimes of these indignities—in the form of catcalls, groping, assault, oppression. These things injure us. They sap our strength. Some of the cuts are so small they're barely visible. Others are huge and gaping, leaving scars that never heal. Either way, they accumulate. We carry them everywhere, to and from school and work, at home while raising our children, at our places of worship, anytime we try to advance.

For me, Trump's comments were another blow. I couldn't let his message stand. Working with Sarah Hurwitz, the deft speechwriter who'd been with me since 2008, I channeled my fury into words, and then—after my mother had recovered from surgery—I delivered them one October day in Manchester, New Hampshire. Speaking to a high-energy crowd, I made my feelings clear. "This is not normal," I said. "This is not politics as usual. This is disgraceful. It is intolerable." I articulated my rage and my fear, along with my faith that with this election Americans understood the true nature of what they were choosing between. I put my whole heart into giving that speech.

I then flew back to Washington, praying I'd been heard.

A S FALL CONTINUED, Barack and I began making plans for our move to a new house in January, having decided to stay in Washington so that Sasha could finish high school at Sidwell. Malia, meanwhile, was in South America on a gap-year adventure, feeling the freedom of being as far away from the political intensity as she could. I implored my staff in the East Wing to finish strong, even as they needed to think about finding new jobs, even as the battle between Hillary Clinton and Donald Trump grew more intense and distracting by the day.

On November 7, 2016, the evening before the election, Barack and I made a quick trip to Philadelphia to join Hillary and her family at a final rally before an enormous crowd on Independence Mall. The mood was positive, expectant. I took heart in the optimism Hillary projected that night, and in the many polls that showed her with a comfortable lead. I took heart in what I thought I understood about the qualities Americans would and wouldn't tolerate in a leader. I presumed nothing, but I felt good about the odds.

For the first time in many years, Barack and I had no role to play on election night. There was no hotel suite reserved for the wait; there were no trays of canapés laid out, no television blaring from any corner. There was no hair, makeup, or wardrobe to be tended to, no marshaling of our children, no late-night speech being prepped for delivery. We had nothing to do, and it thrilled us. This was the beginning of our stepping back, a first taste of what the future might be like. We were invested, of course, but the moment ahead wasn't ours. It was merely ours to witness.

Knowing it would be a while before results came in, we invited Valerie over to watch a movie in the White House theater.

I can't remember a thing about the film that night—not its title, not even its genre. Really, we were just passing time in the dark. My mind kept turning over the reality that Barack's term as president was almost finished. What lay ahead most immediately were good-byes—dozens and dozens of them, all emotional, as the staff we loved and appreciated so much would begin to rotate out of the White House. Our goal was to do what George and Laura Bush had done for us, making the transition of power as smooth as possible. Already, our teams were beginning to prepare briefing books and contact lists for their successors. Before they left, many East Wing staffers would leave handwritten notes on their desks, giving a friendly welcome and a standing offer of help to the next person coming along.

We were still immersed in the business of every day, but we'd also started to plan in earnest for what lay ahead. Barack and I were excited to stay in Washington but would build a legacy on the South Side of Chicago, which would become home to the Obama Presidential Center. We planned to launch a foundation as well, one whose mission would be to encourage and embolden a new generation of leaders. The two of us had many goals for the future, but the biggest involved creating more space and support for young people and their ideas. I also knew that we needed a break: I'd started scouting for a private place where we could go to decompress for a few days in January, immediately after the new president got sworn in.

We just needed the new president.

As the movie wrapped up and the lights came on, Barack's cell phone buzzed. I saw him glance at it and then look again, his brow furrowing just slightly.

"Huh," he said. "Results in Florida are looking kind of strange."

There was no alarm in his voice, just a tiny seed of awareness, a hot ember glowing suddenly in the grass. The phone buzzed again. My heart started to tick faster. I knew the updates were coming from David Simas, Barack's political adviser, who was monitoring returns from the West

Wing and who understood the precise county-by-county algebra of the electoral map. If something cataclysmic was going to happen, Simas would spot it early.

I watched my husband's face closely, not sure I was ready to hear what he was going to say. Whatever it was, it didn't look good. I felt something leaden take hold in my stomach just then, my anxiety hardening into dread. As Barack and Valerie started to discuss the early results, I announced that I was going upstairs. I walked to the elevator, hoping to do only one thing, which was to block it all out and go to sleep. I understood what was probably happening, but I wasn't ready to face it.

As I slept, the news was confirmed: American voters had elected Donald Trump to succeed Barack as the next president of the United States.

I wanted to not know that fact for as long as I possibly could.

The next day, I woke to a wet and dreary morning. A gray sky hung over Washington. I couldn't help but interpret it as funereal. Time seemed to crawl. Sasha went off to school, quietly working through her disbelief. Malia called from Bolivia, sounding deeply rattled. I told both our girls that I loved them and that things would be okay. I kept trying to tell myself the same thing.

In the end, Hillary Clinton won nearly three million more votes than her opponent, but Trump had captured the Electoral College thanks to fewer than eighty thousand votes spread across Pennsylvania, Wisconsin, and Michigan. I am not a political person, so I'm not going to attempt to offer an analysis of the results. I won't try to speculate about who was responsible or what was unfair. I just wish more people had turned out to vote. And I will always wonder about what led so many women, in particular, to reject an exceptionally qualified female candidate and instead choose a misogynist as their president. But the result was now ours to live with.

Barack had stayed up most of the night tracking the data, and as had happened so many times before, he was called upon to step forward as a symbol of steadiness to help the nation process its shock. I didn't envy him the task. He gave a morning pep talk to his staff in the Oval Office and then, around noon, delivered a set of sober but reassuring remarks to the nation from the Rose Garden, calling—as he always did—for unity and dignity, asking Americans to respect one another as well as the institutions built by our democracy.

That afternoon, I sat in my East Wing office with my entire staff, all of us crammed into the room on couches and desk chairs that had been pulled in from other rooms. My team was made up largely of women and minorities, including several who came from immigrant families. Many were in tears, feeling that their every vulnerability was now exposed. They'd poured themselves into their jobs because they believed thoroughly in the causes they were furthering. I tried to tell them at every turn that they should be proud of who they are, that their work mattered, and that one election couldn't wipe away eight years of change.

Everything was not lost. This was the message we needed to carry forward. It's what I truly believed. It wasn't ideal, but it was our reality— the world as it is. We needed now to be resolute, to keep our feet pointed in the direction of progress.

W E WERE AT the end now, truly. I found myself caught between looking back and looking forward, mulling over one question in particular: What lasts?

We were the forty-fourth First Family and only the eleventh family to spend two full terms in the White House. We were, and would always be, the first Black one. I hoped that when future parents brought their children to visit, the way I'd brought Malia and Sasha when their father was a senator, they'd be able to point out some reminder of our family's time here. I thought it was important to register our presence within the larger history of the place.

Not every president commissioned an official china setting, for instance, but I made sure we did. During Barack's second term, we also chose to redecorate the Old Family Dining Room, situated just off the State Dining Room, freshening it up with a modern look and opening it to the public for the first time. On the room's north wall, we'd hung a stunning yellow, red, and blue abstract painting by Alma Thomas—

Resurrection—which became the first work of art by a Black woman to be added to the White House's permanent collection.

The most enduring mark, however, lay outside the walls. The garden had persisted through seven and a half years now, producing roughly two thousand pounds of food annually. It had survived heavy snows, sheets of rain, and damaging hail. When high winds had toppled the forty-two-foot-high National Christmas Tree a few years earlier, the garden had survived intact. Before I left the White House, I wanted to give it even more permanence. We expanded its footprint to twenty-eight hundred square feet, more than double its original size. We added stone pathways and wooden benches, plus a welcoming arbor made of wood sourced from the estates of Presidents Jefferson, Madison, and Monroe and the childhood home of Dr. Martin Luther King Jr. And then, one fall afternoon, I set out across the South Lawn to officially dedicate the garden for posterity.

Joining me that day were supporters and advocates who'd helped with our nutrition and childhood health efforts over the years, as well as a pair of students from the original class of fifth graders at Bancroft Elementary School, who were now practically adults. Most of my staff was there, including Sam Kass, who'd left the White House in 2014 but had returned for the occasion.

Looking out at the crowd in the garden, I was emotional. I felt gratitude for all the people on my team who'd given everything to the work, sorting through handwritten letters, fact-checking my speeches, hopping cross-country flights to prepare for our events. I'd seen many of them take on more responsibility and blossom both professionally and personally, even under the glare of the harshest lights. The burdens of being "the first" didn't fall only on our family's shoulders. For eight years, these optimistic young people—and a few seasoned professionals—had had our backs. Melissa, who had been my very first campaign hire nearly a decade ago and someone I will count on as a close friend for life, remained with me in the East Wing through the end of the term, as did Tina, my remarkable chief of staff. Kristen Jarvis had been replaced by Chynna Clayton, a hardworking young woman from Miami who quickly became another big sister to our girls and was central to keeping my life running smoothly.

I considered all these people, current and former staff, to be family. And I was so proud of what we'd done.

For every video that swiftly saturated the internet—I'd mom-danced with Jimmy Fallon, Nerf-dunked on LeBron James, and college-rapped with Jay Pharoah—we'd focused ourselves on doing more than trending for a few hours on Twitter. And we had results. Forty-five million kids were eating healthier breakfasts and lunches; eleven million students were getting sixty minutes of physical activity every day through our Let's Move! Active Schools program. Children overall were eating more whole grains and produce. The era of supersized fast food was coming to a close.

Through my work with Jill Biden on Joining Forces, we'd helped persuade businesses to hire or train more than 1.5 million veterans and military spouses. Following through on one of the very first concerns I'd heard on the campaign trail, we'd gotten all fifty states to collaborate on professional licensing agreements, which would help keep military spouses' careers from stalling every time they moved.

On education, Barack and I had leveraged billions of dollars to help girls around the world get the schooling they deserve. More than twenty-eight hundred Peace Corps volunteers were now trained to implement programs for girls internationally. And in the United States, my team and I had helped more young people sign up for federal student aid, supported school counselors, and elevated College Signing Day to a national level.

Barack, meanwhile, had managed to reverse the most serious economic crisis since the Great Depression. He'd helped to broker the Paris Agreement on climate change, brought tens of thousands of troops home from Iraq and Afghanistan, and led the effort to effectively shut down Iran's nuclear program. Twenty million more people had the security of health insurance. And we'd managed two terms in office without a major scandal. We had held ourselves and the people who worked with us to the highest standards of ethics and decency, and we'd made it all the way through.

For us, some changes were harder to measure but felt just as important. Six months before the garden dedication, Lin-Manuel Miranda, the young composer I'd met at one of our first arts events, returned to the White House. His hip-hop riff on Alexander Hamilton had exploded into a Broadway sensation, and with it he'd become a global superstar. *Hamilton* was a musical celebration of America's history and diversity, recasting our understanding of the roles minorities play in our national story, highlighting the importance of women who'd long been overshadowed by powerful men. I'd seen it off-Broadway and loved it so much that I went to see it again when it hit the big stage. It was catchy and funny, heart swelling and heartbreaking—the best piece of art in any form that I'd ever encountered.

Lin-Manuel brought most of his cast along with him to Washington, a talented multiracial ensemble. The performers spent their afternoon with young people who'd come from local high schools—budding playwrights, dancers, and rappers kicking around the White House, writing lyrics and dropping beats with their heroes. In the late afternoon, we all came together for a performance in the East Room. Barack and I sat in the front row, surrounded by young people of all different races and backgrounds, the two of us awash in emotion as Christopher Jackson and Lin-Manuel sang the ballad "One Last Time" as their final number. Here were two artists, one Black and one Puerto Rican, standing beneath a 115-year-old chandelier, bracketed by towering antique portraits of George and Martha Washington, singing about feeling "at home in this nation we've made." The power and truth of that moment stays with me to this day.

Hamilton touched me because it reflected the kind of history I'd lived myself. It told a story about America that allowed the diversity in. I thought about this afterward: So many of us go through life with our stories hidden, feeling ashamed or afraid when our whole truth doesn't live up to some established ideal. We grow up with messages that tell us that there's only one way to be American—that if our skin is dark or our hips are wide, if we don't experience love in a particular way, if we speak another language or come from another country, then we don't belong. That is, until someone dares to start telling that story differently.

I grew up with a disabled dad in a too-small house with not much money in a starting-to-fail neighborhood, and I also grew up surrounded by love and music in a diverse city in a country where an education can take you far. I had nothing or I had everything. It depends on which way you want to tell it.

As we moved toward the end of Barack's presidency, I thought about America this same way. I loved my country for all the ways its story could be told. For almost a decade, I'd been privileged to move through it, experiencing its bracing contradictions and bitter conflicts, its pain and persistent idealism, and above all else its resilience. My view was unusual, perhaps, but I think what I experienced during those years is what many did—a sense of progress, the comfort of compassion, the joy of watching the unsung and invisible find some light. A glimmer of the world as it could be. This was our bid for permanence: a rising generation that understood what was possible—and that even more was possible for them. Whatever was coming next, this was a story we could own.

Epilogue

BARACK AND I WALKED OUT OF THE WHITE HOUSE
for the last time on January 20, 2017, accompanying Donald and
Melania Trump to the inauguration ceremony. That day, I was feeling
everything all at once—tired, proud, distraught, eager. Mostly, though, I
was trying just to hold myself together, knowing we had television cameras following our every move. Barack and I were determined to make
the transition with grace and dignity, to finish our eight years with
both our ideals and our composure intact. We were down now to the
final hour.

That morning, Barack had made a last visit to the Oval Office, leaving a handwritten note for his successor. We'd also gathered on the State
Floor to say good-bye to the White House's permanent staff—the butlers, ushers, chefs, housekeepers, florists, and others who'd looked after
us with friendship and professionalism and would now extend those
same courtesies to the family due to move in later that day. These fare-
wells were particularly rough for Sasha and Malia, since many of these
were people they'd seen nearly every day for half their lives. I'd hugged
everyone and tried not to cry when they presented us with a parting gift
of two United States flags—the one that had flown on the first day of

Barack's presidency and the one that had flown on his last day in office, symbolic bookends to our family's experience.

Sitting on the inaugural stage in front of the U.S. Capitol for the third time, I worked to contain my emotions. The vibrant diversity of the two previous inaugurations was gone, replaced by what felt like a dispiriting uniformity, the kind of overwhelmingly white and male tableau I'd encountered so many times in my life—especially in the more privileged spaces, the various corridors of power I'd somehow found my way into since leaving my childhood home. What I knew from working in professional environments—from recruiting new lawyers for Sidley & Austin to hiring staff at the White House—is that sameness breeds more sameness, until you make a thoughtful effort to counteract it.

Looking around at the three hundred or so people sitting on the stage that morning, the esteemed guests of the incoming president, it felt apparent to me that in the new White House, this effort wasn't likely to be made. Someone from Barack's administration might have said that the optics there were bad—that what the public saw didn't reflect the president's reality or ideals. But in this case, maybe it did. Realizing it, I made my own optic adjustment: I stopped even trying to smile.

A TRANSITION IS EXACTLY THAT—a passage to something new. A hand goes on a Bible; an oath gets repeated. One president's furniture gets carried out while another's comes in. Closets are emptied and refilled. Just like that, there are new heads on new pillows—new temperaments, new dreams. And when your term is up, when you leave the White House on that very last day, you're left in many ways to find yourself all over again.

I am now at a new beginning, in a new phase of life. For the first time in many years, I'm unhooked from any obligation as a political spouse, unencumbered by other people's expectations. I have two nearly grown daughters who need me less than they once did. I have a husband who no longer carries the weight of the nation on his shoulders. The responsibilities I've felt—to Sasha and Malia, to Barack, to my career and my country—have shifted in ways that allow me to think differently about what comes next. I've had more time to reflect, to simply be myself. At fifty-four, I am still in progress, and I hope that I always will be.

For me, becoming isn't about arriving somewhere or achieving a certain aim. I see it instead as forward motion, a means of evolving, a way to reach continuously toward a better self. The journey doesn't end. I became a mother, but I still have a lot to learn from and give to my children. I became a wife, but I continue to adapt to and be humbled by what it means to truly love and make a life with another person. I have become, by certain measures, a person of power, and yet there are moments still when I feel insecure or unheard.

It's all a process, steps along a path. Becoming requires equal parts patience and rigor. Becoming is never giving up on the idea that there's more growing to be done.

Because people often ask, I'll say it here directly: I have no intention of running for office, ever. I've never been a fan of politics, and my experience over the last ten years has done little to change that. I continue to be put off by the nastiness—the tribal segregation of red and blue, this idea that we're supposed to choose one side and stick to it, unable to listen and compromise, or sometimes even to be civil. I do believe that at its best, politics can be a means for positive change, but this arena is just not for me.

That isn't to say I don't care deeply about the future of our country. Since Barack left office, I've read news stories that turn my stomach. I've lain awake at night, fuming over what's come to pass. It's been distressing to see how the behavior and the political agenda of the current president have caused many Americans to doubt themselves and to doubt and fear one another. It's been hard to watch as carefully built, compassionate policies have been rolled back, as we've alienated some of our closest allies and left vulnerable members of our society exposed and dehumanized. I sometimes wonder where the bottom might be.

What I won't allow myself to do, though, is to become cynical. In my most worried moments, I take a breath and remind myself of the dignity and decency I've seen in people throughout my life, the many obstacles that have already been overcome. I hope others will do the same. We all play a role in this democracy. We need to remember the power of every vote. I continue, too, to keep myself connected to a force that's larger and more potent than any one election, or leader, or news story—and that's optimism. For me, this is a form of faith, an antidote to fear. Optimism reigned in my family's little apartment on Euclid Avenue. I saw it in my father, in the way he moved around as if nothing were wrong with his body, as if the disease that would someday take his life just didn't exist. I saw it in my mother's stubborn belief in our neighborhood, her decision to stay rooted even as fear led many of her neighbors to pack up and move. It's the thing that first drew me to Barack when he turned up in my office at Sidley, wearing a hopeful grin. Later, it helped me overcome my doubts and vulnerabilities enough to trust that if I allowed my family to live an extremely public life, we'd manage to stay safe and also happy.

And it helps me now. As First Lady, I saw optimism in surprising places. It was there in the wounded warrior at Walter Reed who pushed back against pity by posting a note on his door, reminding everyone that he was both tough and hopeful. It lived in Cleopatra Cowley-Pendleton, who channeled some part of her grief over losing her daughter into fighting for better gun laws. It was there in the social worker at Harper High School who made a point of shouting out her love and appreciation for students each time she passed them in the hall. And it's there, always, embedded in the hearts of children. Kids wake up each day believing in the goodness of things, in the magic of what might be. They're uncynical, believers at their core. We owe it to them to stay strong and keep working to create a more fair and humane world. For them, we need to remain both tough and hopeful, to acknowledge that there's more growing to be done.

There are portraits of me and Barack now hanging in the National Portrait Gallery in Washington, a fact that humbles us both. I doubt that anyone looking at our two childhoods, our circumstances, would ever have predicted we'd land in those halls. The paintings are lovely, but what matters most is that they're there for young people to see—that our faces help dismantle the perception that in order to be enshrined in history, you have to look a certain way. If we belong, then so, too, can many others.

I'm an ordinary person who found herself on an extraordinary journey. In sharing my story, I hope to help create space for other stories and other voices, to widen the pathway for who belongs and why. I've been lucky enough to get to walk into stone castles, urban classrooms, and Iowa kitchens, just trying to be myself, just trying to connect. For every door that's been opened to me, I've tried to open my door to others. And here is what I have to say, finally: Let's invite one another in. Maybe then we can begin to fear less, to make fewer wrong assumptions, to let go of the biases and stereotypes that unnecessarily divide us. Maybe we can better embrace the ways we are the same. It's not about being perfect. It's not about where you get yourself in the end. There's power in allowing yourself to be known and heard, in owning your unique story, in using your authentic voice. And there's grace in being willing to know and hear others. This, for me, is how we become.

Note to Self

Dear Miche,

There you are, in your jean jacket and braids, a long way from that little apartment on the South Side of Chicago. You're at one of the finest universities in the world. You're smiling, and you should be, you worked hard for this. But even now, after you reached your goal, you're still not quite sure if you belong and can't get one question out of your mind: "Am I good enough?" There aren't many kids here who look like you. Some arrived on campus in limousines. One of your classmates is a bona fide movie star, another is rumored to be a real-life princess. Meanwhile, you got dropped off by your father in the family sedan.

Years from now, you'll learn that your parents had to take out new credit cards to pay your tuition. But Michelle, what you'll come to realize one day is that you're seeing only what you lack and not everything that your story has given you.

You grew up surrounded by soul and jazz and a deep, anchoring love. Your parents taught you to keep your word and treat people with respect. They encouraged you to develop your own voice and use it. Those lessons are more valuable than anything material. They'll come in handy in the future, in settings I won't spoil for you right now.

Your father's final lesson will come far too soon. He'll teach you that life is fleeting. So laugh with him until your side hurts. Savor the grip of his hugs, the softness in his eyes. A day will come when those memories are all you'll have. His absence will hit you like a rock. It'll cause you to rethink everything about yourself and your future. But don't worry, you won't have to go through any of this alone.

You'll open your heart to someone whose upbringing was nothing and everything like yours, all at the same time. He's driven by a hopeful set of ideals. He's grounded and kind and absolutely brilliant. And he's pretty good-looking, too. I thought you'd appreciate that.

His certainty about his path will feel like a challenge to yours. You'll learn that even the best relationships take work but that's okay, that's normal and it's what gives your partnership its strength.

Together, you'll be blessed with two perfect little girls who will fill you with so much joy you can barely process it. Yet you'll still struggle to find a balance between your family, your husband's rising career, and your own sense of self. Be patient. You'll get there. And just when you think you've done it, the four of you will be shot out of a cannon into the unknown.

Everything you've fought for so hard—stability, balance, confidence—will feel like it's at risk. You'll be attacked by people who've never met you and don't really care to. They'll try to harm you for their own gain. Don't stoop to their level, no matter how gratifying it might feel in the moment. Hold tight to those values your parents taught you.

Your family will make history, breaking barriers and filling out a more complete picture of the American story. You'll meet two popes and the Queen of England. People will fill stadiums to hear you speak.

It will be easy to think you're something special. Just remember that there are millions of people who grew up like you did and don't get this kind of spotlight. Reflect the light back on them.

There are so many people out there like you, Miche. Black girls and minorities of all kinds, working-class kids from big cities and small towns, people who doubt themselves, who are uncertain about whether they belong but have so much to offer the world. Share your story with them, the struggles and the triumphs and everything else. Show them that there's more beauty inside than they can see right now. That's how you'll answer that question that's following you around, the one that sometimes keeps you up at night.

You're more than enough, Miche. You always have been and you always will be. And I can't wait for you to see that.

Acknowledgments

As with everything I've done in my life, this memoir would not have been possible without the love and support of many people.

I would not be who I am today without the steady hand and unconditional love of my mother, Marian Shields Robinson. She has always been my rock, allowing me the freedom to be who I am, while never allowing my feet to get too far off the ground. Her boundless love for my girls, and her willingness to put our needs before her own, gave me the comfort and confidence to venture out into the world knowing they were safe and cherished at home.

My husband, Barack, my love, my partner of twenty-five years and the most lovingly committed father to our daughters, has been a life partner I could only have imagined. Our story is still unfolding, and I eagerly await the many adventures left to come. Thank you for your help and guidance with this book . . . for reading chapters carefully and patiently, and for knowing exactly when to give a gentle steer.

And to my big brother, Craig. Where do I begin? You have been my protector since the day I was born. You have made me laugh more than any other person on this earth. You are the best brother a sister could ask for, a loving and caring son, husband, and father. Thank you for all the hours you spent with my team peeling back the layers of our childhood. Some of my best memories of writing this book will be our time together, with Mom, sitting in the kitchen reliving so many old stories.

There is absolutely no way that I could have completed this book in my lifetime without an incredibly gifted team of collaborators whom I simply adore. When I first met Sara Corbett a little over a year ago, all I knew about her was that she was highly respected by my editor and knew very little about politics. Today I would trust her with my life not just because she has an amazing and curious mind but because she is a fundamentally kind and generous human being. I hope that this is just the beginning of a lasting friendship.

Tyler Lechtenberg has been a valuable member of the Obama world for more than a decade. He came into our lives as one of the hundreds of hopeful young Iowa field organizers and has been with us as a trusted adviser ever since. I have watched him grow into a powerful writer with an incredibly bright future.

Then there is my editor, Molly Stern, whose enthusiasm, energy, and passion instantly drew me to her. Molly kept me buoyed by her unwavering faith in my vision for this book. I am forever grateful to her and the entire Crown team, including Maya Mavjee, Tina Constable, David Drake, Emma Berry, and Chris Brand, who supported this effort from the beginning. Amanda D'Acierno, Lance Fitzgerald, Sally Franklin, Carisa Hays, Linnea Knollmueller, Matthew Martin, Donna Passannante, Elizabeth Rendfleisch, Anke Steinecke, Christine Tanigawa, and Dan Zitt all helped make *Becoming* possible.

I also want to thank Markus Dohle for putting all the resources of Penguin Random House behind this labor of love.

I would not be able to function successfully in this world as a mother, wife, friend, and professional without my team. Anyone who knows me well knows that Melissa Winter is the other half of my brain. Mel, thank you for being by my side through every step of this process. More importantly, thank you for loving me and my girls so fiercely. There is no me without you.

Melissa is the chief of staff of my personal team. This small but mighty group of smart, hardworking women are the folks who make sure I'm always on point: Caroline Adler Morales, Chynna Clayton, MacKenzie Smith, Samantha Tubman, and Alex May Sealey.

Bob Barnett and Deneen Howell of Williams and Connolly were invaluable guides to the publishing process, and I am grateful for their advice and support.

A special thanks to all those who helped bring this book to life in so many other ways: Pete Souza, Chuck Kennedy, Lawrence Jackson, Amanda Lucidon, Samantha Appleton, Kristin Jones, Chris Haugh, Arielle Vavasseur, Michele Norris, and Elizabeth Alexander.

In addition, I want to thank the incredibly resourceful Ashley Woolheater for her thorough research and Gillian Brassil for her meticulous fact-checking. Many of my former staff also helped confirm critical details and time lines throughout this process—there are too many to name, but I am grateful to each of them.

Thank you to all the amazing women in my life who have kept me lifted up. You all know who you are and what you mean to me—my girlfriends, my mentors, my "other daughters"—and a very special thanks to Mama Kaye. All of you have supported me during this writing process and have helped me become a better woman.

The hectic pace of my life as First Lady left little time for traditional journaling. That is why I am so grateful to my dear friend Verna Williams, who is currently serving as the interim dean and Nippert Professor of Law at the University of Cincinnati College of Law. I relied heavily on the roughly 1,100 pages of transcripts resulting from our biannual recorded conversations during our White House years.

I am so proud of all that we accomplished in the East Wing. I want to thank the many men and women who dedicated their lives to help our nation, the members of the Office of the First Lady—policy, scheduling, administration, communications, speechwriters, social office, correspondence. Thank you to the staffs, White House Fellows, and agency detailees who were responsible for building each of my initiatives—Let's Move!, Reach Higher, Let Girls Learn, and, of course, Joining Forces.

Joining Forces will always hold a special place in my heart because it gave me rare exposure to the strength and resilience of our outstanding military community. To all of the service members, veterans, and military families, thank you for your service and sacrifice on behalf of the country we all love. To Dr. Jill Biden and her entire team—it was truly a blessing and a joy to work side by side with you all on this very important initiative.

To all of the nutrition and education leaders and advocates, thank you for doing the thankless, everyday hard work of making sure all our children have the love, support, and resources they need to achieve their dreams.

Thank you to all of the members of the United States Secret Service, as well as their families, whose daily sacrifice allows them to do their jobs so well. Particularly to those who have and continue to serve my family, I will be forever grateful for their dedication and professionalism.

Thank you to the hundreds of men and women who work hard each day to make the White House a home for the families who have the privilege of inhabiting one of our most treasured monuments—the ushers, chefs, butlers, florists, grounds crew, housekeeping, and engineering staffs. They will always be an important part of our family.

Finally, I want to thank every young person I ever encountered during my time as First Lady. To all the promising young souls that touched my heart over those years—to those who helped my garden grow; to those who danced, sang, cooked, and broke bread with me; to those who remained open to the love and guidance I had to give; to those who gave me thousands of warm, delicious hugs, hugs that lifted me up and kept me going even during my most difficult moments. Thank you for always giving me a reason to be hopeful.

Photograph Credits

INSIDE FRONT COVER: All photographs courtesy of the Obama-Robinson Family Archive

INSIDE BACK COVER: (*top row, both*) Courtesy of the Obama-Robinson Family Archive; (*middle row, from left*) Courtesy of the Obama-Robinson Family Archive; © Callie Shell/Aurora Photos; © Susan Watts/New York Daily News/Getty Images; (*bottom row, from left*) © Brooks Kraft LLC/Corbis/Getty Images; Photo by Ida Mae Astute © ABC/Getty Images

INSERT, PAGES 1 TO 4: All photographs courtesy of the Obama-Robinson Family Archive; page 3 (*top right*) Photo by Kat Peeler

INSERT, PAGE 5: (*from top*) © Public Allies, courtesy of Phil Schmitz; Courtesy of the University of Chicago Medicine; Courtesy of the Obama-Robinson Family Archive

INSERT, PAGE 6: (*from top*) © David Katz 2004; © David Katz 2004; © Anne Ryan 2007

INSERT, PAGE 7: (*from top*) © Callie Shell/Aurora Photos; © Callie Shell/Aurora Photos; Courtesy of the Obama-Robinson Family Archive

INSERT, PAGE 8: (*from top*) © David Katz 2008; © Spencer Platt/Getty Images; © David Katz 2008

Reader's Discussion Guide

1. Mrs. Obama begins her book with a story about making cheese toast on a quiet night at home, a few months after leaving the White House. Why do you think she chose this story to begin her memoir?

2. In *Becoming*, we get to know the constellation of Mrs. Obama's extended family through her eyes. Her grandfather Southside filled his house with music and makeshift speakers and merriment, and the sound of her great-aunt Robbie's piano lessons came up through the floorboards of her bedroom. Years later, Mrs. Obama would fill the White House with music and culture through live performances and several programs aimed at children. How do those kinds of early memories leave an imprint on us as we grow older? What were the sounds, sights, and smells that you remember from visiting grandparents or other elders, and how have they left a mark on you?

3. Early in Mrs. Obama's life, a young relative asks her, "How come you talk like a white girl?" (p. 40). Mrs. Obama came from a home where she was expected to be smart and to "own" her smartness and

"inhabit it with pride" but lived in a neighborhood where "speaking a certain way—the 'white' way, as some would have it—was perceived as a betrayal . . . as somehow denying our culture." What is it like to live straddled across different worlds? What is it like to harbor ambitions that put you at odds with the community and the people you love and trust the most?

4. Mrs. Obama writes that her parents talked to her and Craig like adults, "indulg[ing] every question we asked" (p. 25), from juvenile complaints about breakfast to more serious topics like sex, drugs, and racism. How did Fraser and Marian Robinson's parenting strategy influence Mrs. Obama later in life? Do you agree that parents should answer their children's questions honestly, or do you think it's better to shield them from the messiness of adult life?

5. In discussing her neighborhood on the South Side of Chicago, Mrs. Obama writes, "Failure is a feeling long before it becomes an actual result. It's vulnerability that breeds with self-doubt and then is escalated, often deliberately, by fear" (p. 43). How did this insight shape Mrs. Obama's work and mission as First Lady? What can we all do—as individuals, parents, and community members—to help break this cycle?

6. Early in her senior year at Whitney Young High School, Mrs. Obama went for an obligatory first appointment with the school college counselor. Mrs. Obama was treasurer of the senior class. She had earned a spot in the National Honor Society. She was on track to graduate in the top 10 percent of her class and she was interested in joining her older brother, Craig, at Princeton University. The guidance counselor said to her, "I'm not sure that you're Princeton material" (p. 66). How did Mrs. Obama handle hearing that statement? How does one avoid having one's dreams dislodged by someone else's lower expectations?

7. In high school Mrs. Obama said she felt like she was representing her neighborhood. At Princeton, faced with questions of whether she was the product of Affirmative Action programs, she felt like she was representing her race. Was that more than a feeling? Was she actually representing her communities in those settings? Have you had moments in life where you feel as though you are representing one of your communities?

8. In her early life Mrs. Obama writes about being a "box checker," but as she gets older she learns how to "swerve" to adjust to life's circumstances. What does it mean to swerve and how do we develop that skill in life?

9. When Mrs. Obama's friend Suzanne is diagnosed with terminal cancer, it destabilizes Mrs. Obama's view of "the world as it should be." How does Mrs. Obama cope with Suzanne's death, and the death of her father the following year? How did these early experiences of loss shape her decision to step off the career path of a corporate lawyer?

10. In *Becoming*, Mrs. Obama describes a number of women who have served as mentors for her at different times in her life, including Czerny Brasuell, Valerie Jarrett, and Susan Sher. What do these women have in common? What lessons did Mrs. Obama learn from them about finding a fulfilling career as a parent? Who are your mentors and how do you cultivate those relationships?

11. In describing her relationship with her husband, Mrs. Obama writes, "Coexisting with Barack's strong sense of purpose—sleeping in the same bed with it, sitting at the breakfast table with it— was something to which I had to adjust, not because he flaunted it, exactly, but because it was so alive" (pp. 131-2). How did this sense of purpose affect their life as a married couple? Do you have someone in your life who supports or shares your own sense of purpose?

12. Mrs. Obama writes: "I've learned that it's harder to hate up close" (p. 270). How did her experiences on the campaign trail help her come up with this insight? How do we create spaces where people can come together to talk, listen, and share stories and ideals to build stronger communities, even when people might not agree or share the same history or perspective?

13. In Chapter 15, Mrs. Obama explains why she chose to support her husband's run for the presidency despite her misgivings about politics. What made her change her mind? Would you have made the same choice? How do you balance the competing worlds of family life and work in your life?

14. As Mrs. Obama notes, First Lady is a role without a job description. How did Mrs. Obama choose to approach the role? If you were in charge of writing the job description for the First Lady, what would you include and exclude?

15. In *Becoming,* Mrs. Obama writes candidly about detractors who tried to invalidate her standing or her work. "I was female, Black, and strong, which to certain people, maintaining a certain mindset, translated only to 'angry.' It was another damaging cliché, one that's been forever used to sweep minority women to the perimeter of every room, an unconscious signal not to listen to what we've got to say" (p. 265). What is the root of that "angry Black woman" cliché? How and why does it do damage?

16. When describing her visit to the Elizabeth Garrett Anderson School in London, Mrs. Obama finds herself experiencing "a strange, quiet revelation: They were me, as I'd once been. And I was them, as they could be" (p. 319). What did it mean for the girls to see themselves in Mrs. Obama? Why does she feel such a connection to these girls, and to girls' education more generally? How did she use her visibility as First Lady to bring attention to these issues?

17. Mrs. Obama has surrounded herself with a strong and support-ive circle of friends from an early age. In some cases the circle was within reach; as she got older and busier, she had to work harder to create and maintain her circle of support. She writes, "Friendships between women, as any woman will tell you, are built of a thousand small kindnesses . . . swapped back and forth and over again" (p. 361). How did she create the building blocks of strong friendships in her life? What is the value in creating and maintaining a circle of strength?

18. Mrs. Obama will always be remembered for her fabulous sense of style, but her clothing choices were as much about strategy as about fashion: "Optics governed more or less everything in the political world, and I factored this into every outfit" (p. 333). How did she use this "fashion diplomacy" to send a message to America and the world? How and when do you use clothing or accessories as an ex-tension of your voice?

19. In the epilogue, Mrs. Obama writes, "I've never been a fan of poli-tics, and my experience over the last ten years has done little to change that" (p. 419). Did you find her statement surprising? Do you think politics is an effective way to make social change?

20. Why do you think Michelle Obama chose to name her memoir *Be-coming*? What does the idea of "becoming" mean to you?

A Conversation with Michelle Obama

Q: What was unexpected about the writing process?

A: The process turned out to be really meaningful for me. I spent a lot of time just reflecting and thinking, which is something I just didn't have much time to do for about a decade. Once Barack began his campaign for president, every day felt like a sprint. So it was nice to decompress a little bit and ask myself, "How did I get here? Where did my story take a turn?" I uncovered a lot of smaller moments—moments that folks might not know about, but that I realized were really foundational to the woman I became.

Q: What did you hope to accomplish in writing your memoir?

A: My main hope was to create something that could be useful to other people, to give them something they could use in their own lives. So I focused on telling my story as honestly as I could. I'm not settling scores or giving a political play-by-play. I hoped to bring people inside the experience of growing up a working-class Black girl on the South Side of Chicago who became First Lady of the United States. It's all of me, all right there on those pages, which means I feel a little vulnerable knowing what I'm putting out there. But I hope if

I can share my story, with all its ups and downs, then other people might have the courage to share theirs, too.

Q: You write candidly that your time as a lawyer was not a happy period in your career. What advice would you give people who are unsure about their path and who need a little help figuring out their passion?

A: If you're someone who's lucky enough to think about fulfillment in your career—and there are a lot of people out there who aren't—I think the best thing you can do is listen to yourself. I mean, really, really listen. You've got to make sure you're not acting on someone else's expectations. That's where I got stuck. I spent my early adulthood checking the boxes I thought society expected of me, before I realized that it was making me miserable. I went through a lot of introspection. I did some journaling. And I realized that what I really wanted to do was help people, so I set off on a career of public service. So what I'd say is do your best to listen to yourself and tune out the rest.

Q: During your life you have experienced highs and lows but also so many unimaginable circumstances. How have you adapted to the unpredictability of the journey that has unfolded in your life?

A: I learned that sometimes you've just got to throw your hands up and let the roller coaster do its thing. There's no guidebook for anything, whether you're juggling two little kids, a demanding job, and a husband who's got big goals—or you're parenting two slightly older kids while figuring out which form of address to use with the prime minister seated next to you at dinner.

Q: You write about your inner struggle, at times questioning whether or not you're good enough. Do you have any input on how to quell self-doubt?

A: I may have had some successes in my life, but I can still feel the twinge of embarrassment from when I misspelled a word in front of my class when I was in kindergarten. I still remember the doubts

I had about myself as a working-class minority student on an affluent, mostly white college campus. I think we all carry moments like that—and let me tell you, they don't disappear when you suddenly find yourself speaking to crowded arenas and meeting the Queen of England.

What's helped is getting older and living through some of those doubts, and realizing they're not the end of your life. In fact, they can be a new beginning. It doesn't make the feelings any less difficult in the moment, of course, but in the end, self-doubt can actually be useful, as long as we don't let it overwhelm the way we think about ourselves. It's all a part of becoming.